COSM

Also by Jon King

THE ASCENSION CONSPIRACY: 2013
(a novel)

Cosmic Top Secret

The Unseen Agenda

Jon King

NEW ENGLISH LIBRARY
Hodder and Stoughton

First published in Great Britain in 1998
by Hodder and Stoughton
First published in paperback in 1999
A division of Hodder Headline PLC

A NEL Paperback

10 9 8 7 6 5 4 3 2 1

ISBN 0 340 70822 0

Typeset by Hewer Text Limited, Edinburgh
Printed and bound in Great Britain by
Clays Ltd, St Ives plc

Hodder and Stoughton
A division of Hodder Headline PLC
338 Euston Road
London NW1 3BH

For my Grandfather
One of the few men I ever truly loved
And my Father
One of the many men I never really knew

Contents

Acknowledgements

In compiling the information contained in this book I am indebted to the many brave souls who, in the face of ridicule, persecution and worse, have each in their way contributed to the gradual dissemination of information pertaining to the British and US governments' alleged involvement with extra-terrestrial intelligences and their technology. I should state that I have made every effort to contact the publishers/authors of all works from which I have quoted herein, and I am sincerely grateful for their permissions in this respect (my sincere apologies to those I have not been able to track down, in particular the heirs and/or executors to the estate of Phil Schneider).

In addition to the above I also wish to include the following, which is a list of those individuals who have, either knowingly or otherwise (and in no preferential order) contributed specifically to the writing of this book.

Command Sgt Major Robert O Dean (US Army, Special Forces Ret); Dr John Coleman; Dr Michael Wolf; Whitley Strieber; Timothy Good; Col Philip J Corso (US Army, Ret); Dr Richard Sauder, PhD; Tim Matthews; Jan van Helsing; Stanton T Friedman; Jim Keith; Milton William Cooper; Eris Andys; Michael Hesemann; Martin Redmond MP; Mark Zepezauer; Rodney Atkinson; Russel Warren; Colin Andrews; Art Bell; Jim Mills; Peter Oakley; William H Watson; Kevin Ollier; Tina Dyer; Terry and Alison; 'Jack';

'John'; Stephen Mera; Simon Lewis; Omar Fowler; Malcolm Robinson; Mark Lloyd; Glenn Campbell; Richard Pollock; Lucien Cometta; John Gille; Jimmy Guieu; Peter Sawyer; Matthew Williams; Nimrod; Jacques Vallee; Peter Laurie; Maurice Chatelain; Robert La Mont (MICH); Busty Taylor; Joe Dormer; George Wingfield; Doug Cooper; Bob Boyd and PUFORG; David Dane; Andrew Emerson; Dominic Beglin; 'Steve'; 'Julie and Tom'; Tim Rifat; Martin Cannon; Anna Keeler; Dr James Lin; Dr RO Becker; Alex Christopher; 'Q'; Bill Uhouse; Dr Richard Boylan, PhD; Phil Schneider; 'Mark'; George Vernon; NASA; MoD; White Solar Wind; British and US Intelligence, my thanks to all.

A special thanks to those who must remain anonymous, in particular my Rudloe Manor and Salisbury Plain sources, my Boscombe Down source, my 'Commodore's Daughter' source and one or two other silent voices; also to John Beveridge; Justin Miles-Booy; David Duhig; Candi Collins; Mike Ktomi; and my copy editor Nick Austin for knocking me into shape.

A very special thanks to Stealth, wherever you are; to Yeva for the wine and the peanut butter sandwiches; and most of all to Casey for her inordinate levels of tolerance and support.

Special Notice: Excerpts from *The CIA's Greatest Hits* by Mark Zepezauer are reprinted by permission of Odonian Press, Box 32375, Tucson AZ 85751, USA. Tel: 520 296 4056 or 800 REAL STORY. Fax: 520 296 0936. E-mail: odonian@realstory.com.

Briefing Document

'If I become President I'll make every piece of information this country has about UFO sightings available to the public and the scientists. I am convinced UFOs exist because I have seen one.'

This remarkable statement was made by former US President Jimmy Carter during his election campaign in May 1976. Seven years earlier in 1969, in Leary, Georgia, Carter announced via the press that he had seen a UFO 'the size of the Moon'. He told reporters: 'It was the darndest thing I've ever seen. It was big. It was very bright. It changed colours and it was about the size of the Moon. We watched it for around ten minutes as it travelled across the sky towards us and hovered over some trees. But none of us could figure out what it was . . .'

And further: '. . . One thing's for sure. I'll never make fun of people who say they've seen unidentified objects in the sky.'

Sadly, Jimmy Carter never did fulfil his 1976 election pledge to 'make every piece of information this country has about UFO sightings available to the public and the scientists'. Indeed, when questioned on this matter in a recent television interview, a frail and nervous-seeming ex-President Carter who only moments before had been his customary jovial and communicative self said that although he had indeed ordered the release of certain classified documents pertaining to the

UFO phenomenon he was 'unsure exactly how many had been allowed out into the public domain'.

His face indicated otherwise. It seemed for all the world as if some dark and terrible force had just gripped him. When pushed to explain further, ex-President Carter promptly turned a whiter shade of pale and, surrounded by a small posse of dark-suited bodyguards, shuffled silently off camera, head bowed. He did not say another word. The sight was embarrassing. Though ostensibly once the most powerful man in the world, when push came to shove even the President of the United States was unable to disclose information that he knew by rights belonged in the public domain. Indeed, when push came to shove, even the President of the United States realized he was little more than a pawn in somebody else's chess game. The question is, of course: *whose* chess game?

That Carter's sentiments did not counter the powerful and unseen bureaucratic forces regulating the office of the President of the United States is a great shame. More than this. It is a revelation, clearly indicating that even presidents are subject to someone else's agenda. OK, so politicians are past masters at making promises they later deny having made, but this was never the reason that Carter's election pledge came so woefully undone. As he explained in the abovementioned interview, he did indeed order the release of classified documents pertaining to the UFO phenomenon, but he did not know 'how many had been *allowed* out into the public domain'. [My italics.]

Allowed? Whose authority is it that overrides that of the President? And moreover, whose authority is so omnipotent that for the past fifty years and more it has sponsored the biggest and most insidious cover-up the world has ever known, as well as harbouring its most diabolical secrets?

Perhaps surprisingly, the answer to this question is not so elusive. Said authority belongs to the all-seeing, all-powerful military-industrial complex, a sort of pot-pourri consortium of extremely powerful military, aerospace and intelligence organizations who, together with some of the world's most powerful multinational corporations and financial institutions, are collectively referred to as the Secret Government. In TV's *The X Files* they are referred to more simply as The Group.

But, by whatever name, it is this backstairs consortium of wealth, power and ambition whose operation comes under scrutiny in the pages of this document – in particular, of course, its high-level involvement in the UFO phenomenon. Suffice to say for now that this operation not only lies outside the law – thereby making its activities illegal – but it also funds – and to some significant extent controls – the so-called democratic elective processes of both the United States and Great Britain, to name but two of its major players. In this way it is able to manipulate world affairs to the advantage of its own agenda. Indeed, this fact was alluded to by former President Dwight D. Eisenhower when he warned in his Farewell Address to the Nation of 'the potential for the disastrous rise of misplaced power' inherent within the 'military-industrial complex'. Eisenhower's farewell address was recorded in 1961. Two years later that 'disastrous rise of misplaced power' became only too evident when former President John F. Kennedy was assassinated for daring to challenge the beast.

For now, the plain fact of the matter is this.

A deliberate and ongoing intergovernmental UFO cover-up is today being perpetrated by the non-elected and most highly secret echelons of the British and US governments – i.e. those dark and sinister levels of government that constitute

3

the military-industrial complex, that are not subject to election and re-election by the populace (even though national and international executive and legislative decisions are subject to their approval) and whose activities are protected from public scrutiny by the bogus and illegal manipulation of the laws and restricted priorities applicable to matters of national security. In other words, the illegal misuse of the national security laws (mainly via bureaucratic channels) is the very smokescreen behind which the cover-up thrives, and remains secret. Indeed, it has thrived – with one or two hiccups – and has remained secret – with one or two hiccups – since at least 1947, when it is rumoured that said military-industrial complex first became involved with aliens. This may sound fantastic in the extreme. Nevertheless, for those prepared to undertake the painstaking and often perilous task of serious investigation into this matter, evidence to support this claim is available in tomes. And it is rarely as ambiguous as one might imagine.

The CIA archives, for example, are brimming with UFO-related documents that are classified at a higher security level even than the nuclear weapons programme. (Indeed, these documents are so highly classified that both the CIA and the NSA (the US National Security Agency) denied under oath that any such documents even existed, much less that they had ever possessed them. However, a subsequent Supreme Court action filed under the Freedom of Information Act by the Arizona-based UFO research group Ground Saucer Watch in conjunction with CAUS (Citizens Against UFO Secrecy) eventually forced the release of more than a thousand pages of such documents from the CIA archives alone. (More later.) Similar documents have been secreted away in the bowels of countless military/intelligence facilities worldwide, including the British MoD's own time-musty vaults. Every now and again certain of these documents are 'classification reviewed', following which a small number are made available for public scrutiny. It is the content of these previously classified documents that has revealed undeniable evidence of the UFO cover-up. And more. It has confirmed beyond question not only the US government's role but the *British* government's role in that cover-up too.

The rule of thumb in Britain is that a minimum of thirty years must have elapsed from the time the document was processed and classified to the time it becomes eligible for review. Even then, declassification is not guaranteed. On the contrary, if a document is considered 'too sensitive' for public release even after thirty years, a further seventy-year classification period can be – and often is – imposed. Of course, those documents that might reveal operations the authorities would rather we *never* knew about are simply shredded, never to surface again, leaving the serious investigator to rely either on leaked information or on information made available at a time when the wheels of the secrecy machine were not quite so well-oiled as they are today. Which in effect means that we are forced to excavate archives belonging to the 1940s, 1950s and 1960s in search of clues that just might betray today's conspiracy. The only other alternative, of course, is to turn to America, where the Freedom of Information Act allows far greater and more immediate access. Indeed, this is precisely the reason why so much emphasis is placed on the US cover-up and so little on the British. In Britain secrets are more precious than diamonds.

Whether or not you agree with this process is irrelevant; under current legislation there is nothing you or I can do about it. In Britain we still do not have a Freedom of Information Act: we still do not have a Bill of Rights. And, perhaps even worse, we do not even enjoy the privileges of true democracy, in that the decision as to whether or not certain documents will be declassified and released into the public domain is seldom made by an elected representative such as the Minister of Defence or the Home Secretary. Or even the Prime Minister. Rather it is made by one or another high-ranking civil servant or intelligence chief in response to a directive filtered out from within the murky meeting halls of military-industrial power. No referendum here. No majority opinion even requested, much less considered. That is the deal.

And, moreover, that is why the secrecy machine works. It is why such a massive and ongoing intergovernmental UFO cover-up has succeeded for more than fifty years. And it is why, if left to its own devices, it will continue to succeed for a good deal longer.

So what other evidence is there that indicates such a massive and ongoing UFO cover-up on the part of the world's governments and their intelligence agencies? Well, one would hope that this document is full of such evidence. But to begin, below is a summary of prime cuts . . .

According to former US Army Special Forces Command Sgt Major Robert O Dean, for example, a man who has run covert military operations with the CIA and who once held the highest security clearance in NATO, 'Cosmic Top Secret', the British and US governments are fully aware that at least one extraterrestrial civilization is currently visiting our planet. They are also convinced that the visitors pose no security threat whatever.

In an interview conducted for *UFO Reality* magazine, Sgt Major Dean told me: 'When [President] Nixon was telling people there were no US forces in Laos, I was there with about three thousand men. When he said there were no US forces in Cambodia, I was there with roughly *five* thousand men. But it was in 1963 that the story really began.'

In 1963 Sgt Major Dean was assigned to SHAPE (Supreme Headquarters Allied Powers Europe) where he was informed of a study that had been initiated two years earlier in 1961. According to Dean this study, known as The Assessment, was a Cosmic Top Secret paper evaluating the threat to national and international security from known visiting extraterrestrial intelligences. Part of Dean's assignment at SHAPE was to guard the vaults in which The Assessment was housed.

'I was there at SHAPE from 1963 to 1967. The study initiated in 1961 was published in 1964. Until I left in 1967, when I helped to close the Headquarters in Paris and move it up to where it is now in Brussels, I would pull the document out of the vault and read it, every chance I got. I would literally memorize parts of it. It was shocking to me. It was mind-boggling to me, the implications of it . . .'

And further: '. . . It was a military study that had been undertaken over a period of three years and it concluded that, although we were being monitored by extraterrestrial intelligences, there was no apparent extraterrestrial threat. It concluded that what was going on had been going on for a very long time, and that we were dealing with not one but several extraterrestrial intelligences.'

Though Sgt Major Dean asserts that there are some things he will never divulge concerning issues relating directly to the national security of the United States, he remains to this day convinced that The Assessment is indeed an official classified NATO document and that its contents should be known to all. For this reason he is determined to maintain his struggle to unravel what he calls the 'very high-level bureaucratic web of secrecy' currently in place in the United States and Britain. Indeed, the mere mention of

7

the military-industrial complex and/or the joint British and US intelligence community – its ability to function above the law; its ability to keep secrets from our elected representatives; its ability to make legislative decisions above and beyond the constitutional jurisdiction of the United States and the democratic elective processes currently operating in Britain – brings swear words to his lips. 'These bastards were never elected,' he seethed during our interview. 'You've been lied to. You've been manipulated. You're in the hands of, and being controlled by, an elite group of arrogant bureaucrats to whom the people have never given power. They have no authority.'

Above all else, former US Army Special Forces Command Sgt Major Robert O. Dean is a man of honour. He wants justice.

According to NATO, then, ET is more fact than fiction, more friend than foe, far more likely to be taking an anthropological interest in us than a military or a hostile one. And moreover, it would appear from Sgt Major Dean's testimony that one or more of the extraterrestrial intelligences currently present in our skies could first have visited Earth before *Homo sapiens* even realized he was naked. Perhaps even before that. If this is true then the twentieth-century classification of the UFO phenomenon as a national security threat makes little sense. After all, aliens are either here or they are not. If they are then all the evidence – plus the application of simple logic – points to the fact that they have probably been around for a very long time indeed. If their intentions were hostile (which fact would of course justify the national security classification) then surely they would have done the dastardly deed (whatever it is) long before we invented the means to protect ourselves – long before we invented the kind of devastating weaponry we possess today.

Which leaves one to seriously contemplate the possibility that the governments' national security standpoint with regard to the UFO phenomenon is little more than a smokescreen. Indeed, many now believe that such a standpoint can only represent the *modus operandi* of some backstairs and as yet unseen agenda. And either way, this startling revelation from the mouth of a former US Army Special Forces Command Sgt Major was enough to make me want to know more.

During the course of my own investigations I was soon to learn that Sgt Major Dean is not the only person to have accessed official documentation revealing the British and US governments' involvement with the UFO phenomenon, nor to have reached the same astonishing conclusions regarding the extraterrestrial presence. Indeed, these same conclusions are shared by many other sane, professional people who are only now beginning to publicly admit the fact. And by many others who are not. Some of those who are, however, represent classified government policies and activities most of us would not dream even existed.

Neurologist and pathologist Dr Michael Wolf, for example. Professor Emeritus of the New England Institute for Advanced Research, Member of the New York Academy of Sciences and Patron Member of the American Association for the Advancement of Science, claims that the US government is currently in process of researching the physiological and biological make-up of captured alien life forms. He says he knows this because he has himself worked on such projects at America's most highly secure military-industrial facility, Area 51. Like others before him, however, Dr Wolf has paid dearly for disclosing such sensitive information.

It was Christmas Day 1984 when Dr Wolf and his family were involved in an horrific road traffic accident in Switzerland. Tragically, both his wife and his son were killed. Having been thrown clear of the impact he spent seven days in a coma before making a full recovery, only to learn that his suspicions with regard to the cause of the 'accident' were well-founded: a short while later his intelligence chief informed him that, as a consequence of publicly disclosing certain classified information, he had become a liability. His car had been 'fixed'. His family had been murdered. He was warned not to say anything further. A man in his mid-fifties, Dr Wolf is now dying of a degenerative spinal condition.

With little left to lose, then, Dr Wolf has recently come forward with new information concerning many of the highly controversial 'black-budget' projects allegedly carried out at Area 51, where he was employed as Projects Team Leader. According to Dr Wolf, dissection and autopsy procedures were the order of the day. He also says that the results of his team's work, plus the results of research carried out by other teams at Area 51 – including the study of exotic propulsion systems belonging to captured or otherwise acquired alien spacecraft – form part of an ongoing military-industrial appraisal of Exobiology (extraterrestrial biology) and Exotechnology (extraterrestrial technology). The results of these programs, he says, are recorded in what he calls the *Blue Border Documents*.

But what is even more intriguing about Dr Wolf's claims is this. The Assessment referred to by Sgt Major Dean, he says, is indeed a genuine NATO document, and is officially known as the *Blue Border Assessment*. Wolf says that this document is a record of NATO's ongoing scientific intelligence-gathering program vis-à-vis ETs and UFOs, and that it contains the sum of results obtained from research such as that carried out at Area 51. When asked how he came to know the details of such highly classified material, he replied: 'Because I've seen it.'

It was Dr Wolf's former position as security consultant to the US National Security Council on extraterrestrial matters and head of the US government's Alphacom Team (the leading scientific intelligence-gathering agency within the US government's supersecret extraterrestrial Special Studies Group, Majestic-12) which afforded him access to such highly classified documents as The Assessment which, he says, is classified at either UMBRA, ULTRA or KEYSTONE level, the highest security classifications there are. He adds that Sgt Major Dean is essentially correct concerning the document's contents and conclusions and that, further, the 'in-house' term for anything classified at or higher than ULTRA is indeed COSMIC TOP SECRET.

Sgt Major Dean's claims begin to assume new significance, then . . .

To add further substance, American UFO researcher and author Eris Andys recently obtained a copy of a document entitled The AGARD Report (AGARD: NATO's Advisory Group for Aeronautical Research and Development). Published by the late Robert Maxwell's Pergamon Press, this mysterious NATO document reveals Maxwell's double life as a public figure and international publishing magnate on the one hand, and an intergovernmental intelligence agent via his role as a Mossad/MI5 go-between on the other. His publishing empire acted as a conduit for the report itself.

The report, which reached Ms Andys via the estate of a deceased scientist who had worked on the project, details the results of the US Air Force/NATO's endeavours to reverse-engineer the mechanics of crashed-and-retrieved (or otherwise acquired) alien craft, and reveals that some form of magnetohydrodynamic technology was involved.

In a report for *UFO Reality*, Ms Andys wrote:

'The propulsion system under research was/is one based upon Magneto-Fluid-Dynamics, the same sort of thing as described by Bob Lazar, an engineer who gave accounts of having worked at Area 51. MFD is the science which studies the interaction between flow fields of conducting fluids and electromagnetic fields, simply put. And it's the sort of research which can put an aircraft out of phase with gravity.'

The interesting thing about *The AGARD Report* is that it dates the origination of The Assessment to September 1947, a landmark date in ufology and fourteen years earlier than the date given by Sgt Major Dean. Paradoxically, however, this time-frame would fit comfortably with Sgt Major Dean's claims that the study had been initiated in 1961 and that he had seen the published results in 1964 (it would fit well with what is now known about the US government's initial involvement with the UFO phenomenon, too, which began in earnest in 1947 following the much publicized Roswell 'UFO crash'). By this time said results would have been ready for publication on a 'need-to-know' basis. Indeed, the study referred to by Dean, The Assessment, would seem at that time to have been a sort of generic title for a project that had spanned almost two decades, and which would have involved any number of military-industrial scientific and intelligence studies and their consequent reports, including *Project Sign*, *Project Grudge*, *Project Blue Book* and other *Blue Border* Documents. In this light The Assessment would have represented the collation and extrapolation of findings gleaned over this period from the unknown number of scientific studies undertaken by the various military-industrial components and intelligence departments within the US government and NATO.

Thus, as Eris Andys asserts, *The AGARD Report* would seem to have been an integral part of The Assessment and would therefore have been classified, as Sgt Major Dean claims, at the highest security level known to NATO, Cosmic Top Secret.

It should be said that within the need-to-know framework of such highly classified military-industrial projects, information such as 'origination dates' and the like is a jealously guarded secret, and is therefore prone to 'factual massage' through insertion of a modicum of disinformation. It is highly probable that Sgt Major Dean would have been told that the study had been initiated in 1961 and not 1947 as *The AGARD Report* implies, since Sgt Major Dean's 'need-to-know' status would have demanded that he be informed only according to the needs of his own personal assignment – which was to guard the vaults in which the documents were housed and not necessarily to access the entire database of information concerning the project. Nevertheless *The AGARD Report* and The Assessment undoubtedly share the same bed.

One name mentioned by Eris Andys in her report, and one that springs immediately to mind these days whenever the subject of 'acquired alien technology programs' is broached, is, of course, that of Bob Lazar. Like Dr Michael Wolf (and others) Lazar claims to have worked at Area 51 reverse-engineering the mechanics of acquired alien craft. But before we look at Bob Lazar's claims in detail, first a word about his alleged workplace, the supersecret US government facility, Area 51 – a facility clearly visible to interested parties from certain mountain-peak vantage points surrounding the base; a facility that has been photographed and filmed by researchers and television crews alike from these vantage points and by Russian satellites from space; a facility that, according to the US government, absolutely does not exist.

In brief, Area 51 – otherwise known as 'Dreamland' or

Jon King

'The Ranch' – is an Ultra Top Secret military-industrial facility
spanning a vast area of mountainous desert terrain about
one hundred miles north of Las Vegas, Nevada. Until 1972
it was managed by the CIA (and to some extent it probably
still is) although the official word is that these days the
US Air Force Systems Command is in the hot seat, which
seems reasonable when you consider that one of the major
programmes carried out at this facility is the development of
new and exotic aircraft. As well as the Stealth B2 bomber,
both America's top-secret U-2 spy plane and the later SR-71
Blackbird (a high-altitude, high-performance reconnaissance
aircraft) were developed and test-flown here. To add to
this, America's latest supersecret Stealth prototype, Aurora
(official design name ASTRA – Advanced Stealth Technology
Reconnaissance Aircraft) is currently being developed and
test-flown at Area 51. Indeed, according to *Jane's Military
Aircraft*, sonic booms created by a Mach 3–4 aircraft in the
region of southern Nevada have been tracked by seismological stations since June 1991, while radio intercepts have
confirmed the aircraft's altitude as being at least 67,000
feet. *Jane's* also published an artist's impression of the
supersecret X30 Aurora based on the known performance
and operational parameters of an extremely high-altitude
Mach 8 aircraft. According to 'official rumours', the X30
Aurora is a strategic reconnaissance prototype, developed
at Area 51, whose operational parameters indeed include
an extremely high-altitude Mach 8 capability (100,000 feet
at a speed of around 6,000 mph) and possible space flight.
It is interesting to note that the only pilots – other than US
'top guns' – permitted to fly and test-fly such supersecret
US aircraft are selected from special-operations units within
Britain's RAF. At the highest possible security level, Britain
and America are very intimate indeed.

In addition to this, a series of mysterious 'skyquakes' has been reported over southern California in recent years, fuelling suspicions that the Aurora 'prototype' story is little more than a smokescreen. In fact, it would seem that at least one of the Aurora designs is now operational and that it returns along this set flight path to Area 51 following a once-a-week reconnaissance mission in orbit – a kind of returnable, recyclable, refuellable spy satellite powered by the most highly advanced 'pulse detonation wave' technology and developed at Lockheed's Groom Lake (Area 51) test site. It has been suspected for some time that the US Air Force's most highly secret Stealth aircraft is indeed capable of space flight.

But the most staggering claim so far as we are concerned is that a small fleet of acquired alien 'discs' is today being test-flown above Area 51's hidden nucleus, the vast dry lake bed known as Groom Lake, which satellite photographs have shown boasts probably the longest runway in the world. On 27th April 1984, for example, the *LA Times* reported that US Air Force Lt General Robert M. Bond had been killed – his 'Air Force specially modified test craft' had apparently crashed near Groom Lake at 10:45 a.m. Lt General Bond was at the time a three-star general and Vice Commander of the US Air Force Systems Command, which would have made him one of the most senior military officers at the facility. Naturally the Air Force refused to disclose precisely what type of aircraft the general had been flying, but suspicions were fuelled by the unusual fact that a three-star general and base Vice Commander had been employed as a test pilot. Without doubt this was seen as highly irregular. Perhaps not surprisingly, then, it was the assumption of some conspiracy theorists that Lt General Bond had been test-flying either an acquired alien disc or a US-built advanced technology prototype 'modified' as a result of knowledge gleaned from reverse-engineering the mechanics (in particular the propulsion system) of such an alien disc. In short, word was that the aircraft crashed because 'we' have yet to fully master the alien technologies involved in the construction and propulsion of our own latest prototypes, and *this* was the reason that the experience and skill of a three-star general was called on to test-fly the craft.

And who knows . . . ?

Whatever the truth about Lt General Robert M. Bond, one thing is for sure. Area 51 is home to some of the world's most exotic aerospace technology programmes, and included in those programmes is the development of the strangest, most advanced prototype aircraft this side of the Milky Way. It is perhaps not surprising, then, that unauthorized access to this facility is punishable by death.

Indeed, the facility's outermost perimeter is marked by signs that display the warning 'Use of Deadly Force Permitted', and is patrolled by black, unmarked, fully armed helicopters and ground-based security teams known as Cammo Dudes, who patrol the perimeter in white four-wheel-drive Broncos. But that is only the perimeter. Deeply concealed within this facility – which includes the Ultra Top Secret Nellis Air Force Range and the infamous Nevada Nuclear Test Site – is an even more secret facility known as S-4, where nine acquired alien discs are allegedly being reverse-engineered and test-flown. It is within the confines of this impenetrable inner fortress that both Dr Wolf and Bob Lazar claim to have worked.

According to Lazar, S-4 is the supersecret hub of the US government's acquired alien technology research programme and is so vast that it occupies the innards of an entire mountain range. Indeed, if the stories are to be believed, S-4 is an impermeable netherworld of terrible dark secrets and incredible stories, not the least of which claims that this officially non-existent research facility goes down an incredible forty-two levels below ground, and houses an impressive array of devices straight out of science fiction – including microwave, plasma and particle-beam weapons systems; antimatter reactors; pulse-modulated microwave and neural-chip implant technologies developed for the CIA's ongoing mind-control programs; electromagnetic and magnetohydrodynamic propulsion systems acquired from captured alien craft; the craft themselves . . . and, of course, a smattering of captured and/or visiting alien lifeforms, or EBEs (Extraterrestrial Biological Entities) as they are known to their US hosts. Indeed, if only half of what is claimed concerning this facility is remotely true, then a regular day at the S-4 office must make *Independence Day* look like *Bambi*.

Unquestionably the most famous former S-4 employee is ex-Los Alamos National Laboratories physicist Robert 'Bob' Lazar PhD, who says he worked at the base from December 1988 to April 1989. One month later he revealed live on US television that he had been contracted to 'back-engineer' the propulsion systems of acquired alien craft. He told an astonished American audience that nine such 'discs' were being housed at S-4 and that he had been hired to fathom out how the discs worked. As a safeguard against threats to his life Lazar's face was cast in shadow during the broadcast, in which he used the name 'Dennis' and had his voice electronically distorted so as not to reveal his true identity. The ruse, however, failed.

From this point on both he and his wife began to receive death threats, and at one point his car was shot at by US government agents. Fearing for his life he decided to come out of the closet and go public with his story. Paradoxically perhaps, he figured the best means of protection would be to assume a high-profile persona.

Speaking of his time at S-4 on Michael Hesemann's excellent documentary video *UFOs: Secrets of the Black World*, Lazar says:

'We took off from Las Vegas airport and flew to Groom Lake (Area 51) in a 737 aircraft. There is a bus there that drives about fifteen miles south down to a smaller dry lake bed known as Papoose Lake, and right up against the mountain there is the S-4 installation . . .

'. . . It was very military-like; it was certainly not a scientific atmosphere. There was very high security – wherever you walked you had to have an armed escort, even into the bathroom. All doors lock and open with your badge. It was a very oppressive atmosphere . . .

'. . . When I saw the craft for the first time my impression was, "Well, this explains all the UFO sightings – it's just a secret military aircraft we're working on". When I got to enter it, though, and look over it, and I finally realized what was going on, that this was an alien craft – and of course, this was after I read the briefings – well, that was a totally different feeling. That was not a feeling of excitement; it was almost an ominous feeling, as if you shouldn't even be there . . .

'. . . There were nine craft in total – I only got to work on one of the craft. There was a separate hangar for each of the craft, and each one was essentially different in its visual appearance. A lot of people have speculated about whether the craft had been shot down, or whether they had crashed . . . but the craft seemed undamaged, so I doubt either of those would be correct . . .

'. . . They were absolutely alien craft, there is no question about it. First of all, the scope of the project was to back-engineer them – if they were United States craft we wouldn't have been going backwards trying to find out how they were built and how they worked. And of course, the briefing information stated that they were alien craft.'

Though Lazar's educational and occupational credentials have since been widely discredited by the intelligence community, as well as by many UFO researchers, the crux of the evidence suggests his story is very likely genuine. Front-line US television journalist and UFO researcher George Knapp, for example, spent years endeavouring to substantiate Lazar's claim that, previous to his stint at Area 51, he had worked at the US government's most infamous advanced technology R&D facility, Los Alamos National Laboratories in New Mexico. During this time Los Alamos spokespersons consistently denied that Lazar had ever set foot in the place, thus casting serious doubts over his claims that he had worked at Area 51. After years chasing his own tail, however, Knapp finally received confirmation that Lazar had indeed worked at the facility (a 1982 Los Alamos phone book lists Lazar as an employee at the facility, while a Los Alamos newspaper report from the same year refers to his employment there). It is now widely suspected that a concerted effort on the part of the CIA was responsible for the smear campaign against him.

But then, as we will undoubtedly see as this document progresses, within the field of UFO/ET and secret-technology research, propaganda programmes, disinformation schedules and vicious smear campaigns – as well as direct fear and intimidation tactics, even the odd military-style execution – are par for the course. What this document aims to expose are those responsible for this illegal and wholly unacceptable behaviour.

And, moreover . . . *why* they deem such behaviour necessary.

* * *

It has largely been my work as an investigative journalist and editor of the international bimonthly magazine *UFO Reality* that has afforded me access to the many 'inside sources' who are now prepared to talk openly about government involvement in the UFO phenomenon. These 'inside sources' include military and former military personnel; special forces personnel; British and US intelligence operatives; British and US government officials; employees and former employees contracted to military-industrial facilities such as Area 51; NASA and former NASA personnel; even astronauts. Indeed, several very well-known astronauts have recently declared their knowledge of the extraterrestrial presence, and of the enthusiasm of the governments concerned for absolute secrecy regarding this matter.

Former astronaut Dr Brian O'Leary, for example, speaking at the International Forum on New Science, Fort Collins, Colorado in September 1994, stated:

'For nearly fifty years the secrecy apparatus in the United States government has kept from the public UFO and alien information.' He went on to say, quite unequivocally: 'We have contact with alien cultures.'

Further to this, former US Air Force Colonel and astronaut Gordon Cooper, the last man to fly alone in space, claims that he had two major encounters with UFOs during his military career – the first in 1951 when he was piloting an F86 Sabre jet over what was then West Germany, the second in May 1963 as he was completing the final orbit of a twenty-two-orbit mission of Earth in a Mercury capsule. This second sighting was also tracked by a radar tracking station in Perth, Australia, and was reported by the National Broadcast Company who were covering the space flight live. On both occasions Colonel Cooper was ordered to remain silent about the encounters. He refused, however, and has since spoken publicly in an effort to undo the secrecy web.

Testifying before the United Nations, Colonel Cooper stated:

'[I observed] many flights of different sizes, flying in fighter formation, generally from east to west over Europe . . . several days in a row we sighted groups of metallic, saucer-shaped vehicles at great altitudes over the base [in Germany] and we tried to get close to them, but they were able to change direction faster than our fighters . . .'

And further: 'Every day in the USA our radar instruments capture objects of form and composition unknown to us. There are thousands of witness reports and a quantity of documents to prove this, but nobody wants to make them public. Why?'

Why indeed.

One final example of the fact that information regarding the UFO/ET phenomenon is classified at a very high security level can be found in a statement made by former NASA communications specialist Maurice Chatelain, who designed and built the communications and data-processing systems for NASA's Apollo Moon missions. The late Mr Chatelain's protests are well-known. Indeed, due to his high-level security classification within the military-industrial complex they carry a weight unsurpassed. It should be noted that until his recent death Maurice Chatelain campaigned vigorously against the multibillion-dollar NASA secrecy machine.

As long ago as 1979 Mr Chatelain was publicly voicing his opinion regarding the cover-up. 'All Apollo and Gemini flights,' he revealed, 'were followed, both at a distance and sometimes also quite closely, by space vehicles of extraterrestrial origin – flying saucers, or UFOs if you want to call them by that name. Every time it occurred the astronauts informed Mission Control, who then ordered absolute silence.'

A very close friend of Maurice Chatelain recently explained to me how Chatelain had become extremely angry and frustrated with the secrecy apparatus applied by NASA, and by the US government in general. Anecdotally I was informed of how Chatelain – who was reportedly present at Mission Control for all Gemini and Apollo missions – would hear the live transmissions coming through to Mission Control from astronauts telling of their UFO encounters in space, and how he would 'seethe inside', knowing full well that these transmissions would be immediately jammed and classified.

Like others before and since, Chatelain believed that information concerning a matter with such far-reaching implications as the UFO phenomenon should be available to everyone, and not just to the elite few.

In this respect, Sgt Major Robert O Dean, also a friend of Chatelain's, told me:

'Maurice personally told me . . . he said that: "I was standing there in Houston, Mission Control, when Aldrin and Armstrong were walking the Moon. And I stood there with everyone in that room and listened to them excitedly describe what they were seeing." But, of course, the American public never heard any of that.'

The American public 'never heard that' because what Aldrin and Armstrong described were alien spacecraft parked up on the edge of a nearby crater! (More later.)

Dr O'Leary is not alone in his conclusions, then. Indeed, most of these highly credible sources have told a similar story, while a surprisingly high percentage have seemed more than willing to discuss freely their own UFO experiences and to reveal information they have managed to glean regarding the

UFO phenomenon in an official capacity. This, together with information gleaned from civilian witnesses, has enabled me to document a growing body (perhaps I should say *mountain*) of evidence in support of Sgt Major Dean's claims – i.e. that extraterrestrial intelligences are indeed visiting our planet; that the British and US governments (among others) are well aware of this fact; that highly secretive echelons of the military, while representing some form of behind-the-scenes 'non-elected' administration, are deliberately conspiring to keep this information from the public; and that, moreover, evidence to the effect that the visitors represent a security threat – the official reason for this information being kept secret – simply does not exist. On the contrary, the evidence speaks of a different scenario entirely.

Every relevant declassified document released or statement made by either the British Defence Ministry, the RAF, the US Defense Department, the US Air Force Office of Special Investigations, the US Office of Naval Intelligence, US Army Intelligence, the CIA, DIA, NSA – to name the major players – clearly states that UFOs do not and never have posed a security threat. When presented with this information, plus the NATO conclusions as described by Sgt Major Dean and others, one is left to ponder the inevitable question: why all the secrecy?

When all the evidence points to the fact that some form of human/extraterrestrial interaction has been occurring on Planet Earth for hundreds, possibly thousands of years (as concluded in the NATO study, The Assessment, and as confirmed by recent archaeological finds) and when not one archive extant from either the ancient or modern world has been found to document an aggressive manoeuvre on the part of the visitors, why are the governments so keen to preserve the UFO secret under the bogus jurisdiction of (inter)national security?

As the late Martin Redmond MP remarked following a series of questions he tabled in the House of Commons to the then Secretary of State for Defence, Nicholas Soames MP, 5th November 1996: 'If there is no defence threat, then there is no excuse for secrecy, either.' Before his untimely death in January 1997, Mr Redmond openly accused the government of covering up information on a number of UFO incidents. And like Dr Brian O'Leary before him, Mr Redmond was not alone in his accusations, nor in his quest to pressure governments to come clean on the issue of the UFO cover-up.

Other MPs, including Alfred Morris, Gareth Wardell, Sir Alan Hazelhurst, Barry Field, Dennis Canavan, Roger Gale and in particular Ieuan Wyn Jones, plus such high-ranking luminaries as former Admiral of the Fleet, Chief of the Defence Staff and Chairman of the NATO Military Committee Lord Hill-Norton, have all voiced their concerns over the secrecy issue. In the US, Senators and Congressmen have voiced *their* concerns, too. Indeed, Sgt Major Dean recently informed me that, together with around two hundred other former military and intelligence personnel, including several astronauts, he is currently involved in Operation Stargate, an attempt to force through a Bill of Congressional Indemnity against the operation's members in order that they might be permitted to break their security oaths and reveal their 'inside' UFO information to members of Congress. Such a hearing would be held behind closed doors. Even so, it would be an official 'on-the-record' Congressional hearing and as such the minutes and results of the hearing, under the tenets of the US Constitution, would have to be made available to the public. Also, of course, the success of such an operation as this would surely vindicate the twenty years

Sgt Major Dean has spent endeavouring to make public knowledge the mountain of UFO data currently vaulted in the US intelligence community's *X-Files* archive. It seems the truth really could be out there . . . soon.

In the meantime, rumours of alien/government collaboration abound, suggesting that this is indeed the reason for what many now consider to be a full-scale intergovernmental UFO cover-up. And it may well prove to be the case. However, other evidence points to the fact that an even more sinister agenda lies behind all the secrecy – an as yet *unseen agenda*.

It is this unseen agenda I intend to expose in the pages of this document.

DOCUMENT 01

Cosmic Top Secret
Eyes Only Copy One of One

The Beginning

File 01
Flying Saucers

Though investigations into the UFO phenomenon began officially in 1933 (unofficially, of course, some time before that), it is nonetheless safe to say that the modern UFO era began in 1947. And how.

Following countless reports of UFO sightings – mainly disc-shaped objects – in the summer of 1947, a wave of hysteria swept the United States. Hitherto preoccupied Americans grew wide-eyed at the prospect of alien invasion, while the US military grew edgy for the same reason. Fighter aircraft were frequently scrambled to intercept the UFOs, but to no avail – no successful interception of a UFO was ever recorded. However, according to official reports some aircraft were lost in pursuit of UFOs, the most famous case being that of Captain Thomas F. Mantell Jnr, who was reportedly killed in January 1948 when his P51 Mustang crashed whilst in pursuit of a 'metallic object, tremendous in size, directly ahead and slightly above'. Mantell's last recorded words were: 'I am trying to close for a better look.'

He never did get close enough for a 'better look'. Or if he did, he did not live long enough to describe exactly what he had seen. According to the official files, moments after his final transmission the P51 Mustang crashed two miles south-west of Franklyn, Kentucky – Captain Mantell was dead. It should be added that many anomalies have since been discovered regarding this case, and much distorting detail added to it – for example, there are claims that Mantell's body was never recovered from the crash site because the aliens abducted him from his aircraft; the real content of his final message was that he could see the aliens through the UFO's port-holes; his P51 crashed due to alien attack. I suppose all of these are possible. The more likely explanation, however, is that Mantell climbed too high – while the three other P51 pilots flying formation with him returned to base due to lack of oxygen, Mantell continued his pursuit of the UFO, climbing so high that he finally died of anoxia and thus lost control of his aircraft. Today it is widely suspected that the US military were responsible for embroidering the story of Captain Mantell's death in order to sow the seeds of doubt and panic in the minds of an already wide-eyed American public. The message was unequivocal: *'Yep, aliens are here! But do not be alarmed. They've gotten one of our boys but from now on the US military's gonna be taking care o' business.'* In this way the entire UFO subject would be handled exclusively by the military. Indeed, from now on UFOs were to be considered a national security threat. By 1948 the secrecy machine was already up and running, and the all-powerful military-industrial complex, together with the burgeoning US intelligence community, was fast taking control. No doubt about that.

At the same time that Captain Mantell was allegedly dog fighting with real UFOs, Hollywood was doing its bit to aid in the process of mind-seeding the American public by creating a fleet of belligerent cinematic replicas. While growing ever fatter on the profits of this strange new phenomenon, CIA-sponsored Hollywood moguls were 'encouraged' to make a string of B-rated 'alien invasion' movies in order to further the myth that UFOs were indeed piloted by aliens with hostile intentions. (Indeed, this same policy continues to this day with television programmes such as *The X Files*, *Dark Skies* and blockbuster movies such as *Independence Day*.)

But if this was an attempt to mythologize the truth of what was by now becoming a national epidemic – if not a national emergency – it failed. From here on in the situation intensified.

It was the description of a UFO given to the press by a civilian pilot, Kenneth Arnold, that inspired the media to coin the term 'flying saucer'. Having sighted nine disc-shaped objects flying in formation over the Cascade Mountains in Washington State on 24th June 1947, Arnold reported that the craft moved 'as a saucer would if it was skipped across the water'. For the next few days 'flying saucers' were as popular with the US media as the Spice Girls are today. More so. It is documented that more than 1,000 'flying saucer' sightings were reported in more than forty different states across the US within weeks of Arnold's encounter.

But even this amount of publicity paled to virtual oblivion by comparison with what was to happen next.

File 02
The Roswell Incident

Because one week and one day later, on 2nd July 1947, amidst the squall of a sudden and violent thunderstorm, an incident occurred that even today remains the linchpin of what many consider to be a worldwide UFO cover-up on the part of the US and British governments. Namely: *something* crashed and exploded in the New Mexico desert, and according to the man who was then Commander of the US 509th Composite Bomb Wing and Roswell Army Air Field, Colonel William Blanchard, that something was a 'flying saucer'. Indeed, Colonel Blanchard is on record as saying that the craft that crashed near the sleepy New Mexico towns of Corona and Roswell in 1947 did not originate with the military, nor with any other known terrestrial power or organization. So what was it?

According to the official US Air Force press release immediately following the incident, of course, it was a UFO. But then the US Air Force changed its mind.

Much has already been penned concerning the Roswell incident, so I will limit what I have to say here to the barest minimum.

On 6th July 1947, sheep rancher William 'Mac' Brazel turned up at the Roswell sheriff's office with what he claimed were pieces of debris from a crash site. Evidently he had discovered the debris on the JB Foster Ranch near Corona, New Mexico, where he was employed as ranch manager. He informed Sheriff George Wilcox that the debris was scattered over a large area, and that it comprised materials he had never seen before. Being familiar with weather balloons (which were frequently launched from the area and seen by locals on a regular basis) and experimental weapons and aircraft (which were frequently launched from the nearby White Sands Proving Ground and test-flown over the desert) Brazel was convinced that the debris did not belong to the military. The wreckage, he said, had been in the desert for three or four days, and in that time he had seen no evidence that the military had been out searching for the crashed object – no recovery units, no spotter planes, no military activity whatever. Indeed, the material was so unlike anything he had ever seen that he was convinced it must have belonged to 'one of those flying saucers' that had been making headline news for the past few weeks. 'I've found the wreckage of one of those flying saucers.' Brazel told local radio station KGLF, in a subsequent interview. Consequently Sheriff Wilcox found himself at the centre of what was to become, virtually overnight, a major national incident.

Meanwhile, Roswell Army Air Field Staff Intelligence Officer Major Jesse A. Marcel was enjoying lunch at the officers' club when he received a telephone call from Sheriff Wilcox who, under orders to notify the base about anything that might concern the military, asked Major Marcel to come to the sheriff's office immediately. This Major Marcel did. Once there he examined the debris, and quickly realized that it comprised materials he too had never seen before – extremely lightweight 'metal' I-beams embossed with unrecognizable hieroglyphics; a form of very lightweight 'wood' that could not be burned; a paper-thin 'tinfoil-like' substance that could not be cut, drilled or broken through, even with a sledgehammer, and which, having been screwed up in the hand, immediately returned to its former uncreased state when released. Major Marcel immediately contacted his base commander, Colonel Blanchard, and informed him of the situation. After a moment's consideration Blanchard told

Marcel to go to the crash site and examine the extent of the wreckage for himself. Which he did.

Accompanied by Counter Intelligence Corps (now AFOSI: Air Force Office of Special Investigations) officer Sheridan W Cavitt and, of course, the sheep rancher Brazel, Major Jesse Marcel drove his Buick out of town towards Corona and a remote area of desert on the JB Foster Ranch where Brazel had discovered the wreckage. Upon arrival, however, night had fallen, so the three men decided to wait for daylight so that the wreckage could be more clearly scrutinized. They spent the night in Brazel's ranch house.

As the sun came up over the New Mexico desert it became apparent that, just as Brazel had reported, the wreckage had been strewn over a vast area measuring approximately three quarters of a mile long and several hundred feet wide. Closer inspection showed that it was indeed comprised of the same strange lightweight materials Marcel had seen at Sheriff Wilcox's office the day before. By this time he was beginning to sense something out of the ordinary – for one thing his companion, Cavitt, who had been a friend for some time, became nervous, edgy, stand-offish, while at the same time Marcel, like Brazel, began to suspect that the wreckage had little or nothing to do with the military, but that it belonged to a 'flying saucer'. When he put this theory to Cavitt, however, the counter-intelligence agent showed little enthusiasm for it. Along with many other military and intelligence colleagues, Cavitt would later cold-shoulder Marcel to the point that Marcel would find himself at the wrong end of a bitter hate and disinformation campaign. A lesser man might have crumbled. As it was, however, Marcel would go to his grave protesting the truth of his account.

Later that night, en route back to base, Marcel stopped off at his home where he showed the strange debris materials to his wife and son – his son, now Dr Jesse Marcel Jr, remembers to this day the night his father woke him from sleep in order to show him the strange materials. He also remembers the way in which those materials acted, in particular the 'tinfoil-like' substance that when crumpled in the hand returned to its pristine, uncreased state as soon as it was released. He also remembers seeing strange symbols embossed on small 'I-beam' sections of the material which, he says, 'resembled hieroglyphics'. In a sworn affidavit Dr Jesse Marcel Jr stated:

'. . . [the debris consisted of] a brittle, brownish-black plastic-like material, like Bakelite, and there were fragments of what appeared to be I-beams. On the inner surface of the I-beam there appeared to be a type of writing . . . composed of curved geometric shapes. It had no resemblance to Russian, Japanese or any other foreign language. It resembled hieroglyphics, but it had no animal-like characters.'

Like that of his father before him, Dr Jesse Marcel Jr's story has remained consistent over decades.

As it turned out, Major Marcel had been showing the materials to his wife and son for only a short time before military personnel arrived with orders for Marcel to return to the base immediately. Which he did. Samples in hand, Marcel drove back to Roswell Army Air Field where he was immediately summoned to the office of his base commander, Colonel William Blanchard. It was now the late evening of 6th July 1947.

On 7th July 1947, Colonel Blanchard ordered the crash site to be cordoned off; within hours the site had been completely sealed and, according to local witnesses, was crawling with very high-ranking military, FBI and intelligence personnel, as well as 'other' government officials. Many of the witnesses have subsequently claimed that they were told, on pain of death, or worse, not to say anything about what they had seen. William Woody, for example, a local pig farmer who was thirteen years old at the time of the incident, was one of more than 350 witnesses who said that they saw the craft in distress, flying erratically beneath the low cloud cover on the night of the violent thunderstorm, but that they were warned in no uncertain terms not to say anything about what they had seen. 'It was so bright it was like looking at the sun,' Woody said, describing the craft moments before it crashed, while Frankie Rowe and Loretta Proctor, personal friends of the Marcels, said that they actually handled the debris materials and that they felt 'real light, weird'. Mrs Rowe said that when she dropped the material on the table it seemed to 'spread out like water'. It should be added that Mrs Rowe was subsequently visited and threatened by the military at her home. Intelligence officers told her: 'I want you to know you were never there. You never saw anything. You don't know anything.' And further: 'We can take you out into the middle of the desert and nobody will know you're there.' Both Mrs Rowe and Sheriff George Wilcox later testified to the fact that a cover-up had indeed been initiated by the military. 'Yes, it was a flying saucer,' Wilcox admitted, 'but the Air Force threatened me not to say anything.' He added that several bodies and one still-living alien were also recovered from the crash site.

Sheriff George Wilcox was not the only witness to make such a claim.

According to Master Sgt Frank Kaufmann of the Roswell Army Air Field Personnel Department (1947) who was subsequently assigned to a covert counter-intelligence unit code-named 'The Nine' (specifically formed to deflect unwanted interest in the incident), five alien bodies (at least one still living) plus the wreckage of an extraterrestrial craft were indeed recovered from the desert and housed over-night inside Roswell Army Air Field's Hangar 84. Kaufmann explained that the bodies had been recovered from a second site, a few miles from the debris site, where the main body of the craft had been found intact and virtually undamaged even though it had become 'embedded' in the side of a rock face. The paper-thin 'tinfoil-like' material discovered at the first site, he said, appeared to have been a protective 'skin' or 'coating' of some kind, seamless, no rivets; the craft had seemingly come down at the first site, 'bounced' on impact (leaving a great gouge in the desert floor and littering the site with slivers of its shredded 'skin') and had then been discovered several miles away by spotter planes, complete with occupants. Master Sgt Kaufmann also revealed how the military had contacted local mortician (undertaker) Glenn Dennis who subsequently advised on how to preserve the bodies and provided 'child-sized' coffins to house them.

Indeed, when interviewed Mr Dennis confirmed Master Sgt Kaufmann's story, and went on to tell how, even though he had been officially invited onto Roswell Army Air Field in order to offer his advice regarding the preservation of the 'child-sized' bodies, he had been manhandled and 'thrown off the base' by overly aggressive military police. He testified that the base was alive with activity, that everybody seemed on edge, and that security at the base was tighter than he had ever before seen. He also told the story of how a 'lady friend', a nurse at Roswell Army Air Field at the time of the incident, had been assigned to assist in the autopsies carried out at the base prior to the alien bodies being transferred. 'The bodies smelled so bad that military personnel [participating in the autopsies] became very ill,' she told Dennis. She also sketched a drawing of the aliens she had seen, depicting them as frail in stature with large heads and large black almond-shaped eyes. She then burned the drawings and told Dennis that she would be in 'great danger' if the authorities ever found out that she had given him this information. But by this time, it seems, it was too late; evidently someone at the base had noted and reported her indiscretions. According to Mr Dennis, his 'lady friend' died in an air crash soon after the incident. 'At least that's what they told me,' he said.

Other witnesses included former Roswell Army Air Field employees Ruben and Pete Anaya, who both testified that the recovered alien craft was indeed housed overnight in the base's Hanger 84, along with its occupants. Both men stated that they saw at least one still-living alien. Another base employee, Dan Dwyer, also stated that he saw at least one still-living alien and two dead aliens – which he referred to as 'little people', 'not human people' and people who 'did not come from this world'. Dwyer said that he saw the still-living alien 'walking around' inside Hangar 84.

For the record, Colonel Philip J. Corso, head of the Pentagon's Foreign Technology in Army Research and Development during the early 1960s (where he was in charge of the US government's official 'Roswell Files') has since come forward and confirmed that the Roswell incident indeed involved the crash and retrieval of an alien craft and the survival of at least one of its occupants (see Document 06, File 23). He also says that the US-based military-industrial complex has been 'reverse-engineering' the mechanics of crashed-and-retrieved alien vehicles for the past fifty years, and that many of today's most advanced technologies are the direct result of this programme.

Considering the extremely tight security and cover-up procedures that followed in the wake of this incident, then, it is perhaps surprising that on 8th July 1947 Colonel William Blanchard instructed the Roswell Army Air Field press officer, Lt Walter Haut, to issue a press release stating that debris from a crashed 'flying saucer' had been recovered by the US Air Force in the New Mexico desert. Naturally this press release made front-page news. At the same time Major Marcel was ordered to organize a B29 crew and accompany the wreckage to what was then Wright Field (now Wright-Patterson Air Force Base) in Dayton, Ohio, the home of the US government's Foreign Technology Division (FTD). In 1947 Wright Field was certainly the US Air Force's most highly secure facility for the storage and scientific analysis of captured enemy equipment and technology. It was thus the prime candidate for housing crashed-and-retrieved alien craft, plus their pilots, dead or alive. Indeed, there are many witness statements in circulation acquired from former Wright Field personnel that tend to substantiate this claim (see Document 02, File 05 and Document 06, File 23). It seems aliens might be more familiar with Dayton, Ohio, than many humans are.

En route to Wright Field, Marcel was ordered to make a stopover at Fort Worth Army Air Field (subsequently Carswell Air Force Base), Texas. Here he was to receive further instruction from his base commander's immediate superior, Major General Roger Ramey, Commander of the US 8th Air Force division of which Marcel's now-famous 509th Composite Bomb Wing was perhaps the most notorious subdivision. It was here that the cover-up was initiated.

Instead of continuing his flight to Wright Field, Marcel was ordered to remain behind in Texas while the wreckage was sent on without him. Pseudo-wreckage – allegedly that of a ripped-up weather balloon and its 'tinfoil-like' radar reflector – was brought in to replace the genuine wreckage. In a subsequent briefing Major General Ramey ordered Marcel to keep silent about the true nature of the wreckage he had seen, and instructed him to comply with the new cover story being disseminated by the military – namely that the wreckage was in fact the result of a crashed weather balloon and its radar reflector; that it was not, as first thought, that of a crashed alien disc. In response to orders from a 'higher level' the crashed flying saucer story was to be withdrawn immediately.

An example of how quickly and effectively the authorities can prevent a story reaching the public domain is cited in Timothy Good's book *Beyond Top Secret*. Good states that a news broadcast from Albuquerque describing the 'crashed disc' incident was picked up by at least two radio stations who immediately broadcast the incredible story. However, their transmissions were simultaneously interrupted with a warning from 'on high' not to continue the broadcast, as the following transcript reveals:

'ATTENTION ALBUQUERQUE: CEASE TRANSMISSION. REPEAT. CEASE TRANSMISSION. NATIONAL SECURITY ITEM. DO NOT TRANSMIT. STAND BY . . .'

One wonders why a crashed weather balloon and its radar reflector would be deemed a 'national security item'.

Meanwhile Radio KGFL, New Mexico, reported that it received a call direct from the Pentagon on the afternoon of 8th July 1947. The radio station was told that if it went ahead with the broadcast it would lose its licence to transmit. Assuming the wreckage was that of some secret US military aircraft the radio station complied with the request. But, of course, if the wreckage *had* been that of some secret product of 1947 US technology it would by now almost certainly have taken pride of place in some or other military museum or other where today it would be on show to the public. And it is not. On the contrary, if it still exists then it is still the property of the US government's FTD department. Strange that the US military would transport the wreckage of one of its *own* aircraft to the Foreign Technology Division, it has to be said.

In a later testimony, Frank Joyce, presenter with KGFL at the time of the incident, said that he had received a telephone call direct from the Pentagon on 8th July 1947. 'You put that story out about flying saucers and you'll be in a lot of trouble,' the Pentagon voice told him. It added: 'I'll show you what we can do.' KGFL had already broadcast an interview with ranch manager Mac Brazel, who had stated in no uncertain terms that the wreckage he had discovered was indeed that of a crashed flying saucer. As a consequence of the Pentagon telephone call, however, KGFL broadcast a second interview with Brazel, who this time said that the debris was definitely that of a weather balloon. Further investigations by Frank Joyce led him to discover how Brazel had been paid a sum of $3,000 by the US government (an awful lot of money in those days) in order to change his story. Brazel had been bought off.

From here on in, then, the national press disseminated what was now to be the official story, the 'weather balloon' story. But of course this was sham. Indeed, according to Thomas Jefferson DuBose, Chief of Staff to Major General Ramey at the time of the incident, the 'weather balloon' story was all part of a 'containment strategy' initiated from Washington DC by Major General Clements McCullen, Deputy Commander, Strategic Air Command. According to DuBose: 'McCullen said, "You are not to discuss this – this is more than Top Secret. You will say nothing. This is the highest priority you can imagine".' And further: 'We were in a real bind. McCullen said, "Look, why don't you come up with something, anything you can use to get the press off our back?" So we came up with this weather balloon story.' And until the release of the official US Air Force report in August 1994, which declared that the Roswell crash vehicle was not, after all, a weather balloon, but a Top Secret Project Mogul spy balloon, the story remained the same. One wonders how long it might take the relevant authorities to change their minds again.

[Note: In the summer of 1997 the US Air Force made what is perhaps its biggest blunder to date concerning this case: it released a press statement declaring that 'bodies' had indeed been recovered from the Roswell crash site, but that said 'bodies' were in fact 'dummies' used in high-altitude parachute tests. It has to be said that this must have been the first and only time that high-altitude parachute tests had been conducted from a Top Secret spy balloon!]

Back in July 1947, however, the weather balloon story stuck. Major Marcel was ordered to appear before reporters and press photographers over the next few days (together with pieces of the pseudo-wreckage strewn all about him) as a living testimony that the new story was indeed authentic. He was told that, in order to 'keep an eye on proceedings', he would be accompanied at the press conferences by senior military officials (including Major General Ramey) who would ensure that he rectified the 'mistake' and confirmed to the world the new story. This was done. As a result the 'crashed flying saucer' story was indeed withdrawn, Marcel ended up on the front page of every newspaper from here to eternity – along with official statements to the effect that indeed the debris was that of a crashed weather balloon and its radar reflector – and a rebuffed and ridiculed Major Jesse Marcel returned to Roswell Army Air Field with his name, and his reputation, undone.

In short, Major Jesse Marcel drew the short straw: he was the patsy.

File 03
Immaculate Conception

The Roswell incident, however, was not to be so easily forgotten. Word of the incident had reached the then President, Harry S. Truman, who ordered an immediate inquiry, or at least an immediate consultation with his top military and scientific advisers vis-à-vis the 'flying saucer problem', official government investigations into which had begun in earnest under the Franklin D. Roosevelt administration in 1933. (There is even some evidence that Roosevelt's predecessor, former President Herbert H. Hoover, had heard whispers of the phenomenon, and his term in office had begun as early as 1929.) Indeed, there are rumours that a pre-World War II British intelligence report (now shredded) alluded to the fact that Nazi scientists had been involved in reconstructing alien technology as early as 1935. It is said that the report ended up in the hands of top-ranking US military officials, and although this may sound irregular, further evidence I will present later also implies that Britain's official UFO investigations are monitored and overseen from Washington DC and Langley, Virginia, home of the CIA. The joint British and US intelligence machine may well present different exteriors, but it is driven by the same executive.

Intriguingly enough, these same rumours resurfaced a decade later as the CIA's infamous 'Operation Paperclip' became responsible for ferrying untold numbers of Nazi scientists to the United States in lieu of facing war crimes charges. They were to be employed at Ultra Top Secret Research & Development (R&D) facilities in the United States in order to continue the work of reverse-engineering the mechanics of acquired alien craft and adapting this technology for terrestrial military use. The CIA, of course, has always denied that Operation Paperclip ever took place. But then, what is the CIA's job if not to deny its own existence, much less the existence of aliens and their technology? As always, the Good Ol, US of A was innocent of all charges, the CIA maintained.

But if the Americans were unaware of the UFO situation in the mid-1930s – which seems unlikely – the Vatican was not. A quote from Pope John XXIII – from a statement made by him in 1935, before he became Pope – reads:

'The signs are increasing. The lights in the sky will appear red, blue, green, rapidly. Someone is coming from very far and wants to meet the people of Earth. Meetings have already taken place. But those who have really seen have been silent.'

Little wonder, then, that President Truman took the Roswell incident very seriously indeed.

Among the brief list of luminaries present at the Truman meeting was the infamous Dr Vannevar Bush, the leading US government scientist responsible for organizing the National Defense Research Council in 1941 and the Office of Scientific Research and Development in 1943 (later the Joint Research & Development Board) which in effect became the Manhattan Project, which in effect became the first atomic bomb. It is interesting to note that at the time of the Roswell incident, Roswell Army Air Field housed the only atomic bomber wing in the world, the 509th Composite Bomb Wing. Was the crashed disc there to monitor our newly acquired atomic capability, one wonders?

Also present at the meeting were Rear Admiral Roscoe H. Hillenkoetter, Director of Central Intelligence and the first Director of the CIA (which was, interestingly, formed on 18th September 1947, some say in response to the growing 'flying saucer problem') and former Secretary of the Navy James

V. Forrestal, who was aptly appointed Defense Secretary in July 1947, the exact same time as the Roswell incident. In effect this meeting witnessed the birth of the CIA and its supersecret Special Studies Group concerning the UFO situation, Majestic-12 (see Document 02).

The UFO era and the day of the government cover-up had truly arrived.

As we have already seen, and as further evidence will show, by the mid-1950s the British and US governments (both independently and as part of the NATO UFO study) had concluded that although UFOs and extraterrestrial intelligences were indeed visiting our planet, and that they therefore constituted a genuine phenomenon, they did not – and have not since – constituted a threat to either national or international security. Seems straightforward enough. Indeed, even today a simple enquiry to either the Ministry of Defence in Britain or the US Defense Department will provoke a similar response: i.e. that no UFO sighting investigated by the relevant departments has ever proven to be a defence threat. Seems even more straightforward.

However, a similar request for information regarding the British government's and/or the US government's active involvement in the phenomenon over the years – the military action they have taken against UFOs; the amount of crashed or otherwise downed UFOs they have retrieved; the amount of UFOs they have otherwise acquired; plus, of course, what they have managed to glean from the visitors themselves – their culture, their society, their technology – will be met with a barrage of silence and a veritable maze of still-classified documentation. Which makes no sense whatever. After all, if the phenomenon poses no threat, then why is there a need for secrecy? And moreover, if official military and scientific evaluations had, by the 1950s, already concluded that UFOs pose no threat then why is the phenomenon still classified at a higher security level even than the nuclear weapons programme?

Which it is.

This is not to say that I am either confused or surprised that both the British and US governments might consider penetration into their airspace by aircraft of unknown origin a defence threat. Logic dictates that indeed this would be the case. What *confuses* me is the fact that, in the face of incontrovertible evidence to the contrary – in the form of official military and intelligence documents declassified and released under the Freedom of Information Act in the United States and under the thirty-year Secrecy Act in Britain – both governments consistently deny any involvement in the phenomenon whatever. And what *surprises* me is the fact that they expect us to sit back and accept these lies as Gospel.

It is contradictions such as these that ignite public suspicion and so give rise to conspiracy theories. And unquestionably the most notable incident carrying by far the greatest implications to the effect that a massive UFO cover-up indeed exists at government level is the pivotal Roswell incident.

It is the Immaculate Conception of ufology.

DOCUMENT 02

Cosmic Top Secret
Eyes Only Copy One of One

Majestic-12

File 04
MJ-12 Briefing Document

Following recovery and removal of the crashed Roswell disc, then, the first of what was to become an ongoing series of containment and disinformation strategies was initiated. At the same time a series of official intelligence gathering studies was proposed. This was achieved mainly via CIA channels and was further accomplished via the various Secret Service and Military Intelligence agencies of the day, not the least among them the US Air Force Office of Special Investigations (AFOSI), the Office of Naval Intelligence (ONI) and US Army Intelligence. As I was soon to learn, however, the CIA was – and still is – the grand-daddy of them all.

Ostensibly a US Air Force *Estimate of the Situation* study, Project Sign was the first in a long line of official classifications for what in truth were CIA/MJ-12 studies into the UFO phenomenon. 'Sign' was later replaced by Project Grudge, then Project Blue Book, and today continues –

despite denials to the contrary – as Project Old New Moon. The Defense Intelligence Agency (DIA) has its own version of this study, which it calls Project Moon Dust. It is interesting to note that, although the above-ground complex at Area 51 is known to those who work there as 'Dreamland', the vast deep-underground complex seething beneath the desert there is code-named 'The Dark Side Of The Moon'. The connection between the US government, the UFO phenomenon and the Moon will become even more evident in Document 04.

Perhaps because he knew how difficult a task it would be to keep tabs on the sum of information gathered by these various agencies, President Truman decided to initiate a move that would see the collation of all UFO/ET data housed under one roof; there are many military, intelligence and civilian personnel of the era who have since testified to this fact. But it was the sudden and unexpected appearance in the UFO research arena of certain leaked documents that finally offered hard evidence that indeed a central military and scientific intelligence group had been established under the Truman administration. Indeed, some would go so far as to say that these documents offered not merely evidence but proof. Tentative proof. Proof, nonetheless.

According to said documents it was the combined advice of Dr Vannevar Bush, Rear Admiral Roscoe H. Hillenkoetter and Defense Secretary James V. Forrestal that persuaded Truman to form such a supersecret group, which came to be classified well above Top Secret under the code name 'Majestic-12' (MJ-12 and/or Majic-12). It is this group, formed by Presidential Executive Order on 24th September 1947, that the TV series *Dark Skies* has recently fictionalized (some would say as a damage-limitation exercise against the leak of the MJ-12 documents) and in so doing has of course undermined the many years of meticulous research undertaken by the central investigators in this case. When the content and the context of the *Dark Skies* series is set against the evidence now available it takes little imagination to see how the intelligence community's containment and disinformation strategy operates – that it is still in operation. TV fiction bears its message very well.

The containment of information sometimes fails; information is sometimes leaked and, when it is, disinformation is employed as a means to recover the secret lost as a result of the leak. A standard disinformation strategy, by its nature, would indeed include a skeleton of true facts fleshed out with strips of disinformation, or non-facts, as witness *Dark Skies*. This is standard intelligence procedure. As a still-active British intelligence source recently informed me: 'Once something has leaked out, if you still want to keep it secret, tell the world about it, especially in a fictitious form, a book, a film, that sort of thing. And then discredit it. In this way it becomes a bit of a joke, or at least it's seen as fiction, and although people know about it, nobody takes it seriously any more.' The fact that *Dark Skies* would seem to be a response to the leak of the MJ-12 documents appears to substantiate this policy, especially when you consider the purpose of such a group as Majestic-12 – to keep secret from the public the true facts about the UFO/ET phenomenon so that any scientific and/or technological advances made as a result of the study can be used in covert operations and turned to military advantage (such as the highly secret Stealth aerospace programme). The fact also that the 'hive' in *Dark Skies* are depicted as *'evil aliens whose intention it is to take over the world'* means for certain that another little pocket of humanity is being slowly but surely conditioned against the idea that the visitors could be anything but hostile. This in turn is sufficient to convince many that the UFO phenomenon should remain a national security issue. A perfect double bluff.

At the same time, of course, the existence of such groups as MJ-12 is wholly justified.

But wait a minute . . . Majestic-12 is pure fiction, right . . . ?

File 04: Appendix 01
Case Study: Cosmic Top-X01 Eyes Only Leaked Documents

Wrong.

In December 1984 US UFO investigator Jaime Shandera received a roll of undeveloped black-and-white 35 mm film in the post. Though the package arrived anonymously it was stamped with an Albuquerque, New Mexico postmark. This was notable for the fact that Kirtland Air Force Base, Los Alamos National Laboratories and White Sands Proving Ground are all Ultra Top Secret facilities located near Albuquerque, New Mexico, and all figured prominently in the furore surrounding the Roswell incident. Indeed, Roswell itself is a mere hop-and-a-skip distant. Could this document have been leaked by an insider who wanted the facts known? If so, it would not have been the first time.

According to nuclear physicist and longstanding UFO researcher Stanton T. Friedman, who has worked closely with Shandera regarding this issue, when the film was developed it revealed duplicate sets of eight pages of documentation classified TOP SECRET/MAJIC. (It should be noted that Mr Friedman's painstaking research and equally rigorous scientific analysis of these and further leaked MJ-12 documents is largely responsible for their verification. For this alone he deserves the applause of the entire UFO research community.) In his excellent book *Top Secret/Majic*, Friedman goes on to say:

'[The title page reads]: "Briefing Document: Operation Majestic-12 Prepared for President-Elect Dwight D. Eisenhower: (Eyes Only) 18 November, 1952." ' And further: 'The second page of the set listed the members of the Majestic-12 group, all of whom were dead. Then they read me the third page: "On 24 June, 1947, a civilian pilot flying over the Cascade Mountains in the State of Washington observed nine flying disc-shaped aircraft travelling in formation at a high rate of speed . . . In spite of these efforts, little of substance was learned about the objects until a local rancher reported that one had crashed in a remote region of New Mexico . . . On 07 July, 1947, a secret operation was begun to assure recovery of the wreckage of this object . . ." '

The document goes on to reveal that four small alien bodies were also recovered along with the wreckage. They had apparently ejected and were found two miles east of the crash site (an interesting correlation with some of the witness statements, including that of former US Army Intelligence man Master Sgt Frank Kaufmann). Also mentioned is the fact that the US government sequestered both the wreckage and the bodies for analysis. The document also contained a list of the operation's major players (see below).

Though this document has been both revered and ridiculed by members of the UFO research community – virtually in the same breath – nevertheless it continues to titillate interested parties. And so it should. As we shall see later, further MJ-12 documents have since been leaked and are now available in the public domain – documents that tend only to confirm the authenticity of the original document, the Briefing Document prepared by the then President

Harry S. Truman for President-Elect Dwight D. Eisenhower in 1952.

The US National Archive record of this document reads: 'Operation Majestic-12 is a TOP SECRET Research and Development/Intelligence operation responsible directly and only to the President of the United States. Operations of the project are carried out under the control of the Majestic-12 (Majic-12) Group, which was established by special classified executive order of President Truman on 24th September 1947, upon recommendation by Dr Vannevar Bush and Secretary James Forrestal. Members of the Majestic-12 Group were designated as follows:

Dr Vannevar Bush [prominent US government scientist and head of the Joint Research & Development Board in 1947. Four years earlier he was responsible for the Manhattan Project, which developed the first atomic bomb. As noted earlier, Bush's involvement in the production of the world's first atomic bomb cannot be removed from the fact that in 1947 Roswell Army Air Field housed the only atomic bomber group in the world, the 509th Composite Bomb Wing. Circles within circles . . . Dr Vannevar Bush was reputedly head of the Majestic-12 Group. Indeed, in a Top Secret Canadian Department of Transport memorandum, dated November 1950, Canadian government scientist Wilbert Brockhouse Smith is quoted as saying that flying saucers are 'the most highly classified matter in the United States Government, rating higher even than the H-bomb'. This senior secret defence projects engineer went on to confirm that Dr Vannevar Bush headed a 'small group' established to investigate the flying saucer problem. That 'small group' could only have been MJ-12];

Rear Admiral Roscoe H. Hillenkoetter [Director of Central Intelligence and first Director of the CIA. It is worth noting that the CIA and MJ-12 were established in the same week, 18th–24th September 1947, just two months after the Roswell incident. Well, well . . . Hillenkoetter was also on the board of directors of the National Investigations Committee on Aerial Phenomena, and in later years was thought to have softened on the secrecy angle. In a letter to Congress in 1961 he stated: 'It is time for the truth to be brought out . . . Behind the scenes, high-ranking Air Force officers are soberly concerned about the UFOs . . . But through official secrecy and ridicule, many citizens are led to believe the unknown flying objects are nonsense.' Rear Admiral Hillenkoetter was not the only one to become deeply affected by the information made privy to him as an MJ-12 Group member; it cost Defence Secretary James V. Forrestal his life];

Secretary James V. Forrestal [formerly Secretary of the Navy, which in 1947 was reportedly the overseeing body on matters of national security. This of course included the 'flying saucer problem'. Forrestal was appointed Defense Secretary in July 1947, the exact same time as the Roswell incident. More circles within circles . . . Following an alleged mental breakdown due to information overload associated with the US government's contact with extraterrestrials – which by this time had allegedly occurred – in March 1949 Forrestal was committed to Bethesda Naval Hospital in Washington DC. Two months later he (allegedly) committed suicide. According to former US Naval Intelligence man Milton William Cooper, however, Forrestal's death was no suicide.

Already embroiled in negotiations with at least one visiting alien embassy, President Truman was becoming increasingly concerned about Forrestal's ability to keep the 'secret' secret. Cooper says that Forrestal had been spilling secrets to members of Congress about the alien presence, and so had become something of a liability. Truman demanded

Forrestal's resignation. Forrestal refused to go. A short while later Forrestal was said to have suffered a 'mental breakdown' and so was admitted to Bethesda Naval Hospital where he was denied all visits, even from his family. Concerned for his welfare, on 21st May 1949 Forrestal's brother notified the authorities that he intended to remove his brother from the hospital the following day. But he was too late. According to Cooper, in the early hours of 22nd May 1949, CIA agents paid Forrestal a visit. Having first tied a sheet around his neck they then threw the former Secretary of Defense out of the window. The sheet ripped; Forrestal plummeted to his death. Later that day his tragic 'suicide' was announced to a shocked and disbelieving world. This, then, is an alternative account of the alleged suicide of MJ-12 Group member and former Secretary of Defense James V. Forrestal, according to Milton William Cooper. It should be noted that Cooper is a former member of the Intelligence Briefing Team of the Commander-in-Chief of the US Navy Pacific Fleet, and that the documents Cooper himself accessed whilst in service have convinced him utterly that the US government is indeed in conference with alien visitors];

General Nathan F. Twining [Commander of Bombing Operations during World War II, Twining was later appointed Commanding General of Air Materiel Command (AMC) based at Wright Field (Wright-Patterson AFB), Dayton, Ohio. It has been substantiated that between 8th July 1947 (the day of the first press release concerning Roswell) and 10th July 1947, General Twining was indeed in New Mexico 'due to a very important and sudden matter'. Wonder what that was . . . ?]

General Hoyt S. Vandenburg [second Director of Central Intelligence 1946–1947, and US Air Force Chief of Staff. Vandenburg by account, was in favour of 'destroying' the

UFOs – he saw them as a threat to both national and inter-national security. Indeed, it was Vandenburg who ordered the original US Air Force's *Estimate of the Situation* report to be burned on the grounds that UFOs were more likely to be Russian than alien – '*god-damned outer-space commies!*' He was evidently hand-picked for his military position, but his 'need-to-know' status obviously did *not* include information gleaned from his own government's scientific evaluations of the visitors nor the fact that more senior members of the MJ-12 Group regarded the 'problem' in a somewhat different light. And in any case, when one's own politics include 'thermonuclear democracy', well now . . .];

Dr Detlev W. Bronk [Chairman of the National Research Council and member of the Medical Advisory Board of the Atomic Energy Commission. Bronk enjoyed close affiliations with Dr Edward Condon, who headed the fabled US Air Force-sponsored scientific investigation of UFOs at the University of Colorado, 1966–1968. *The Condon Report* was published in 1969, and concluded that UFOs were of little scientific significance. Both Bronk and Condon later became members of the Scientific Advisory Committee of the Brookhaven National Laboratory, famous for its research into acquired alien 'beam weapon' technology];

Dr Jerome C. Hunsaker [Head of the Departments of Mechanical and Aeronautical Engineering at the Massa-chusetts Institute of Technology (MIT: renowned US gov-ernment scientific intelligence institute and favoured CIA stomping ground). Hunsaker was acclaimed as a genius in aircraft design. He also chaired the National Advisory Committee for Aeronautics];

Rear Admiral Sidney W. Souers [first Director of the Central Intelligence Group – January–June 1946 – Souers became Executive Secretary to the National Security Council in

September 1947, the very same time MJ-12 and the CIA were formed, barely two months after Roswell. Another coincidence . . . ?];

Mr Gordon L. Gray [despite his name, Mr *Gray* was not an alien – at least, I don't think so! He was, however, Secretary of the Army until 1950, when he was appointed Special Assistant to the President for National Security Affairs concerning the 'psychological warfare implications of UFOs'. And then again, on second thoughts, perhaps he *did* resemble one of those little almond-eyed critters . . . !];

Dr Donald H. Menzel [executive CIA operative under the Directorate of Operations' Covert Action Staff – function: disinformation and propaganda schedules. Menzel was also Director of Harvard College Observatory. He is remembered specifically, of course, for his untiring work in attempting to debunk the UFO phenomenon. Indeed, he was America's number one UFO/ET debunker and in this respect mentor to Philip Klass, who has since succeeded him in this role. However, as Timothy Good remarks in his book *Above Top Secret*, Menzel's scientific qualifications – which were plentiful in the fields of astronomy, wave mechanics, atomic spectra and planetary atmospherics – would have made him a great asset to the MJ-12 Group. But his biggest contribution would have been his reputation and expertise in coordinating covert-action debunking and disinformation schedules: keeping the public eye trained on anything but UFOs];

General Robert M. Montague [Base Commander at the Atomic Energy Commission installation at Sandia Base, Albuquerque, New Mexico. Interestingly enough, Montague held this position from July 1947 (now there's a surprise!) through February 1951];

Dr Lloyd V. Berkner [key member of the CIA-sponsored

Robertson Panel, a scientific advisory group on UFOs set up by order of the White House in 1953. He also worked under Dr Vannevar Bush as Executive Secretary of the Joint Research & Development Board in 1946].

Following the death of Secretary James V. Forrestal on 22nd May 1949, *General Walter B. Smith* was designated as permanent replacement. His appointment to the MJ-12 Group became official on 1st August 1949.

General Smith was Director of the CIA from 1950 through 1953 under President Truman. Like Hillenkoetter and Forrestal before him, however, Smith evidently had problems. In a memorandum to the National Security Council in 1952 he gave voice to his mounting concern regarding what he believed had become a precarious US government/alien stand-off: '. . . It is my view that this situation has possible implications for our national security which transcend the interests of a single service . . .'

The document concludes:

'. . . The Majestic-12 Group remains of the unanimous opinion that the imposition of the strictest security precautions should continue without interruption into the new administration [i.e. from the outgoing Truman administration into the incoming Eisenhower administration, 1952/3]. At the same time contingency plan MJ-1949-04P/78 (Top Secret – Eyes Only) should be held in continued readiness should the need to make a public announcement present itself.'

File 05
The Cutler-Twining Memo

'14 July 1954 was probably a day like so many others in Washington. James Lay came back to his office from a meeting with President Eisenhower at 2:30. p.m. At 4:30, he took a short call from Eisenhower. When he put down the phone, he perhaps beckoned to a secretary and started dictating some work. The secretary took down the dictation, most likely returned to her desk and typed up the material, including the following memo:

```
Memorandum for General Twining


SUBJECT: NSC/MJ-12 Special Studies Project
   The President has decided that the MJ-12 SSP
briefing should take place during the already
scheduled White House meeting of July 16, rather
than following it as previously intended. More
precise arrangements will be explained to you
upon arrival. Please alter your plans accord-
ingly.
   Your concurrence in the above change of ar-
rangements is assumed.
   ROBERT CUTLER
   Special Assistant
   to the President
```

When it was finished, the security marking TOP SECRET RESTRICTED SECURITY INFORMATION was typed on the memo, and it was sent on its way. A perfectly normal occurrence.'

The above extract is from Stanton T. Friedman's superb book *Top Secret/Majic*, in which Friedman details the years of painstaking research he has undertaken – together with fellow researchers William Moore and Jaime Shandera – in a tireless endeavour to uncover the truth regarding the

Majestic-12 Special Studies Project. Indeed, the above memo did not come gratis. It was the end result of a very long, very frustrating investigation.

In July 1985 William Moore and Jaime Shandera flew to Washington DC in order to further their search for declassified MJ-12 files. Three months previously, in March 1985, Stanton Friedman had also been in Washington, and had learned from Ed Reese at the Modern Military Branch of the US National Archives that the Air Force Headquarters intelligence files were up for classification review. By the time Moore and Shandera returned in July the review had been completed. Together they began their laborious task of sifting through the files.

It was while Shandera was busy searching through the newly reviewed material – Entry 267 from the US Air Force Record Group 341 – that fortune paid him a visit. While placing a file folder back in its box and pulling the next file out he discovered a sheet of innocuous-seeming paper that, somewhat mysteriously, had been misplaced between the files (did someone *want* Shandera to discover this information?). As he carefully retrieved this mysterious sheet of 'onion-skin' paper he discovered that it was a memo from one Robert Cutler to Majestic-12 Group member General Nathan F. Twining, dated 14 July 1954.

Shandera had struck gold. This was clearly an authentic document. It was unequivocally marked NSC/MJ-12 (National Security Council/Majestic-12) Special Studies Project and unlike President Truman's Briefing Document for President-Elect Eisenhower, which had arrived anonymously in the post eight months previously, this document had been discovered at the Modern Military Branch of the National Archives in Washington DC, the home of all declassified US military documents. To add to this, in 1954 Robert Cutler was Special Assistant for National Security to the President, which meant that he was the official liaison between Eisenhower and the National Security Council. It should be said that in 1954 the NSC enjoyed a far lower profile than it does today, and was essentially set up to advise the president on matters of national security. The Executive Secretary of the National Security Council at that time was James Lay, who dictated the memo and who worked very closely with Cutler – together they were responsible for the preparation and collation of all classified paperwork relevant to the President, in particular material concerning foreign affairs and national security. In brief, they were civil servants of the highest order. But above and beyond this they had unwittingly provided the most telling piece of evidence thus far that Majestic-12 was indeed an official 'Top Secret Restricted Security Group responsible directly and only to the President of the United States'. And between them they had unwittingly struck a near-fatal blow to the endeavours of the world's most notorious debunkers. They would live to fight another day.

Though even more convincing documents were yet to emerge, the discovery of the Cutler-Twining memo was a rich reward for the many years the Friedman/Moore/Shandera team had spent chasing paper. But there was more work, more paper-chasing to be done. Tests had to be carried out in order to authenticate the memo. Was this strange 'onion-skin' paper from the same stock as that used at the White House in 1954? Was the typeface the same? What about the style in which the memo had been written? The language? The grammar? The format?

And how did it compare to other memos known to have been prepared by Cutler?

It all checked out. When compared to other memos from Cutler that did not mention MJ-12 but that were known to be authentic, the similarities in style, format, language and grammar were seen to be consistent. This in itself was sufficient to substantiate beyond question some very important points hitherto under debate:

a) that the Majestic-12 Group existed;

b) that it was directly responsible to the President of the United States, and was not, therefore, some renegade backstairs intelligence cell whose authority undermined that of the White House and the US Constitution, as has been claimed by many researchers: on the contrary, it would seem that MJ-12 was set up in order to counteract this possibility;

c) that at least one of its members – General Nathan F. Twining – was one of the highest-ranking military officials of the period, indicating that whatever the nature of the projects undertaken by this group they were more than likely to have been classified at the highest possible security level. The fact that the memo itself was classified Top Secret Restricted Security Information was sufficient to show this. Indeed, the only thing this memo did not show was the precise nature of the 'special studies' the Majestic-12 Group was set up to administrate. Or did it?

At the time this particular memo was written Twining was Commanding General of Air Materiel Command based at Wright Field (now Wright-Patterson Air Force Base), Dayton, Ohio, where it is said the Roswell UFO wreckage was taken for storage and analysis, along with four dead aliens. It has already been established that between 8th July and 10th July 1947, Twining was in New Mexico 'due to a very important and sudden matter'. This 'very important and sudden matter' could only have been related to the Roswell incident.

Where the authenticity of certain leaked or officially declassified documents may remain in question, the fact that Twining was indeed Commanding General of AMC and that he held the above-described post at Wright Field during this time-frame may not. Though of course the US government is not about to admit the fact that alien technology and biology was stored and analyzed at Wright Field in the late 1940s (until the bulk of this work was transferred to Area 51), nevertheless numerous military and former military witnesses to this fact have since testified positively. Wreckage from at least one UFO crash together with at least four dead aliens were indeed present at the base during the Roswell time-frame, they say.

Not the least of these witnesses is former US Air Force Colonel Edward Strieber, Whitley Strieber's uncle. Whitley Strieber is possibly America's most famous 'abductee', and to judge by the success of his book *Communion* (later a successful Hollywood movie), he is probably the wealthiest, too. Perhaps because of this he has suffered all the run-of-the-mill in-house snipes and accusations regarding his own integrity and, perhaps more pertinently, his standing in relation to the intelligence community. It is worth mentioning here that, according to former US Naval Intelligence operative Milton William Cooper, Whitley Strieber is a CIA agent. Whether this be fact or fiction – or pure paranoia on the part of Mr Cooper – I do not know. What I do know is that, due to the phenomenon's extremely high-level security classification and the consequent attention given it by certain elements of the intelligence community, paranoia within the field of UFO research is as rife as church on Sunday. Everybody's immediate conclusion seems to be that everybody else is a government agent. Research is dogged by such in-house bickerings and accusations. It is a minefield. But then, to my mind this situation only adds weight to the suspicion that the intelligence community – in particular counter-intelligence agencies such as the CIA, AFOSI and MI6 – takes the phenomenon very seriously indeed. The paranoia and the bickering, I am convinced, are the result of an insidious backstairs manipulation on the part of those who do not want anyone else to know their big secret. Whatever it is.

I felt it pertinent to mention Mr Cooper's assumption of Whitley Strieber because the following testimony originated with Strieber himself. I should add that I have spoken personally to Whitley Strieber and that I am sufficiently convinced of the sincerity of his motive that I am able to include his testimony here with confidence.

In a taped interview with me, Mr Strieber referred to several aspects of the UFO phenomenon and, in particular, its connection to the US intelligence community, within which he admits to having high-level contacts. He told me that his uncle, Colonel Edward Strieber, had spent much of his career at Wright-Patterson and that, as a result, he had been aware of the Majestic operation. He told Strieber that, in the summer of 1947, Wright Field was indeed the recipient of the Roswell crash wreckage that included 'alien materials, artefacts and biological remains'. He also confirmed that concern over what should be done with the wreckage 'had been debated at the highest levels of the government'.

Strieber also told me about another officer who had worked at Wright Field in 1947. This man claimed that he had actually handled the decomposed alien remains. According to Strieber, the officer described the remains as 'vegetative' in quality, and spoke of the internal organs as being 'unformed'. Though of course even the most enlightened scientist, at first sight, would be stretched to accurately describe the inherent and functional qualities of extraterrestrial physiology and biology, nevertheless the officer in question claimed he had seen enough to conclude that the remains were not indigenous to Earth.

'Certainly not.'

One further snippet worth mentioning concerns a man by the name of Dr Robert Sarbacher, who told the authors of *The Roswell Incident*, William Moore and Charles Berlitz, that he too had seen the Roswell wreckage. In a letter published in *The Roswell Incident*, he said: 'I still do not know why the high order of classification has been given and why the denial of the existence of these devices.'

Though we did not broach this subject during the interview, in Whitley Strieber's *Breakthrough: The Next Step* he tells the story of how he sought out Dr Sarbacher. In a telephone conversation with him Strieber says that Dr Sarbacher confirmed that the contents of the letter were indeed true, and that the materials he had worked on 'had some very unusual properties'.

Dr Sarbacher went on to say: 'That fabric we obtained at Roswell had molecular welds so small that you couldn't even identify what they were until the Sixties, when the microscopes to do it became available.' He also said that the knowledge gleaned from working with these materials was later used by defence contractors to manufacture seamless coatings for 'radar-proof' aircraft such as the Stealth. Strieber also enquired as to whether Dr Sarbacher thought the material could possibly have been of 'nonhuman origin'. Dr Sarbacher replied: 'What I can be certain about is that it was not produced by any technology that we were aware of in 1947. Or now.' This conversation took place in 1986. However, the story did not end there.

When Strieber later sent Dr Sarbacher a package, he received a telephone call from the freight company telling him that the package could not be delivered. The reason?

The recipient was deceased. Evidently Dr Sarbacher had 'fallen' from his boat and drowned.

A reminder, perhaps, of just how desperate certain parties are to keep secrets secret.

To conclude – for the moment – our investigation into the role played by Wright Field in the Roswell incident, and therefore its connection to the Majestic-12 operation via Base Commander and MJ-12 member General Nathan F. Twining, I should mention here the testimony of Bill Uhouse, who claims that he worked on covert government projects for more than thirty years.

Uhouse, who these days uses the pseudonym 'Jarod 2' (pronounced 'Jay-rod') claims to have worked on covert government projects from the mid-1950s through to his retirement in the late 1980s. He told US researcher Glenn Campbell (no relation to the *Rhinestone Cowboy*) that he worked at Area 51 on the mechanical design for the avionics of simulators for US-built spacecraft, or UFOs. He also said that four aliens survived a UFO crash in Arizona in May 1953 and were taken to the supersecret deep-underground facility at Wright Field before being transferred to Area 51. He described the aliens as being around four feet tall with two eyes, two ears, a nose and a small round mouth. Though vaguely humanoid in appearance, he said, their arms were longer than normal. The 'guests' were subsequently transferred to Area 51 where, assuming their continued survival, they are still being held today. Uhouse confirmed that communications had been established between the aliens and their captors once they were ensconced inside Area 51.

Like that of many other witnesses, including Colonel Edward Strieber and Dr Sarbacher, Uhouse's testimony cannot be substantiated. The subject to which he refers is highly classified and the relevant authorities will of course neither confirm nor deny such claims. They would rather we kept stabbing in the dark – keep us all guessing: that's the way any need-to-know operation works.

However, the above testimonies do imply that something out of the ordinary *was* going on at Wright Field during the late 1940s, and General Nathan F. Twining *was* Base Commander during this period. In my opinion this strongly suggests that the nature of the projects undertaken by the Majestic-12 Group – of which General Twining was an executive member – was at the very least directly related to whatever the military scientists at Wright Field were working on. And according to the testimonies of Colonel Edward Strieber, Dr Robert Sarbacher and Bill Uhouse (Jarod 2), they were working on exobiological and exotechnological projects – the study of extraterrestrial biology and technology – projects so secret that knowledge of their existence was restricted to Majestic-12 clearance level only.

Thus the memo, by implication, does indeed allude to the nature of the 'special studies' that the Majestic-12 Group was set up to administrate.

File 06
The Robertson Panel and The Alleged Instruction Paper

I have decided to include here what I believe to be a very significant extract from an alleged instruction paper prepared by MJ-12 Group member Rear Admiral Roscoe H. Hillenkoetter, then Director of the CIA, for President-Elect Eisenhower in January 1953. Essentially this paper was prepared as a result of the CIA/USAF-sponsored Robertson

Panel Report of the same month, and seems to have been an appendix to the original Briefing Document prepared two months earlier in November 1952.

In short, the so-called Robertson Panel Report came about as a result of the CIA's mounting concern over the UFO problem. By order of the White House and the OSI (Office of Scientific Intelligence) a panel of very prominent scientists was convened over a period of several days, 14th to 17th January 1953, in order to ascertain whether the phenomenon should be considered a serious national security threat. Meetings were held at the Pentagon. Among the list of luminaries sitting on the meetings' Scientific Advisory Panel were weapons systems expert Dr H. P. Robertson, after whom the report was named, and Dr Lloyd V. Berkner, eminent geophysicist and MJ-12 Group member. Others present included experts in the fields of physics, astrophysics, radar, astronomy, atomic structure, missiles and rockets, plus a panel of America's highest-ranking military and intelligence officials whose task it was to interview the scientists. The interview panel included Brigadier William H. Garland, Commanding General of ATIC (Air Technical Intelligence Centre), Dr H. Marshall Chadwell, Assistant Director of the CIA/OSI, Ralph L. Clark, Deputy Assistant Director of the CIA/OSI, plus other high-ranking members of the CIA and OSI and members of US Air Force Intelligence and US Naval Intelligence. It is clear that in 1953 the US government took the UFO phenomenon very seriously indeed.

What is interesting about this report is the fact that, among other conclusions reached, the panel decided after four days of discussion and debate that 'there was no evidence of a direct threat to national security'. To add to this, though the panel was reluctant to admit officially to the possibility that UFOs could be of extraterrestrial origin, it did note statements made by Major Dewey Fournet of US Air Force Intelligence in this respect:

'Mr Fournet, in his presentation, showed how he had eliminated each of the known and probable causes of sightings, leaving him "extra-terrestrial" as the only one remaining in many cases.'

Of equal interest was the Panel's recommendation to initiate a policy that included the debunking of all UFO sightings and a schedule of public 'education'.

'The "debunking" aim would result in reduction in public interest in "flying saucers" which today evokes a strong psychological reaction,' the panel concluded. And further: 'This education could be accomplished by mass media such [as] television, motion pictures, and popular articles. Basis of such education would be actual case histories which had been puzzling at first but later explained.'

But perhaps the most sinister recommendation made by the panel was to monitor and discredit the activities of civilian UFO groups. Infiltration was a method both proposed and still employed by the CIA, as we shall see later. The reasons given for this illegal activity included the need to prevent the 'great influence on mass thinking' that, it was deemed, continued widespread sightings would inevitably induce, and in this respect the panel concluded that 'the continued reporting of these phenomena does . . . result in a threat to the orderly functioning of the protective organs of the body politic'. In other words it upsets the status quo's apple cart.

In addition, Captain Edward J. Ruppelt, Chief of the ATIC's Aerial Phenomena Branch – who also sat on the interview panel – reported that the CIA had directed the Air Force to debunk all reports of UFO sightings and to discredit all witnesses. 'We even have to discredit our own pilots,' he disclosed.

Little wonder, then, with all this brouhaha concerning UFOs, that Rear Admiral Hillenkoetter deemed it necessary to prepare an instruction paper for the incoming President Eisenhower.

Which reads: 'On the last day the panel adopted a "public education program" supported by all government agencies concerned with two main objectives: Educate and Trivialize. The aim of trivialization was to reduce public interest in "flying saucers" and could be accomplished via the mass media [such as] television, motion pictures and popular articles. The basis would be actual cases that would first cause confusion, but would then be explained. As with magic tricks, there is scant interest once the trick has been revealed.'

And further: 'The National Security Council was to start immediately the necessary action to strip the unidentified objects of their special status, the aura of mystery they enjoy.'

The paper goes on to report on remarks made by Albert M. Chop, US Air Force press officer for all reports concerning UFOs, who also sat on the interview panel. According to a copy of the report obtained by German conspiracies author Jan van Helsing, Mr Chop stated: 'We [the Air Force] have been ordered to collaborate in a country-wide disclaiming campaign, to publish articles in newspapers and to give interviews to ridicule UFO reports.' ATIC's Captain Ruppelt added: 'If we could not find a plausible explanation, we were just to ridicule the witnesses.'

Perhaps disillusioned by these recommendations, both Chop and Ruppelt resigned their military careers within months of the Robertson Panel Report.

File 07
Operations Manual

Following the discovery of three new MJ-12 documents by California researcher Tim Cooper in 1992, Stanton Friedman and his team once again set to work endeavouring to establish their authenticity, or otherwise. The documents seemed to check out. Consistencies were found in typeface, style, language and format. The doubts surrounding the existence of the Majestic-12 Group were further diminished.

But it was two years later that Friedman learned of yet another MJ-12 document, the *Majestic-12 Operations Manual*, which he enthusiastically describes as 'the mother of all Majestic-12 documents!' If this document could be authenticated it would not only substantiate beyond doubt the existence of the Majestic-12 Group – it would substantiate the nature of the projects undertaken by the Group, too.

Like the Briefing Document for President-Elect Eisenhower, this document also arrived on a roll of 35 mm film. Evidently it had been sent anonymously to researcher and member of the board of the Fund for UFO Research Don Berliner, who told Friedman in December 1994 that he had received it nine months earlier in March 1994. It had taken him this long to develop the film as he thought it was one of several other rolls of 35 mm film he had taken of aircraft at the Experimental Aircraft Show he had attended in Oshkosh, Wisconsin. As the package in which it had been sent bore a Wisconsin postmark, Berliner thought he had obviously left it behind and somebody had forwarded it to him. He thought nothing more of it.

Until he finally developed it. It was then that he realized what a jewel he had in his possession.

The document was dated April 1954, and was marked

'TOP SECRET/MAJIC: Eyes Only'. The heading *Majestic-12 Group Special Operations Manual: Extraterrestrial Entities and Technology, Recovery and Disposal* left no doubts as to the nature of the MJ-12 operation. As Stanton Friedman euphorically explains in his book *Top Secret/Majic:* 'The report outlined how to secure, package, ship and store artefacts and extraterrestrial biological entities from recovered alien flying saucers!'

The document goes on to corroborate information pertaining to the Eisenhower Briefing Document and other leaked and/or declassified MJ-12 documents. Indeed, the wording in some places is identical to that of the other documents. The same can be said of its style, language and format. Investigations and analysis of the document are ongoing, but surely even the more pedantic in the field of UFO research cannot seriously continue to question the authenticity of these documents, nor the sum of information gleaned from them. Barring an open admission on the part of the US government that indeed Majestic-12 existed – and probably still does, even if under a different code name – and that the purpose of its operation was the recovery and analysis of extraterrestrial vehicles and their pilots, I would say these documents prove beyond reasonable doubt that the US government and aliens are indeed more than just good friends.

DOCUMENT 03

Cosmic Top Secret
Eyes Only Copy One of One

The CIA
And The Secret Government

File 08
The Beast

'In order to survive, nations need strong intelligence services. But the idea that the CIA is primarily an intelligence-gathering operation is itself one of the agency's greatest propaganda triumphs.'

The above quote is taken from a superb little booklet I picked up recently, *The CIA's Greatest Hits* by Mark Zepezauer. Anyone with even the slightest interest in real-life X-File operations should read it. Essentially, this booklet, written in concise two-page chapters, will tell you at a glance all you ever needed to know about the CIA's direct involvement with Nazi war criminals; international terrorism: high-finance scandals; the rigging of elections; Watergate; Iran/Contra; drug trafficking; the assassinations of popes, presidents and other high-ranking politicians and officials; acts of genocide; infiltration of the media and other relevant organizations . . .

indeed, think of your worst political nightmare and you will find that the CIA, at some time or another, has brought it to terrifying life. And then some.

But it is this last point that brings us to the real crux of Document 03: the infiltration by the CIA of civilian UFO groups and organizations in a major US government initiative to keep all of the most pertinent information regarding UFOs secret.

That, and to establish the fact that behind what has become somewhat erroneously known as the 'Government UFO cover-up' lurks a beast more powerful even than Congress or Parliament. Or even the White House. It is this beast, known collectively as the military-industrial complex – and otherwise as the Secret Government – that stands like some megalomaniacal Mother Superior behind the world's elected Governments, and that therefore should be brought to account for withholding information pertaining to the extraterrestrial presence – information that, after all, must surely be the property of every freethinking adult on the planet.

It is this non-elected beast that holds the secrets, then. And the CIA is the receptacle in which this beast's secrets are kept.

File 08: Appendix 01
Case Study: Cosmic Top-X02 Eyes Only
Secret of the Ages

In 1978, Todd Zechel made history.

In an attempt to prise open the CIA's X-File archives he formed a civilian UFO organization with a remit to pressure the US government to release classified UFO documents. He called this organization *Citizens Against UFO Secrecy* (CAUS). In December of the same year CAUS put out a press release announcing that the CIA had indeed released previously classified UFO-related documents. This press release was distributed throughout the US media.

Together with William Spaulding of the Arizona-based UFO research group *Ground Saucer Watch* (GSW), the previous year – 1977 – Zechel had hired New York lawyers Peter Gersten and Henry Rothblatt to sue the CIA under the Freedom of Information Act for the release of the documents. Previous to this the CIA had firmly denied withholding any such documents, except those relating to the Robertson Panel Report of January 1953 which the CIA had itself instigated. These documents totalled fifty-seven. Following the court ruling, however, the CIA was forced to release a staggering one thousand pages of documents (still only one-twentieth of the quantity thought to be held in the CIA archives). This discrepancy is almost as big as the lie upon which the agency was built.

According to Zechel (and Milton Cooper and a host of others) the CIA has been centrally and continuously involved in the UFO phenomenon since 1948. He says the CIA archives are stuffed with photographic data, witness reports and even physical evidence, proving beyond question that UFOs are part of a genuine phenomenon that has been around for at least fifty years, and that forms part of the biggest and most well-kept government secret ever. He also says that during this time the CIA has been the most senior and certainly the most central player in the collation and analysis of UFO/ET evidence, gathering reports from the National Security Agency and the Defense Intelligence Agency, to name but two. But perhaps the most disturbing claim made by Zechel is that the CIA's Directorate of Operations (counter-intelligence) has been actively involved in the interrogation and intimidation of witnesses for decades, while the domestic Collection Division's role (internal security) has been that of 'silencing' those witnesses who refused to comply with the agency's wishes. Zechel maintains that the CIA is without question the nut to crack if you want to know about alien/government secrecy.

The problem is, of course, this nut is a multifaceted, multibillion-dollar rhinestone.

Whether or not Zechel's court action was a genuine civilian victory over the US government's secrecy policy is, of course, debatable. Zechel is himself a former National Security Agency employee. The possibility that Zechel was acting on behalf of the NSA, either wittingly or otherwise, must be a consideration. After all, there is little doubt that the CIA is in possession of information and materials that the NSA covets dearly, in particular concerning the UFO phenomenon. It could be that a civilian battleground such as the US Supreme Court was simply the one the NSA considered the most likely to produce results. If this be the case then it seems the NSA was right. It was the first time since the CIA's inception that civilian law had prised open at least one of the agency's X-File vaults. For this fact alone Todd Zechel should be commended; it is not every day the CIA's secrecy veil is breached.

Indeed, ever since its formation under President Harry S. Truman the CIA has remained the world's most dubious, sinister and probably its most compartmentalized intelligence agency. Certainly its most powerful. Formed on 18th September 1947, out of the now-defunct Office of Strategic Services, the Overseas Secret Service and the Central Intelligence Group, the CIA soon became a government in its own right.

But it was with no small amount of help from its British counterpart MI6 (or SIS: Secret Intelligence Service, as Britain's own counter-intelligence agency is officially known) that the agency became the monster it is today. Indeed, it would be fair to say that, in the first instance, the CIA modelled itself on the template of British espionage. One might say that MI6 is to the CIA what Charles Atlas is to Arnold Schwarzenegger: role model and mentor supreme, with the added similarity that the protégé has in the long run outstripped the achievements of its forerunner by a country mile. In this respect the more covert echelons of MI6 these days comprise little more than a British CIA outlet. And there are many such outlets worldwide. Indeed, the CIA's role today is more that of an international policing agency, a kind of latter-day Gestapo and, like its Nazi predecessor, is sponsored and governed by a global consortium of the world's most powerful financial and political groups, most notably today the Council on Foreign Relations, the Royal Institute for International Affairs, the United Nations, NATO's ruling elite, the Trilateral Commission, The Round Table, P2 Masonry, the Club of Rome, the Policy Committee (Bilderberg Group) and the overseeing Committee of 300. Within these highly exclusive political circles global policy is debated, determined and implemented, and the CIA – again, like its Nazi predecessor – is there to ensure this policy remains intact. In this respect it is simply impossible to calculate the number of foreign security agencies on the CIA payroll, much less the total number of its personnel. Officially the CIA staff numbers around eleven thousand, but this figure is of course a nonsense. Its foreign agents and contracted personnel alone number easily in excess of this figure. And then some. The CIA's official budget is classified; its unofficial budget is incalculable. But no matter how many taxpayers' dollars find their way into the CIA coffers each year, the figure, whatever it is, would pale to insignificance when compared to the real power invested in this faceless monster.

Greater than faith in a pope.

In a nutshell, then, this is a break down of the world's most powerful intelligence agency. And in a nutshell, it is this intelligence agency that holds in its X-File archives the key to the 'secret of the ages': the government/alien agenda.

File 09
X File Supreme

Before we take a close look at the CIA's infiltration schedule, first a thing or two about the agency's grand entrance onto the UFO scene – how influential it has become with regard to US government security policy, how autonomous its directive with regard to the UFO phenomenon in general. After all, if the CIA's 'above-the-law' security clearance is sufficient to conceal such damnable actions as the assassinations of the brothers Kennedy, the odd pope, the human rights activist Dr Martin Luther King Jr *et al*; the toppling of governments; the orchestration of internecine conflicts in order to furnish the coffers of the arms-trade magnates (a percentage of whose inconceivable profit margins form a sizeable chunk of the CIA's black budget) and the covert instigation of convenient civil and international wars (the Gulf War, for example, and Angola, Panama, Bosnia) in order to test the US government's latest biological, chemical, laser and particle-beam weapons systems, then who is to say this same agency would not enjoy a little light relief in setting about the UFO phenomenon, too? Remember that the UFO phenomenon is classified at a very high security level indeed. It involves not only the so-called 'cranks' who claim they have received 'messages from the gods', but also the possibility that some of the most highly advanced technologies in governments' possession originated with alien intelligences. Surely any government in possession of such highly advanced technologies as these would wish to keep them under wraps. Which is where the CIA enters the frame.

Without question the CIA is the intelligence agency most closely associated with the UFO/ET cover-up. Indeed, there is more than a little evidence to suggest that America's most 'above-the-law' intelligence agency was established for this very reason – as a negotiating table for the unpublished dialogues taking place between alien intelligences and the US government (in particular Majestic-12) and, of course, as a disinformation, propaganda and bully-boy operation with a directive to keep these dialogues under wraps. Sounds far-fetched, I know. But this is certainly the claim of former US Naval Intelligence operative Milton William Cooper, who, like Robert O. Dean before him, says he has seen the documents to prove it. In his book *Behold A Pale Horse*, Cooper states:

'A special group of America's top scientists were [*sic*] organized under the name Project SIGN in December 1947 to study the phenomenon. The whole nasty business was contained. Project SIGN envolved into Project GRUDGE in December 1948. A low-level collection and disinformation project named BLUE BOOK was formed under GRUDGE. Sixteen volumes were to come out of GRUDGE. 'Blue Teams' were put together to recover the crashed disks and dead or live aliens. The Blue Teams were later to evolve into Alpha Teams under Project POUNCE.

'During these early years the United States Air Force and the Central Intelligence Agency exercised complete control over the 'alien secret'. In fact, the CIA was formed by Presidential Executive Order . . . for the express purpose of dealing with the alien presence.'

My own standpoint on this (and other similar claims) is that either all of these former military and intelligence personnel are gaga, or they are lying – or there is at least some truth underpinning their claims. (It should be said here that Mr Cooper has suffered in the most horrendous way as a result of disclosing the contents of the documents he claims to have seen whilst attached to US Naval Intelligence. His car has twice been run off the road by the same black government limousine. The first time he was left for dead, but survived. The second time he lost a leg. He was visited in hospital following the second 'accident' and told that if he did not 'shut up' the next 'accident' would indeed be fatal. As a protection, Mr Cooper spent $27,000 on a mailshot informing the greatest number of people he could about the UFO cover-up and its attendant backstairs plan to invent an artificial threat from outer space in order to unite humanity under the banner of a New World Order, a One World Government. It is for reasons such as these that the claims of former military and intelligence personnel are taken seriously by the author, at least until proven otherwise.)

It should also be said that the point of this document is neither to prove nor to disprove these claims, but to study the evidence and to draw the relevant conclusions. And in order to achieve that, we must throw *all* the evidence in the pot and sample the brew. That the CIA was formed as a counter-intelligence screen to protect a formal treaty allegedly signed between a visiting alien embassy and the US government is a claim to be considered, then. Indeed, if proven, it is the CIA's *X File Supreme*.

But whatever the truth behind the UFO/ET scenario and its connection to the US intelligence community, one thing is clear: the Central Intelligence Agency and the Majestic-12 Group were both established within a week of each other (September 1947) and less than three months after the world's most famous UFO incident ever, the Roswell incident. The chain of coincidences begins here.

File 10
The Nazi Connection

Before outlining the CIA's direct connection to the UFO phenomenon, I would like to include here one or two of the agency's most notorious 'hits'. The reason for this is to establish the nature of the beast, so to speak – that in fact the CIA's history file looks more like a serial killer's casebook than the record of a reputable intelligence agency.

For example, according to the author of *The CIA's Greatest Hits*, Mark Zepezauer, 'one of the most important of all CIA operations began before the agency was even born'.

The connection between the US government and Nazi Germany, via CIA channels, is well-known to many UFO researchers. Indeed, this connection has been highlighted in TV's *The X Files*. Under the code name 'Operation Paperclip', so the storyline informed viewers, top Nazi scientists were shipped to the US and South America towards the end of World War II instead of facing war crimes charges. It seemed the US authorities had better use for the likes of Klaus Barbie (the 'Butcher of Lyon'), for example, than did the criminal justice system. And the reason? Well . . . Scully seemed content to believe it was all down to genetics and the cloning of a super 'Aryan'-race (indeed, it is now known that Nazi scientists experimented on concentration-camp internees – in particular Jews and Gypsies – and the evidence suggests that, even in the 1940s, the experiments were linked to research into genetics and cloning procedures). Mulder, on the other hand, was convinced of an alien connection.

What is known for certain is this. Towards the end of World War II many high-ranking Nazis realized that Germany was about to lose the war. Negotiations for their future began as early as 1943, when prominent Wall Street lawyer and future CIA Director Allen Dulles moved to Bern, Switzerland, in an official capacity as an agent of the Overseas Secret Service (OSS, the CIA's predecessor). But as Mark Zepezauer points out in his book, Dulles had his own agenda with the Nazis, 'many of whom he had worked with before the war'. It is suspected that Dulles's sole purpose for moving to Bern was to begin negotiations with his 'clients' in order to secure their futures as US collaborators.

The yarn spun by the Nazis in order to attract US attention to their plight was that the USSR was planning to attack the Allies. This was a clever ploy: paranoia between the two future superpowers was already simmering. The fact that the US finally swallowed this ruse, however, was largely due to the efforts of Hitler's intelligence chief for the Eastern Front, General Reinhard Gehlen, who was flown to Fort Hunt, Virginia in 1945, where he convinced the US authorities that the Russians were indeed planning to attack the Allies. He also convinced them that, in exchange for allowing him to carry on living, he could be of use to them as a European and Soviet intelligence 'eye'. The US agreed. In the end it was the US who funded the setting up of

Gehlen's intelligence organization which, before it evolved into the BND (Germany's present-day 'CIA') was known as the Gehlen Org. For a full decade following the war Gehlen's intelligence machine was the CIA's Cold War eye on Eastern Europe. At the top end of the chain, even today Germany's BND is little more than a European CIA outlet.

But Gehlen was not the only Nazi to forge a treaty with the Americans. The CIA also contracted the likes of Holocaust mastermind Otto von Bolschwing and SS Colonel Otto Skorzeny, as well as the Lyon butcher, Klaus Barbie. Top Nazi scientists and aviation experts such as the infamous Wernher von Braun were also poached by the CIA and given their freedom – in exchange for 'services rendered'. The reason so many top Nazi scientists and aviation experts were included on the CIA payroll was that major scientific advances had been made by them in matters of flight propulsion, many believe as a result of some covert Nazi/alien alliance, and the Americans wanted to develop rather than destroy the new technologies on offer. It is no secret that the Nazis had forged major breakthroughs in 'flying saucer' technology, for example, and it is suspected that the so-called 'Foo Fighters' observed by both German and Allied pilots towards the end of the war were indeed the result of Nazi technology. The question on everyone's lips was: did the Nazis forge this kind of supertechnology alone?

Or did they receive a little help from an off-planet source?

The idea that, in conjunction with some of the world's most powerful corporate and occult-based Secret Government groups, some renegade alien intelligence sponsored Hitler's rise to power is of course absurd. More than this. It is downright ludicrous. Yet evidence presented later will show beyond question that the British and US military are today in possession of technologies – in particular those concerning some very strange and exotic forms of aircraft propulsion – that make the latest Stealth aircraft look like steam engines. As we will see, this fact is not in doubt. What *is* in question is the origin of these technologies. Were they developed purely by human artifice (and if so, why are they not available today in the public domain?) or were they developed by a visiting alien intelligence that, having failed in its bid to gain world domination by sponsoring the Nazis during World War II, turned its attention instead on what was to become the most dominant superpower in the post-war world: the United States of America?

And moreover, is this same alien intelligence presently in league with the US/neo-Nazi/Secret Government-controlled military-industrial complex, as so many researchers and witnesses have claimed? Indeed, if this scenario turns out to be – frighteningly – correct, then the agenda lurking behind government secrecy policies over UFOs and the intimately linked New World Order takeover bid begins to take on very serious implications indeed.

File 10: Appendix 01
Case Study: Cosmic Top-X03 Eyes Only
The Vril Society

That the Nazi dream of a New World Order and/or a One-World Government was born of occult beliefs is today widely accepted. That Hitler himself was obsessed with the supernatural and with the idea of establishing what some commentators have termed 'profitable contact' with extraterrestrial intelligences is also substantiated by much hard evidence. As, for example, researcher and author Russel Warren comments: 'From the very beginning the embryonic National Socialist movement was heavily influenced by various occult ideas – as was Hitler himself during his early, desperate days in Vienna. The Thule Society, from which Nazism largely developed, was a melting pot of various occult orders, attracting a ragbag of occultists ranging from Theosophists to Neo-Templars.'

But the occult organization with the most influence on Nazi policy was undoubtedly the Vril Society, whose major ambitions included the development of new and radical technologies based on the teachings of 'Occult Wisdom'. Together with Hitler and his band of megalomaniacs the Vril Society was obsessed with stories of space travellers and descriptions of flying machines found in ancient Sanskrit texts and other scriptures from antiquity. Indeed, the society claimed to have harnessed the means to recreate this ancient space-faring technology. And more than this. The most covert and masonic echelons within Hitler's Third Reich claimed, together with the Vril Society, to have been *given* this wisdom (and its attendant technology) by an extraterrestrial intelligence from Aldebaran, a solar system in the constellation of Taurus sixty-eight light years from Earth. While this may sound absurd in the extreme, it is now known that – as early as the 1930s – Hitler and the Vril Society were indeed involved in the development of saucer-shaped aircraft that displayed highly advanced aeronautical capabilities.

The US authorities, of course, were well aware of this. They were also aware that a similar situation existed in pre-war Japan. Evidence has recently come to light that implicates Japanese scientists in Nazi-style experiments involving rudimentary research into genetics and cloning. Once again, alien involvement is cited. Some say this is the real reason America joined the war in 1941–1942 to prevent the combined might of Nazi Germany and Imperial Japan from developing these technologies to their fullest potential. Indeed, it was only the ultimate victory over Nazi Germany that prevented the production of Hitler's infamous 'Andromeda Machine' – described as a giant space station built from acquired alien technology and based on the science of electrogravitics, a new and exotic form of propulsion beyond scientific development even today. Or so we are told.

But the point is that, when the full extent of available evidence is freely considered, the idea that Hitler was in league with extraterrestrials as long ago as the 1930s becomes a little less absurd, a little more plausible. Which in turn gives more credence to the idea that today the US government and the military-industrial complex are indeed in possession of alien technology, either 'gifted' or otherwise 'acquired', and that in return for this technological enlightenment the aliens are in receipt of something that we have and they want. Precisely what this 'something' might be is, of course, still open to investigation. But in any event, this situation would indeed explain why such a massive conspiracy of secrecy today surrounds the UFO/ET phenomenon at government level.

And the CIA is the agency detailed to keep it that way.

File 11
The Bilderberg Connection

To further the ambitions that had driven Hitler's Third Reich towards the establishment of a one-world state, a New World Order, the CIA recruited in the early 1950s many still-young right-wing war veterans and sold them the idea of an imminent communist takeover. The young guns were told that a strong and united anti-Soviet European Superstate would be the only effective countermeasure to the threat of world domination by an increasingly hostile – and powerful – Soviet regime. To this end the CIA funded the campaign for 'European Unity' to the tune of £1.34 million, an awful lot of money in the 1950s. Behind the scenes, of course, this figure was exceeded countless times over.

As part of this move to establish a European Superstate and to bring it in line with plans for a One-World Government, the CIA funded Polish-born philanthropist and political philosopher Dr Josef Retinger to establish what became known as the American Committee on a United Europe. When Prince Bernhard of the Netherlands showed interest, the movement took on major new proportions, and gained new momentum in the process. Between 29th and 31st May 1954, a meeting was convened at the now-famous Bilderberg Hotel in Oosterbeek, Holland. The CIA-funded Bilderberg Group was born.

Essentially, the Bilderberg Group – sometimes referred to as the Policy Committee – is a veritable pot-pourri of international financiers and industrialists, corporate bigwigs, academics, statesmen, high-ranking military and intelligence chiefs, politicians (both left and right), publishing magnates, CIA-payroll editors/journalists . . . all boasting the same collectivist ideals for a One-World Government complete with a world bank, centralized administration and all the relevant trimmings, such as an electronic single currency and ID tagging. The Bilderberg Group is as Big Brother as you can get. Affiliations with other members of the Big Brother family, other Secret Government organizations – the US-based Council on Foreign Relations, the British-based Royal Institute for International Affairs, the UN, the overseeing Committee of 300, etc – are incestuous, to say the least. But today the Bilderberg Group stands alone as the most influential body of backstairs policy makers in the world.

And the CIA is its cat's paw.

Perhaps this is one reason why Bilderberg policies are always discussed behind closed doors – a policy adopted from the CIA. Journalists attending Bilderberg meetings, for example, are requested not to report on the group's policies and activities. The journalists always comply (but then, their bosses are some of the most influential Bilderbergers around). To counter this, though it is considered to play a central role in secret, behind-the-scenes world government, the Bilderberg Group is not so secretive that it denies its own existence. On the contrary, included among its impressive and publicly accessible list of attendees are, for example, well-known politicians – such as Margaret Thatcher and Tony Blair, an unlikely political duet. A political duet, nonetheless. Though ostensibly worlds apart, both might be considered high-profile agents of the same central agenda: to serve the Bilderberg directive and, at the same time, of course, to climb its political tree.

It is reputedly Bilderberg influence that makes or breaks politicians, decides which party needs to be in power and for how long, and dictates policy to US and European administrations as though orchestrating some global chess game. It was no surprise, for example, that the Labour Party won the 1997 British General Election under Tony Blair – it is reported that Tony Blair had attended a Bilderberg meeting prior to his appointment as Labour leader, some say for a final 'briefing'. ('*Now we really do need to get this business of Europe satisfactorily sorted out, Tony, and for that we need a mildly socialist platform. Naturally you'll have to revamp your image, make yourselves more appealing to the middle classes, but I'm confident you can handle that. What do you say?*') It was of course well known that Britain under a socialist Government would be far more easily manipulated into a European Superstate than under a Conservative one. It was obviously time for one final shove in this direction. Margaret Thatcher's sudden and brutal political demise is also attributed to Bilderberg chicanery, much the same as will be Tony Blair's, I feel certain, just as soon as he has fulfilled his sponsors' requirement of him.

The question of UFOs arises in connection with the Bilderberg Group in that it seems to all intents and purposes as if the group's formation was a direct move to continue Nazi policy aimed at the establishment of a One-World Government and the continuation of secret-technology projects, which are themselves the alleged product of an alien/Secret Government alliance. (It is important to note that Secret Government politics is not partisan towards specific nation states or their political proclivities. Though the evidence seems to suggest a transfer of allegiance on the part of the visitors from pre-war Nazi Germany to post-war America, in truth – if such a transfer indeed occurred – it would have been little more than cosmetic. As can be seen in the example set by Rockefeller's Standard Oil, for example, the Secret Government was instrumental in financing both sides during World War II. This is how fortunes are made, and sustained. And increased. It is how the dynamics of global administration remain efficacious. A transfer of allegiance is irrelevant to this kind of backstairs politics. As Secret Government architect Mayer Amschel Rothschild said when formulating his plan of 'economic inductance': 'Give me control over a nation's currency, and I care not who makes its laws.' In this respect it is likely that any alliance between aliens and governments would be precisely stage-managed by organizations such as the Bilderberg Group to optimize their economic and political viability – never mind which nation the alliance appears to favour. Any scientific and/or technological advances made as a result of such an alliance would of course be utilized to a similar end, and to further bolster the group's influence on world affairs. If there truly is a worldwide UFO cover-up, the Bilderberg Group and its spawn of sister lodges – plus, of course, its executive cabal, the Committee of 300, the Policy Committee – is central to its implementation. No doubt about that.)

Certainly the most exotic and advanced technology projects undertaken by the CIA/Secret Government-sponsored military-industrial complex are funded and overseen by some of the most powerful and influential members of the Bilderberg Group. Likewise the nature of the projects undertaken is decided by this group. Indeed, many of the major multinational corporations have strong Bilderberg connections. Most are fully-fledged members.

The aim of the group's membership is to abolish democratic nation states and to form a centralized One-World Government.

File 12
JFK

There is another secret in the hands of the CIA. It is the CIA's greatest hit; and it is this:

The CIA assassinated JFK.

In conjunction with CIA-controlled factions within the FBI and the Mafia it was the CIA who ordered and carried out the assassination of President John F. Kennedy. This fact has today been largely substantiated; indeed, it is widely accepted. What is not widely accepted, however, is the motive given for the assassination which, according to many researchers – most notably Milton William Cooper – was directly related to the US government's secret involvement with the UFO phenomenon. Should this claim turn out to be little more than some wildly inaccurate outburst on the part of a few 'UFO cranks', then the question must surely be asked: why is this case still to be proven? And moreover: why do the very foundations of CIA Headquarters, Langley, Virginia still shudder at the mere mention of Kennedy's name?

Should this claim turn out to be even only partially true, however, it would certainly explain why such confusion, controversy and secrecy still surround this case, some thirty-five years on.

It is worth noting at the start that the formation of the Defense Intelligence Agency (DIA) under President Kennedy in 1961 was met with no small amount of paranoia and hostility, in particular on the part of the CIA and FBI Directorships. In 1961 the FBI under the Directorship of John Edgar Hoover and the CIA under Nazi sympathizer Allen Dulles enjoyed something of a monopoly on US security and intelligence policy. (And despite all the brouhaha about the mighty National Security Agency and the equally powerful National Reconnaissance Organization, this same situation continues today.) In this respect the forming of the DIA was seen as a threat. Allen Dulles was not about to let his grasp on security policy slip easily through his fingers, while FBI Director John Edgar Hoover was simply outraged at the fact that the young upstart Kennedy would even dare attempt to muscle in on matters in which, according to Hoover, he had no business interfering. Indeed, the power war between Hoover and the Kennedys was no secret. Neither was the fact that, at least to some degree, Hoover held the President to ransom over 'acquired' photographs and 'private' correspondence disclosing Kennedy's infidelities. It is suspected that Dulles also had plans for Kennedy's downfall; indeed, that he too possessed compromising documents on Kennedy's not-so-private life. Part due to his wish for retaliation, perhaps, part due to the fact that Kennedy wished to regain at least some portion of control over the CIA/FBI monopoly on security policy – thus re-establishing the President's direct authority in this respect – Kennedy pledged to 'splinter the CIA into a thousand pieces and scatter it to the winds'. In 1961, the Kennedys and the intelligence community were at war, make no mistake.

In his fervour to sweep the intelligence carpet clean President Kennedy, perhaps unwisely, then fired CIA Director Allen Dulles and Deputy Director Charles Cabell (who just happened to be the brother of the Mayor of Dallas, where Kennedy was assassinated). Top names within the intelligence community began to seethe. As did Richard Nixon, Vice President under Eisenhower and longstanding CIA conspirator and Mafia associate via [name deleted by publisher for legal reasons]. As did Kennedy's Vice President, Lyndon B. Johnson, behind-the-scenes adversary to Kennedy and someone who would later be implicated as accomplice in the President's assassination, the preparation for which was already under way. To add to this, looming darkly above the horizon was a situation Kennedy had inherited from Eisenhower, the Cuba situation, which would ultimately be cited as the reason for Kennedy's murder. It is a well-known fact that Kennedy had all along opposed the Bay of Pigs invasion.

During the years leading up to Cuban revolutionary Fidel Castro's victory over the US-sponsored Batista regime in 1959 (a victory which saw Castro claim power) a backstairs consortium involving the CIA, the Mafia and other US-based multinationals ran a sizeable string of casinos and brothels out of Cuba, the profits from which were enormous and, of course, tax-free. However, when Castro established his own communist government in Cuba he closed down the casinos and the brothels and nationalized all the businesses. Enraged, the consortium pulled out. It was then that Vice President Nixon came to the fore.

The Secret Government, itself divided into factions – some to the left who fund and sponsor the Democrats, others to the right who fund and sponsor the Republicans – had fully expected Richard Nixon to succeed President Eisenhower in 1960. Indeed, this was the plan. Nixon had been working closely with the CIA and the Mafia since 1959 to conjure up ways of assassinating Castro and re-establishing the illegal 'free-enterprise' situation which they had enjoyed in pre-Castro Cuba. When, by no small twist of fate – and of course a little behind-the-scenes outmanoeuvring on the part of the Secret Government 'lefties' – Kennedy won power, the whole Cuba situation was cast in shadow. Naturally the CIA, the Mafia and a host of very influential crime barons still wanted rid of Castro. Under pressure Kennedy agreed, but he was not prepared to use US forces to achieve this. Rather, a force comprised of Cuban exiles who had opposed Castro's forces in 1959 was selected to spearhead an invasion planned for April 1961 – the now-infamous Bay of Pigs invasion. The CIA was furious. In order to sabotage the invasion and make Kennedy look a fool, both politically and in the eyes of the American public, at the last minute a crucial supporting air strike was cancelled behind Kennedy's back. The invasion failed. Castro retained power. Kennedy's future looked grim.

A combination of the above, then (the formation of the DIA and the failure to get rid of Castro – plus the Kennedy brothers' rather public crackdown on organized crime), is generally the reason given for JFK's assassination. However, there is another aspect to all of this which is rarely included in the equation.

It is known that President Eisenhower inherited the Majestic-12 Special Studies Group from the Truman administration. When Truman formed the group in September 1947 the CIA was less than a week old. By the time Eisenhower took over the office of President in 1953 the CIA was five and a half years old, and was already showing signs of becoming a precocious and decidedly delinquent child. By 1961, at the tender age of fourteen, puberty had set in – the CIA was out of hand.

Had Majestic-12 continued to enjoy the same presidential power and privilege under Eisenhower that it had under Truman, perhaps the CIA's development into some wild, unbridled adolescent could have been checked, at least so far as the projects undertaken and overseen by Majestic-12 were concerned. The problem was, of course, that Majestic-12 and the CIA were virtually Siamese twins. Almost every member of the Majestic-12 Group enjoyed close ties and connections with the CIA. Indeed, MJ-12 Group member Rear Admiral Roscoe H. Hillenkoetter was the first Director of the CIA. Though Majestic-12 had been designated 'responsible only and directly to the President of the United States', the CIA by this time had become something of a renegade agency independent of the President's authority. To add to this, the vast military-industrial complex of which the CIA was – and still is – the linchpin (if not the Head Office) was fast becoming the fat and overfed cow it is today, with many of its covert projects and operations being undertaken without the President's knowledge, much less his authority. The designation 'responsible only and directly to the President of the United States' had become a sham, and this fact was reflected in Eisenhower's Farewell Address to the Nation, in which he warned of 'the potential for the disastrous rise of misplaced power' within the 'military-industrial complex'. Evidently Eisenhower's eight years in office had witnessed the CIA's 'coming of age'. It was now a fully fledged monster.

By the time Kennedy assumed office, then, US security policy had been usurped, lock, stock and barrel. To be sure, the Majestic-12 operation had been absorbed into the CIA's own agenda, along with the authority normally associated with the office of the President. Majestic-12 was no longer responsible to the President (and therefore to the people); on the contrary, it had become responsible only and directly to the authority of the military-industrial complex. Kennedy knew this. He also knew that information regarding the alien presence – information which, a decade earlier, had been subject 'only and directly' to the President and the original Majestic-12 Group – had now become the property of extremely high-ranking intelligence chiefs, military officials and other Secret Government godfathers such as Nelson Rockefeller and future CIA Director and President George Bush. Something had to be done. Kennedy told his confidants that if the situation could not be redeemed 'in-house' he would inform the American people that their liberty was in process of being violated and that therefore their constitution was little more than ink on paper. And worse. According to Milton William Cooper, he threatened to spill the beans about the aliens, too.

But Kennedy was not the first president to threaten such a disclosure. It is alleged that his predecessor President Eisenhower, following a meeting with an alien embassy at Muroc Air Force Base, California, in 1954 (now Edwards AFB), had threatened to make a public announcement regarding the alien situation. As we have seen, Eisenhower had witnessed the steady decline in presidential power and the concurrent rise in what he called 'misplaced power' within the military-industrial complex. He too – like his successor – was being manipulated and outmanoeuvred by an entity more ferocious and powerful even than the office of the President. It is perhaps no surprise, then, that his decision to go public with news of the aliens was overridden. Instead he was allegedly coerced into signing a covert formal treaty with the aliens on 20th February 1954, a treaty that included a pledge on the part of the visitors to service the US government with new and exotic 'alien' technologies. Perhaps this was the point when the aliens officially transferred their allegiance to the US. But then, by 1954 the US-based military-industrial complex was so rife with former Nazis that the aliens must have felt as though they were still on home ground. And either way, this was the situation inherited by Kennedy.

More than this. This was the situation Kennedy had threatened to expose.

Whether this be fact or fantasy, perhaps we will never know. But the evidence certainly now points to the fact that President John F. Kennedy was callously and brutally gunned down by a joint CIA/FBI hit squad (with a little help, of course, from the Mafia – but then, at the top end of the chain, the CIA, the FBI, the Mafia . . . what's the difference?). If this is indeed true then the only missing piece of the argument is: why? What was the *real* motive behind the decision to assassinate Kennedy? After all, presidents have made political blunders before, and since, but none as a result have become the victim of such a massive and covert conspiracy on the part of the US intelligence community. It would seem without doubt that some as yet unseen motive (one far more powerful than the somewhat flimsy 'Bay of Pigs' explanation) could well have been behind the assassination. The evidence speaks for itself.

*   *   *

The official explanation for Kennedy's death is surely as absurd as any talk of aliens and governments collaborating. More so. The Lee Harvey Oswald story, for example, is these days treated with the contempt it deserves by anyone who has seriously investigated the case. Indeed, even the 'official' version of the now famous Zapruder film footage clearly shows Kennedy being shot by at least three different bullets travelling in at least three different directions, while the 'unofficial' – *uncut* – version also shows the President being shot by the driver of his own car, Special Agent William Greer. (The sanitized 'official' version of this footage, which *does not* show Greer shooting the president, is available for public scrutiny; the original 'unofficial' version, which *does* show Greer shooting the president, is now back in the hands of the CIA, although I am led to believe that there are still a few 'leaked' copies around. If you can track one down, check it out.) It should be added that more than two hundred material witnesses to the event and/or those otherwise involved in the conspiracy died within two years of the President's death. As Milton Cooper points out in his book *Behold A Pale Horse*: 'The odds against this happening are so high that no one has been able to calculate them.' Cooper goes on to say that 'the odds against [even] the first eighteen to die within two years of the assassination were calculated at one hundred thousand trillion to one'. Anyone willing to risk a buck?

The point of this exercise is not simply to show that the CIA murdered JFK. So far as I am concerned this is a foregone conclusion. There are many more details involved in this affair that are not really relevant to our investigation; for this reason I have chosen not to include them here. Nevertheless, when studied, they prove beyond all reasonable doubt that the assassination of President John F. Kennedy was the result of a backstairs conspiracy that involved the CIA, the FBI and the Mafia, and possibly even some other quasi-official agency too powerful to name. These details also point to the fact that Kennedy's longstanding adversary and successor, Lyndon B. Johnson, was involved to some or other degree. It is easy to see why; his complicity earned him the presidency. But then, as history has shown, Johnson – unlike his predecessor – was a *manoeuvrable* puppet, and thus represented a far more attractive proposition to the consortium of puppeteers at his back.

Indeed, perhaps this is the reason Kennedy was 'advised' to name Johnson as his Vice President in the first place.

File 13
Project Aviary

And so to the crux of the matter: the infiltration by CIA agents of the world's leading UFO-related groups and organizations.

That the CIA's official 1953 'Educate and Trivialize' policy – 'debunk, discredit, disinform' – continues to this day is irrefutable (see Document 02, File 06). That this policy also includes a programme of infiltration is equally certain. Indeed, infiltration of the world's leading UFO groups and organizations by CIA agents began in earnest in the 1950s and continued at a pace during the '60s and '70s (see *Above Top Secret*, Timothy Good). In the early 1980s the crop circle phenomenon began to impress itself on interested parties hanging out at CIA Headquarters, Langley, Virginia, and by the late 1980s/early 1990s the crop circle research arena had been flooded by agents from both the CIA and British military and defence intelligence. This is the situation as it stands today.

In his book *Secret Societies and Their Power in the 20th Century*, Jan van Helsing quotes from 'an open letter by the initiative "Justice for Military Personnel" (JMP) of September 4, 1987, to then President Reagan' which reads: 'The national UFO trivialization campaign ordered by the CIA in 1953 fabricated books and infiltrated the press with hundreds of articles to surround the subject of UFOs with an aura of ridicule through false contacts and obvious UFO hoaxes. This ongoing campaign had CIA agents infiltrate civil UFO research groups to ridicule them by certain manipulations or to guide their efforts towards "other explanations". This cover-up policy was more successful than the CIA ever expected, thanks to the brilliant manipulation of the press with the strategy of ridicule . . .'

The letter concludes: 'The established press, for fear of ridicule, proved to be only too gullible towards "official statements".'

Following the initiation of this policy in 1953, then, it is alleged – and strongly substantiated – that a covert CIA cell was formed with a special directive to infiltrate, contain and disinform: to *infiltrate* known UFO organizations worldwide, to *contain* the extent of the information gleaned by said organizations as a result of independent civilian research into the phenomenon, and to inject wherever necessary a modicum of *disinformation* into the equation in order to confuse and discredit. (It is thought this cell was initiated by a covert CIA Special Studies Group that had been established the previous year – August 1952 – the same study group that instigated the Robertson Panel Report of January 1953.) At the same time this cell was authorized to gather whatever UFO/ET information it could from the organizations it had infiltrated. According to several well-known UFO and conspiracy investigators, including Jaime Shandera, William

Moore and Armen Victoria (among others), this cell, a kind of latter-day Majestic-12 working group, began operations under the code name *Project Aviary*.

Whether or not Project Aviary ever really was the code name for this operation has to remain open to debate. So far as I am aware no documentation bearing this code name has ever been released. Indeed, the first anyone ever heard of this name was when Jaime Shandera and William Moore were investigating the MJ-12 documents back in 1980, and were approached by US Air Force Office of Special Investigations (AFOSI) Master Sergeant Richard Doty, whom they referred to as 'Sparrow' (his mysterious superior as 'Falcon') as a means of identification. Thus the idea of an 'aviary' intelligence cell became seeded in the public domain.

I should add that although this operation – by whatever name – has been active for some years, I feel it is pertinent to reiterate here its primary objectives and agendas as they are ongoing and so directly relate to events and agendas detailed later in this book. And in any case, information I gleaned from one particular source would suggest that, far from becoming obsolete, within the last decade Project Aviary has been resurrected and its activities stepped up. The arrival of the crop circle phenomenon, my source said, has given rise to renewed interest and increased activity on the part of the intelligence community, in particular the CIA and the Project Aviary cell. Though technically two distinct phenomena, as far as the intelligence community is concerned UFOs and crop circles have become one inseparable phenomenon. For this reason crop circles have attracted similar interest from the military and the intelligence community today as was shown in UFOs in the 1940s and 1950s (see Document 07). Evidence to this effect can be clearly seen in the way that crop circles have been received by the intelligence-sponsored media – debunk; discredit; ridicule; yawn, yawn . . .

One intriguing aspect of the way in which the intelligence community views UFOs and crop circles was pointed out to me by this same source, who claims former affiliations with the CIA and US Special Forces and who is today assigned to a joint British/US counter-intelligence cell stationed in Britain. This is all I am permitted to say about this source. No buts. I will call him 'Stealth'.

Stealth confirmed to me that, so far as he is aware, Project Aviary is indeed a likely misnomer, but that the intelligence community's objectives concerning UFOs and crop circles remain consistent with the objectives associated with Project Aviary – debunking, disinforming and discrediting wherever and whenever these methods are deemed appropriate. We agreed to employ the name Project Aviary anyway.

According to Stealth, a further directive of Project Aviary was, and still is, to monitor and manipulate public reaction to the UFO/ET/crop circle phenomenon in order to both measure and contain its apparent metaphysical implications and their effect on the collective psyche, the common mindset. Stealth told me that certain elements within the military-industrial complex and the intelligence community are today convinced that some kind of full-scale interaction with extraterrestrial intelligence is imminent and that such an interaction, unless carefully monitored and controlled, would undoubtedly cause widespread panic and hysteria within fundamentalist religious and political organizations. The effects of this, he said, could so easily lead to social and economic decline, if not collapse. In turn this would of course irretrievably weaken the position of the military and the government in dealing with the 'problem'. According to Stealth, the major concern of the military and the intelligence community over human/extraterrestrial interaction is that the military's capability to defend against 'alien invasion' should in no way be compromised. If a third of the world is lost in euphoria at the arrival of the 'space brothers' while another third is fairly pissed off because the aliens do not fit into their fundamentalist belief systems (and the remaining third is simply lost in confusion and panic), he said, then social order would face a rapid decline and the military's capability to implement its defence strategy would indeed be compromised. More than this. The entire ship would be rocked to its rudder. International banking concerns would collapse, as would most – if not all – of the major socio-political structures currently in place. Chaos would ensue. And worse still, power would be compromised, if not forfeited altogether. The billions upon billions of dollars invested in the perpetuation of the present socio-political system would be up in smoke. And all because some inconsiderate alien council decided it was time to visit Planet Earth.

According to Stealth this is what the 'powers-that-be' fear most of all. And moreover, this is why they deem it necessary for operations such as Project Aviary.

File 13: Appendix 01
Case Review: Cosmic Top-X04 Eyes Only
Sleeper Agents

One further nugget of information imparted to me by Stealth – one that will perhaps seem less than directly relevant at first, but which will nevertheless become entirely relevant as our investigation progresses – did not surprise me. But it horrified me, even so. It is unofficially known as the CIA's 'sleeper agents' programme.

According to Stealth, certain individuals in the armed forces are 'selected out' from their military careers and surreptitiously 'worked on' by specialized units within the intelligence community. This happens in both Britain and America, as well as in many other countries worldwide. These people are very often 'unstable' in some way; the examples given were of those who were seen to suffer from mental and/or emotional hang-ups or those who were known to suffer from some or other form of sexual deficiency or deviance – in short, any weakness that can be used to manipulate and control. Over a period of some years, Stealth said, these people are gradually 'destroyed' and 'reprogrammed' by means of remote electronic stimulation of neural implants and other 'psychotronic warfare' techniques employed against them (see Document 10). Special 'psy-ops' (Psychological Operations) units exist to execute and monitor these operations. At the end of an unspecified 'incubation period', Stealth said, the 'sleeper agent' is born.

Sometimes the 'sleeper agents' remain 'asleep' for the rest of their lives, even after leaving the military. These are the lucky ones. Those who are 'woken up' are woken up for a reason. And it is normally for a very unpleasant reason indeed. One example of a sleeper agent being 'woken up' (his 'chip-in-brain implant' being remotely triggered by some or other high-technology electronic microwave device – see Document 10) Stealth said, is Sirhan Sirhan, who was falsely convicted of assassinating Robert Kennedy in 1968. Another, surprisingly, was Mark Chapman, who murdered John Lennon outside his famous New York home, the Dakota Building, in 1980. Stealth said that Lennon had been on the CIA hit list for years before the shooting. He had apparently upset the US authorities by becoming involved in some way with the IRA, although Stealth was convinced that even this was a cover story. His own view was that the former Beatle had simply pissed off certain quarters of the Secret Government's 'extremely right-wing KKK initiative' who had sanctioned the burning of all Beatle records in America's Deep South during the mid-1960s, and that Lennon had finally paid the penalty for influencing a generation of minds against the status quo. (Indeed, it is now known that a jealous and fading Elvis Presley worked closely with the CIA in an attempt to have the Beatles expelled from America during this period.) Stealth said that there were those within this and other CIA/Secret Government groups who would have woken up Chapman 'just for the hell of it'. He added with a shrug: 'They probably had nothing better on the agenda for that day.'

File 13: Appendix 02
Case Report: Cosmic Top-X05 Eyes Only
The Bennewitz Affair

One example of Project Aviary's *modus operandi* can be found in the tragic story of electronics expert and UFO investigator Dr Paul Bennewitz.

In 1980 Dr Bennewitz found himself at the centre of a considerable UFO flap near Albuquerque, New Mexico, where he ran a science and electronics company, Thunder Science Corporation. Most of the UFO activity seemed to be centred around the nearby Manzano Weapons Storage Area at Kirtland Air Force Base, Sandia, New Mexico, and it was here that Dr Bennewitz succeeded in eavesdropping on classified radio communications at the base and capturing some of the UFO activity on video. He also claimed to have recorded electronic and magnetic activity that he believed was caused by the UFOs, and had informed senators, congressmen and even the president of this. The military were less than pleased. Via researcher William Moore, Bennewitz was subsequently fed false documents and other disinformation aimed at discrediting his name. But despite this Bennewitz persisted in his endeavours to discover the connection between the operations carried out at the base and the UFO activity taking place there, activity that he had, of course, filmed. It was then that the Project Aviary 'final solution' directive came to the fore. Following a series of 'psychotronic warfare' techniques employed against him (anything from pulsed electromagnetic and microwave 'brain-scrambling' weapons – see Document 10 – to threats of blackmail and extortion) Dr Bennewitz ended up in a psychiatric clinic.

It is interesting to note in this respect that the US government's Non-Lethal Weapons programme – which includes the development of ELF (Extremely Low Frequency) pulsed microwave and particle beam weapons technologies, plus other exotic 'psychotronic warfare' techniques – is based largely in New Mexico, in particular at Los Alamos National Laboratories and Kirtland, where the Bennewitz UFOs were observed and filmed. It is suspected that Dr Bennewitz, having ignored the warnings given him under the directive of Project Aviary, became one of the first known UFO-related victims of the Non-Lethal Weapons programme.

Indeed, one of the Aviary's most prominent members was until recently head of the US government's Non-Lethal Weapons programme at Los Alamos National Laboratories. He goes by the name of 'Penguin'.

File 13: Appendix 03
Case Study: Cosmic Top-X06 Eyes Only
The Birds

The Aviary is so called because each of its members goes by the code name of a bird: Penguin, Owl, Falcon, Oriel, Bluejay, Pelican, etc – 'birds' whose real names and affiliations were due to be published here. However, due to 'official' warnings ranging from DA-Notice and libel threats to physical intimidation (and not wishing to compromise the rest of this book for the sake of publishing a few ignominious names belonging to a few ignominious CIA/MI6 agents) I have been advised to delete the contents of File 13, Appendix 03. Reluctantly I have done so. I should state, however, that the Bennewitz Affair (above) is but one of several incidents I have on file (all more recent) concerning the treatment suffered by independent researchers at the hands of Aviary policy. For the safety of those researchers concerned, these accounts have also been omitted from File 13.

File 14
The Autopsy

And so to the present . . .

One further CIA 'hit' that should be included here concerns the so-called Ray Santilli alien autopsy footage, a must for all dedicated followers of the macabre!

This 16 mm film footage of what appear to be military surgeons performing an autopsy on a dead alien found its way into the public domain by way of a retired US military cameraman – he says he filmed the autopsy of an alien that had been killed in the Roswell UFO crash. For some reason, this cameraman claims he was able to 'smuggle' a copy of the film away from the crash site and keep it for himself. As with the Roswell incident, however, so much has already been penned concerning the cameraman and his alleged autopsy footage that I will restrict what I have to say to the CIA operation that produced the film in the first place.

In May 1995 businessman Ray Santilli held a press conference in London. The purpose of this press conference was to show for the first time to a public audience film footage of an alien autopsy that had allegedly taken place in 1947. I should state from the outset that in no way do I intend to implicate Mr Santilli as part of the CIA operation that produced and disseminated the footage. So far as I am aware, Mr Santilli simply seized upon the chance to make a profit from what he saw as a highly commercial and viable opportunity. He is a clever and astute businessman.

For some months following the release of this footage all hell broke loose. Public reaction ranged from '*Proof at last!*' to '*Downright hoax!*' The fact that the footage had been whispered about within the UFO community for a full eighteen months before it finally reached the public domain (for reasons best known to themselves, the hierarchy of BUFORA – the British UFO Research Association – had requested that knowledge of the footage remain within 'appropriate circles' until such time as they deemed it judicious to release it) was enough to rouse the sceptics. Other discrepancies only added to their ammunition. First it was announced that there were three hours of footage to be viewed; when it was finally shown, however, there were barely three minutes. Next, Kodak confirmed that the film stock was indeed 1947 vintage (matching the date to the time of the Roswell incident); then Kodak denied confirming this date, although finally the photographic processing giant gave three dates, assuring interested parties that the film stock could be dated to either 1927, 1947 or 1967. Next came revelations that President Truman could be clearly seen on a segment of the footage that covered the actual crash retrieval. Wrong again. Though a few bits of metal could indeed be seen lying on a table top, one embossed with hieroglyphics, no footage of either President Truman or the crash retrieval operation ever came to light. To add to this, the featured bits of metal resembled not in the least the description given by Major Jesse Marcel who had handled the debris back in 1947 (see Document 01). There were many other anomalies, contradictions and talking points, all of which only added to the hullabaloo already surrounding the case. By the time it had all died down, most within the UFO community were left none the wiser as to whether the footage was genuine or a hoax. Indeed, most were left dazed and confused by the whole affair. For the record, most of those who *had* managed to form an opinion had come down on the side of hoax.

Which must have brought a whoop and a holler from the boys back at CIA HQ, Langley, Virginia. The scam had gone according to plan. The footage had been discredited. Roswell had been fictionalized. Mission accomplished. All that was needed now was for the US government to make some or other pronouncement on the case and the whole Roswell saga could be put to bed, once and for all. We didn't have to wait long.

Because later that same year (July 1995), following investigations made in the US by Senator Walter Schiff, the US General Accounting Office (GAO) finally announced that the

Roswell incident probably was the result of a crashed Top Secret Project Mogul spy balloon – as had been announced by the US Air Force the year before (August 1994), a sudden about-turn on the part of the USAF, who for forty-seven years had held that the crash debris had been that of a *weather* balloon and its radar reflector, and that therefore no alien bodies had been recovered from the crash. To confuse matters further, however, a more recent USAF announcement (1997) claimed that 'bodies' had indeed been recovered from the Roswell crash, but that they were not 'alien'. On the contrary, the announcement claimed that the recovered 'bodies' were 'rubber dummies' used in 'high-altitude parachute tests'! (This explanation was immediately scorned by UFO investigators due to the fact that 'high-altitude parachute tests' were not initiated until the mid-to-late 1950s, and even then it is highly unlikely that such tests would have been conducted from either weather balloons or Top Secret spy balloons.) Official explanations become more ludicrous by the decade.

At the same time (July 1995) the GAO also announced to an enraged UFO research community that all relevant documents concerning the Roswell incident had been mysteriously 'destroyed', and that therefore 'no firm conclusions could be drawn' (although the announcement also included the fact that, even though records of every Project Mogul spy balloon flight had been logged and vaulted, no records existed of a similar flight having occurred at the time of the Roswell crash in July 1947). The Roswell incident and the autopsy footage, it seemed, would remain forever unproven, and the UFO phenomenon in general would become little more than home entertainment, being featured in a host of new Hollywood and TV dramas as an interesting but fictitious storyline. It was a sad day for ufology.

But then came news of where the footage had really originated.

File 14: Appendix 01
Case Report: Cosmic Top-X07 Eyes Only
CIA Productions Inc

One of the principal investigators into the autopsy footage case was my good friend and world-renowned crop circle researcher Colin Andrews, one man amidst the wolves who all along had the courage and integrity to keep an open mind on whether or not the footage might be genuine and, indeed, where it might have originated. And perhaps because he did, it would seem he was able to sift the evidence more thoroughly and clearly than perhaps one or two others I could name. This in turn led him to uncover what is probably the most damning piece of evidence to date in support of the likelihood that the so-called 'Santilli footage' was indeed all part and parcel of the CIA's ongoing 'Educate and Trivialize' – debunk, discredit, disinform – programme concerning UFOs and government secrecy. On this occasion, though, it seems the CIA might just have shot itself in the foot.

Both Colin and rock singer Reg Presley (of The Troggs) had been centrally involved in the autopsy affair from the outset. Indeed, it was during an interview for BBC TV about the success of his song 'Love Is All Around' (which had just been recorded by the group Wet Wet Wet and had become a massive worldwide hit) that Presley first announced to the world the existence of the footage. Evidently Presley knew Ray Santilli – a rock music and video entrepreneur – from past dealings, and had been one of the first people to view the footage. Colin Andrews was one of the first people he had told about it.

When I spoke to Colin about the footage saga he told me that he had just received some very interesting information regarding the film's source. It appeared the case was not so open and shut as first it might have seemed.

'Shortly after I had finished a lecture at the UFO Expo West in the Hotel Hilton, Los Angeles, Sunday 11th June 1995,' Colin told me, 'I was asked to interview Johsen Takano for a forthcoming video.'

Colin went on: 'Johsen Takano is Head of Construction and Director of Planning for the Space and UFO Museum project in Hakui City, Ishikawa Prefecture, Japan, and is one of two Japanese delegates to have addressed the United Nations on the subject of UFOs. During the interview I specifically asked Mr Takano for his opinion on the footage, and to my utter surprise he proceeded to tell me something which could be extremely important.

'Mr Takano said that as he began to watch the autopsy footage he realized he'd seen it before. He had been shown the film in CIA Headquarters in America about one year earlier. He said his government had asked the US authorities for UFO research material for their upcoming Museum project and, as a result, were visited by an official from the CIA.

'The CIA man met with three Japanese government officials, including Johsen Takano. They were then flown together to CIA Headquarters in Langley, Virginia, and were shown not only what was to become known as the 'Santilli footage' but also six hours of movie film showing several different alien autopsies, one in full colour! I was stunned . . . I should add that Mr Takano was not the only person to tell me this and similar stories.'

To recap . . . Colin told me that three members of the

Japanese government had been shown film footage of the Roswell and other UFO crash retrievals and alien autopsies by the CIA. They had been shown this footage either just prior to or around the same time that Mr Santilli had announced to the world the existence of his own copy of the autopsy footage. The very least this evidence shows is that the day Mr Santilli went public with his copy of the footage the CIA was already in possession of the same and other autopsy/crash-retrieval material. The likelihood is, of course, that the CIA had been in possession of the footage all along, and had deliberately 'leaked' the film via the anonymous 'cameraman' in the first place. For some reason the US authorities wanted this footage in the public domain, and it would seem that this reason was directly linked to the announcements made by the US Air Force (August 1994) and the GAO (July 1995) concerning the Roswell incident.

After all, if the CIA was willing to supply the Japanese government with film of alien autopsies and UFO crash-retrieval operations (knowing full well that said footage would reach public attention at the very least by July 1996 – when the Hakui Space and UFO Museum was due to be opened) then it is reasonable to conclude that indeed it wanted this footage made available for public scrutiny, either as part of the Roswell-debunk exercise or as a public-opinion gauge to the alien presence. Probably both. In short, if the Santilli conduit had failed to bring the footage to public attention then the Hakui Space and UFO Museum would have provided a back-up conduit that would have seen the footage in the public domain a year or so later. It is therefore most likely that the CIA supplied Mr Santilli's 'retired military cameraman' with the Roswell autopsy footage in the first instance – just as this same agency supplied the Hakui Space and UFO Museum with same – fully intending for this cameraman to sell the footage on to the first innocent businessman with the appropriate entrepreneurial skills. Which is precisely what he did.

Of course, this does not necessarily mean that the footage is a hoax. On the contrary, the 'alien' featured in the footage could still be genuine, as could the footage itself. Disinforming the public is often about presenting genuinely 'leaked' artefacts and documents (which have perhaps undergone a little cosmetic surgery) with a view to debunking and discrediting them once they are in public view.

But to judge by the evidence now on offer (and by the known nature of official disinformation schedules, the way they are strategized, the way they are implemented) it is certainly clear that the CIA was indeed responsible for the dissemination of the Ray Santilli Autopsy Footage – which had either been stored for the past half-century in a CIA lock-up or had been made more recently by 'CIA Productions Inc', perhaps employing a film-prop model, perhaps a genuine alien corpse. The implications of it being the latter possibility, of course, are both enormous and despicable.

Like the power invested in the CIA itself.

DOCUMENT 04

The Secret NASA Files

File 15
Mission Control

'All Apollo and Gemini flights were followed, both at a distance and sometimes also quite closely, by space vehicles of extraterrestrial origin – flying saucers, or UFOs if you want to call them by that name. Every time it occurred the astronauts informed Mission Control, who then ordered absolute silence.'

So claimed former NASA communications specialist Maurice Chatelain, who designed and built the communications and data-processing systems for NASA's Apollo Moon missions and was present at Mission Control, Houston, Texas, for all Gemini and Apollo space flights during the 1960s and early 1970s. All of these flights, he claimed, were followed by 'space vehicles of extraterrestrial origin'. He also said that all Gemini and Apollo astronauts reported close encounters with 'unidentified space vehicles', a fact that has been confirmed by subsequent statements made by some of the astronauts concerned. Recent film footage of UFOs obtained from NASA's STS-48 and STS-80 Space Shuttle missions (plus similar footage obtained from the Russian 'Mir' Space Station) only tends to confirm Mr Chatelain's claim.

He went on to say: 'I think that Walter Schirra, aboard Mercury Eight, was the first of the astronauts to use the code name 'Santa Claus' to indicate the presence of UFOs . . . However, his announcements were barely noticed by the general public. It was a little different when James Lovell on board the Apollo Eight command module came out from behind the Moon and said for everybody to hear: 'Please be informed that Santa Claus does exist!' Even though this happened on Christmas Day 1968, many people sensed a hidden meaning in those words . . .'

Despite these claims, however, plus the accidental release of some very interesting NASA photographs depicting UFOs in space and other deep-space and lunar anomalies, it should be said that the most famous space agency in the world still denies any knowledge of the extraterrestrial presence. Indeed, an information paper issued by NASA in 1978 states:

'NASA is the focal point for answering public inquiries to the White House relating to UFOs. NASA is not engaged in a research program involving these phenomena, nor is any other government agency. Reports of unidentified objects entering United States air space are of interest to the military as a regular part of defense surveillance. Beyond that, the US Air Force no longer investigates reports of UFO sightings.'

And further, in an updated paper entitled *The US Government And Unidentified Flying Objects* issued by NASA in February 1996, the space agency states:

'No branch of the United States Government is currently involved with or responsible for investigations into the possibility of alien life on other planets or for investigating Unidentified Flying Objects . . . During several space missions, NASA astronauts have reported phenomena not immediately explainable; however, in every instance NASA determined that the observations could not be termed "abnormal" in the space environment.'

A highly ambiguous statement, to say the least. After all, what *would* be considered ' "abnormal" in the 'space environment'?

The paper concludes: 'With the termination of Project Blue Book, the USAF regulation establishing and controlling the program for investigating and analyzing UFOs was rescinded . . . Since the termination of Project Blue Book, nothing has occurred that would support a resumption of UFO investigations by the USAF or NASA.

This would be all well and good, if only it were true. Which it almost certainly is not. That an organization set up, in part, to investigate aeronautical and space phenomena should distance itself from what could prove to be the Rosetta Stone of interstellar travel and communication is, quite frankly, laughable. It is like the FBI suddenly announcing it no longer investigates crime. And who would believe that?

Later in this document we will scrutinize the many anomalies and unanswered questions that together comprise the bulk of the evidence in support of the fact that NASA is indeed involved in a worldwide UFO cover-up. More than this: that it is one of the major players.

But first, perhaps the greatest cover-up of all . . . the Apollo Moon landings. Did they really take place? Did Neil Armstrong really walk on the Moon in July 1969? Or could the most famous space flight ever undertaken by NASA in fact represent one of the biggest and most insidious backstairs counter-manoeuvres ever deployed against the human race?

As fantastic as this idea might seem, there is more evidence in favour than against. Indeed, if the evidence were presented in a court of law then NASA would be in deep trouble deeper than space itself.

File 15: Appendix 01
Case Study: Cosmic Top-X08 Eyes Only Faked Landing

To be clear from the outset, the evidence contained in File 15 suggests that NASA, together with the CIA, the DIA and other US government agencies faked a series of Moon landings during the late 1960s and early 1970s. The reason? To convince the rest of the world – in particular the Soviet Union – that America was the leading technological power on Earth. In so doing, of course, America would instantly gain an irreversible strangle hold on the manipulation of the international power games that, in essence, fuelled its black-budget economy. After all, if America could send a manned mission to the Moon – something the Soviets had failed to do, even though they were the undisputed leaders in the so-called 'space race' up to this point – then the Soviets' own aerospace technology programmes would be seen to represent a less attractive investment potential than that publicly demonstrated by the Americans. International investment in US black-budget projects would – and did – increase dramatically, while the same backstairs investment in Soviet technology – which was to this point very healthy – would diminish in equal proportion. Which it did. The United States would become the most technologically advanced – and therefore the most feared – superpower on Earth.

Which it did. And still is. The scam worked. The Soviet space programme, on the other hand, faded into comparative oblivion.

For these reasons alone File 15 insists that the Apollo Moon landings programme was little more than a scandalous hype, a propaganda exercise, a covert counter-intelligence operation and perhaps the greatest and most insidious deception ever perpetrated on the global population.

The sad thing is we all fell for it, hook, line and sinker. And the black-budget US space programme lives on . . .

The evidence, then . . .

According to Neil Armstrong, the first man to walk on the Moon, there was good reason for the US government's sudden 'about-turn' decision to cancel the Apollo Moon landings programme prematurely in 1973: it was the result of a warning given by extraterrestrials.

On 21st July 1969 millions of goggle-eyed people watched the 'live' televised transmission of Neil Armstrong's historic Moon-walk. Though the transmission was not broadcast live in Britain – and therefore I did not see it – I have nevertheless spoken to at least a dozen people who did, as well as obtaining first-hand confirmations from the television networks involved. All of them told me the same story – that shortly after the now-famous 'One small step, one giant leap' announcement, one of the astronauts was heard to say that he could see a 'light' on the rim of a nearby crater, following which Mission Control was heard to respond with a request for further information. All of America heard this dialogue. However, only a select few heard what was to follow. Because the minute the authorities realized what the astronaut was saying the transmission was shut down for a full two minutes. America fell silent, as did the airwaves. Nothing further was heard.

Or was it? According to former NASA employee Otto Binder, who was a member of the NASA team during the Apollo 11 mission, someone other than Mission Control was eavesdropping on the conversation that followed the transmission's shut-down. Radio hams across America had evidently managed to bypass the jamming signal and had recorded the following transcript:

Armstrong: 'What was it? What the hell was it? That's all I want to know!'

Mission Control: 'What's there? . . . [garbled transmission] . . . Mission Control calling Apollo Eleven . . .'

Apollo 11: 'These babies are huge, sir . . . enormous. Oh, God! You wouldn't believe it! I'm telling you there are other spacecraft out there, lined up on the far side of the crater edge. They're on the Moon watching us . . .'

It should be said at this point that NASA denies the authenticity of this transmission. And one has to say, of itself it amounts to the flimsiest of evidence – it would be the easiest thing in the world to fake an alleged radio transmission such as the above Mission Control/Apollo 11 talk-talk. Indeed, if Otto Binder and his radio hams were the only ones to have reported this incident then I would probably not have mentioned it. But they were not. The encounter was also witnessed by Russian scientists secretly eavesdropping on the transmission from 'KGB Central', Moscow.

It was reported by Dr Aleksandr Kasantsev, for example, that Buzz Aldrin took colour-movie footage of several alien craft that he says were 'parked up' on the edge of a nearby crater. The footage was allegedly shot from within the lunar module on its descent to the lunar surface, and again from outside the module once Aldrin and Armstrong had taken their historic 'giant leap for mankind' and stepped down onto the Moon's crust. Armstrong later confirmed in secret that this footage had indeed been shot by Aldrin, but that the CIA had confiscated it on Apollo 11's return to Earth. Fearing for his own well-being, it is claimed, Armstrong refused to go into further detail, except to confirm that the CIA were indeed behind an extensive cover-up regarding the US space programme and its consequent encounters with UFOs and extraterrestrial intelligences. Certainly Maurice Chatelain agrees with Armstrong: 'The encounter was common knowledge in NASA,' he revealed in 1979. 'But nobody has talked about it until now.'

A second Russian scientist, Dr Vladimir Azhazha, physicist and Professor of Mathematics at the KGB-sponsored Moscow University, reported the following: 'According to our information, the encounter was reported immediately after the landing of the module. Neil Armstrong relayed the message to Mission Control that two large mysterious objects were watching them after having landed near the Moon module. But his message was never heard by the public, because NASA censored it.' Dr Azhazha went on to say that the UFOs departed soon after the astronauts had disembarked from the lunar module.

Further to this, world-renowned UFO researcher Timothy Good claims that a former British military intelligence agent informed him of the following conversation that took place between Neil Armstrong and an unnamed professor at a NASA symposium in Europe. The intelligence agent told Good that he had 'overheard' the conversation, which took place in an adjoining hotel bedroom:

Professor: 'What really happened out there with Apollo Eleven?'

Armstrong: 'It was incredible . . . of course, we had always known there was a possibility . . . the fact is, we were warned off. There was never any question then of a space station or a Moon City.'

Professor: 'How do you mean, "warned off"?'

Armstrong: 'I can't go into details, except to say that their ships were far superior to ours, both in size and technology. Boy, were they big! . . . and menacing . . . No, there is no question of a space station.'

(Which is strange. NASA had already invested millions of dollars at this point in research into the construction of a futuristic Moon City, plans for which – according to officially released papers containing blueprints and an artist's impression of how the finished construction would look – were already at a very advanced stage.)

Professor: 'But NASA had other missions after Apollo Eleven.'

Armstrong: 'Naturally. NASA was committed at that time, and couldn't risk a panic on Earth . . . but it really was a quick scoop and back again . . .'

Indeed it was. And more than this. If Armstrong's alleged secret testimony bears any truth at all then the fact that the Apollo programme was prematurely curtailed in 1973 begins to make sense. Of course, these claims are shrouded in uncertainty, some say fantasy. They are without hesitation denied by NASA's official PR department and by Armstrong himself, who refuses to discuss the matter. But then so are the thousand and one other claims regarding the US space programme and the joint NASA/CIA/NSA/DIA cover-up, some of which have now been proven (by the release of previously classified documents under the Freedom of Information Act) to have been genuine. As fantastic as these claims may seem, then, there is sound reason behind them. Indeed, official NASA film footage and photographs of the astronauts on the Moon are riddled with still-unexplained conundrums and anomalies, as detailed in File 17. There are countless inconsistencies regarding the Moon's gravity and atmosphere, for example – the artificial lighting on the photographs; the way the Lunar Rover chucks up dust that streams behind the vehicle in its wake in what is supposed to be a vacuum (according to NASA, remember, the Moon has no atmosphere); the fact that no evidence of a rocket thrust can be seen when the Lunar Excursion Module lifts off from the Moon's surface on its way back to dock with the Command Module . . . while other photographs seem to show artificial constructions of enormous proportion dotted around the Moon's plains and 'oceans'. In an article published in April 1995, Maurice Chatelain claimed that 'several mysterious geometric structures of unnatural origin' had been discovered and photographed by the Apollo astronauts. The *question* of a cover-up no longer existed, he said; it was now cold hard fact. Indeed, many researchers who have studied this material in depth – including Britain's foremost authority on the NASA cover-up, researcher and author David Percy – are now convinced of the real possibility that the Apollo programme was, at least in part, faked.

And after studying the evidence for myself, I have to say I agree.

Consider this scenario, for example:

21st July 1969: despite prior warnings from an extraterrestrial intelligence not to go to the Moon (where ET bases and/or colonies already exist) NASA successfully lands Apollo 11 on the lunar surface and Armstrong and Aldrin encounter the now-famous 'light' on the rim of that nearby crater. (Included also in this scenario is the likelihood that the Soviets had been given the same extraterrestrial warning; unlike the Americans, however, they had heeded it. After all, what other reason would have prevented the Russians from sending their own manned mission to the Moon? They had the technology. They had the will. Most of the world fully expected the Russians to send a manned mission to the Moon before the Americans. But they did not. Indeed, they *never* sent a manned mission to the Moon, period. Why?) On reaching the Moon NASA is warned by a show of strength not to return. Due to financial and other commitments, however, NASA is forced to ignore the warning.

14th November 1969: as stated in secret by Neil Armstrong (to Timothy Good's 'anonymous' British military intelligence agent) Apollo 12 makes a 'quick scoop [to the Moon] and back again' and, so far as we know, manages to avoid further confrontation with the ETs. But NASA is still committed; plans for a further mission are already under way. The ETs, however, have other plans . . .

11th April 1970: Apollo 13 leaves Earth's atmosphere and, two-thirds of the way to the Moon, is disabled by a mysterious explosion that rips the side of the module and causes a dangerous oxygen leak. (NASA would later claim that a damaged coil inside the oxygen hold was responsible for the explosion.) The module begins to lose power. It is decided back at Mission Control that, due to a damaged engine that might explode if used to power the module home, the crew should not 'abort' and return home immediately but should continue their journey in order to gain added velocity by orbiting the Moon and utilizing its gravity as a means of propelling the module back towards Earth. Which it does.

NASA calls this a 'free trajectory' or a 'slingshot' manoeuvre. The disabled Apollo 13 orbits the Moon and heads for home. But there is more trouble ahead.

Further instrumentation failure brought on by further loss of power means that mission commander James Lovell is forced to pilot the module manually across thousands of miles of deep space . . . *by eye!* (Surely a feat more implausible even than the idea that aliens kicked NASA's butt!) Even so, this seemingly impossible feat is accomplished. Against all possible odds James Lovell manages to guide the module successfully on a perfect course and trajectory for re-entry (within a two-and-a-half-degree re-entry corridor), still piloting blind, and so miraculously manages to avoid 'bouncing off' Earth's atmosphere into outer space, never to be seen again. (Whichever way you look at it, *someone* seems to be taking care of this ill-fated mission and its crew.) Apollo 13 splashes down in the Pacific Ocean and the American public enters a state of euphoria. Meanwhile NASA plans its next mission . . . in Hollywood.

1970–72: as a consequence of the US government now taking the extraterrestrial warning a tad more seriously, the Apollo 14, 15, 16 and 17 Moon landings are faked in a Hollywood studio (or more likely, of course, in a studio specially constructed at one of America's *Ultra Top Secret* aerospace facilities). Bogus film and photographic evidence of the faked missions is circulated; according to plan, the public buys it, lock, stock and barrel. This course of action gives the 'powers that be' time enough to conjure up a convincing and convenient argument against the continuation of the Apollo programme, an argument that must at all costs ensure the least public and political backlash. The argument decided on is a combination of 'lack of funding' and 'non-justification of further funding'. The argument works. The Apollo programme is cancelled and the American public goes back to work, content in the knowledge that Good Ol' Uncle Sam beat those damned Russkis to the Moon anyway. NASA refocuses its attention on Mars.

The US government in the meantime refocuses *its* attention on a Star Wars-style 'Strategic Defense Initiative' (SDI) to be located in permanent orbit (complete with laser-guided nuclear warheads and an electromagnetic beam-weapon system) and HAARP (High-Frequency Active Auroral Research Project) designed officially for 'upper atmospheric research' and weather-pattern control – unofficially, however, as a ground-based electromagnetic weapons system augmented by the use of strategically deployed satellites. The reason for the US concentrating its efforts on the development of these new and highly sophisticated space-age weapons systems is this: it is known from past experience that the most effective weapons for disabling and bringing down the visitors' craft are electromagnetic in nature. (This is thought to have been the case with the Roswell incident in 1947, when America's newly deployed pulsed high-frequency electromagnetic radar capability proved sufficient to cause havoc with the ETs' own finely balanced electromagnetic propulsion systems and bring the craft to earth.)

The powers that be do not intend to have their space programme disrupted again.

OK, so on the face of it this may well seem little more than paranoid ranting. But there are several other factors to be considered, not the least of which is the fact that some scientists maintain that human travel beyond the Van Allen belt is quite simply impossible without extremely thick radiation shields (not included in the design of the

Apollo modules). The Van Allen belt is a region of intense solar radiation situated several thousand miles above the Earth – *between* the Earth and the Moon. To add to this, if the Moon's atmosphere is non-existent as NASA says it is then the astronauts should by rights have been fried alive in the furnace of undiluted solar radiation the minute they disembarked from the Lunar Excursion Module and stepped out onto the Moon's surface. (Assuming, of course, that they had escaped being cooked to a cinder as they travelled through the Van Allen belt en route.) Indeed, if the Moon's atmosphere is non-existent as NASA says it is then it should not be able to produce water and support life. If this is true then one wonders what prompted world-renowned astronomer and well-known UFO debunker Patrick Moore to let slip the following gem of information to author John Noble Wilford for publication in his book, *We Reach The Moon*: 'On the whole moon there is no living thing, apart from a few scattered patches of lichens or moss-type vegetation on the floors of some of the craters.' Official NASA photographs of 'clouds' above the Moon and, indeed, vegetation growing in and around some of the craters not only confirm Patrick Moore's hypothesis, they also add weight to the claims that, in one way and another, the entire Apollo programme was a propaganda stunt from the outset.

And that what NASA tells us about the Moon, the Sun, the planets and the stars is not necessarily the way it is.

File 16
The Lie

Ostensibly NASA (the National Aeronautics and Space Agency) is a civilian space agency. So the publicity literature implies. But as we have previously seen with the CIA, the fact that the general public believes this line is in itself the agency's most successful publicity stunt. The truth of the matter is less sharply defined.

Established on 1st October 1958, under President Dwight D. Eisenhower, NASA's official role is that of coordinating and administering the United States' space programme, simply put. This involves the management of all Research & Development programmes to do with aeronautical and space technology and, of course, space travel. According to the US Constitution these programmes should all be conducted in the public eye. They are not. On the contrary, NASA's major contractors include the US Department of Defense, the National Reconnaissance Office, the US Air Force, the US Navy, the NSA and the CIA, as well as the world's largest and most powerful US-based aerospace multinationals and corporations, such as McDonnell Douglas, Lockheed Martin and Northrop, the two latter being the pioneers of the world's only known operational Stealth aircraft, including the so-called Aurora (see Document 05, File 22). Given that all of the above-named are involved in highly classified new technology programmes, it is easy to see why many investigators perceive the agency's claim that it is a 'civilian space agency' as a lie. And worse – a lie perpetrated on the very people who fund its operations: the American public. In this respect NASA's activities stand open to serious investigation.

For example, the recently unveiled *LoFlyte* prototype (Low Observable Flight Test Experiment), a futuristic triangular-shaped aircraft whose 'wave rider' design gives it the ability to 'surf' the air rather than having to plough through it and which is capable of speeds in excess of 3,000 miles per hour (or Mach 5), is itself the product of a joint NASA/USAF secret technology programme. Nothing civilian about that. Indeed, this aircraft is so secret, and so futuristic, that the front page of the *Sunday Times* (11th August 1996) implied that it was probably responsible for most if not all sightings of triangular-shaped 'UFOs' in recent years. A ludicrous claim, to be sure. Especially when you consider that reports of triangular-shaped UFOs date back more than a hundred years (see Document 05, File 18). Even so, it provides at least one shred of evidence to the effect that NASA is more than just a civilian space agency, that many of its projects are classified well above Top Secret and that, as a consequence, information pertaining to these projects is not available to the civilian population.

What is little known to the majority of this civilian population in this respect is that the 1958 US Space Act contains a very interesting clause that, in effect, gives NASA the right to do whatever the hell it damned well chooses. To begin, the Space Act states that NASA was set up to 'coordinate national space activities'. Nothing out of the ordinary there. Also stated, however, is the reason for the seeming paradox overshadowing the agency's proclivity towards the military agenda – that one of the major reasons for establishing the agency in the first instance, and for further expanding the space programme over subsequent decades, was to take 'full advantage of the *military* potential of space', while at the same time to 'administer the *civilian* space program' [my italics]. Seems clear enough. Indeed, this clause alone places NASA under the same security regulations as any other US government agency and, in one fell swoop, dismisses the idea that any space data gathered by the agency automatically belong in the public domain. On the contrary, according to former Lockheed Missile and Space Company scientist Dr Norman R. Bergrun, who claims in his astonishing book *The Ring Makers of Saturn* that in 1980/81 the NASA *Voyager* probes 1 and 2 obtained photographs of massive cigar-shaped UFOs 'approximately the size of Earth' orbiting Saturn: 'The 1958 Space Act states that the public should only be informed of space data and photographs if it is determined "non-hostile".' If NASA truly has obtained photographs of what Dr Bergrun believes is at least one UFO large enough to accommodate 'an entire civilization', and that, as he further claims, the UFO is thought to be an electromagnetically powered, intelligently controlled vehicle, then it is perhaps understandable that the US government considers this information pertinent only to the military, despite the moral issues involved here. A craft this size, Dr Bergrun said, would undoubtedly be classified 'hostile', and any relevant information and/or photographs depicting the nature of the craft would not, therefore, be released to the public. 'It would have far too great a military significance,' he said.

That may be so. But the same argument surely cannot be applied to information about the Moon.

Though ostensibly a non-military project, the Apollo programme, by its nature, was classified a Top Secret programme, with much of its technology and personnel originating with the US-based military-industrial complex. All Apollo astronauts, for example, were – and still are – subject to US military security regulations, as are all NASA astronauts and personnel, no matter the mission or the programme. In addition, I have it on very good authority that all film and photographic material obtained during NASA flight missions plus all radio communications are screened by the National Security Agency before being allowed out into the public domain. Even the so-called 'live' transmissions such as the famous 'One small step, one giant leap' transmission are subject to several seconds 'screening delay' before they are relayed via the networks to the listening world. Indeed, more than one NASA source has told me that very little information, whether film, video, photographic or audio, reaches the public domain until it has been thoroughly screened and, where necessary, 'sanitized' by the US intelligence community, in particular by the NSA, the CIA and the Department of Defense. This policy has been effective since 1958 when the space programme began. Even so, it was not until the historic Apollo 11 transmission that security was increased to the level it enjoys today – that of manic paranoia. For this reason we are forced to dredge the archives of NASA's formative years for the more solid evidence of what I believe to be an ongoing and insidious cover-up.

Support for the veracity of this claim comes from many sources, not the least of which is former NASA photographic technician Donna Teitze, whose work included sifting the 1.6 million photographic images of the Moon sent back to Earth by the 1994 US Defense Department/NASA *Clementine* probe. Barely a handful of these images have found their way out into the public arena, and it is easy to see why. When interviewed by WOL-AM Radio in Washington DC on 6th May 1995, Donna Teitze revealed:

'The job of a co-worker in a restricted area was to airbrush out any anomalies found on the Moon photos.'

A staggering disclosure, and meticulous analysis of many of NASA's publicly released photographs has indeed revealed signs of these photographs having been either tampered with or, more simply, faked. Perhaps we should be grateful, then, that on occasion the odd 'gem' does seem to slip what is otherwise a very carefully monitored and watertight security net.

This is especially true when you consider the claims of yet another 'inside' source, who recently informed me that NASA's 'unofficial' library is brimming with the most startling photographic and film evidence of UFOs to be found anywhere in the world. To a large degree this claim is also supported by NASA's former data and photographic documentation supervisor Ken Johnston, who claims that hundreds of photographs in NASA vaults seem to show structures of unnatural origin on the Moon. Film footage shot by Apollo 14 astronauts, he says, also shows these same anomalies – indeed, he says that this 16 mm footage clearly shows 'five or six lights' in a crater on the far side of the Moon, corroborating Armstrong's and Aldrin's claims that they had seen a 'light' on the rim of a nearby crater following their historic Moon landing in 1969. Johnston says that he showed this footage to other NASA personnel the day after discovering these anomalies, but that NASA subsequently erased the relevant frames. When Johnston questioned this policy he was told by NASA executive [name deleted]: 'I don't know what you're talking about.' Johnston is now convinced that the footage was either locked away or destroyed. He is also convinced that a serious NASA cover-up is in operation, and that it has been ever since the space programme was officially launched in 1958. He adds that, during his time at NASA, [name deleted] has ordered copies of many other Moon images from the Apollo missions to be destroyed.

Speaking to one of America's best-known radio talk-show hosts, Art Bell, on 21st March 1996, Johnston revealed: 'Without the aid of any kind of instrumentation you can actually see some of the anomalies on just the raw film and pictures itself.'

And further: 'One of the most striking things I have found, and one of the comments that one of the analysts was making is – if you really want to see what somebody doesn't want you to see on the Moon, look in the visor of the person being photographed. And it was a rather unique experience. We started looking at . . . the reflections on the curvature of the face masks of the astronauts on the lunar surface . . .

'. . . And there's some rather striking pictures that show what appears to be constructed structures, ladders, portals; some very, very interesting things in the visor in a number of pictures.'

Johnston concluded: 'So the answer is, yes, there are definitely things you can see with the naked eye.' He added that some pictures even seem to depict astronauts walking among either the ruins of lunar constructions or lunar constructions still in use. If this is true then it would further explain why NASA was forced to withdraw its plans for a Moon City – there is *already* a Moon City. And it belongs to somebody else. And whoever that 'somebody else' might be, it would seem they are less than keen to share their celestial motel with Earth's primary space agency. And, frankly, who can blame them?

In addition to this, retired NASA and McDonnell Douglas engineer Marvin Czarnik, a one-time self-confessed sceptic who started out on a mission to *disprove* the 'cover-up', is himself now convinced that the Moon anomalies depicted on the secret NASA photographs are real. This opinion is also shared by geologist Ronald Nicks, who has studied the geological processes that could account for the natural formation of such anomalies as the so-called 'shard', a tall needle-like construction clearly seen to protrude high above the Moon's surface. After meticulous research Nicks is now convinced that this structure could in no way be the result of natural geological processes, an opinion shared by other reputable geologists. On the contrary, as former NASA consultant Richard Hoagland (who has discovered similar structures on Mars, including pyramids and a sphinx-like 'Face') asserts, the so-called shard and other anomalous constructions are indeed artificial and could therefore represent the 'signature' of extraterrestrial visitors to our planet and our planet's satellite, the Moon. This is further corroborated by the recently 'leaked' video footage shot from NASA's STS-80 Space Shuttle, which shows several unexplained objects entering and leaving Earth's atmosphere. And then again, the 1991 video footage shot from NASA's STS-48 Space Shuttle *Discovery* which also shows unexplained objects entering and leaving Earth's atmosphere (one in particular that, having taken evasive action in order to avoid being struck by what appears to be a missile fired at it from Earth, is seen to accelerate away at an incredible speed – estimated at 900,000 mph!). For the record, NASA later claimed that these objects were 'ice crystals'. I don't know about you, but I've yet to see an 'ice crystal' turn a 900,000 mph right-angled escape trajectory, much less perform in the way many other anomalous objects are seen to perform on this official NASA video footage. And as if this were not enough in itself there is also the video footage shot from the Russian space station Mir to be considered. This official Russian Space Agency video footage clearly shows an elliptical object – in Earth's upper atmosphere – so huge it could only have been a floating iceberg, never mind an ice crystal. To my mind, the 'fob-off' becomes more ludicrous by the second.

In support of the anomalous photographic and video evidence, several sources – including Maurice Chatelain and former Gemini astronaut Brigadier General James McDivitt – have said that all astronauts are briefed and debriefed before and after every mission, during which they are warned not to discuss in public information about their encounters. Most comply.

Some, however, do not. Former astronaut Dr Brian O'Leary, for example, has spoken out vehemently against what he calls the 'Cosmic Watergate'. Speaking at the International Forum on New Science, Fort Collins, Colorado, September 1994, Dr O'Leary could not have been more explicit: 'We have contact with alien cultures,' he told an astonished audience.

Dr O'Leary went on to say: 'The suppression of UFO and other extraterrestrial intelligence information for at least forty-seven years is probably being orchestrated by an elite band of men in the CIA, NSA, DIA and their like. This small group appears able to keep these already hard-to-believe secrets very well.'

And further: 'Those who have investigated this hydra-headed beast believe that the Cosmic Watergate of UFO, alien, mind-control, genetic-engineering, free-energy, antigravity-propulsion and other secrets will make Watergate or Irangate appear to be kindergarten exercises.'

And then some.

Other astronauts who have spoken out about the cover-up include Edgar Mitchell, the sixth man to walk on the Moon, and former astronaut and US Air Force Colonel Gordon Cooper, who recently announced on American TV that what he was about to reveal would probably send shockwaves throughout the US Defense Department and the intelligence community. Gordon Cooper, the last American to travel alone in space, told America in no uncertain terms that its government was indeed involved in a very high-level UFO cover-up, and that film of a disc landing at Edwards Air Force Base in California in the 1960s had been confiscated by Pentagon officials and locked away in the dungeons beneath Washington DC, never to be seen again. Speaking of another incident that involved the landing of a UFO in Florida in 1973, Colonel Cooper disclosed:

'I happen to know that Authority did just about everything to keep this incident from the press and TV in fear of a panicky reaction from the public.' I feel sure that this 'panicky reaction' will be far more evident when the public finally discovers, not that extraterrestrials are visiting our world, but that governments have deliberately and illegally concealed this fact for more than fifty years.

One final astronaut story concerns the pre-Apollo space flight of Brigadier General James McDivitt, who was piloting NASA's Gemini 4 mission over Hawaii in 1965 when he saw and photographed a UFO. The claim of Maurice Chatelain that 'all Apollo and Gemini flights were followed . . . by space vehicles of extraterrestrial origin' are further substantiated by McDivitt's report.

By 1965 America's plans to land a man on the Moon were well under way. In light of this – and the evidence presented thus far – it is perhaps not so absurd to postulate that the ETs had by this time stepped up their own reconnaissance of NASA's activities in space. Certainly according to Chatelain this is so. And if Brigadier General McDivitt's official report is to be considered here, then this possibility becomes even more plausible. Because on 4th June 1965, while in orbit over Hawaii, McDivitt spotted something anomalous out of Gemini 4's window. Responding swiftly he shot two films of what was later described as a 'beer can-shaped object' with two different cameras before Gemini 4's orbit took him into the glare of the sun, whereupon he lost sight of the object. Like Colonel Gordon Cooper before him, and Neil Armstrong after, McDivitt was ordered to remain silent about the encounter on his return to Earth. He refused. Indeed, in his attempt to make this information public McDivitt broke the NASA code of silence and informed the press that he had taken photographs of a UFO in space. The story was out. NASA responded in the only way it knew how – by releasing the photographs to the public.

However, when McDivitt saw the newly developed photographs he immediately realized *why* NASA had agreed to release them – they were not the photographs he had originally taken. Rather they were fakes put out by NASA in response to McDivitt's public disclosure and the consequent media interest. Indeed, McDivitt says that both he and NASA knew full well that the released photographs were fakes. In an effort to beat the secrecy agenda and find the real photographs, McDivitt spent days searching through the thousands of official mission photographs taken by Gemini 4, but without success. The photographs had mysteriously 'disappeared'. Reluctant to admit that a backstairs cover-up was responsible for 'misplacing' the photographs, however, McDivitt's subsequent stance regarding this incident was that the original photographs had probably not developed properly due to sun-glare, the official NASA story (one wonders if someone had words in McDivitt's ear). Even so, the UFO phenomenon is to be taken seriously, he says: 'They are there without a doubt. But what they are is anybody's guess.'

It is my contention that for as long as NASA and the US government is permitted to retain the monopoly on the sum of the world's space data we'll all be kept guessing for a very long time to come.

File 17
One Small Step

'Many people now feel that we have been told less than the truth regarding NASA's space programme, in particular the

Apollo Missions of the late Nineteen Sixties and early Nineteen Seventies. Recent research has shown that conditions
on the Moon could be very different indeed to the 'official-line'
announcements fed to us by the well-oiled NASA propaganda
machine.'

The above quote is taken from an article penned by
researcher Jim Mills for the August/September 1996 edition
of *UFO Reality*, in which he also states: 'Dr Farouk El Baz,
for example, one of NASA's foremost scientists, confirmed
public suspicions when he stated that "not every discovery
has been announced to the public". As I see it, this could
turn out to be the understatement of the millennium!'

I couldn't agree more.

Indeed, as we have already seen, and despite official
statements to the contrary, investigations have shown that
there is no shortage of 'anomalous information' concerning
the Moon and the US space programme. Many of the original
photographic images obtained by NASA, for example, are
extremely well-defined. By the time they have been 'cleaned
up' and reduced in size to fit the pages of a comparatively small
paperback, however, and the clarity has been further reduced
by copying processes and other 'in-house methods', the
images tend to become pretty meaningless. In many cases
researchers are left with little more than 'smudges' and 'blurs'
where once detailed definitions of the anomalous images
existed. With the state-of-the-art technology at the disposal
of agencies such as NASA, there is no scientific reason why
copies of these images should become so ill-defined. But,
mysteriously, they do.

Another problem for researchers is, of course, that of
access. Relatively few people have ever been permitted to
view the massive photographic archive existing somewhere
in NASA's secretive depths. And of those who have, all

have been subject to the US government's national security regulations – *Disclose This Information At Your Peril!* This being the case we are forced to make do with the two or three dozen poor-quality reproductions that NASA deems fit for public release (which appear in all the official textbooks) and this despite the fact that NASA has obtained literally millions upon millions of photographic images since 1958. Indeed, as stated above, the 1994 joint NASA/US Defense Department *Clementine* probe sent back a staggering 1.6 million photographic images of the Moon alone. Something is seriously amiss.

Even so, and despite all of these apparent obstacles, abundant evidence still exists that, when scrutinized under the proverbial – and literal – microscope, points to the very probable fact that virtually everything NASA has told us about the Moon and the US space programme is an outright fiction. Before I present this evidence in full, however, I should own up to the fact that I am no scientist, and that therefore some of the evidence presented may well be open to scientific amendment. Nevertheless much of the evidence relies more on the faculty of common sense than on science. And in any case, until such time as NASA and other government agencies open up their 'X Files' to public scrutiny I will maintain the right to question the motives and activities of such agencies, and this includes the right to be told the absolute truth concerning information held, in secret, by the powers who sanction the authority of said agencies in the first place.

That said, the evidence . . .

To begin, if the testimonies of such high-ranking luminaries as former NASA communications chief Maurice Chatelain and former US Army Special Forces Command Sgt Major

Robert O. Dean are to be taken seriously, then the classified NASA photographic library houses anomalous descriptions of every shape and proportion. According to Maurice Chatelain, for example, the original Moon photographs show all kinds of structures existing on the lunar surface, seemingly both old and new – domes, rectangles, pipelines, crystal towers, even pyramids. But who outside the confines of NASA knows about these photographs, much less their contents?

To add to this, in several segments of official NASA film footage of astronauts on the Moon the American flag is seen to 'flap in the wind' (and yet the Moon, according to NASA, has no atmosphere: it is a vacuum). One film clip that I have seen clearly shows a desperate astronaut trying his level best to hold the flag still! Some commentators have suggested that this could have been caused by the solar wind. But of course, there is no solar *wind* as such. The term is used to describe the continuous flow of charged particles radiated by the sun, a phenomenon which would be hard put to disturb a feather at ninety-three million metres, much less a flag at ninety-three million miles! Another explanation is that the flag is suspended on wires or springs to give it the appearance of flapping, but again, the flag is clearly seen to flap independently, while the astronaut is seen to make a fairly desperate attempt to hold it still. So what *is* the mysterious cause of this flag-flapping incident? Perhaps there is a perfectly logical explanation. But if there is, NASA has yet to share it with the rest of us.

In the same breath we are told that the classic Neil Armstrong 'footprint' will remain etched on the Moon's surface for ever and a day. We are told this precisely because the Moon's 'atmosphere' is a vacuum (which is fair enough – the laws of physics, I am reliably informed, demand that dust becomes hardened and compressed in a vacuum, thereby ensuring the 'footprint' remains undisturbed). What is confusing in this respect, however, is the fact that, on a different segment of this same film footage, great plumes of dust can be clearly seen spewing up from the back of the Moon Buggy as it travels across the lunar surface. As I have already said, I am no scientist. But in this instance it is plain and simple common sense that raises the question: Is the so-called 'vacuum theory' all part and parcel of the same wild hoax being perpetrated by NASA? Again, I stand open to scientific amendment on this one.

But not on *this* one. According to Jim Mills, Peter Oakley and other well-known and respected researchers, cloud formations have been photographed above the Moon, confirming astronomer Patrick Moore's unexpected disclosure that indeed primitive forms of life – such as 'lichens or moss-type vegetation' – can and indeed do exist 'on the floors of some of the [Moon's] craters'. However, the problem arises when we consider NASA's official line in this respect, that the Moon's atmosphere is a vacuum and cannot therefore produce moisture in any quantity, much less produce cloud formations. But it does. Indeed, perhaps one of the least talked about Moon anomalies is the *one-hundred-mile-wide cloud of vapour* detected above the Moon by NASA's own instruments. This embarrassing anomaly was promptly explained away by NASA scientists as 'the result of the considerable volume of urine ejected by the Apollo astronauts'! (One wonders . . . what in heaven are they given to drink?!)

To further confirm the 'moisture on the Moon' theory a series of colour photographs taken by the Apollo 8 astronauts clearly depicts areas of green vegetation on the lunar hills (photographs that surely give a whole new meaning to the song *There Is A Green Hill Far Away*!) and, as Patrick

Moore rightly predicted, inside some of the craters. This in itself is evidence enough to substantiate the fact that the Moon does indeed have an atmosphere of some density and that, contrary to the official NASA hand-out, it is not a vacuum. The question is: Why should NASA wish us to believe otherwise?

Further unexplained anomalies include the many strange lights and objects and apparent structures that have been observed and recorded on the Moon by independent astronomers and scientists. Science writer Joseph Goodavage, for example, observed the fact that over two hundred white 'dome-shaped' structures had been seen and catalogued on the Moon, but that 'for some strange reason they often vanished from one place and reappeared somewhere else'. Are these structures spaceships? Mobile space stations? What?

Unfortunately, only NASA has the answer to these questions. And until such times as the specious space agency decides to let us all in on a few of its more intimate secrets, all we can do is keep rummaging away and firing the questions.

Questions like:

If NASA was indeed formed primarily as a civilian space agency (in order to explore space on behalf of us poor uninformed souls) then why are so many NASA programmes funded by the US Defense Department? The CIA? The military-industrial complex?

Why are all astronauts subject to US military security regulations?

Why is all video and photographic evidence screened by the National Security Agency?

Why are all radio communications screened by the National Security Agency?

Why, after spending millions of taxpayers' dollars planning the construction of a Moon City, was the Apollo program suddenly and prematurely curtailed in 1973?

And further, apart from the US Defense Department-funded *Clementine* probe, launched in the spring of 1994, why hasn't NASA been back since?

Or has it?

Indeed, why hasn't *anybody* – including the Russians – been back since?

Or have they?

Why are some of NASA's top photographic technicians assigned to 'airbrush out' space anomalies caught on film by astronauts and other agencies, such as the Hubble telescope?

Questions in need of immediate attention.

File 17; Appendix 01
Case Review: Cosmic Top-X09 Eyes Only
NASA Fact File

In the meantime, a fact file:

For example, *did you know* . . . that the spacesuits and face shields worn by the astronauts on the Moon would have had to protect the astronauts from temperatures ranging from approximately –180 degrees to +180 degrees Fahrenheit, the difference between a lunar night and day. No such material was available in 1969. Indeed, no such material is available today, at least not in the public domain.

And *did you know* . . . that in every officially released NASA Moon photograph there is a conspicuous absence of background stars. The sky is pitch-black. According to some scientists and independent photographic technicians and analysts this could only be the case if the Moon had an atmosphere, which NASA claims it does not.

According to others this seeming anomaly is due to sun-glare and the fact that the cameras were focused on infinity when the photographs were taken. Perhaps the many top photographic experts still confounded by this effect have overlooked such a simple explanation.

And *did you know* . . . that in many photographs there are several light-sources illuminating the astronauts on the Moon's surface. This kind of lighting is consistent with that used on a film set. Remember, when a particular area of the Moon is neither lit by the Sun, nor by reflected light from Earth, it is pitch-dark. This is so because according to NASA the Moon has no atmosphere. Yet several NASA photographs of astronauts on the Moon clearly show them being illuminated from behind as well as from the front. According to many photographic experts, this simply does not tally.

And *did you know* . . . that around the same time as the Apollo 11 mission in 1969, investigative journalists in Holland uncovered evidence to the effect that indeed the Apollo programme was little more than a propaganda exercise designed by the US administration to gain psychological – and thereby military and technological – superiority over the Soviet Union. Remember, up to this point the Russians were leading the space race by a good furlong and a half. Perhaps understandably – given the timing of this story – the evidence was never taken seriously enough to cause the US authorities any major problems.

And further, *did you know* . . . that prior to the official Moon landings the prime reasons given for wishing to travel to the Moon were to do specifically with mining and mineral rights?

This begs its own question: bearing in mind the fact that rich deposits of titanium, aluminium, uranium, helium-3 and heaven-only-knows-what-else were found on the Moon, are we seriously to believe that Uncle Sam would have broadcast to the world: '*Hey, come on up, boys, there's gold in them there hills, for all the world to share!*'?

No, I don't think so, either.

In his book *Men From Earth*, the second astronaut to walk on the Moon, Edwin 'Buzz' Aldrin, states: 'Another exciting energy resource on the moon is . . . an ample supply of the isotope helium-3 (He-3), which is very rare on Earth but has been deposited on the lunar surface over billions of years by the solar wind. It is now estimated that at least a million tons of He-3 are readily recoverable from the regolith formations where lunar solar power stations would be practical. This He-3 offers a key to safe, practical nuclear fusion energy on Earth. It is estimated that a single ton of He-3 delivered to Earth would be worth at least $1 billion.'

I'll leave you to draw your own conclusions . . .

Again, *did you know* . . . that, as well as the 'footprint' and 'flag-flapping' anomalies, official NASA film footage also shows one astronaut disembarking from the lunar module rather 'heavily'? After descending the ladder at a cautious rate of knots he leaps from the last rung (which appears to be around eighteen inches from the ground) and hits the lunar surface with a hefty thud! But wait a minute . . . isn't the Moon's gravity supposed to be one-sixth of the Earth's own gravity? Or is this hogwash, too? Even taking into account their weighted spacesuits that, NASA says, weighed around 185/190 pounds, the astronauts would have been so light on the Moon they should have been able to jump over six feet in the air (the weight of the spacesuits plus the astronauts' body weight would have made their combined weight relative to Earth about sixty-two pounds, or around four and a half stone – a fact further corroborated by another quote from Buzz Aldrin's book *Men From Earth*, in which he states: 'I weighed only 60 pounds'). Official film footage, however, clearly shows the astronauts struggling to jump more than 18 inches. Is this another NASA oversight?

And *did you know* . . . that no crater was formed when the Lunar Excursion Module (LEM) touched down on the Moon's surface? According to an official statement by NASA, the reason for this was to do with the combination of the LEM's weight (seventeen tons), its rocket-engine thrust (10,500 pounds) and the fact that there is no atmosphere on the Moon. No, I don't get that one, either. Nevertheless, NASA said that this was also the reason no dust was kicked up when the LEM landed – because the Moon's atmosphere is a vacuum. Yet we have already seen that official NASA film footage shows great plumes of dust being kicked up as the Lunar Rover travels across the Moon's surface. More lies?

And if anybody is still unconvinced that something is seriously amiss here, official NASA statements confirm Buzz Aldrin's claim that the astronauts weighed only sixty pounds – or thereabouts – whilst on the Moon. And yet, while a seventeen-ton Lunar Excursion Module and its 10,500-pound rocket thrust made no impression whatever on the Moon's surface, Neil Armstrong's sixty-pound 'footprint' is supposedly still there to this day. Something just does not add up.

And finally, *did you know* . . . that official NASA film footage clearly shows the LEM taking off from the Moon's surface, evidently *minus* any conventional form of propulsion system? Despite the official artist's impression of this event (which rightly depicts great plumes of thrust and flame as the rocket-engines ignite) on the film footage no such ignition is evident. Instead, a series of what appear to be 'bolts' clamping the module to the Moon's surface are seen to explode – small explosions, like Guy Fawkes bangers. The module then simply 'floats' back up into space, again leaving no impression on the Moon's surface whatever.

Is this evidence of some kind of antigravity propulsion system already in use in 1969? Or were we instead shown a computer-simulated takeoff from Hollywood's *Moon Landing* studios? I suggest you check it out for yourself, because it sure as hell beats the logic out of me. It defies the laws of physics entirely.

But then again, defying laws seems to be what NASA is all about.

DOCUMENT 05

Cosmic Top Secret
Eyes Only Copy One of One

The Black Triangle Enigma (Part 1)
Sightings

File 18
Dark Skies

While the skies of the 1940s and 1950s seemed infested with mainly saucer-shaped objects, the skies of the 1990s have become darkened by what many consider to be a relatively new phenomenon – the 'Black Triangle', sometimes referred to as the 'Flying Triangle' or the 'Silent Vulcan'. The question on everyone's lips today is:

Is this strange and massive triangular craft reported by so many sane, professional witnesses extraterrestrial? Or is it some supersecret military prototype? Or both . . . ?

Perhaps the collection of following reports will help determine the truth concerning the origin of what many are now calling 'the UFO of the 1990s' – the already infamous Black Triangle.

Though some researchers and commentators are convinced that the Black Triangle is indeed some new and highly

not so easily persuaded. For one thing, sightings of triangular-
shaped aircraft have been reported for more than two hundred
years. Indeed, the first report I have managed to obtain is
dated 29th August 1871, when a French astronomer sighted
formations of triangular – as well as circular and multifaceted –
objects hovering and otherwise manoeuvring in Earth's upper
atmosphere. According to Australian researcher William H.
Watson, this same astronomer together with a colleague also
observed 'numerous round and triangular objects crossing
the face of the Sun on 3rd August 1886'. Watson goes on
to present other astronomical observations of unidentified
triangular craft, including that of a 'huge illuminated equilateral
triangle' that appeared within the Moon's crater Plato on 23rd
November 1887.

Reporting for *UFO Reality* magazine, Watson states:
'Tiny points of light were observed to originate in Craters
Aristarchus and Kepler and in the Lunar Alps. The lights
converged on Plato and traversed its high walls to unite in
the colossal floodlit triangle.'

If the military-industrial complex were flying aircraft to the
Moon more than one hundred years ago, then I would say
we are in some deep trouble!

On the other hand, these reports tend to support the
idea that not all triangular or delta-winged aircraft sighted
in our skies belong to the military. Surely even the most
paranoid conspiracy theorist cannot seriously believe that
any terrestrial power or agency possessed the technology to
build and fly space-faring triangular aircraft in the nineteenth
century. Yet there are reports of such sightings on record that
continue to appear throughout the first half of the twentieth
century and, indeed, to this day. William H. Watson, for
example, has collated forty-seven independent reports of

Flying Triangle sightings ranging from 1871 to 1963. From 1963 to the present day this same phenomenon has grown to immense proportions.

Before we investigate the present-day situation, however, first a brief look at the phenomenon over the years. On 29th March 1950, for example, a small delta-winged aircraft was sighted by three Spanish Army Air Corps officers stationed at Villafria Airfield. The officers observed the strange craft as it flew in from a south-south-easterly direction over the control tower and then turned east-wards. Its altitude was estimated between 1,600 ft and 3,200 ft while its speed was recorded at approximately 1,125 mph. As William Watson rightly notes, 'a ridiculous velocity in 1950'.

Further to this, at 3:40 p.m. on 24th July 1952, two USAF colonels flying a B-25 at 11,000 ft over Nevada sighted three objects in clear skies. According to the report the objects resembled F-86s flying in a tight 'V' formation. Both colonels noted, however, that if these craft were indeed F-86s, then they should have been flying at a lower altitude over that particular area due to civil aviation regulations. Indeed, this fact made the colonels wonder what type of aircraft they *were* observing. They did not have to wait long to find out.

Because within seconds the strange craft were close enough to the B-25 to be clearly visible, and both colonels reported seeing silver delta-winged aircraft with no tails and no pilot canopies. They estimated the speed of these craft to be around 2,000 mph (or three times the speed of an F-86). Though possible, it is highly unlikely that the US military possessed such craft in 1952.

Another report from 27th January 1953 surely dispels any lingering thoughts that the so-called Black or Flying Triangle could be anything but extraterrestrial. As William

Watson reports in his excellent article, *Delta Volant – Flying Triangles In History*. 'Over Albany, Georgia [USA] at 6,000 ft . . . an F-86 pilot spotted an unusually bright, white light at 10 o'clock high. He watched it for a few minutes, trying to decide whether it was a star or another aircraft – but it had too definite a circular shape for either.

'He climbed above it, proving it could not have been a star, and began to nose down close to Mach 1. Seeing no navigation lights he continued the pursuit, converging rapidly on his target. Then, in about a two-second cycle, the light changed from white to red and back again two or three times. Next it resolved into a triangle, thereafter splitting into two triangles, one above the other.'

The report concludes: 'The whole incident had been followed on radar as the initially slow-moving UFO had sped up to keep ahead of the aircraft, and had then shot off the scope at tremendous speed.'

Years before the US had even conceived the plans for a delta-winged stealthy aircraft, then, it would seem that someone else was already flying one.

File 18: Appendix 01
Case Report: Cosmic Top-X10 Eyes Only Belgium

Though impressive for its day, this was not the only Black Triangle case to have been monitored on radar.

Following a spate of Black Triangle sightings in the Hudson Valley area of New York State in the early part of the 1980s – during which time encounters with this strange new UFO were reported on an almost daily basis – the phenomenon visited Europe. And how.

Literally hundreds of independent Black Triangle sightings had been reported in the US during the Hudson Valley flap (including several simultaneous mass sightings) and many of these reports had been submitted by groups of disbelieving motorists who had stopped their cars and climbed out to view the massive triangular UFOs that appeared to hover above highways and freeways as though on public display. Even so, when the Triangles turned up in Europe some six years later, the number of reported sightings increased to thousands.

The biggest, most famous and certainly the best-documented series of Black Triangle sightings occurred, of course, in Belgium over a five-month period from November 1989 through March 1990. Indeed, it is estimated that some 13,000 independent witnesses observed the 'football-pitch-sized' UFO on one night alone (30th/31st March 1990). Many of these sightings were corroborated by the Belgian Air Force's radar operators and pilots. Between 29th November and 2nd December 1989, for example, massive UFO activity reported across Belgium led to the Air Force scrambling F-16 jet fighters in order to attempt an intercept, but to no avail. Although the radar operators – who had been alerted by the local gendarmerie – could see the craft on radar clearly enough, as soon as the F-16s approached the target area the echo disappeared from the screen. The F-16s lost contact. Not for the first time the terrestrials came off second best.

But it was on the night of 30th/31st March 1990 that the fun really began.

To judge by the sheer volume of independent Black Triangle sightings (around 13,000, of which 2,600 were officially received and logged) it is clear that something extraordinary occurred in the skies over Belgium and northern Germany on this unprecedented night. Among the impressive list of witnesses were local police officers, the gendarmerie and officials from the Belgian Air Force and NATO. No 'UFO cranks' there. But what is even more impressive is the fact that virtually all of these witnesses reported seeing the same remarkable phenomenon – three lights in triangular formation that, when viewed from fairly close range, appeared to be illuminating the underbelly of an immense black or dark-grey triangular craft. According to a very high percentage of reports, this craft was seen flying at very low altitudes – 100 to 200 ft – and at very slow speeds – thirty to forty mph; it was also seen to stop and hover over residential areas and was clearly visible from the ground. Some reports – including the official Air Force and NATO radar returns – stated that, although the craft was inexplicably capable of such 'slow-flight' and 'standstill' manoeuvres, it was also capable of speeds many times faster than, say, an F-16 (whose top speed is around 1,100 mph). And as the pilots of two scrambled F-16s were about to find out, it was also capable of manoeuvres that defied the laws of physics entirely.

Following a request from the Wavre gendarmerie to NATO radar stations at both Semmerzake and Glons – both of whom had by now encountered unexplained echos on their radar screens – the NATO air defence system's sector commander authorized two *Quick Reaction Alert* F-16 fighter jets to be scrambled immediately, their mission to intercept the unidentified radar target. But although the F-16s were giving chase within minutes, and although their own radars locked on to the target easily enough, as soon as they got within sight of the unidentified craft their radar-lock was inexplicably broken. Indeed, the target-craft – whatever it was – performed manoeuvres surely beyond the capabilities of any known terrestrial aircraft, and this notwithstanding the probability that the US-based military-industrial complex is currently developing technologies beyond most of our wildest dreams. At one point, for example, this immense triangular craft – which, according to several thousand reports, remember, was the size of a 'football pitch' – dropped from around 10,000 feet to somewhere below 500 feet in less than two seconds, an action recorded on no less than five NATO and Belgian Air Force radar screens! Needless to say, the F-16s were unable to continue their pursuit. The craft was suddenly lost to radar and the pilots were called back to base, bested. They had given chase for over an hour.

Back on the ground thousands of incredulous Belgians and Germans were watching the display with some awe. Many of their detailed reports were later confirmed to have been corroborated by NATO's radar returns, including the sudden and inexplicable manner in which the craft seemed simply to disappear. Indeed, ground witnesses reported that, as the F-16s approached the target area, the craft simply vanished – the three lights, which were located one at each of the Triangle's points, suddenly converged on the centre of the craft's underbelly and 'dissolved' into one another. Some say the remaining single light then took off at an inestimable speed and disappeared into the heavens.

It should be added that top-ranking officials from the Belgian Air Force considered this incident real – the craft was no apparition, they say, and neither could it be explained away as laser light shows, weather balloons, atmospheric anomalies or any other kind of natural or man-induced phenomena. Indeed, according to then Colonel – now General – Wilfried De Brouwer, Chief of Operations for the Belgian Air Force, the craft was solid and intelligently controlled. 'There was a logic in the movements of the UFO,' he said.

Indeed there was, as has been corroborated by the many

hundreds of similar reports from England and Scotland over the past few years, many of which seem so consistent with the Belgian incident that it is now beyond question that this same massive black triangular phenomenon has turned its attention to Britain.

File 19
Southern Skies

In August 1995 alone more than one hundred independent reports of encounters with a massive and truly sinister-seeming black triangular aircraft were received by local UFO groups in the south of England. Further investigation showed that this same phenomenon had been occurring on a regular basis for some years. Most reports detailed the craft's unusual flight characteristics – a 'standstill/hover' capability; silent and/or virtually silent flight/propulsion system; extreme low-altitude capability; extreme slow-flight capability; the ability to simply 'disappear' and 'reappear', often spontaneously; top speeds beyond those of any known conventional aircraft. A researcher's dream. Other sightings (some of which have been filmed and/or photographed) included reports of mysterious black spheres, massively long cylindrical objects, luminous diamond-shaped objects, flying 'Vs', 'Hs', discs, rhomboids, boomerangs . . . all displaying similar flight characteristics to the aforementioned Black Triangle. Indeed, when reports from all over the UK appeared to match those occurring in the south it seemed a British UFO wave of mammoth proportions was under way. And so it was. The wave continues to this day.

File 19: Appendix 01
Case Report: Cosmic Top-X11 Eyes Only
Jack

The first report I received was submitted by a well-known British rock musician who lives in Somerset, and who, due to his high-profile career, wishes to remain anonymous. I will call him Jack.

It was around 10 p.m. one night in July 1989 when Jack and a few friends were seated around a camp fire; two of the party decided to go back in to the house to fetch some water. According to Jack, it was a clear, cloudless night and still partially light – the sun had not long gone down behind the hills to the west. Some brief time after the two had returned to the house, those still seated around the camp fire began to feel a little 'strange'.

As the two returned with the water they were suddenly stopped in their tracks. Looking up, they saw what appeared to be an object hovering directly above the trees where the camp fire was still burning. According to their account the object was hovering low, and made no sound whatever.

Closer inspection of the object determined its shape as triangular, and it 'appeared to pulse white and red beams of light that reflected on the trees where the others were'. It should be said that by this time 'the others' were feeling 'tired and drained' for no explicable reason. Indeed, when I interviewed Jack he told me that they found themselves 'slumping' on the ground where moments before they had been seated upright and talking.

Meanwhile, the craft was still being observed by the two friends on their way back to the camp fire. At some point one of the two eyewitnesses flashed his torch [flashlight] in the direction of the craft, and then watched in utter disbelief as the craft suddenly flew off at lightning speed. According to both witnesses the craft went from standstill to enormous speed with no evidence of acceleration, and finally disappeared behind the Mendip Hills – about ten miles away – 'within two seconds'. On their return to the camp fire – where the others were still feeling 'strangely tired' – the two who had seen the craft were notably shaken and excited. 'It was the weirdest thing I've ever experienced,' Jack confided. And who could argue with that?

File 19: Appendix 02
Case Report: Cosmic Top-X12 Eyes Only
The Future Of Earth

This next report was submitted by an entire family who encountered the Black Triangle on their way home from visiting relatives. Indeed, this story made the front page of the local *Mid-Somerset Gazette* on 24th August 1995.

It should be said that when I spoke to 'John' about this incident it was immediately apparent that he and his family had been seriously unnerved by their experience, which began as the family approached the small, rural village of Butleigh Wootton in Somerset while driving home from London. It was a clear, hot summer's night at around 10:45 p.m., 17th August 1995. In the car with John was his wife, his son and his nephew – all four were about to experience something none of them had ever believed possible.

As they drove past several grazing fields near the local church, John suddenly noticed a large airborne object hovering just above the field to his left. He observed the object as being triangular in shape with three pulsating red lights, one in each corner. Immediately he slowed down to take a closer look.

It was then that he saw the triangular craft moving 'very slowly' above the field – 'far too slow for something that big' he said, quietly shaking his head as though still deeply affected by the experience. He added that the craft was 'about the size of a large Jumbo Jet'.

After observing the craft for several moments, John told me that it then suddenly rose upwards and banked over a nearby row of silhouetted trees. As it performed this manoeuvre John was able to confirm without question that indeed the craft was triangular in shape, and 'massive'. It was also silent. He said the two children were so frightened at this point that they both began to cry. 'They were terrified,' he said. 'Indeed, we all were. Although I have to say, myself and my wife couldn't help but feel intrigued by what we were seeing.'

Of all the witnesses I have interviewed regarding sightings of this strange black beast, John was the first to speculate on the craft's origin. 'I had this strange feeling,' he told me nervously, 'this inexplicable feeling when I was watching that thing that it wasn't alien, but from the future of Earth. It just felt so like Earth technology, the kind of technology they might have in a hundred years time.'

Or perhaps even now, somewhere . . .

File 19: Appendix 03
Case Report: Cosmic Top-X13 Eyes Only
Terry-fied!

On 15th June 1995, at around 1:30 a.m., Terry McDonough of Street, Somerset, was sitting in his back garden. It was a perfectly clear night dappled with stars, and very hot. Indeed, it was the start of the 1995 heatwave and Terry was finding it difficult to sleep, which was why he found himself sitting outside in his garden instead of being curled up in his bed, dreaming. He was soon to find himself in the middle of a dream anyway. The only difference being that this dream would reveal itself as a real-life nightmare.

Because suddenly Terry saw a very bright light in the sky, far brighter than any of the stars, he said, and it seemed to be moving towards him. As the light drew nearer Terry was able to determine the shape of a large triangular craft, 'about the size of a Jumbo Jet'. He could now see that the single light he thought he had first seen was in fact one of three lights illuminating the craft, one at each corner. According to Terry the craft was either very dark grey or black, and at one point hovered directly and noiselessly above him at an altitude of around 400/500 ft. By now Terry was little short of terrified.

Next, the craft started to make what Terry described as a 'strange high-pitched sucking sound', like a 'giant vacuum cleaner', which was loud enough to wake his girlfriend, Alison, from sleep. As she came out into the garden to investigate, the craft suddenly flew off at incredible speed, and according to both Terry and Alison, it flew off 'flat end first'. Both Terry and Alison were extremely shaken by their ordeal.

When questioned further about the craft's 'strange high-pitched sucking sound', Terry produced a newspaper cutting he had found in the 31st August 1995 edition of the *Bristol Evening Post* (two and a half months after Terry's encounter). The headline read: *Mystery Noise Wakes City Families*. The report went on to say how families in Bristol – about twenty-five miles from Street – had been awakened at 5:30 in the morning by a noise that sounded like a 'jet aircraft in trouble'. One of those awoken by the sound was store manager Lyndon Allen of Easton, Bristol, who told the *Bristol Evening Post*:

'It was a low engine noise that reminded me of an aircraft falling out of the sky. All of a sudden the sound of the engine became very high-pitched.' Mr Allen added: 'Whatever was making the noise suddenly shot off at high speed.'

This, said Terry, described the sound (and the capability) of the Triangle very well.

But what Terry did not know was that the sound he described had been heard and reported by many others in the south-west of England during this same summer period (1995). Most of these reports described a mysterious 'high-pitched boom-and-rumble' sound that seemed to occur late at night or in the early hours of the morning. The term 'skyquake' has been coined to describe these strange sounds.

Indeed, this would perhaps be an appropriate place to mention the series of similar 'skyquakes' reported in California in recent years. And then again the same phenomenon reported in Pordenone, north-east Italy, in 1995, where over one hundred thousand people were startled half to death by what is presumed to have been a sudden and terrifying sonic boom, but which, according to local reports, sounded more as though an earthquake had just ripped through Italian skies. Indeed, the sound shattered windows and scrambled brain cells to the point that locals thought some great and terrible 'end' had suddenly been visited upon them. In California, of course, the sound has been monitored and investigated, and is now suspected to be associated with the re-entry of Aurora, the supersecret US space-reconnaissance aircraft based at Groom Lake, Nevada. Indeed, videotape evidence shot by California researcher Sean Morton tends to support this conclusion. But what of the Italian quake?

Perhaps not surprisingly, the highly Top Secret USAF Aviano Air Base is located close to Pordenone where the 1995 skyquake occurred. Indeed, due to its strategic military position and the fact that either UFOs or secret experimental aircraft have on previous occasions been reported in connection with this Italian-sited USAF base, Aviano has become known as Europe's 'Area 51'.

I recall author Timothy Good's story (*Above Top Secret*) of American soldier James Blake and nightwatchman Benito Manfre who, in 1977, witnessed a strange 'glowing disc' hovering above the hangars at Aviano Air Base, causing a total power blackout. When the disc finally glided noiselessly away from the base the lights came back on and normal activities were resumed. The security alert caused by the incident – and reported by the base's personnel – was later denied by NATO headquarters in Brussels. Those same headquarters were unable to give any explanation for the 1995 Italian skyquake.

We can only wonder, then, at the sound reported by Terry and Alison, and by the residents of Bristol in August 1995. I have it on very good authority, for example, that Aurora overflies British and European airspace on a regular basis, and that Britain has its own supersecret 'Stealth' prototype which is currently being developed and test-flown (see File 22). If either of these two 'non-existent' aircraft were responsible for the skyquakes – or indeed, for the 'strange high-pitched sucking sound' reported by Terry – then come very serious questions need to be asked at Government level (an issue we will discuss in more detail later). For now the most immediate question that springs to mind is: If this immense black triangular aircraft is indeed some super-duper new military prototype, then what in God's name do the authorities think they are playing at, test-flying over such densely populated areas? The *Bristol Evening Post* article, for example, concluded by telling how another Bristol resident reported 'windows rattling in Old Market as the area was swept by the sound'. It should be added that British Aerospace (which is secretly developing Britain's new Stealth aircraft) has a runway at Filton, near Bristol. As expected, however, the military-industrial giant said it had 'nothing to do with the noise'.

No surprises there, then.

File 19: Appendix 04
Case Report: Cosmic Top-X14 Eyes Only
Low-Flying Exercises

This next report might just shed some light on the ET/military conundrum: Is the Black Triangle extraterrestrial? Or is it military? Freelance journalist Kevin Ollier saw it, and he is convinced it is not the latter.

In May 1994 the RAF announced in the local Somerset press that 'overnight low-flying training exercises' would be undertaken by Hercules C-130 transporter planes. According to the newspaper article these exercises were to be held over a three-week period in June 1994. It is perhaps not surprising, then, that a string of UFO sightings was reported at this time.

However, so many of the reports were so detailed in their descriptions, and the witnesses seemed so adamant that what they had seen had not been a military or any other kind of known aircraft, that I decided to include this following report for the reader's appraisal. It should be said that it is very unusual for the RAF to announce their plans for night exercises in the local press. Helicopters, jets and Hercules C-130 tactical transport aircraft are frequently seen and heard low-flying at night over the Somerset moors and levels, the point being that it is not such an unusual occurrence that the RAF should deem it necessary to publicly announce the fact. Indeed, what is more unusual is that the RAF *did* announce the fact. With this in mind one wonders: Was the RAF's objective to pre-empt what was to become a sizeable UFO flap by announcing its intentions to conduct night exercises? Was the military simply covering its tracks? According to freelance journalist Kevin Ollier, this is a very likely scenario.

On Sunday 5th June 1994, at around midnight, Kevin Ollier was out walking with his brother-in-law Duncan Gaukroger, who was in Glastonbury visiting with his family. At some point the two men decided to take a rest; Kevin sat himself down on a roadside bench while Duncan remained standing, facing Kevin. Through the trees, approaching over a high rise known as Chalice Hill, Kevin suddenly noticed a very bright light in the sky. When I spoke to him he told me that his initial reaction on seeing the light was: 'It must be Venus.' But the light seemed to be getting brighter, and closer, and so Kevin finally pointed it out to Duncan. He then got up from the bench and both men walked a few yards further along the road to gain a better view.

'By now the light looked like something from a Nativity scene,' Kevin told me. 'Duncan said: "*What is that*?" I told him it was probably a Hercules, but admittedly I wasn't convinced, because there was no sound and the night was perfectly breezeless. It kept getting nearer and we both began to wonder what would happen next. At this point I felt exhilarated and terrified, both at once. After three or four minutes the object passed overhead, very slowly. We were able to see it very clearly.

'It was big, dark, triangular, had lights underneath and was moving in a northeasterly direction. After it had passed overhead Duncan said: "I don't know what that is, but it's definitely not a Hercules!" '

The two men went home convinced they had seen something other than an RAF night exercise. Indeed, they went home wondering what had prompted the RAF's press announcement in the first place.

File 19: Appendix 05
Case Report: Cosmic Top-X15 Eyes Only
HMS Heron

One further report from File 19 that also suggests a military connection to the Black Triangle phenomenon is the account of Tina Dyer, who claims to have seen the craft taking off from a highly secure Royal Navy base in Yeovilton, Somerset: HMS *Heron*, the flagship of the Navy's Fleet Air Arm . . .

Dotted around the length and breadth of Britain are a host of highly secure military bases. Some would argue that, in the interests of national security, military bases should indeed enjoy the strictest security measures, if only to ensure that 'prying eyes' be kept at a safe distance. However, this argument rests on the assurance that the activities carried out at such bases are themselves in the interests of national security. Much evidence now points to the possibility that this is far from the reality.

Well-stocked UFO archives contain countless reports of unexplained aerial phenomena being observed over military bases. I call your attention to what were formerly the joint RAF/USAF Woodbridge/Bentwaters twin bases near Ipswich, for example, where in 1980 a UFO was seen to land in Rendlesham Forest (an area of woodland that separates the two bases). The incident was witnessed and reported by both regular and high-ranking military officers and was subsequently covered up by the MoD, much to the concern of Admiral of the Fleet and former Chief of the Defence

Staff and Chairman of the NATO Military Committee, Lord Hill-Norton. One wonders why such a high-ranking military luminary, though aware of the cover-up, is unable to breach its defences.

In his excellent book *Revelations: Alien Contact and Human Deception*, longstanding UFO researcher Jacques Vallee puts forward the theory that the Woodbridge/Bentwaters case was probably no more than a psychological operations exercise perpetrated by the US military. The reason? To monitor the response of the military personnel involved in anticipation of a similar incident occurring for real. Though I beg to differ with one or two conclusions drawn by Vallee, nevertheless this hypothesis, I believe, should not be dismissed out of hand. Indeed, if this turns out to be the case then the question must surely be asked: Just what exactly *is* going on behind those barbed-wire perimeter fences? And moreover, if the answer to this question is 'covert operations perpetrated on unwitting subjects' (military or otherwise) then I argue that this activity is illegal and the regular national security laws should not therefore apply. On the other hand, should the answer be 'the test-flying of advanced-technology experimental aircraft, such as Aurora, Halo, etc', then why are these aircraft being test-flown over residential areas? Either way, the activities of the military in this respect are highly illegal and should therefore be brought to account.

By way of adding spice to this seeming conundrum I received a telephone call at around 9:30 p.m. on 17th April 1996 from Tina Dyer of Shaftesbury in Somerset, who told me she had just witnessed something very strange indeed above HMS *Heron*, RNAS Yeovilton, the Fleet Air Arm's 'Flagship' air base located at Yeovilton, Somerset. It is suspected that some very exotic aircraft indeed are frequent visitors to this base, as well as to RAF Boscombe Down in Wiltshire, the allegedly deserted RAF Machrihanish in Scotland and a list of others. But it is to HMS *Heron*, RNAS Yeovilton that we turn our investigations for the present.

At around 8 p.m. that same evening, Tina said, she had been out walking when her attention was taken by a 'yellow light' that rose slowly up into the sky. Tina said that at first the light seemed 'diffused', but that as it rose up into the sky it became brighter and sharper, until it became about the same brightness as, say, Venus on a good night. What is intriguing is that, at the time, Tina was looking in the direction of HMS *Heron*, the Royal Naval Air Station at Yeovilton.

'I was looking towards the air base,' Tina told me. 'What I saw was a fuzzy yellow light that rose up very, very slowly. I watched it for about ten minutes continuously, until it was quite high in the sky. What made me keep watching was the fact that it rose up so slowly; that's what made me think how strange it was.

'I continued to observe the light, and watched it rise up through some clouds [the evening was quite clear with sparse cloud cover]. As it rose up it had a short trail underneath that wasn't like a normal aircraft trail. It didn't *leave* a trail in the air like a normal aircraft – the trail remained attached to the object. It's really quite difficult to put into words.

'Then, quite suddenly, it changed into a sort of cylinder shape, and became a brighter yellow. As it rose up even further it was angled slightly, still looking like a cylinder shape, but by now it looked longer and darker. I can't tell how high it was, but I assume it was quite high because it had been ascending now for about fifteen minutes. When it reached a certain point it jettisoned something, a small black object that fell straight to earth and disappeared from view. It was then I caught sight of what I was really looking at.

'Because at this point the thing changed direction and

started flying towards me. It was about 8:20-8:25 p.m. as it flew over me, and by this time it seemed incredibly high, much higher than a normal military aircraft, and yet it was still clearly visible. What struck me was how incredibly black it was [Tina emphasized the word "black"] and very sharp, a very sharp-angled shape. There was no sound until it had passed over me, and then there was a sort of "soft thunder", again not like the noise made by either a jet or a helicopter, or any other kind of aircraft. It was all a little strange. As it flew overhead I could see that, what had appeared from a distance to be cylindrical, was in fact triangular. It was a black triangular craft, very sharp and thin. My gut feeling was this was some secret military craft, and that it was perhaps being test-flown at Yeovilton.'

When Tina got home she rang HMS *Heron*, RNAS Yeovilton and explained what she had seen. She spoke to the Yeovilton control tower and asked if they knew of any unusual aircraft that might explain her sighting. According to Tina, the man she spoke to was very abrupt, to the point. 'No,' was all he said. Feeling intimidated by this man's attitude, and still quite shocked by what she had just seen, Tina said 'Thank you' and hung up. She then called my business number and left a message, explaining what had happened.

The next morning at around 10 a.m. I contacted the Yeovilton base myself, and was told that pilots from the base had indeed been night-flying the previous evening. The night-flying had continued until 10:30 p.m., I was told. When I asked why they hadn't told Tina Dyer this the night before, the woman I spoke to said she didn't know.

I then told the woman that the sighting had taken place between 8 p.m. and 8:30 p.m. The woman giggled and said: 'But it was still light then.' I told her: 'I know it was still light then, and that's what makes this sighting all the more intriguing.'

I then explained that there had been an awful lot of reports lately of a black triangular aircraft flying and hovering over the local area and in other parts of Somerset and the South-West, and could she say anything about this. Again she reiterated that aircraft from Yeovilton had been 'night-flying' the previous evening, and explained that they'd had 'jets and helicopters' in the air. When I told the woman that Tina Dyer had heard no noise from the aircraft except the 'soft thunder' she had reported after the aircraft had departed (remember, the aircraft had hovered and ascended for around fifteen minutes prior to its departure) and that most of the local reports filed recently seemed to tell a similar story, and *could she comment on this*, the RNAS spokeswoman promptly said: 'OK, then. Sorry I couldn't help you,' and hung up.

I was in no position to take this report any further. NATIONAL SECURITY took care of that.

File 20
Northern Skies

If the skies of southern England have been darkened by sightings of the so-called Black Triangle over the past few years, then those of northern England and Scotland must by now be sheer fearful black. Reports from Derbyshire, Yorkshire and in particular Lancashire, plus those from the Bonnybridge and Falkirk areas of Scotland have doubled and redoubled in recent times. I would like to take this opportunity to highlight the dedicated and often perilous research carried out by investigators in these areas, in particular Stephen Mera, Simon Lewis and Tim Matthews in Lancashire, Omar Fowler in Derbyshire and Malcolm Robinson in Scotland, plus of course researchers everywhere, without whom the story of the British Black Triangle phenomenon would not have been told.

File 20: Appendix 01
Case Report: Cosmic Top-X16 Eyes Only Police Report

Very often people seem more convinced of a UFO sighting if it is reported by a police officer. For those of this disposition the first of our *Northern Skies* sightings should satisfy well enough. It was reported by no less than *four* police officers whilst on duty on the Stretford/Old Trafford border in Manchester.

According to the report, submitted by the Manchester Anomalous Phenomena Investigation Team (MAPIT), it was just after midnight on 8th February 1996 that the four on-duty police officers reported seeing a 'strange low-level craft' above the Lancashire Country Club. They described it as being triangular in shape with a 'girder' structure running the length of its underside. According to the officers the craft was 'massive' and had red and white lights set into it. They reported that the craft made no sound whatever, and that it performed aerobatics that the Red Arrows would have been proud of! All four officers watched the strange craft for several minutes until it eventually sped off in a southerly direction.

To support the testimonies of the four on-duty police officers, the MAPIT report also included testimonies to this same sighting from thirty civilian witnesses. The report went on to say that some of these witnesses contacted Air Traffic Control at Manchester's Ringway Airport, who in turn alerted RAF West Drayton (as their directive demands). Some reports suggested that jets had been scrambled (from RAF Valley on

Anglesey) to intercept the anomalous craft but, as the MAPIT report rightly points out, this would have depended on West Drayton picking up a radar return. The MoD later confirmed that its Secretariat (Air Staff) 2a1 office had received several reports from civilians that coincided with those filed by the police officers. It should be added that other UFO groups across the north-west subsequently investigated reports of what appears to have been the same craft on the same night.

File 20: Appendix 02
Case Report: Cosmic Top-X17 Eyes Only
Civil Reports

Another report I received from the north-west shows that police officers are not the only respected members of society who see UFOs. This same phenomenon also visits itself upon civil servants – like Pieter Smit of Morcambe.

Mr Smit was in his back garden on 18th April 1995 when, once again, according to a very well-researched MAPIT report, 'a huge dark triangular craft came and hovered above him'. He described the craft as being 200 metres in length (twice the size of a Jumbo Jet) and hovering at an altitude of between 300 and 500 ft. He said there was a cabin-like structure running nearly the entire length of the craft which was 'illuminated with soft lights'. Mr Smit also reported seeing 'four soft lights' glowing on the craft's underbelly, and said that the craft made no sound whatever. After about fifteen seconds, the report says, the craft moved slowly away in a west-north-westerly direction.

It should be stated here that this and other reports of Black Triangle sightings published in this document have been selected from hundreds more filed away in the *UFO Reality* archives, and in the archives of research groups across the entire British Isles. Of these, Lancashire has certainly had its fill. Indeed, according to Lancashire investigators Tim Matthews and Jason Carradus, the so-called 'modern wave' of UFO sightings and encounters in the Morcambe Bay area dates back to the 1940s, once again casting serious doubt on the possibility that the Black Triangle is a military aircraft. However, for the purposes of our investigation, I will keep to the most up-to-date reports.

According to a report I received from the Lancaster UFO Network, for example, at 9:30 p.m. on an April evening in 1995 four people witnessed the arrival of a 'huge black triangular craft' that hovered over the town of Carnforth in Lancashire. Evidently one of the four witnesses, a woman, had worked at Heysham Harbour for many years (prior to the development of a nuclear facility on the site) and so she was used to seeing triangular-shaped Vulcan bombers flying over the harbour. However, according to Tim Matthews and Jason Carradus, she described this particular triangular craft as being 'much bigger, particularly graceful and completely silent', while all four witnesses reported that the craft 'blocked out the light and created a shadow over the area', despite the fact that the sighting occurred in the late evening. Indeed, this is becoming a very common theme with Black Triangle sightings (i.e. that the craft appears to be even darker than the darkest of nights). The Lancaster UFO Network also reported that a craft of very similar description was responsible for many of the *two hundred* reports received over the three-month period from January to April of the same year (1995).

Indeed, a mechatronics engineer from Bare in Lancashire saw the craft from her backyard. She said it was flying so low that she was able to provide the local UFO investigation team with a computer-aided diagram of the craft. Once again the witness reported that the craft was completely silent and flying at an altitude of around 500 ft. As well as its distinctive shape, a red light was seen to glow from the centre of the craft's underbelly.

Further to this, a man from Morcambe's West End saw a black triangular craft hovering over Morcambe Bay and illuminating the water with its light. This was in August 1995. On this occasion the craft approached the witness's car and, to the amazement of the driver and his daughter, hovered briefly at a distance of no more than 100 ft. It then followed the promenade and moved off at high speed in a south to south-easterly direction.

To add to this, a report I received from the Birmingham UFO Society (BUFOS) detailed a sighting of the Black Triangle over the M6 motorway. According to this report three witnesses observed the strange craft as they travelled between Junction 7 of the M6 and the M5 motorways. The craft was described as triangular with a central white light beneath and smaller white lights at each corner, with the added detail of red lights being seen 'along the edges'. The report stated that the craft hovered above 'two carriageways of the motorway at a height of approximately 200–250 ft'.

A second report from BUFOS described the sighting of a 'huge black triangular object' that hovered over a lorry park in Strensham, Worcester, 'for about thirty-five seconds'. This sighting occurred at 9:50 p.m. on 7th March 1996. According to the witness, the craft had a central red light and a red light at each corner, and a 'green flashing light on top'. The object was said to be 'completely silent' and moving slowly southwards. At one point during the sighting the witness, an aviation expert, heard an aeroplane approaching which, on visual contact, he identified as a Hercules C-130. The Hercules was forced to 'bank left' in order to avoid a collision with the UFO which then 'sped away at a very high speed'. The report goes on to explain that the witness immediately reported his sighting to the MoD, but to no avail. Like countless eyewitnesses before and since he received nothing more than the standard 'no defence significance' reply, and this despite the fact that one of the Ministry's Hercules C-130 aircraft had almost bumped into an aircraft of unknown origin in British airspace.

The question everyone is eager to have answered is: If the UFOs reported are indeed of 'no defence significance', and so are not deemed a threat to national security, then why all the secrecy within the MoD's hallowed halls?

As the late Martin Redmond MP commented following questions he tabled in the House of Commons (5th November 1996) concerning UFOs and Government secrecy: 'The answers I've been given lead me to think there is something more to this.' And further: 'The only thing I know for sure is this whole issue is shrouded in secrecy.'

And so it is.

File 20: Appendix 03
Case Report: Cosmic Top-X18 Eyes Only Scotland

The above reports account for only a small handful of the countless Black Triangle sightings and encounters reported in the Midlands and the north of England over the past few years. In support of this, what follows is a summary of what has been happening further north in Scotland where, if the truth be told, the British Black Triangle epidemic fairly began.

*   *   *

To begin, a taster . . .

A regular evening's radio broadcast became transformed into a bizarre and interesting event in May 1996, when James Lyon presented a 'phone-in' live on air. At some point during the show a woman telephoned and said that she had just seen something quite extraordinary in the sky. She went on to describe a huge black triangular aircraft, apparently noiseless, and distinct in every sense from anything the woman had ever previously seen. At first James Lyon decided to ignore the call, but then for some reason reversed his decision as he suddenly felt that the woman 'had sounded sincere'. During the course of proceedings he asked his listeners if any of them had witnessed something similar in the sky that evening. He was not disappointed by the response.

Almost immediately people from all over the Inverness broadcast region started to telephone in with their stories of UFO sightings. James was suitably stunned by such an eager response. 'We were inundated with calls,' he said. 'So much so that our phone lines were jammed for more than an hour and a half. More than forty people rang in, all saying that they had seen the triangular-shaped craft. Many said they saw unusual colours being emitted from the back of it.'

James has since pledged to keep an eye on the sky from now on!

This is a mere snippet. Over the past few years literally hundreds of independent reports of Black Triangle sightings have emerged from Scotland, in particular from the Bonnybridge and Falkirk regions. Indeed (following the now-famous Belgian sightings of 1989/90, when Belgium seemed to be the Triangle's favoured hunting ground), by the mid-1990s Bonnybridge had become known within the UFO research community as the veritable hub of Black Triangle activity. Alas, however, there is simply not the room here to include the many reports I have on file regarding these sightings. Suffice to say for now that the reports thus far presented in Files 19 and 20 are wholly representative of what has been occurring in Scottish skies during this same time-frame. The following account, as well as being one of the most impressive Black Triangle reports ever logged, should likewise be seen to represent the many other reports which, sadly, must be omitted here. Nevertheless it should be reiterated that Scotland has seen more than its fair share of this mysterious black invader.

File 20: Appendix 04
Case Report: Cosmic Top-X19 Eyes Only
The Fife Incident

Due to its location, this particular sighting has been aptly named the 'Fife Incident'.

According to Scotland's foremost UFO investigator, Malcolm Robinson of Strange Phenomena Investigations (SPI), the Fife Incident is certainly one of the most remarkable UFO cases to have occurred in Scotland over the past few years. 'Not only are we dealing with observations of large, silent black triangle-shaped UFOs,' he said of this case, 'but also observations of many small grey "beings".' What follows is a summary of a report compiled by Mr Robinson for *UFO Reality*.

On the evening of 23rd September 1996, Mary Morrison, accompanied by her ten-year-old son Peter and her friend Jane, left her farmhouse to travel to a nearby town in order to purchase some coffee. The time was around 8:05 p.m. On the way they observed a huge white stationary light in the sky. Initially they thought that this was either a helicopter or a plane, but after a few seconds this bright light split into two. They stopped the car, got out, and were further amazed to see bright spotlights illuminating the ground in front of them. All three of them then observed a huge black triangular-shaped object with a number of red lights attached to it. The object was slowly turning in the air, and they could see what appeared to be a small dome on top of this triangular shape. They couldn't hear any noise, which made the close appearance of this object all the more strange. After a few moments the object gradually drifted away and was lost to view. On their journey back from the shop they observed the same (or a similar) object, but on this occasion it appeared to rush towards their car. Ten-year-old Peter was so scared that he began to cry, a fact that seemed somehow to be conveyed to this object, for as soon as he started crying it disappeared.

Although they were all shaken by the sighting Mary and Jane were also intrigued, and so they decided to return home and drive back to the spot with Susan, Jane's very sceptical daughter. While the car was heading back out to where they'd had their initial sighting they became aware of a tremendously bright white light on the ground, beside a group of trees. They also saw a bright blue glow shining from the ground and upwards towards the sky. It was at this point that events took a really dramatic turn, for silhouetted against the lights were lots of small grey figures running around and busily picking up what looked like boxes or cubes, and also cylinders. To the right of this amazing scene was a taller, brown-coloured 'being' who appeared to be watching intently what was going on. There was also what appeared to be a dark triangular shape further back into the woods. The small figures kept scurrying back to it, then running out again, like something out of *Star Trek*. But to Mary, Jane and Susan, of course, this was cold stark reality.

Just then they observed what appeared to be a 'cocoon of mist' floating out of the trees towards them. Contained within this mist were several of these small beings, who did not appear to be moving but were being *propelled* along the farmer's ploughed field in their direction. That was it; they had seen enough. Accompanied by a few choice expletives they leapt back into the car and sped off home.

It should be reiterated that this is only a brief summary of what occurred that night, and indeed for several nights thereafter. Following through with their investigations, Mr Robinson and his team discovered that there had been many UFO sightings in the Fife area during this same time-frame, and that both families concerned with the aforementioned report witnessed a number of UFOs near their property in the weeks to follow.

Which leaves one to ponder, if the Black Triangle is indeed a supersecret military prototype, why this one carried a crew of aliens . . . ?

[My special thanks to Mr Robinson and the SPI team for allowing me to reproduce this story.]

And thus the *Northern Skies* File comes to a close, for now . . .

File 21
Hostile Skies

On 2nd February 1996, the Civil Aviation Authority (CAA) released a report detailing an 'unexplained air miss' between a 'wedge-shaped' UFO and a British Airways Boeing 737. According to the report, the near air miss occurred at about 4,000 ft as the 737, en route from Milan, was on final approach to Manchester's Ringway Airport.

The incident was reported by Captain Roger Willis and First Officer Mark Stuart, who both saw the futuristic triangular-shaped craft as it scorched past their cockpit at phenomenal speed. They described the craft as 'wedge-shaped' and 'lit with a number of small lights, rather like a Christmas tree.' They also said that the craft was 'silent', and that it had a 'black stripe down its side'. As well as the crew, around sixty passengers were on board the 737 when the near air miss occurred.

The report, compiled by the CAA's Joint Air Miss Working Group and which took a year to complete, stated that both pilots were absolutely convinced about what they had seen. 'The object made no attempt to deviate from its course,' the report revealed, 'and no sound was heard or wake (wind turbulence) felt ... He (the co-pilot, First Officer Mark Stuart) felt certain that what he saw was a solid object − not a bird, balloon or kite. Despite exhaustive investigations, the reported object remains untraced.'

CAA spokesperson Chris Mason added: 'A small proportion of near-miss situations involving untraced aircraft remain unsolved.' As is now beginning to come to light, however, most remain unreported.

The report also included details of the two-way conversation that took place between the Boeing 737 cockpit and air traffic controllers at Ringway Airport.

Cockpit: 'We just had something go down the right-hand side, just above us, very fast!'

Control: 'Well, there's nothing seen on radar. Was it . . . ahhh . . . an aircraft?'

Cockpit: 'Well, it had lights. It went down the starboard side very quick.'

Control: 'And above you?'

Cockpit: 'Ahhh . . . just slightly above us, yeah.'

Control: 'Keep an eye out for something . . . ahhh . . . I can't see anything at all at the moment, so . . . ahhh . . . must have been very fast, or gone down very quickly after it passed you, I think.'

Cockpit: 'OK. Well, there you go!'

The report concluded that:

'The object, seen by both pilots, was highly unlikely to have been a hang glider, paraglider or microlight aircraft;

'There was no evidence of official military aircraft in the area;

'Any unknown military or civil movement in the area would almost certainly have been picked up on radar;

'It is most unlikely that military activity would have been conducted in CAS [Civilian Air Space] and so close to a busy international airport.'

And further that: 'The nature and identity of this object remains unknown.' The report also claimed that there were 'no other eyewitnesses' to the incident.

However, during the course of my own investigations into this case I soon discovered that the two British Airways pilots were *not* the only ones to witness the elusive craft – it was also seen by at least one other person, Mark Lloyd of Gatley near Manchester, who told me that the craft was 'the size of Wembley Stadium'. Mark told me he was driving along Styal Road (which runs adjacent to Ringway Airport) at approximately 3:30–4 p.m. on 6th January 1995, just three hours before the near air miss occurred. Suddenly, out of his car window, Mark spotted something unusual in the sky above the airport – so unusual, in fact, that he almost crashed his car. Fortunately he managed to stop the car and pull over to the side of the road where, for the next fifteen to twenty minutes, he watched in disbelief as a massive triangular-shaped 'spaceship' performed aerobatics above the busy airport. Mark remains astonished at the fact that, officially, only one aircraft crew reported seeing the craft (the crew of the Boeing 737 piloted by Captain Roger Willis); he believes many more pilots, air crews and airport ground staff must have seen the display, but that their reports were somehow kept quiet.

Describing the craft, Mark, an aviation enthusiast, told me: 'I knew it wasn't Concorde because it had no wings. It looked like a massive spaceship the size of Wembley Stadium, flying at about four thousand feet. I know it was about this altitude because that was the height of the cloud on that day.'

He added: 'I saw it through the clouds. It was shaped like a Christmas tree and was so huge it must have cost billions of pounds. To see just how big this thing was I held a sheet of A4 paper at arm's length, and it barely covered it.'

Mark concluded that, in some ways, the craft resembled a NASA-style space shuttle, although he added that it was far bigger, silent, and far more advanced technologically. So what on Earth *was* this mystery aircraft?

I first noticed Mark when he appeared on ITN's *News At Ten* on the night the CAA report was released. It was then that he told the reporter: 'It was able to move sideways, right and left, and tilt over backwards, doing manoeuvres no other aircraft could do.' When I later spoke to Mark he told me he had watched the craft 'darting around the sky, doing flips, turns, spins and spirals' before it finally disappeared.

Being a regular visitor to air shows and the like, Mark was somewhat used to seeing the latest technology putting on its best performance for an audience. But according to Mark, this craft was something else. He also said that, although the day was overcast, there was a sizeable break in the clouds above the airport, and this enabled him to observe the craft's incredible manoeuvrability unhindered.

In an attempt to find out what the authorities might know about the incident, Mark contacted Kerry Philpott at Secretariat (Air Staff) 2a1, MoD, Whitehall, the government's official 'UFO Desk'. Perhaps it will come as little surprise to learn that Mark's enquiry was met with disdain and derision.

'She just kept talking about *Independence Day* [the movie],' Mark told me. 'Have you seen *Independence Day*? It was as if she was implying I was making it all up, that it was just some fantasy I'd dreamed up . . .' He added: '. . . And by the way, I *hadn't* seen *Independence Day* – it hadn't even been released in England, not at that time.'

One wonders whether the two highly trained British Airways officers had seen *Independence Day*, too. Or whether Ms Philpott would have dared pose the same question to them.

Next, Mark visited Dr Clive Saunders, a thermonuclear physicist at Manchester University. He explained what he had seen in some detail and asked Dr Saunders his opinion on whether or not the craft in question could possibly have been developed by, say, the military, or anybody else for that matter. Dr Saunders' reply was emphatic. He said that the kind of nuclear technology necessary to power a craft of the size and proportion Mark had described would not be available, in his estimation, for at least another one hundred and fifty years. Dr Saunders's conclusion, therefore, was that the craft could not possibly have belonged to the military.

However, to counter this argument, here is another interesting snippet to add to the equation.

Around the time that the official CAA report was released (February 1996) Mark was invited to talk on various radio and TV talk shows. It was during one of his TV interviews that he learned of an alleged DA Notice (a 'reporting restriction' notice) which the government had ordered with regard to the so-called Black Triangle. This nugget was particularly interesting to me as some months previous to my interview with Mark I had been reliably informed by a top BBC executive that the BBC had indeed been 'heavily DA-Noticed' with regard to reports which in any way refer to sightings of, or encounters with, the Black Triangle. The reason given was because the so-called Black Triangle (or something just like it, particularly in shape) is indeed a current Top Secret military prototype.

It was certainly interesting to watch the news unfold on TV on the day the CAA report was released. Although the BBC reported the near air miss on its six o'clock news programme, the report was conspicuously missing from the BBC's main *Nine O'Clock News* that same evening. I am myself a journalist, and it has to be said that a story as big as this one (a UFO almost colliding in British airspace with a commercial airliner complete with sixty passengers) would normally be considered one of the major news items of the day. Indeed, on ITN's *News At Ten* the story was aired in about third slot. It should be remembered that UFO stories, if aired at all, always seem to fill that 'and finally' slot, and are generally treated in such a way as to leave the viewer with a sense that not all the news is depressing. At least you can have a chuckle at the UFO story at the end of the programme.

Not so with the near air miss report, at least not so far as

ITN was concerned. For once they treated the story with the respect it deserved. The BBC, on the other hand, for some inexplicable reason, decided not to run the story at all. If my information (together with Mark's) is correct, then the reason the story was cut was due to the DA Notice. Any other explanation simply does not make sense.

However, in fairness to the BBC, I should perhaps include here one or two points highlighted in a letter I received from Richard Fair, a broadcast journalist with *BBC GMR Talk* in Manchester, who disputes that a DA Notice has been enforced.

> 'Dear Mr King . . . At no time have I, or any other members of staff, been under any kind of reporting restriction on this or similar stories.
>
> 'All stories are judged on merit and despite certain discrepancies between his original statement and his current standing of how the events unfolded, Mark [Lloyd] appeared again on GMR Talk on Monday 27 January 1997.
>
> 'Your statement that a "top BBC executive" told you that the BBC "has been heavily DA-Noticed" has been repeated in many places, but for reasons best known only to your anonymous source, has not been passed down to the reporters and producers within the rest of the organisation.'

Stories of NASA personnel come to mind, personnel who claim it is nothing short of lunacy to think that an organization as big as NASA could possibly be involved in covert and/or conspiratorial activities without the workforce finding out. This is of course sheer nonsense. I recall, for example, the Manhattan Project, wherein thousands of workers had not a clue what they were working on until after the first atomic bomb to be dropped on an enemy target had wiped out half the population of Hiroshima. And then again the Stealth F-117A, which undertook its first 'official' test-flight on 18th June 1981 out of Groom Lake, Nevada – but who in the world ever heard of it until its futuristic design filled our TV screens during the Gulf War in 1990? The answer: no one outside of those who were *supposed* to know about it. I do not and have not ever worked for the BBC. I do not know what reporting restrictions its personnel may or may not be subject to. But I do know what I was told, and by whom, and that the reason my very reliable and high-ranking source must of course remain anonymous is due to the fact that the information was passed to me in confidence, and that a breach of that confidence would undoubtedly see my source's career down the tubes, to put it mildly. I also know that any government agency or establishment organization such as the BBC will be very adept indeed at keeping secrets, especially from those most closely involved. I do not doubt the ability of those who control the BBC to keep secrets from those in their pay.

With regard to Mr Fair's letter, then, all I can say is it comes as little surprise to learn that he and 'other members of staff' are unaware that they might indeed be under some form of reporting restricting. To imagine that the DA Notice would be enforced across the board, of course, with notice of its enforcement written in stone and posted on the canteen walls, is to miss the point altogether – which is precisely the objective of those with the authority to enforce such restrictions. With respect, of course a regional radio talk show will be exempt from the restrictions governing the main national television news programme. Government and intelligence agencies work with a sound knowledge of psychology on their side;

they are scarcely concerned about what might be discussed on a regional talk show. Indeed, such talk-talk is seen by the authorities – from a psychological standpoint – as little more than entertainment, and rightly so. Kilroy, Opra Winfrey, Richard and Judy *et al* do not pose a threat to national security, no matter the topics under discussion. Should similar material enjoy prime-time BBC news coverage, however, a different psychological effect entirely is experienced by the viewer.

In short, people believe without question what they are told on the *BBC News*, and the authorities are fully aware of this fact. Hence the DA Notice. What is discussed on a talk show, on the other hand, is trivia, no matter the significance to those either listening in or those directly involved in the debate. Hence the apparent lack of a DA Notice.

So far as the authorities are concerned, talk-show topics amount to little more than garden-wall gossip. In this respect it is very probable that a BBC DA Notice could and indeed does exist with regard to credible, mainstream reporting of Black Triangle sightings (and that even the BBC's television newsreaders are unaware of its existence) but that Mr Fair and his regional radio talk-show colleagues have no knowledge of it whatever.

File 21: Appendix 01
Case Review: Cosmic Top-X20 Eyes Only
Johnny Radar

To judge by the evidence thus far scrutinized, then, it must surely be the conclusion of most – if not all – level-headed, open-minded investigators that a phenomenon is occurring in our skies that does not seem to comply with the conventional laws of physics, and thus is highly unlikely to have originated with any known terrestrial power, including America. The Belgian case alone testifies to that. However, we have yet to study the evidence *against* this conclusion, as detailed in File 22 below. And until we have done that we should perhaps refrain from forming absolute conclusions about anything.

As for Mark Lloyd, he simply wanted his story heard, and for the truth to be told regarding this case. He felt all along that, despite the CAA's apparent 'honesty' in releasing the report publicly (something it was bound by constitutional regulations to do) a cleverly managed cover-up had been set in place in order to hide the true facts. Rumours of airline pilots being threatened and intimidated, for example, and of radar tapes going missing (or being confiscated by the military) abound, even though the authorities claim that the airport's radar system did not detect anything out of the ordinary on the day in question, and that the pilots were commended for coming forward and reporting the incident.

It should be pointed out here, however, that since the release of the CAA report, Captain Roger Willis has refused to talk to *anybody* about the incident. One is left to wonder: is this of his own choice?

It should also be added that, although two professionally trained pilots reported seeing a solid aircraft cross their flight path, no radar returns were recorded. Supposedly. Yet I was secretly told by another airport official that, within hours of the reported encounter, two uniformed intelligence officers arrived at the airport and left with the radar tapes in a briefcase. Someone is simply not telling the truth.

But then, faced with the kind of animal we are undoubtedly up against – an animal as fearsome as the military-industrial complex and its attendant quasi-military/intelligence agencies – is it any wonder that *Johnny Radar* is prepared to tell a few porkies, if only to protect his own butt?

File 22
Northern Exposure

Files 18 through 21 detail the evidence in support of the Black Triangle being extraterrestrial, or at least the result of, and powered by, technology that is unlikely to have originated on Earth. As a counterbalance, File 22 will detail what evidence there is to suggest that the Black Triangle might be of terrestrial/military origin.

Or indeed, that it might be the result of some joint military/alien alliance.

Perhaps the most reliable and respected publication in the field of cutting-edge aeronautics technology is *Jane's Military Aircraft*, the 1995–1996 edition of which alluded to the existence of Britain's own Stealth Technology programme (page 452). While numerous US media reports quoting Washington sources have tended to confirm that Britain is indeed developing an aircraft 'optimized for frontal area stealthiness', *Jane's* took the argument one step further by describing the aircraft under development as being of the 'Low Observable combat' type and stating that it was being developed in a 'secure hangar' at the British Aerospace (BAe) Special Projects site at Warton, Lancashire. The new aircraft was to replace the obsolescent Tornado GR MK4, the report said.

Also included in *Jane's* report was the fact that, between 1992 and 1994 alone, £100 million had been spent on Britain's 'stealth aircraft development' programme, unofficially code-named 'HALO' (High Altitude, Low Observable). The report concluded that the programme was 'nearing completion . . . in 1995', that BAe was 'urging government go-ahead for stealth demonstrator in 1997' and that 'production aircraft [were] then to be available in 2013'. International collaboration on the programme was likely, it said.

Less than inclined to face the music regarding the covert expenditure of more than £100 million of taxpayers' money, however, the government staunchly denies that this programme exists. No surprises there. The £40 billion of British taxpayers' money already pledged to the development of *Eurofighter 2000*, NATO's new all-singing, all-dancing fighter-bomber warplane (curiously, also scheduled to replace the obsolescent Tornado at the turn of the millennium) is surely sufficient for the government to have little option but to deny, deny, deny the existence of an aircraft that, even though still classified, already makes the multibillion-pound Eurofighter seem Jurassic. After all, what could possibly be the point of contributing forty billion big ones to the development of a flying dinosaur when you already have a spaceship? Indeed, one could be forgiven for thinking that the Eurofighter is little more than an exorbitant smokescreen for the development of something far more exotic, far more costly.

And one would probably be right.

Even so, for now we must restrict our own investigation to the matter in hand, namely: is Britain (or anybody else for that matter) in possession of an aircraft that could possibly be mistaken for the 'UFO of the 1990s', the seemingly ubiquitous Black Triangle? And if so, is it being secretly developed and test-flown in Britain's North-West?

In search of corroborative evidence of this, I contacted one of Britain's foremost UFO and black-projects investigators, Tim Matthews of the Lancashire UFO Society (LUFOS), who lives in Lancashire and has been monitoring events at BAe Warton for some years. Mr Matthews told me that many people in the area claimed to have seen a new and exotic triangular-shaped aircraft taking off and landing at the site, that it appears to be powered by some form of electromagnetic propulsion system (this because of the strange 'humming' sound emitted by the aircraft whilst in flight) and that security at the BAe Warton site had become unusually oppressive over the past few years. Indeed, sources informed Mr Matthews that the site's security had been 'extensively upgraded' since 1995, while Nick Cook (writing for *Interavia Business and Technology*, July/August 1995) stated that the new security regime at BAe Warton was comparable to similar regimes operating at America's infamous Advanced Stealth Technology facilities, such as the Lockheed Martin, McDonnel Douglas and Northrop facilities in southern California and, of course, Area 51 in Nevada.

'BAe officials reveal that engineers recruited for the South Side facility are being screened as rigorously as any employee of the Lockheed Martin Skunk Works – an entity that has become synonymous with Stealth.' So claimed Nick Cook in his *Interavia* article.

Certainly it seems that security at BAe Warton is equal to the extreme levels of secrecy surrounding what goes on there. While strategically placed security cameras monitor every square inch of the place (making it both hazardous and virtually impossible to gain access to even the remotest perimeter vantage points) security guards have been seen to chase off those who attempt to dodge these cameras in order to gain a sneak preview of the work carried out inside what is undoubtedly one of Britain's most highly secure R&D hangars. To add to this, the programmes carried out at BAe Warton are so secret that sources say many employees are unaware of the nature of the projects they are working on, although some sources claim to have heard rumours about the development of a triangular-shaped Stealth aircraft at the site. One source told Mr Matthews that a 30ft-long triangular Stealth prototype is indeed being test-flown there, and Mr Matthews has since learned that this same prototype is also being test-flown at three other sites, code-named Delta 405, 406 and 407. These sites are situated at Marshside Sands (near Southport, Lancashire), Walney Island (off Barrow-in-Furness) and a third site north of Kendall in Cumbria, where numerous sightings of the new aircraft being escorted by a Tornado (sometimes two) have been reported in recent years. In support of these claims I have myself received further reports of a strange triangular-shaped aircraft being escorted by Tornados in other parts of the country, in particular East Anglia and the South-West. It should be added that, although the government denies any knowledge of a British Stealth programme, reputable aviation writers have already started to disseminate what appears to be the 'official party-line introduction' to the idea that a Stealth development programme is indeed under way in Britain; however, thus far the most they are prepared to admit to is that it exists 'at the design stages only'.

To counter this 'official party-line introduction', information received from a number of reliable sources suggests that Britain's own black-budget Stealth development programme is in fact well beyond the 'design stages'. One source with an inside view, for example, told me that although America (as well as Russia) is undoubtedly leading the way with regard to Advanced Stealth Technology programmes, Britain's own dabblings in this area are nevertheless 'two decades beyond anything you're likely to see in the civilian sector'. Indeed, if the countless eyewitness reports detailing sightings of the BAe prototype in the Lancashire and Cumbria skies (as well as elsewhere) are to be believed, then Britain's first Stealth aircraft is already being flown. No doubt about that.

The question, however, remains: Is it comparable in both

dimension and capability to the Black Triangle? Tim Matthews thinks it could be.

'We should not fall into the trap of arguing that the Triangles perform manoeuvres beyond the leading edge of technology,' he told me. 'The technology being developed behind closed doors in Britain's Top Secret research labs is clearly much more than we might believe.'

Let us, then, consider the facts.

File 22: Appendix 01
Case Study: Cosmic Top-X21 Eyes Only
HALO

In the 5th January 1997 edition of the *Sunday Mirror* it was reported that a 'Stealth sci-fi aircraft' had been spotted and photographed flying across the Lancashire moors. The report claimed that the 'mysterious triangular-shaped object' was approximately 30 ft in length, silver in colour, that it flew silently, had no wings and no visible engines. It had apparently been photographed by a landscape photographer who was out taking shots of winter snow scenes on the moors. The photographer in question (who did not want his name published) said that he had not seen the aircraft with his naked eye; until his film was developed some short while later, he said, he'd had no idea that the aircraft had flown over him. The report implied that this was the world's first photograph of Britain's new supersecret Stealth-type warplane, HALO, said to be generations in advance of America's already operational B-2 and F-117A Stealth planes. The report further implied that the many sightings of 'triangular-shaped UFOs' over the past few years could likely be attributed to HALO test-flights.

The photographs depicted a triangular-shaped aircraft

clearly enough, but as stated above it was silver in colour and considerably smaller than the countless eyewitness descriptions of the Black Triangle – to my mind, there is no way a 30 ft-long silver triangle could be so consistently mistaken for a 'football-pitch-sized' black one. True, by its nature a prototype is likely to be a scaled-down version of the intended production model; if a full-scale production model exists then it could well be much larger than its prototype and black in colour. But then again, if a full-scale production model exists then this implies that the aircraft is already operational, and if this is so then why is the military still test-flying a prototype? Also, of course, there is no evidence whatever to suggest that a full-scale production aircraft more than ten times the size could perform similar manoeuvres to its prototype demonstrator, any more than the largest of Jumbo Jets can do what the nimblest of military fighter jets can do. To my mind, the argument that promotes HALO as the answer to the Black Triangle enigma is thus far a delicate one, to say the least. As one inside source confided to me: 'What you're referring to as HALO has been around for years but, so far as I'm aware, there are no production aircraft yet. The problem is it still can't do the things it was built to do. They have the technology; they've had it for decades. But they still can't get it to perform in the way it's supposed to.' Wryly he added: 'But they're working on it.'

Indeed they are. According to Tim Matthews, the BAe Warton prototype is capable of Vertical Take Off and Landing (VTOL) manoeuvres, and some reports say that it can even hover silently and attain remarkable speeds from a standstill position. These manoeuvres are certainly associated with the Black Triangle, and indeed suggest that the BAe prototype could be powered – as has been suggested – by some form of electromagnetic or magnetohydrodynamic (or even electrogravitic) propulsion system. It is known, for example, that the three US-based aerospace giants, Lockheed Martin, McDonnell Douglas and Northrop, as well as British Aerospace, are currently experimenting with this kind of technology, and that the Military Advanced Technology Division at BAe Warton is currently engaged in research into future Stealth weapons and propulsion systems based on microwaves, lasers and soundwaves. It is claimed that such a propulsion system could generate speeds in excess of Mach 25, or more than 18,000 m.p.h.!

It has to be said, though, that the most likely form of propulsion system (currently being developed in both Britain and the US) is known as a Pulse Detonation Wave Engine (PDWE), which detonates the fuel in the jet pipe and expels some of the gases produced through inlets at the forward end of the pipe. Those who have heard this engine in flight have indeed commented on the 'strange' and 'relatively quiet' pulsed electromagnetic-type sound it seems to emit. This relatively exotic propulsion technology would certainly facilitate the extremely tight-angle turns and vectored-thrust capabilities so often reported with regard to UFO sightings, plus the virtually silent VTOL manoeuvres and speeds in excess of Mach 5. Even so, it has to be said that it remains highly unlikely that an operational military aircraft the size of a 'football pitch' (possibly 500 ft across) or even a 'Jumbo Jet' powered purely by electromagnetic means and capable of seemingly antigravitational manoeuvres is yet in existence, at least in Britain.

But what about America? If indeed sightings of the so-called Black Triangle can be explained by the development of exotic terrestrial technologies, then my guess is that the US is the place to look for those technologies.

So far as is known, the US-based military-industrial

complex currently has two contenders under development, LoFlyte (Low Observable Flight Test Experiment) which is essentially the US version of HALO, and ASTRA (Advanced Stealth Technology Reconnaissance Aircraft) otherwise known as Aurora. LoFlyte is the product of a joint NASA/US Air Force programme and is based on a design known as the 'wave rider' that, according to official reports, allows the aircraft to 'wrap its own high-speed shockwave around the fuselage and trap a cushion of air below it', which in turn means that, essentially, the aircraft is able to 'surf' the air rather than having to plough through it (thus facilitating speeds in excess of Mach 5). Details of the LoFlyte prototype were officially 'unveiled' in August 1996.

ASTRA, on the other hand, is still a highly classified aircraft; like Area 51 it does not officially exist. It is suspected that this hypersonic spaceplane was developed – with CIA/black-budget funding – at Northrop's Advanced Technology and Design Centre in southern California, and that it is capable of Mach 5+ (some reports say Mach 8, or nearly 6,000 m.p.h.). ASTRA is certainly capable of extremely high altitudes (100,000 ft+ supercruise capability) and evidence to suggest that it is also capable of space flight is now overwhelming.

Though LoFlyte is still thought to be in the design and development stages, evidence suggests that ASTRA, even though still classified, is now an operational aircraft, and that it has been since 1994. Indeed, the *Jane's Military Aircraft* report alluded to the fact that a Low Observable Stealth aircraft 'assumed to be American' had been involved in an accident at RAF Boscombe Down in Wiltshire on the night of 26th September 1994, and further evidence suggests that the aircraft concerned was indeed an operational ASTRA. It is well known, of course, that many Top Secret US aircraft utilize British RAF bases, in particular supersecret bases such as Boscombe Down, which boasts a sizeable BAe presence and is the new home of the Defence Testing and Evaluation Organization (DTEO), a subsidiary of the Defence Research Agency (DRA) which is itself heavily involved in developing seamless anti-thermal coatings for Stealth aircraft. Indeed, one very high-ranking source let slip to me that aircraft displaying flight capabilities he 'did not believe possible' were 'occasional visitors' to Boscombe Down. But although he was aware of a 'serious incident' that had occurred at the base on the night in question, that extremely high security measures had been enforced for some nights thereafter, and that the aircraft involved was indeed American, he was unable to identify the aircraft by name. I think we might be able to help him out there.

Evidence has since come my way that certainly points to the fact that this 'serious incident' indeed occurred, and that it involved the aborted take-off of an already operational ASTRA – it is claimed that the accident was due to a nose-wheel collapse that occurred as the multimillion-dollar aircraft began its take-off run along Boscombe Down's Runway 23.

Investigations undertaken by journalists Ren Hoek and Marco P. van der Valk have indeed shown that the aircraft involved in the Boscombe Down incident was referred to during radio communications as AV-6 (Air Vehicle 6) and that it was allocated the US Air Force serial number 90–2414 (thus indicating that it was not a British aircraft). This is interesting because Northrop always refers to its prototype aircraft as PAVs (Prototype Air Vehicles) and to its production aircraft simply as AVs (Air Vehicles). As the aircraft concerned was officially designated AV-6 it is reasonable to assume that it was an operational and not a prototype aircraft. Further investigations and much tuning-in to military wavebands on the night of the incident and for several days and nights thereafter (revealing the involvement of the SAS, the CIA and the US Air Force in the damage-limitation exercise that followed the incident, plus the fact that the damaged aircraft was transported by a USAF C-5 Galaxy back to its base at Air Force Plant 42, better known to the UFO community as Northrop's Palmdale facility in southern California) subsequently identified the aircraft as an ASTRA. Thus it seems now beyond question that America's Advanced Stealth Technology Reconnaissance Aircraft is indeed operational, and that it has been since at least 1994.

But can it do what the Black Triangle can do?

ASTRA – whose first official Pentagon code name was Aurora – is certainly America's latest and most highly advanced operational Stealth Technology aircraft which, according to *Air Forces Monthly* (March 1997 edition), first took to the air in 1989 – and this despite Pentagon denials that the aircraft even exists. It is suspected that ASTRA has a flight ceiling of at least low-orbit, that it also utilizes the PDWE propulsion system (or perhaps some form of auxiliary electromagnetic, magnetohydrodynamic or electrogravitic propulsion system, though this remains doubtful) and that it is thus capable of manoeuvres consistent with those many people might associate with UFOs. When you consider that CIA-operated U-2 spyplanes were flying at well over 70,000 ft as far back as 1955, and that considerable advances in aeronautics have been achieved since then (including, of course, the development of NASA's Space Shuttle) the idea that ASTRA boasts both space flight and hypersonic flight among its numerous capabilities is not so absurd.

With regard to Black Triangle comparisons, I have been reliably informed by two independent 'inside sources' (one

British, one American) that ASTRA overflies Great Britain on a regular basis (and has done since at least 1992) and that its main British stopover point is the reactivated RAF Machrihanish located on the west coast of Scotland. This would certainly explain the high-intensity sonic booms measured by seismological stations in Holland since 1992 (including one on 19th August 1992, which prompted questions in the Dutch Parliament). It would also explain why ASTRA has been linked to the Belgian Black Triangle incident of 1989/90. Indeed, seismological studies of the sonic booms caused (allegedly) by ASTRA have plotted a seemingly routine flight path southeast from Scotland, which would indeed suggest that ASTRA utilizes RAF Machrihanish and subsequently overflies both Holland and Germany fairly regularly, skirting northern Belgium en route. If indeed ASTRA *was* the so-called Belgian Black Triangle then it would certainly explain how it was so easily able to outmanoeuvre the Belgian Air Force F-16s which, by comparison, are the product of some pretty outdated technology. Also, of course, it would explain why it was necessary not to reveal the fact that the radar-tracked 'UFO' was in fact an American aircraft – the US authorities would not have wanted it known that their latest and most supersecret Stealth spyplane had strayed into unauthorized territory.

On the other hand, of course, we have to remember that, with regard to the so-called Black Triangle, we are talking about an aircraft that has been seen (and filmed) to stand silently on end, perfectly still in the sky, a manoeuvre that gives it the appearance of a Christmas tree. The fact that ASTRA crashed during its take-off run at RAF Boscombe Down suggests that it is not a VTOL aircraft, casting serious doubt on its ability to hover at all, much less silently at both high and extremely low altitudes.

To add to this, hundreds of eyewitness reports at the time of the Belgian incident stated that, as the Belgian Air Force F-16s approached, the Triangle simply dissolved into itself and 'disappeared'. At the same time it vanished from NATO radar screens. Whatever technology powers ASTRA, and indeed whatever radar-invisibility capabilities it may possess, I seriously doubt that it includes optical-invisibility capabilities such as those reportedly demonstrated on the night in question (30th/31st March 1990).

Further, according to both NATO and Belgian Air Force radar operators the Black Triangle dropped from an incredible 10,000 ft to under 500 ft in less than two seconds. Even if the technology necessary to perform this kind of manoeuvre exists (which is doubtful in the extreme) the human pilot who could withstand the G-forces involved does not. (It is estimated that such a manoeuvre would generate G-forces well in excess of 20 G, way beyond the 9 G limit of a fully trained military pilot.) But what about the possibility that the aircraft in question was unmanned?

If General Wilfried De Brouwer, Chief of Operations for the Belgian Air Force at the time of the incident, is to be believed, then the Belgian Triangle was solid and intelligently controlled. 'There was a logic in the movements of the UFO,' he said following NATO's attempts to intercept the mysterious craft. Could an aircraft that is reportedly at least the size of a Jumbo Jet be remotely controlled? The answer is, *yes*, of course it could. Indeed, both the USAF and the RAF are known to possess Unmanned Air Vehicles (UAVs) and Uninhabited Combat Air Vehicles (UCAVs) though the official line is that UCAVs will not be operational until around 2015. But if the Belgian Black Triangle was indeed a military UAV remotely piloted from some supersecret command post somewhere, then the question arises: Who was the remote controller?

And moreover, who was giving him his orders, aliens or presidents? Or both?

One thing we can be certain of is that it wasn't NATO chiefs; they were too busy trying to catch the thing.

DOCUMENT 06

Cosmic Top Secret
Eyes Only Copy One of One

The Black Triangle Enigma (Part 2)
The Alliance

File 23
Alien Technology

So what on Earth is going on?

Does the combined British-and-US-based military-industrial complex truly possess technology so far in advance of that commercially available that it can fly 'Wembley Stadium-sized' triangular aircraft?

Aircraft with the kind of capabilities detailed in Document 05?

Capabilities witnessed and reported by such highly trained observers as police officers, military personnel/pilots, commercial airline pilots, NATO and civilian radar operators?

Capabilities that include silent or virtually silent flight?

A standstill/hover function?

Speeds ranging from 30 m.p.h. to infinity?

The ability to descend so rapidly from high to very low altitude that radar is incapable of tracking the manoeuvre?

Plus the ability to dissolve into itself and disappear?

If the answer to these questions is, unbelievably, *yes*, the military-industrial complex *does* own this kind of technology, and the craft to go with it, then far from answering the great UFO conundrum it merely poses a series of further and rather more serious questions. Questions like:

Where did this technology originate?

Why is it not available in the commercial sector?

If the governments are test-flying aircraft which utilize some form of electromagnetic, (magneto)hydrodynamic and/or electrogravitic propulsion systems, then why is the rest of the world still existing on fossil fuels?

Is it all down to the global economy?

Or is there an even more diabolical reason?

Who has the authority to withhold this kind of technological enlightenment from the general public?

Why are our children not being taught this advanced level of physics in our schools and universities?

And moreover: what on Earth is the military playing at, test-flying its supersecret 'alien technology' prototypes over residential areas and in known commercial flight paths?

Once again, whichever side of the fence you find yourself on, something somewhere simply does not add up.

In order to gain some purchase on whether or not the joint British-and-US-based military-industrial complex might be in possession of acquired alien technology, let us take a look at some facts.

It is alleged that in 1947 an aircraft of unknown origin crashed near Roswell, New Mexico. Although this case does not stand alone (indeed, there are numerous accounts of such 'crash/retrievals' having occurred over the years) it is nevertheless well known and equally well documented.

Also, of course, it marks the beginning of what I believe to be a fifty-year (ongoing) worldwide UFO/ET cover-up. For this reason alone Roswell stands supreme as *the* UFO/ET watershed.

Conflicting reports suggest that either the crashed Roswell craft was some form of secret new US Air Force prototype, a new kind of rocket or some other new weapon fired out of nearby White Sands Proving Ground, a Top Secret Project Mogul spy balloon (the official story), or that it was extraterrestrial. And whichever one of these proves ultimately to be correct, one thing is now beyond question: *something* did indeed crash in the New Mexico desert on 2nd July 1947. There can be no doubt about that. Even the US authorities have admitted this much, and they have done so publicly.

Assuming then – for the moment, and for the sake of our investigation – that the crashed object was an alien craft of some kind, one might further assume that the US authorities would not have wanted to suffer the embarrassment of having to admit that an 'unknown' craft had come down, unnoticed, in US airspace. Remember, the US authorities were unaware of the crash until local rancher William 'Mac' Brazel (who discovered the debris) informed them some three or four days after the event. Until then the military had no idea that the crash had even occurred. This fact alone is sufficient to rule out the possibility that the crashed object was either a prototype aircraft (*any* kind of military aircraft, for that matter) or some new 'misfired' weapon – had the object been either of these, it is inconceivable that the might of the US military/intelligence machine would have remained unaware of the fact that it had crashed or misfired. Also the fact that, on hearing of the incident, the military immediately cordoned off the area and transported the debris – in secret – to the Foreign Technology Division (FTD) at Wright-Patterson Air Force Base (formerly Wright Field) in Dayton, Ohio, suggests that it wasn't a spy balloon either. One does not sequester one's own hardware in one's own 'foreign technology' department.

Which leaves us with just one possibility . . .

Taking our working hypothesis to its own natural conclusion, then, and assuming that not only was the crashed object some form of extraterrestrial spacecraft but that it was taken into custody along with its occupants, then the possibility that some form of dialogue could have been established at this point between the US authorities and their alien captives must be a consideration. This scenario is of course based on the supposition that at least one of the craft's occupants survived the crash. But there are now sufficient eyewitness reports to at least entertain the possibility that one or more of the aliens did indeed survive the crash (and that other aliens survived further, lesser known crashes). And if this is so, then we have at least established a basis for the feasibility of some form of deal being struck at this point between the captor and the captive – maybe even an 'alliance'.

There are now many witnesses to the fact that the Roswell 'disc' was indeed taken – along with some dead aliens, and at least one still-living alien – to Wright-Patterson AFB in Ohio. Many former Wright Field personnel have testified to this end. Not the least of these (as mentioned in Document 02) is Whitley Strieber's uncle, Colonel Edward Strieber, who told his nephew in no uncertain terms that he had seen both the crash debris and what he described as the 'biological remains' of the aliens. He also told Strieber that 'he had knowledge of the Majestic-12 project' (the setting-up – immediately following the Roswell crash – of a military-cum-scientific intelligence group code-named

Majestic-12 (MJ-12 or Majic-12) whose task it was to ensure that the alien presence remained a tightly held secret, and at the same time to glean as much scientific and technological information from the aliens as possible – see Document 02).

According to another former USAF officer stationed at Wright Field in 1947 (who claimed to have actually handled the alien bodies) the aliens were 'vegetative' in quality, presumably meaning that they displayed asexual processes akin to those of plants, and that their constitution was based more on the photosynthetic processes of plants than the digestive processes of humans. And either way, according to Whitley Strieber, the aliens and their crashed aircraft were indeed observed by these two former USAF officers at Wright-Patterson Air Force Base in 1947.

To add to this, in late June 1997 former US Army officer, Colonel Philip J. Corso released a book entitled *The Day After Roswell*, in which he also tells the story of how the military retrieved a 'flying disc' from the scene of the Roswell crash in July 1947. A former intelligence officer on the staff of General Douglas McArthur during the Korean War, a member of the National Security Council during the Eisenhower administration, and head of the Pentagon's Foreign Technology in Army Research and Development during the early 1960s (where he was in charge of the Roswell Files), Colonel Corso retired from the Army in 1963 with no less than nineteen medals and ribbons to his name. These kinds of credential simply cannot be bested.

According to Colonel Corso, included in the Pentagon's Roswell Files are pieces of debris from the crash and full reports of the incident from the military perspective. These, says Corso, form an incredible cache of data and UFO parts that 'an Army retrieval team . . . pulled out of the wreckage of a flying disc that had crashed outside the town of Roswell in the New Mexico desert in the early-morning darkness during the first week of July 1947'. Corso goes on to explain that he was Post Duty Officer at Fort Riley, Kansas on the night a shipment of Roswell artefacts arrived from Fort Bliss on its way to Wright Field. It was Colonel Corso's job to examine the shipment that, he says, contained a dead extraterrestrial preserved in a 'thick light-blue liquid'. According to Corso – who also claims to have seen many memos to Presidents Truman and Eisenhower referring to the Roswell incident and the 'goods' it provided – no less than five extraterrestrials were recovered from the crash, three dead, two still living. Of the two still-living ETs, one was shot and killed by jittery soldiers while attempting to escape; the other was barely alive on its arrival at Roswell Army Air Field. All five ETs were described by Colonel Corso as having greyish-brown skin, four fingers, oversized heads, no body hair and standing around four and a half feet tall. Their build was said to be slight.

This former hard-headed military colonel, who saw extra-terrestrials in the same light as he did *those damn Commies*', goes on to reveal how he was chosen to spearhead the Army's supersecret 'reverse-engineering' project that ultimately 'seeded' the military-industrial complex with new and exotic alien technologies. The corporations who benefited from this 'seeding' process, he says, included IBM, Hughes Aircraft, Bell Labs, Dow Corning and others. The US-based aerospace corporations had a field day. Corso also describes the devices found aboard the crashed alien craft that, he says, were the precursors for today's laser technology, fibre optics, computer hardware/microchip technology, super-tenacity fibres and night-vision equipment . . . plus a host of still-secret, still-classified discoveries, including various psychotronic devices capable of translating human thoughts and emotions into electronic signals, and vice versa (see Document 10) and Star Wars-style electromagnetic and microwave particle-beam weapons systems. Like Dr Robert Sarbacher before him (who, before he mysteriously 'fell' from his boat and drowned, revealed that the 'fabric we obtained from Roswell had molecular welds so small that you couldn't even identify what they were until the Sixties, when the microscopes to do it became available', and further, that these 'non-human' technologies were used by defence contractors to manufacture seamless coatings for 'radar-proof' aircraft, such as the Stealth), Corso also claims that today's Stealth technologies were derived from this project. He goes on to explain how the acquired alien technology helped to shape post-war geopolitical policies and events – how it helped to ensure that America finally won the 'space race', for example (and so became the recognized leading superpower), and how it inspired further initiatives such as SDI (Strategic Defense Initiative, more popularly known as Star Wars) that, he says, was designed specifically as an early-warning defence system against possible alien invasion; Project Horizon (the construction of a military base on the Moon) which, as we have seen, probably did not happen; and HAARP (High-frequency Active Auroral Research Project) designed 'officially' for 'upper atmospheric research' and weather-pattern control – 'unofficially', however, as a ground-based electromagnetic weapons system augmented by the use of strategically deployed satellites. Colonel Corso also claims that it was this acquired alien technology that ultimately decided the outcome of the Cold War.

These days, Corso says, the captured alien craft are housed at three specified US Air Force facilities – Norton AFB, Edwards AFB and Nellis AFB (Area 51) – and that the alien technology R&D programmes undertaken at these and other facilities are still overseen by the supersecret military and scientific Special Studies Group, Majestic-12. He says that Majestic-12 was indeed formed in September 1947 by Executive presidential Order under the Harry S. Truman administration, that it was known simply as *The Group*, and that this same group (with new members) now operates under President Clinton. He claims that two proto-type 'antigravity craft' powered by nuclear-fission generators were constructed and test-flown in the 1950s, but with little success. The new propulsion systems were inefficient and leaked radiation, he says. Nevertheless, these and similar projects continued throughout the ensuing decades and were (and still are), according to Corso, kept secret due to the fact that the extraterrestrials are deemed – at the highest level, and by certain high-powered right-wing military, intelligence and quasi-political chiefs – to pose a security threat. The reverse-engineering projects are being carried out, he says, so that extraterrestrial technologies can be matched by those possessed by terrestrial (military) agencies.

In short – according to Corso – if and when *The War of the Worlds* scenario finally comes to pass, the military intends to have transformed itself into a technological match for the invaders.

It should be added that Colonel Corso is the highest-ranking military official ever to come out of the closet and make this information public.

There now exists an ever-expanding catalogue of witness claims and confidentially leaked evidence that suggests that at least one still-living alien was secretly transferred from Wright Field to Area 51 at some point during the early 1950s. We have already heard the testimony of Bill Uhouse (Jarod 2), for example (Document 02), a man who worked for more than thirty years on covert government projects and more specifically on the mechanical design for the avionics of simulators for US-built spacecraft. Uhouse claims that four aliens survived a crash that occurred in Arizona in 1953, and that they were subsequently taken to the supersecret deep-underground FTD facility at Wright Field before being transferred to Area 51. Uhouse, who worked at Area 51, described the aliens as being around four feet tall with two eyes, two ears, a nose and a small round mouth. Though vaguely humanoid in appearance, he said, their arms were proportionally longer than those of humans. He revealed that the aliens were later transferred to a facility at Area 51 where communications were indeed established.

Further to this, former US Naval Intelligence man Milton William Cooper says that he saw documentation to the effect that, between January 1947 and December 1952, at least sixteen downed or crashed alien craft plus sixty-five alien bodies and one still-living alien were recovered by the US authorities. He also says that communications that led to the establishment of a formal treaty/alliance between the US government and an alien civilization from the Zeta Reticuli solar system were initiated in the early 1950s, but that communications have since broken down to the extent that an unhealthy and precarious 'agreement' now exists. The aliens are these days treated more as prisoners than guests, he says.

Also, of course, nuclear physicist Bob Lazar says that he thinks he saw an alien whilst working at S-4, the supersecret

R&D facility concealed deep inside the desert mountain range surrounding Area 51's Papoose Lake. This claim is supported by the testimony of another former Area 51 scientist, Dr Michael Wolf (see Briefing Document) who says that his job as both head of MJ-12's lead scientific intelligence unit, Alphacom Team, and as senior Projects Team Leader at Area 51 was to study extraterrestrial biology by implementing autopsy and other related procedures. The 'in-house' term for this form of scientific study, he says, is 'exobiology', while the reverse-engineering of alien spacecraft is known as the science of 'exotechnology'. Dr Wolf, former consultant to the President and the US National Security Council on extraterrestrial matters and member of MJ-12, says that the US government is indeed playing host to not one but several species of alien. He agrees that the breakdown in relations between the US government and the Zeta Reticuli aliens (as well as another race of humanoid ETs from the Altair Aquila system) in 1975 means that, these days, all species of extraterrestrial visitors are treated as hostile. Like Milton William Cooper, Dr Wolf says that Earthbound ETs are today treated as 'prisoners' rather than 'guests'. He also says that many extraterrestrial spacecraft have been 'downed and captured' rather than 'gifted', that elite special forces within the US military are today flying 'antigravity' spacecraft, and that a superelite right-wing fundamentalist 'Cabal' that exists within the US and British governments – and which is 'top heavy with the military' – is responsible for deploying 'Star Wars-type' weapons against the visitors in an ongoing effort to prevent full-scale human/extraterrestrial contact.

It should be reiterated that Dr Wolf's wife and son were murdered as a result of him revealing this information.

File 24
Nightmare On Salisbury Plain

That the US-based military-industrial complex, at least to some limited degree, has been involved in the reverse-engineering of captured or otherwise acquired alien space-craft (or that this, for one or another strategic reason, is what the US authorities want us to believe) must now be considered a very real possibility. That some limited form of communication has been established between the US authorities and an extraterrestrial intelligence must also be considered in a similar light. But what is perhaps even more disturbing from the British point of view is that, according to some very reliable 'inside sources', these same acquired alien-technology programmes are now being carried out on British soil. Or perhaps more accurately, *beneath* British soil (see Document 12). And perhaps what is most disturbing of all is the fact that this same diabolical secret is being kept from not only the British public but from some of the highest-ranking political and military chiefs in the country.

This in itself – even if it can be substantiated – does not prove that either the British or US governments have formed some kind of alliance with a visiting alien intelligence of course. Indeed, if such an alliance truly exists, it is surely a secret so jealously guarded that 'concrete proof' of its existence will never be forthcoming, at least not until those involved decide that it is time to let us all in on their pernicious little game. After fifty years of absolute silence, this eventuality must be viewed as very unlikely.

However, what *is* implied here – both in the evidence documented in File 23 and that documented here in File 24 – is that some dark 'invisible' arm of the British and US military-industrial-intelligence complex has at the very least had some limited contact with an alien intelligence and, moreover, that this same body of megalomaniac minds has had more than fifty years to research and develop any extra-terrestrial technologies 'acquired' from reverse-engineering the mechanics of retrieved alien spacecraft.

To my mind, this possibility alone is worth a full and rigorous investigation.

And so to the present . . .

I have several reports on file that strongly suggest that some form of alien/government 'alliance' is indeed still operational, that the reverse-engineering programmes employed by the US government's black-budget scientists have been more successful than perhaps we might think, and that, more-over, the whole alien/government alliance scenario these days includes some dark and covert echelon of the *British* government, in particular of course the British-based military-industrial complex. Indeed, the reports in question point to the fact that either a joint British/US secret military aircraft is being flown in British skies (and that it displays the same extraordi-nary flight characteristics as we might expect from a UFO) or that alien craft are being permitted to fly in British airspace as part of some extremely covert joint alien/NATO exercise.

Take this File 24 Case Report, for example . . .

File 24: Appendix 01
Case Report: Cosmic Top-X22 Eyes Only
Night Manoeuvres

In May 1996 I received a telephone call from a former British soldier who, in several further communications by letter and telephone, told me that during the winter of 1989/90 (exact date unknown) he and five other soldiers had encountered a massive black triangular UFO whilst on night manoeuvres on Salisbury Plain, Wiltshire. The soldier told me that this incident had so distressed him that he had subsequently suffered a series of nightmares and headaches.

According to his report the encounter occurred close to a place called Dunch Hill Plantation, which separates the well-known Bulford Ranges army-training area from a highly Top Secret MoD compound on the south-eastern border of Salisbury Plain. The soldiers (all names on file) were hiking from a place called Beach's Barn to Dunch Hill Plantation when the encounter took place.

In October 1996 I finally interviewed the soldier at his home; for his own security I will refer to him as 'Mark'.

'It really did my head in,' Mark told me, still visibly shaken by what he and the others had witnessed, even though some six years had passed since the incident occurred. 'It was weird, really weird. We were about four hundred metres from our destination [Dunch Hill Plantation] when suddenly this craft just appeared there above the tree tops. It was massive. And black. Very black. The next thing I remember we were six hundred metres away from where we were supposed to be, all six of us bending over a map trying to figure out where we were and how the hell we'd ended up there. I still can't remember how we ended up that far off course.'

According to Mark, the entire manoeuvre was a mystery from the outset. 'We all thought what a total waste of time it was,' he told me angrily. He then confirmed to me that his platoon had never before, and never since, been required to perform such a 'bloody useless exercise'.

The six soldiers had been 'volunteered' to walk four or five kilometres, out in the open, in a virtually straight line, from

Beach's Barn to Dunch Hill Plantation. According to Mark, although it was around two o'clock in the morning and very dark, the exercise was so straightforward they barely needed a compass.

They had been told the reason for this unusual exercise was that a reconnaissance unit positioned around Sidbury Hill (a high-plateau vantage point about two kilometres north-east of Dunch Hill Plantation) was testing night-vision equipment. The purpose of the exercise, the soldiers were told, was to see if the night-vision equipment could detect the soldiers in the dark. As Mark told me, he has himself used this same equipment, and it was obvious to all and sundry that, being out in the open, even in the dead of night, the soldiers were bound to be detected. 'This night-vision gear is brilliant,' Mark said. 'It's just like looking through binoculars in broad daylight. There's no way they wouldn't have seen us. It was a pointless exercise.'

Which leaves one to wonder: What could have been the *real* reason behind this 'pointless exercise'? I put the question to Mark.

'I don't know,' he said grimly, shaking his head. 'But it sure as bloody hell wasn't to test the night-vision gear. No way.'

Could they have been testing *new* equipment? Could it have been equipment Mark was unfamiliar with?

'Possibly. But if it was then the whole thing was even more ridiculous. If the equipment *I'd* used could pick us out, then any new equipment would, presumably, be even better than the old equipment. And anyway, that's just not the way you test night-vision gear. On a normal exercise of this type we would have been made to duck and dive a bit, you know, made it a bit more difficult for the recce unit to spot us. It just didn't make any sense. It was a total waste of time.'

During the course of the interview Mark told me exactly the sequence of events as he remembered it. As I was about to discover, this sequence of events led to what can only be described as one of the most unprecedented cases in the history of British UFO investigation. What follows is Mark's story . . .

File 24: Appendix 02
Case Review: Cosmic Top-X23 Eyes Only
Mark's Story

'The six of us were volunteered from the rest of the platoon. We were always the ones that got the naff jobs, but this one was a total waste of bloody time. We set off from Beach's Barn at around two o'clock in the morning, the corporal at the front; I was about the fourth in line. All we had to do was walk the four or five kilometres across the plain to Dunch Hill Plantation, completely out in the open. We were told that a recce unit was positioned up at Sidbury Hill, testing their night-vision gear, and that all we had to do was walk from A to B . . .

'. . . When we got to about four hundred metres from our destination, this craft suddenly appeared there above the tree tops . . . Dunch Hill Plantation is right next to an MoD area that's sectioned off from the army land. There's a copse there that marks the boundary of the MoD area . . .

'. . . Suddenly this craft was just there. It just appeared there above the trees. It was massive. And black. Very black. The strange thing was no one said anything. All of us could see this thing, and yet none of us said anything. I guess we were all stunned, afraid – I know I was . . .

'. . . All of a sudden it [the craft] started beaming down this light onto the trees, onto the copse, where I sensed some kind of movement. There were lights in the copse, like torch [flashlight] lights as if some people were milling around in there. Then suddenly this huge black craft was beaming down this really powerful light, like a searchlight, onto the copse. I couldn't make out the shape of the craft at this point, but it was massive and black. You know, the night was really dark – it was two or three in the morning by this time – but the craft was even blacker than the night . . .

'. . . It was about the size of, say, a Hercules C-130, or even bigger, maybe even as big as a football pitch. But it was just hanging there, making no noise whatsoever. Then suddenly it just took off at incredible speed, still silent, and flew off in the direction of Tidworth [to the east]. The next thing I remember we were six hundred metres away from where we were supposed to be, all six of us bending over a map trying to figure out where we were and how the hell we'd ended up there . . .'

Mark added: 'We have these red night torches . . . we were all bending over the map trying to ascertain our position. It was ridiculous. We only had to walk in a straight line. There was no way we should have been where we were. I still can't remember how we ended up that far off course.'

I then asked Mark if he thought it possible he could have hallucinated the incident. He said he truly wished that had been the case, but it was highly unlikely as he'd only had to walk a maximum of three and a half miles (four or five kilometres). He told me that he knew the feeling of hallucinating from participating in longer, twenty-five-kilometre hikes, and from being forced to stay awake for up to forty hours at a time on some exercises. But a three-and-a-half-mile walk? He also told me that, being somewhat used to night manoeuvres, his night vision was good, as was that of the other soldiers with him. So far as Mark is concerned, what happened that night was a real event, and whatever the soldiers had seen had actually been there. He had little doubt on that score.

So what happened next?

All Mark could remember was being picked up by an Army Land Rover (driven by another member of his platoon who had not participated in the exercise) and then being ferried back to barracks. So far as he can recall, he was not debriefed on his return. Indeed, nothing was ever said about the incident, period.

It was apparent from speaking with Mark that he had suffered at least some loss of memory concerning the event. He could remember approaching Dunch Hill Plantation clearly enough, then being confronted by what he described as a 'massive black craft' that simply 'appeared' in the night sky above the copse (or, at least, it arrived so swiftly that it *seemed* simply to appear); people milling around inside the copse; the craft beaming its light down onto the copse; the craft then taking off at incredible speed towards Tidworth; and then . . . blank.

The next thing he could remember was being 600 metres from his position, poring over a map with the rest of his colleagues, trying to figure out where they were and how they had suddenly arrived somewhere else, 600 metres off course. He was then picked up by an Army Land Rover and ferried back to barracks where, he made a point of telling me, no one said a word about what they had just experienced. Indeed, according to Mark, none of the other soldiers ever spoke to him about the incident. But what was even more unusual, Mark never said a word, either.

Until later, that is. Much later. Over the years Mark began

to recall the incident that seemed to have wiped itself from his memory. The incident occurred in the winter months of 1989–1990, but it wasn't until some years later that Mark began to remember the incident more clearly. The memory of the manoeuvre itself remained with him, of course, but the detail only started to come back to him a couple of years ago and even then the finer details were patchy. The time-loss period – the period between the six soldiers approaching the copse and seeing the craft, and then finding themselves 600 metres off in the wrong direction – never came back at all.

File 24: Appendix 03
Case Report: Cosmic Top-X24 Eyes Only Hypnotic Recall

It was at this point that I called on the assistance of Robert La Mont (MICH) a very highly regarded Harley Street hypnotherapist and Member of the Institute of Clinical Hypnosis. Over recent years Robert has helped many 'abductees' to recall memories of their encounters. On hearing of this case, Robert kindly agreed to 'regress' Mark in order to see if he could unlock his missing-time memory.

During the regression session (which I attended) Robert proved to be a very thorough and professional hypnotherapist. I would say he took a good fifteen to twenty minutes to put Mark 'under', so to speak, working slowly and methodically to ensure Mark was completely relaxed and responsive to command. Indeed, from where I was seated, Mark looked fast asleep.

I should add that at no point did Robert lead by suggestion. Rather, if anything, he led by counter-suggestion – making absolutely certain that Mark was telling his own story, and not the story we all may have wanted to hear. What came out of the session was remarkable, to say the least.

Under hypnosis, Mark recounted the sequence of events which had led to his sighting of the 'UFO' – how the officer had called on them out of the blue, with no prior warning, to hike the several kilometres to Dunch Hill Plantation; how their route had taken them across open ground, in full view of the reconnaissance unit allegedly positioned on Sidbury Hill to the east; how the soldiers had become 'bored', 'cold' and 'agitated' en route.

What follows is a minimally edited transcript of what Mark was able to recall under hypnosis, from the point where he and the five other soldiers were approaching Dunch Hill Plantation, their ill-fated destination . . .

'. . . So where are you now?' Robert put to Mark.

'I can see the woods . . . all dark and thick . . . lights . . . in the copse . . . people milling around in the copse.'

Robert then told Mark to continue on towards the copse, as he had done six years previously.

'Could the lights you're seeing be a helicopter?' Robert said.

'No.'

'Is it an aeroplane, then?'

'No. The lights are in the woods.'

'How high off the ground are the lights?'

'They're in the woods . . . they're in the woods.'

'And do you go to investigate the lights?'

'No.'

'You're not bothered about the lights?'

'No.'

'OK. Walk on a little bit further.'

At this point Robert told Mark to 'freeze-frame' and 'zoom in' on the lights. (Mark had been told that he was watching a replay of the event on an imaginary screen in his mind, and that he had a 'remote control' in his hand, with 'pause', 'rewind' and 'zoom' facilities, etc.)

'What can you see now?' Robert asked.

'Don't know . . . don't know what it is . . . big thing.'

'Big thing?'

'Yeah.'

'Can you describe the big thing for me?'

'Just dark.'

'In the woods?'

'Above the woods . . . the woods are illuminated.'

'The whole of the woods?'

'The copse, yeah.' At this point Mark started to show signs of distress.

'OK, Mark. You're back on the path. Describe to me what you can see.'

'The light's shining on us . . . I'm cold . . .'

'What can you see, Mark? Where is the light that's shining on you coming from?'

'From above.'

'Above? So you're looking up now?'

'Yeah . . . It's shining in my eyes . . .'

'And then what happens?'

'I . . . I can't see . . .'

Again Mark became visibly distressed; Robert spent the next short while reassuring him.

A few moments later: 'Tell me what you can see now, Mark.'

'A Yank . . .'

'An American?'

'Mmm . . .'

'Where did the American come from?'

'Out of the woods . . .'

This time Mark's distress became very apparent indeed; Robert again took a short time out to reassure him everything was OK, that what he was seeing was only a 'replay' of something that had happened a long time ago and that, as such, it could not harm him. Eventually Mark settled down again.

Then: 'OK, Mark. The American's come out of the woods now . . .'

'He's poking at us . . .'

'What is he poking at you?'

'A stick thing . . .' Mark's voice was still trembling; he sounded very afraid and, once again, for a few moments he was too distressed to continue. Once again Robert spent a few moments calming him down.

Then: 'OK. Can you describe what this American's wearing?'

'A black zip-up thing . . . like a flying suit.'

'How do you know he's an American?'

'His accent . . . he's swearing and stuff . . .'

'What is he actually saying?'

'Fucking British!'

'And what are the rest of the guys saying?'

'Nothing. We're all backing away.'

'How many Americans are there?'

'One.'

'Just one?'

'Yeah.'

'So you've got six guys backing away from just one guy?'

'Yeah.'

'Don't you find this strange?'

'He's pointing at *me*.'

'He's just pointing at *you*?'

'Yeah.'

'Describe the stick to me, Mark.'

'It's a . . . pointer . . . like an aerial . . .'

'And what's he doing with it?'

'He's just pointing at me . . . and pushing me and prodding me in the chest.'

Robert now told Mark to use his imaginary remote control, and to move through this particular sequence 'frame by frame'.

'What's the American doing in this frame?'

'He's just stood there . . . but there are lights on us.'

'He's on his own, you're stood in a group, and there are lights on you. Is that right?'

'Yeah. We're huddled together.' Next frame: 'It's like a beam . . . encircling us . . .'

'And where's the American?'

'He's outside of the beam.' Next frame: 'We're all getting moved by the beam . . . we're moving with the beam.'

'Where to?'

'To the right.' Next frame: 'We're right by the edge of the wood . . . by the edge of the copse.'

'And where's the American now?'

'He's not there any more.'

'OK. Are you actually walking? Can you feel yourself walking as you move?'

'Yeah . . . shuffling . . .' Next frame: 'We're all being moved by the beam.'

'And then what happens?'

'We're all just stood there . . . with the light on us.'

'And the object is still there?'

'Above us, yeah.' Next frame: 'We're just underneath it.'

'Can you make anything out as you look up?'

'It's a triangle . . . black metal . . . it's not smooth or anything . . . it's like . . . wedgy . . . sort of wedged.'

'Whereabouts is the light in which you're standing emanating from?'

'From the middle [of the craft's underbelly].'

'Any other details?'

'Black . . . it's just dark . . . at the bottom end it's like an aircraft light . . '

'Any other details?'

'We're just covered in this light. It's like pulses of light . . . directed at us . . . I feel sick, dizzy . . .' Next frame: '. . . I'm surrounded in light . . . pulsating light . . . and there's a noise . . . almost like a generator . . . like a humming, pulsating, continuous . . .'

Again Mark became very distressed.

Mark went on to recall how the craft had finally departed, slowly at first and then at incredible speed, but with no apparent acceleration. He was then able to recall how the six soldiers had wandered off in the wrong direction, stunned, dazed . . . finally explaining how they had ended up 600 metres from where they were supposed to be. They had walked, although none of them had remembered doing so.

In summing up this case Robert La Mont sent me the following report, detailing his professional conclusions.

'My professional opinion on this case is that the subject did in fact have an encounter, along with his colleagues. This conclusion is based on the visual reactions to the regression session, and the following observations:

'1) The traumatic reaction to the situation;

'2) The apparent lack of communication between "command" and the soldiers;

'3) Identification of the "ground crew" of the Triangle [the

American]. Because no one was seen entering or leaving the craft, I cannot call him an "occupant".

'4) The now familiar geographical location of this type of craft, close to military activity;

'5) The amnesia induced in all the victims, almost instantly;

'6) The identification of the small insignia on the left upper-chest area of the suit worn by the "ground crew".' (Though not included here, Mark did indeed describe a 'small insignia on the left upper-chest area of the suit worn by the American', whoever he was.)

I could pick out further findings, but I feel the point has been made.'

If Mark's story is true – and there is every reason to conclude that it is – then there are some very serious and pertinent questions to be asked.

One: Since when did our alien neighbours take to wearing black flying suits and speaking with American accents?

Two: What was the *real* agenda behind this highly unusual manoeuvre? To test some new beam-weapon capability, perhaps? A weapon developed as a result of reverse-engineering acquired alien hardware?

And three: What was the craft and where did it originate? Was this 'massive' triangular craft extraterrestrial? Terrestrial? The result of some joint US/British reverse-engineering programme?

Or evidence of an alien/government alliance?

It should be added that one of Britain's most highly secret air bases, RAF Boscombe Down (the scene of the 1994 ASTRA incident – see Document 05, File 22) is situated less than two miles – as the crow files – from the scene of Mark's encounter.

*   *   *

So were Mark and his colleagues used as some kind of human guinea pigs on the night in question?

Mark now feels certain that this is precisely what happened. 'I feel bloody angry,' he told me. 'Sick . . . and bloody angry. I feel like I've been used.'

This is not the only such incident on file involving British military personnel. But it is perhaps the most revealing to date.

File 25
Operation Blackbird

Another similar incident, which also involved the arrival of a huge black unconventional 'aircraft' in the midst of a heavy military presence, forms the story of George Vernon. George's chilling account surely implies some kind of collaboration between the military and the craft's 'occupants', whoever they were. This time the unknown craft appeared in the middle of a joint civilian/military exercise called *Operation Blackbird*. The reason for me citing this case is to offer more evidence in favour of the military/alien alliance, and in so doing help corroborate Mark's story.

Sponsored by BBC TV and Nippon TV (Japan), Operation Blackbird took place in July 1990 and was the brainchild of Colin Andrews and Pat Delgado, Britain's two leading crop circle researchers of the late 1980s. Indeed, although Pat Delgado has since withdrawn from the scene, Colin Andrews is still recognized as one of the world's leading authorities on the crop circle phenomenon.

The purpose of Operation Blackbird from the civilian point

of view was to try and catch a crop circle being formed on camera. And no expense was spared in this endeavour. It is said that the hi-tech surveillance equipment used in the operation – which included state-of-the-art video equipment, infra-red cameras and image intensifiers strategically positioned around a sizeable parcel of land at Bratton Castle in Wiltshire – was worth somewhere in the region of £1 million. According to the experts this equipment should have recorded anything and everything that moved within the cordoned-off area. In the event, however, this did not prove to be the case. (Or if it did, film of what occurred is now for the exclusive viewing of the military and top BBC chiefs – not for the public.)

It should also be pointed out that the operation was conducted under the scrutinizing eye of the world's media. As well as the BBC and Nippon TV, numerous reporters and cameramen from both the local and national press were present. It was said at the time that the only event likely to have attracted an even larger media presence would have been something involving the Royal Family, such was the extent of media interest. If the government was ever to prove crop circles a 'man-made phenomenon', this was the time to do it – in front of a world audience. Indeed, it was rumoured from the outset that this may have been the very reason the military became involved in the operation. It is known, for example, that secret meetings had already taken place between the Ministries of Defence, Agriculture and the Environment concerning the crop circle phenomenon and what to do about it. As a result of these meetings the matter had been placed squarely in the hands of the Ministry of Defence – both MI5 and MI6 had been alerted to the situation and even the services of DI55 and DI61 had been called upon, two of the government's most 'non-existent' DIS (Defence Intelligence Staff) departments. The Directorate of Scientific Intelligence had also been alerted. The outcome was that a direct disinformation and debunking programme should be initiated via television and the tabloid press – make the experts look like fools . . .

. . . And waiting smugly in the wings, of course, was the government's ace card: two elderly gentlemen by the names of 'Doug and Dave'. But that's another story (see Document 07).

Perhaps predictably, then, the operation culminated in the discovery of a hoaxed formation, the arrival of which had apparently been caught on camera. Unaware that he was being set up, Colin Andrews was called to the site from his bed at around 3:30 a.m. and, upon his arrival, was told by the military that a crop circle had appeared. An hour or so later (amidst a flurry of media excitement and military pressure) he announced on nationwide breakfast television that a 'major event' had occurred and that it had indeed been caught on camera.

'We do have a major event here,' Colin announced to the world. 'On the monitor a number of orange lights taking the form of a triangle . . . we have high-quality equipment here and we have indeed secured on high-quality equipment a major event . . . we have everything on film and we do have, as I say, a formed object over the field . . .'

However, when the formation was finally examined in daylight it was found to be a set of six very well-made – though *man-made* – circles, complete with rings and a few bars. But that was not all. It seemed that whoever had been responsible for the hoax had left what the press described as a 'Ouija Board' and a roughly made wooden cross in the centre of each of the six circles. There was also a length of red wire that corresponded in size to the diameter of some of the circles, presumably to let people know how the circles had been made – army boots for trampling the crop and a length of wire for a measuring tool. In short, this was anything but a 'major event'.

Indeed, my contention is that the only 'major event' to have occurred that night was the cleverly planned and executed government/military operation designed specifically to debunk the phenomenon, not only on site but in the blaze of media publicity surrounding the project. In short, Colin Andrews and his team were set up. And they were set up in a big way.

The question is, by whom? The military? Aliens?

Or both . . .?

In Document 07 further evidence revealing how the intelligence communities of both Britain and America were behind the media's crop circle debunking campaign of the early 1990s will be presented. Indeed, as we shall see, the CIA in particular wanted this phenomenon discredited out of hand (and the agency was prepared to make enormous sums of money available to those involved in order to achieve its goal). For the present, however, we must focus our investigations on the military's unexpected involvement in Operation Blackbird – that, and the truly chilling encounter experienced by a man called George Vernon.

At some point during the preparation stages of the operation Colin Andrews was approached by two senior Army officials who offered the Army's assistance in the form of manpower and equipment. Unaware of hidden agendas Colin gladly accepted the offer (an action he would later regret). From this point on the military presence became very apparent indeed.

As researcher George Wingfield wrote at the time: 'The

Army, who apparently own the land on which the observation post was situated, were deeply involved in Blackbird . . .'

He went on to say: 'The soldiers at Blackbird, though officially off duty, did not wear civilian clothes. The Army also carried out considerable additional night surveillance of its own, using night-sights and the like which gave far clearer vision of the fields being watched than anything in the observation post. This equipment was manned by soldiers with blackened faces hiding in camouflaged dens. Rather curiously, the two corporals assigned for duty at the Blackbird observation post were absent on the night of the hoax, though they were there on every other night of the project.'

[I would urge you to keep in mind George Wingfield's above commentary, in particular the fact that 'the equipment was manned by soldiers with *blackened faces* . . .' (my italics).]

One of the most damning pieces of evidence with regard to the military's involvement in Operation Blackbird was incautiously divulged to the press by one of the soldiers taking part. During the operation Corporal Darren Cummings unequivocally told reporters: 'We are here to prove that they [the circles] are caused by people; the scientists are here to prove otherwise.' Seems clear enough to me.

Further evidence in this direction – that the military had infiltrated the operation purely to debunk the phenomenon in the public eye – came from a senior military (MoD) official, who revealed at the time that the hoax had indeed been carefully planned in advance and executed at short notice by a 'Special Operations' military unit. (Subsequent information suggested that this unit belonged to the SAS.) He also disclosed the fact that the operation had been ordered from a very high level within the MoD. For obvious reasons the senior military official in question must remain anonymous.

To add to this, it is also known (as Colin Andrews said) that the 'event' – whatever it was – was caught on film by the BBC (who, incidentally, still refuse to allow anyone to view it, even though they spent considerable sums of taxpayers' money in their endeavours to secure the footage). Apparently the film shows some 'orange lights' hovering above the field where the crop formation was found. According to the military these 'orange lights' belonged to a helicopter. According to an eyewitness who is now ready to tell his story, however, they belonged to something else entirely . . .

File 25: Appendix 01
Case Report: Cosmic Top-X25 Eyes Only
Merlin

George Vernon's name first came to light during the media blitz immediately following Operation Blackbird. The fact that he had invented an astrology-based board game and that in the process of marketing his new game he referred to himself as 'Merlin' made him the perfect media fall guy.

The *Sunday Sport*, for example, reporting on the events of Operation Blackbird back in 1990, brazenly told the world that George Vernon had claimed to have made all the crop circles through the power of his mind, and that he had discovered this ability some years previously when he'd slept in a crop field near Stonehenge and had woken up to find that a circle had formed around him. The *Sunday Sport* also claimed that Vernon had admitted to hoaxing the Blackbird formation by 'rolling around in the corn'. It should be added that this story was written by the *Sunday Sport* reporter, B. Ollocks. I'll leave you to draw your own conclusions.

George Vernon categorically denies all of these bizarre

claims. Having spoken to him on a number of occasions on the telephone, and having met and interviewed him at his home, I have to say that I believe him. His story is compelling and coherent, and has remained consistent throughout my investigations, even though the terrible traumas he has suffered over the past seven or eight years have taken their toll. Though fully cognizant, George is now in fragile mental health. Nevertheless he is determined to clear his name and get to the truth of what really happened on the night of 25th/26th July 1990.

In brief, George's story begins with the mysterious deposit of some £10,000 in his bank account. This occurred shortly after he was involved in a car accident in December 1985. According to George, all he can recall about the accident is being picked up by an 'ambulance crew' and an 'ambulance man' bending over him, touching his forehead and asking his name. For some reason that, at the time, even George could not fathom, he replied: 'Merlin.'

Some short time following the accident George became inspired to invent a board game based on astrology and megalithic sites, such as Stonehenge, but he did not have the money to do this. The next thing he knew £10,000 had been deposited in his bank account. To this day he has no idea where the money came from. When questioned about this his bank manager explained that there was no mystery attached to the deposit – George had taken out a personal loan and must have *forgotten* that he had done so. When asked to produce evidence of the loan – a signed document of some kind – the bank was unable to do so, however.

Bemused by this rather mysterious set of circumstances, in October 1988 *HTV News* revealed that they too had investigated the deposit: as it turned out, their findings differed slightly from George's own account. In a two-and-a-half-minute segment correspondent Jonathan Meredith reported that, when questioned, Lloyds Bank had admitted to having made a sizeable blunder – their computer had deposited the £10,000 in George's bank account by mistake! As a consequence, Lloyds were now treating the so-called 'mistake' as a personal loan and expected George to pay it all back. In the meantime, however, George had treated himself to a holiday in Greece with some of the money, while the balance had been invested in the development of his board game. In short, he no longer had the £10,000.

And here's another twist. While travelling back from Greece, George was stopped by Customs officials and questioned about the sizeable amount of cash he was carrying. When George attempted to explain that the money had mysteriously appeared in his bank account he was arrested and held for further questioning; he spent the entire weekend in custody while the CID endeavoured to trace the money – where it had come from, who had been responsible for the deposit, etc. The strange thing is that the CID drew a complete blank; they could not find any details as to where the money had come from or who had deposited such a large sum in George's bank account. George was subsequently released without charge.

'I had to sign a statement that said they could go through my account to find out where the money came from,' George told me. 'But even the CID couldn't find out where the money came from, so they let me go.'

In the meantime George followed his inspiration and invented his new board game. The reason I mention the board game is because it plays a very central role in the plot, and the mysterious deposit of such a large sum of money in his bank account certainly suggests that perhaps someone *wanted* him to create this new board game very badly. Why this should be so remains to be seen. Perhaps what happened next may throw some light on the mystery . . .

. . . On the night of the now infamous Operation Blackbird 'hoax' (25th/26th July 1990) George Vernon happened to be in Wiltshire (he was a removals man and was working in Wiltshire on the day in question). So far as George is concerned, what happened to him that night not only changed his life completely, it virtually *destroyed* him.

That evening, at around 11:30 p.m., George says that a 'voice' or an 'inner communication' told him to drive to a particular place and a particular field, which he did.

'I was driving the van and this thing came in my head to go to Bratton, to turn left, to turn right . . . it was about 11:30 p.m. and I was told to turn left and go over a little bridge, and drive about four hundred yards. Then the engine cut out. I pulled in to the grass verge by a farmhouse gate and I was told to get out of the van. I wasn't scared at this point. I was being controlled, totally taken over.'

It just so happened that this field in which George had 'arrived' (and in which he now stood, in Bratton, Wiltshire) bordered part of the perimeter of the operation's cordoned-off surveillance area, although George had no idea that this was the case. Indeed, he had no idea that Operation Blackbird was even taking place, much less that he had stepped slap-bang into the middle of it, and that, as a consequence, his every move was being monitored by hi-tech military surveillance equipment. So far as George was concerned he was simply responding to a 'command' given him by some 'inner voice'. His mind was numb to all else.

So there was George, suffering the effects of what might be

described as an 'altered state', standing in a field at midnight in the middle of Wiltshire because he had been ordered to do so by an 'inner voice'. Sounds bizarre, I know. It gets even more bizarre.

Next, George was suddenly confronted by a human-like 'being' who, he says, came out of the bushes and proceeded to make contact with him 'telepathically'. He asked George his name, to which George once again replied: 'Merlin.' But what is strange is the fact that, when George asked the being *its* name, it replied: 'I am Merlin, too.'

George told me: 'I climbed over the fence and this being came out, this shape, this black shape . . . it was a little bit smaller than me and I couldn't see a face. It was human-shaped. It climbed the fence . . . it did everything human.'

The being then instructed George to fetch six of his board games from his van (wrongly described as 'Ouija Boards' by the press) and to place one at the centre of each of the six crop circles which were, by this time, present in the field. This George did. The being also ordered George to place some stones in the circles which, again, he did. By this time, however, George was becoming frightened, and so he also placed a wooden cross in one of the circles 'as a protection'. The wooden cross was later described by the press as 'evidence of some kind of ritual', which indeed it was not, and 'roughly made', which indeed it was. George had fashioned it there and then out of his own staff – the staff he used when marketing his board game under the guise of 'Merlin'. He simply snapped the staff in two and placed it in the form of a cross in one of the six circles.

According to George, the circles – which later became known as the 'Bratton Castle Hoax', or the 'Operation Blackbird Hoax' – had just been made by the being and his 'colleagues', and not by some arbitrary team of hoaxers. Perhaps one interpretation of this might be that they had been made by the 'special forces' military (SAS) to whom this being belonged, and who were there – as Corporal Darren Cummings had already confided to the press – as part of a pre-planned operation to 'prove that they [the crop circles] are caused by people'.

Indeed, considering this formation was so well-made, and that it was manufactured in the space of approximately one hour, it is highly improbable – indeed *impossible* – that one man (George Vernon) could have made it by 'rolling around in the corn', as the *Sunday Sport* subsequently claimed. It is equally improbable that it was made by a team of drunken young farmers after a night at the local pub, or even by a team of practised hoaxers for that matter – who, it should be said, were not nearly so *practised* in 1990 as they are today (bless their tiny little agendas).

Another possibility at the time was that the hoax had been made by the pop group KLF, who in the same year had created a hoaxed formation in the form of a pyramid crossed by a large ghetto blaster, the band's logo; film of this formation was later used in the promo video for their single *What Time Is Love*.

The reason KLF were suspected of creating the Blackbird hoax was that on the day following Colin Andrews's ill-fated TV announcement he received a letter that seemed to have been sent by the band's members. 'Colin,' the letter read. 'The circles on Wednesday were just a hoax, but we can't help to play jokes. Inconvenience caused? We're sorry. Catch us, you'll have to hurry. Yours, in total control, the Justified Ancients of Mu-Mu – the JAMMs. Try not to worry too hard. We find it very funny while you sit back and rake in the money.'

Although it is known that KLF members Bill Drummond and Jimmy Cauti (alias the JAMMS) expressed a healthy interest in what they termed the 'landscape art' aspect of the crop circle phenomenon, and that they paid farmer David Read £350 to create the now-famous 'pyramid and ghetto blaster' formation on his land, it is highly unlikely that they were responsible for either the letter to Colin Andrews *or* the Blackbird hoax. Indeed, when George Wingfield spoke to the band on the telephone they categorically denied involvement, period, an uncharacteristically discreet disavowal for a pop group (*any publicity is good publicity*) unless of course it was true. And in any case, it is known that the 'pyramid and ghetto blaster' formation took them six hours to make in broad daylight. The Blackbird hoax consisted of *six* circles and was made in approximately *one* hour in the *dead of night* – and under the watchful eye of the military.

Every indication, then, points to the fact that this was a pre-planned operation performed with military precision, SAS precision, and that George Vernon, Colin Andrews, Pat Delgado *et al* were destined from the very beginning to be the fall guys.

Back to the plot . . .

According to George Vernon, the being that confronted him was about six feet tall, dressed all in black with a blackened face, and was somehow able to reach inside his mind and take control. As if by some form of 'mental hijack' this being was able to lead George across two more fields towards a railway embankment, George following behind like an obedient puppy, unable to break the grasp this being seemed to have on his mind. Despite the fact that the being had a human-like build and, according to George, walked like any human might walk (and indeed, had to climb over fences and stiles in the same way as any human would) George believes to this day that the being was a 'spirit' or an 'alien' of some kind. But then, George – like most people – has little idea of what the military is these days capable of, much less the motives for executing this kind of covert operation. Perhaps understandably he is also reluctant to accept the possibility that the military might be working with aliens (or at least with secretly developed 'acquired alien technologies' capable of creating screen memories in one's mind – memories that act like screens to block out what really happened and at the same time replace one's true memory with a false one – see Document 10). But if the military is *not* working with aliens and/or their technology, then what happened next beggars the very fabric of sanity itself.

Because as George approached the railway embankment – still following the strange black being – he was suddenly confronted by a sight that has dogged him to this day. His still-recurrent nightmares are a testament to this end.

According to George, what happened next was that a massive black 'craft' suddenly arrived and hovered above the field in which he stood. And then landed.

'All of a sudden, from the left-hand side, looking up at Bratton Fort, this black object came at us at the speed of light, then circled around and landed. It was so fast and silent – I couldn't believe my eyes. The being in front of me said (telepathically): "Stand still." And I just froze.'

In a later interview George described the craft as 'massive, very black, and silent', eerily similar in every respect to the craft described by Mark, the craft that had zapped him and five other soldiers on Salisbury Plain only six months previously. The jigsaw begins to form a picture, then . . .

It seems the arrival of the unknown craft was sufficient to snap George out of his mental stupor, at least to some small degree – enough that he suddenly became aware of what was happening to him and, perhaps not surprisingly, started to become very frightened. In the meantime the being continued to try and coax George on towards the craft which, by this time, had landed silently in the field. But George remained rooted to the spot. When a second being emerged from the landed craft, however, and started to walk over towards him, George instinctively felt that he was about to be abducted. At which point the 'spell' on him came loose and he was able to turn and run away, lacerating his hand and arm on a barbed-wire fence as he did so.

'The being approached this black object (the craft) and I saw an orange ball come out of the craft and turn before my eyes into another black entity . . . At this point panic set in and I ran like hell from the middle of this field (200–300 yards) straight into a barbed-wire fence . . . when I got up he was there. He got me again.'

Despite his efforts, then, George did not get away; the being caught up with him and, in order to prove that it wasn't 'human', proceeded to 'melt' in front of his eyes, and then reassemble itself. At least this is George's 'memory' of the event. This is also, of course, one of the main reasons George is reluctant to believe that this could have been anything but an 'alien' or a 'spiritual' experience, and understandably so. After all, if what your mind 'remembers' is some strange being 'melting' before your eyes the last thing it will want to be told is that this being was 'human' – that this particular part of your memory is a false one that has been so cleverly woven into your *true* memory of what *really* happened that discrimination between *false* and *real* is virtually impossible. Of course, in order for this to have occurred George must surely have been 'taken' and 'worked on', at least for some short period of time. And if this was the case then equally he must have experienced some missing time.

Sadly he did. The next thing George remembers is waking up, slumped over the driving wheel of his van with a head full of nightmares that felt like memories, *his* memories – memories which to this day he believes are perfectly accurate and authentic. Most of them probably are.

It should be added that George has subsequently suffered no less than three nervous breakdowns, all due to this event, and is still on prescribed medication for his condition (although, being teetotal, he normally refuses to take even an aspirin).

File 25: Appendix 02
Case Review: Cosmic Top-X26 Eyes Only
Summing Up

Evidence points to the fact that a crack SAS (Special Air Service) psy-ops unit was indeed active on the night of the Operation Blackbird hoax, and that it had been ordered at short notice to execute a specific 'mission' at Bratton Castle (or perhaps even two specific missions – see Document 26). The evidence also seems to point to the fact that this psy-ops exercise demanded the involvement of a 'remotely controlled' or 'mind-controlled' stooge. Sadly, I believe George Vernon *was* that stooge, and that he had for some years been unwittingly prepared and programmed for the task, or another one just like it. (See the 'sleeper agents' information in Document 03, File 13.) Let us not forget that the military is these days perfectly capable of achieving such abominations.

Let us not forget, either, that – assuming he *was* used – George Vernon would not have been the first British subject to have suffered at the hands of the military's – the Alliance's? – psychological warfare programme.

Remember Mark?

The point of me relating George's story, of course, is to offer further evidence of the fact that either the military is capable of controlling people's minds at will, as seems to have been the case with George – Mark and his five colleagues, too – or they are in league with those who can. The arrival of the massive black craft that hovered and landed silently in the midst of such a heavy military presence seems to point to the latter as the most likely scenario. Remember, in Mark's case the craft was seen *before* his apparent 'missing time' experience; it was not part of the information he recalled under hypnosis. And in George's case, the craft was captured on film by the BBC. It is unlikely that the craft itself was part of any 'screen memory'.

The conclusion I am heading towards here goes something like this:

Had Mark's account been a simple UFO sighting, intriguing as it might have been I would probably not have taken George's story quite so seriously. Mark's account, however, was *not* a simple UFO sighting. On the contrary, it constitutes one of the most telling pieces of evidence to date in support of British involvement in the government/alien alliance scenario. According to Mark, remember, he too witnessed the arrival of a 'massive black' craft, in the dead of night, and in the midst of a sizeable military presence (indeed, in the middle of a night-manoeuvres exercise on Salisbury Plain). It is inconceivable that such a craft – assuming for one moment it was alien – would have been allowed to enter British (military) airspace and perform its experiment without some unseen cooperation from the government/military – indeed, without the craft and its occupants being part of some backstairs 'alliance'.

But what makes Mark's account even more similar to George's is the sudden and mysterious appearance of the 'being' dressed all in black and with a *blackened face* (see George Wingfield's commentary above).

In Mark's account, the being brandished a 'stick' or an 'aerial', spoke with an American accent and was somehow able to intimidate and control the soldiers to such an extent that they were unable to resist in any way. In George's account, the being was also dressed in black with a *blackened face*, and was able to reach into George's mind and take control of him. The similarities are very apparent. Remember, there were no less than six soldiers involved in Mark's encounter, all of whom were unaccountably unable to defend themselves against the being's prodding and poking and verbal abuse. One man against six combat-trained soldiers, and yet all six soldiers became 'frightened' and 'disoriented' in the being's presence. Though retold in a different way (because George believes the being was an alien and that his experience was in some way 'spiritual', while Mark believes the being was human and that his experience was nothing short of some heinous advanced-technology experiment) the fact that the being was able to reach into George's mind and take control of him is nonetheless also a fact in Mark's case. Perhaps the 'stick' or 'aerial' was instrumental in influencing the soldiers' minds, perhaps not. But what is clear is that this mysterious being, whether alien or special forces, was somehow able to take control in both situations.

All of which leads us to one of three inevitable conclusions:

1) Mark and George – who approached me quite independently, neither having heard of the other, and both coming
from quite different backgrounds, one military, the other not
– are blatantly lying, and by chance just happen to have
concocted chillingly similar stories;

2) The joint British and US military-industrial complex has
developed an aircraft the size of a football pitch that utilizes
some form of unconventional silent propulsion system and
carries on board some form of inconceivable beam weapon
designed to immobilize trained soldiers instantly, causing
them to become confused and to lose their memories.
This craft is also capable of breaking the sound barrier
from standstill (in a matter of seconds) with no apparent
acceleration and without creating a sonic boom;

3) The joint British and US military-industrial complex is
working with – or has worked with – aliens, and so is in
possession of alien technology.

The possibility that this was solely the work of aliens is
largely ruled out by the fact that, in Mark's case, the being
spoke with an American accent, implying the involvement of
a US and/or joint British/US or multinational special forces
unit. The fact that, in both cases, the being was dressed all in
black with a *blackened face* would seem to support this view.
However, the fact that this same being was – in both cases –
associated with the arrival of a 'massive black craft' capable
of manoeuvres that simply defy the laws of physics as we
know them implies something altogether more sinister.

To my mind, and notwithstanding the fact that the military-
industrial complex is in possession of some very future-tech
aircraft indeed, it is nonetheless inconceivable that such a
vehicle – as described above in conclusion (2) – could be
the result of terrestrial technology alone. Which leaves only
one of two possibilities:

Either the military has become very adept indeed in the science of holographics (and the craft, perhaps even the being, was a hologram) or some highly secretive elite within the government/military-industrial complex has indeed formed an alliance with a visiting alien race.

And remember, whichever conclusion proves ultimately to be correct, this all happened on British soil: if an alliance truly does exist between aliens and governments, then one of those governments is British.

File 26
The Bratton Castle
White Horse Mutilation

As startling as George Vernon's encounter was, yet further – and equally bizarre – events were to unfold before Operation Blackbird was complete. File 26 describes one of those events.

In the summer of 1997 I received the following report from UFO and crop circle researcher Joe Dormer. Following my lengthy investigations into events related to Operation Blackbird (see also Document 07, File 28), the arrival of this report could not have been more timely, and filled me with a sense of renewed intrigue regarding the motives and agendas played out via this overemphasized crop circle watch, Operation Blackbird. With Joe's kind permission I have decided to reproduce the report in its entirety. Personally I find it extraordinary (not to say suspicious in the extreme) that the following could have happened only three nights after George Vernon's unbelievable encounter – and in virtually the same field in Wiltshire.

File 26: Appendix 01
Case Report: Cosmic Top-X27 Eyes Only Macabre

In the early morning of 29th July 1990, a white male horse was found dead and mutilated near an Iron Age hill fort at Bratton, Wiltshire. Its left ear and its penis had been cleanly removed, in a manner redolent of the mysterious cattle mutilations that have been occurring in various parts of the US. There was no sign of blood on the animal.

News of the horse's macabre death quickly reached the ears of 'Operation Blackbird' (a team of crop circle researchers who were keeping watch at a site nearby) then spread to other circle watchers who had come down just for the weekend. Within hours of the discovery, however, the police were issuing statements, later circulated among members of the Blackbird team, that the horse had simply died of natural causes.

This explanation was accepted almost unquestioningly by ufologists and anomalies researchers, so that to this day the case is treated as a classic example of how the natural inclination to embellish a story can turn a perfectly ordinary occurrence into a mystery. An investigation by researcher Clive Potter and myself, however, has shown that this is quite the opposite of what happened.

I would almost certainly never have questioned the official explanation were it not for an incident that occurred at the 1991 International UFO Congress at Sheffield.

During question time following TV producer John MacNish's talk on crop circles, a member of the audience raised his hand and asked if the speaker had any news on the Bratton horse mutilation. Now, as I have said, most of us were of the persuasion at that time that there was no truth in this story. And MacNish's reply did nothing to dispel that view. 'The horse died of natural causes', he said. 'We know this to be true since we got this information from the police.'

At this point a man in the audience stood up. 'Excuse me', he said. 'I was the one who – with a colleague – discovered the horse. Its penis and its left ear were cleanly removed . . . it was we who gave this information to the police. It's a cover-up!'

At the end of the session I managed to manoeuvre my way through the crowd just in time to catch up with the man on his way out onto the street. Could he tell me more? I asked. He hesitated. What exactly was my interest in this case? he wanted to know. His apprehension over the possible consequences – real or imagined – of revealing any information at all was evident enough.

Only when he was satisfied that my request was genuine, and that I wanted to look further into this case, did he volunteer to send me further details. These arrived by post two days later: a four-page (A4) report written in longhand, along with a sketch pinpointing the exact location at which the horse was discovered.

The report describes how on the morning of 30th July 1990, at about 7:15 a.m., he and his friend went 'in search of a toilet' and came across the horse: 'It was a white male horse lying dead on its side. Its feet were all caught up in a large link fence. Its sex organ was cleanly removed, along with its left ear. There was a mass of foam protruding from each nostril and its eyes were bulging, both indicating that the horse had died . . . in agony.

'The whole area around the horse was free of blood – only one drop could be found about four feet away, no bigger than a ten-pence piece. This struck us as very odd . . . We looked for the missing organs but found nothing. There was also a pile of dung about twelve feet away. The horse must have died only a couple of hours before our discovery (or less) as the foam suggested . . . rigor mortis was beginning to set in.'

Here then was a first-hand account by the original witness. Not some second-, third- or umpteenth-hand account by a friend of a friend of a cousin on his brother's side, but primary-source information. That was what had been needed all along, and that was what I now had. I wrote immediately to Clive Potter, whom I knew had already made some preliminary enquiries. His interest was sufficiently rekindled for him to wish to look further into this and he suggested we work together.

We began by writing to Trowbridge Police Station, where officers investigating the case would have been based. Not surprisingly, Trowbridge denied all knowledge of a mutilated horse. Less predictably they claimed to have no record of *any* incident involving a dead horse on the day in question. Their reply reads: 'We have checked our records and enquired of our officers, but can find no trace of any such incident.' We also wrote to Wiltshire Constabulary, which should have held copies of all Trowbridge's records, but their reply was the same: *'We have checked our records, but can find no trace . . .'*

This is impossible to reconcile with what the police told MacNish: that there *was* a dead horse, but it had died of natural causes. MacNish's account, which we transcribed (verbatim) from an audio recording of his talk, is as follows:

'Basically, the white horse mutilation . . . we checked with the police . . . And the police report . . . I rang the police and said: "Can you tell me a bit more about the horse mutilation?" And they said: "What, you mean the alien encounter with three beings from outer space and the woman was abducted and the horse got mutilated?" And I said: "Well it might be." And they said: "Well, the farmer went over to where the horse was . . . It turned out that it actually . . . our post mortem on it was the horse died of natural causes." Now that's what I know about that . . . That was the police report . . . [inaudible] . . . actually had suggestions of UFOs and aliens in it . . . the actual police report!'

So we have, according to MacNish, a police inquiry, a post mortem, an official police report – and no one recalls a thing: neither the officers who investigated it nor those who found the joke about aliens such a source of amusement. And not a trace on record? How was this possible?

We put this question mischievously in a second letter to Trowbridge. We also put it to them that 'whoever performed the autopsy would surely have kept a separate record'. And, further, that: 'In the – hypothetical, shall we say – event of such a horse being discovered, who would have performed the autopsy?' They chose to ignore both questions. So did a computer error wipe out the records? Or do all the police officers at Trowbridge suffer from poor memories? Or were the 'pigs' telling porkies?

If the police would not be straight with us, might members of the 'Blackbird' team be persuaded to tell us what they knew? We wrote to several leading members of the team, but were met with a wall of silence.

Clive and I had to agree that this was one of the most frustrating cases either of us had investigated. Most refused even to talk about it; nobody was prepared to go on record as saying anything at all about it. This reluctance to say very much, incongruously coupled with requests for anonymity, was the recurring theme of anyone who might have been able to provide us with information.

Finally, one 'Blackbird' member told us: 'I can give you a contact address but please don't mention my name'. The contact turned out to be a crop circle researcher by the name of Rita Gould, who had come down to the area that weekend from Leicester. Rita had struck up a friendship with the two men [who discovered the horse] and was actually the first to be told of their discovery. It was she in fact who had informed the 'Blackbird' team.

Rita described to Clive how the two men were then allowed to enter the 'Blackbird' site and describe what had happened. They were then escorted to the horse by stewards, the site manager and people dressed in military uniform. No one else was allowed to visit the site until after the police had arrived and removed the carcass.

It has now emerged that the police quickly adopted a policy of secrecy and persuaded the 'Blackbird' team to go along with it. This much has now been admitted to me by one leading 'Blackbird' member. No doubt cogent reasons were given for concealing this information from the public – and who knows whether we, too, might have complied in similar circumstances? Nevertheless it is our duty as researchers to ferret out the facts, and that is what we have done. And the facts are that the macabre killing and mutilating of a male white horse did indeed take place that weekend at Bratton.

The questions remaining are: Why? And: Who was responsible?

I discussed the incident with American researcher Linda Moulton-Howe during one of her visits to Britain. Linda thinks it fits the pattern of the animal mutilations in the US. Further, she believes there is sufficient evidence to link this phenomenon with UFOs – though that is another matter. I must confess, though, I find this explanation rather more plausible than MacNish's: that the horse did indeed die of natural causes and only subsequently 'had nasty things done to it'.

Why do I find MacNish's explanation so far-fetched? Because the condition of the horse suggests that it died only hours before it was found: and in fact corroborative evidence has been provided by pilot and crop circle researcher Busty Taylor (among others), who recalls being woken in the middle of the night by a colleague who had heard what sounded like the cries of an animal in pain.

Are we to take seriously the suggestion that someone stumbling around in the dark came across the horse, quite by accident, and then spontaneously decided to mutilate it – having by happenstance the tools and the extraordinary skills necessary to perform this gruesome operation? I think not! The unanswered question, though, is: Who, or what, did?

File 26:
Appendix 02
Case Review: Cosmic Top-X28 Eyes Only

Further to receiving the above report I contacted several members of the Operation Blackbird team plus the Trowbridge and Westbury police stations and quizzed them on the allegation that the Bratton white horse had been mutilated by aliens. The officer at Trowbridge police station certainly mumbled something to the effect that, yes, he did seem to remember the incident, vaguely, though he could not help throw any light on the details. When I asked him if he could check back through the files I was told that records are kept on site for a maximum of three years; there were no files extant regarding this case, at least not at Trowbridge. He advised that I talk to someone at Westbury. This, he said, was the police station nearest to where the incident had occurred – if anybody knew anything at all it would more likely be someone stationed at Westbury.

I called Westbury police station.

Unlike the officer at Trowbridge, the woman I spoke to there was both friendly and helpful, at least initially, and offered to check back through the missing files. She told me she was under the impression that a horse had indeed been mutilated on the date given, but that the dastardly deed had actually been performed on a prehistoric 'White Horse' hill figure, of which there are any number of prominent examples in Wiltshire – including, she said, the so-called 'Bratton White Horse'. This reply, however, while perfectly feasible, did not concur with the testimony of either Rita Gould or TV producer John MacNish. On the contrary, MacNish claimed that, according to the Wiltshire Constabulary, the horse had been of the living, breathing, mammalian type, that it had died of natural causes and that it had been autopsied and 'mutilated' (had had various parts removed) after its death. A strange confession from the Wiltshire Constabulary, it has to be said, especially if all that had really happened was that a prehistoric hill figure had been disfigured by vandals. (It should be added that information I received from several other sources, including Operation Blackbird participant and longstanding crop circle researcher Busty Taylor, revealed that the disfigurement of a nearby hill feature had indeed occurred some years ago, but 'absolutely not at the time of Operation Blackbird'.) After speaking to nearly a dozen people about this incident, including the two police officers, it seemed that, like Joe Dormer before me, I had drawn a blank. Certainly if anybody at either Trowbridge or Westbury police stations remembered the incident they were not talking about it, at least not to me. Despite the initial helpful attitude I encountered when speaking to the woman officer at Westbury police station, and a further assurance from the Westbury police that they would furnish me with a detailed account of this case, at the end of the day I met with the usual wall of silence. The case details were never forwarded to me as promised and further attempts to tease information from the police were to no avail. Indeed, a similar response was offered by almost everybody who had been involved at Operation Blackbird; curiously, it was as if nobody wanted to talk about this incident. Though of course I was not able to talk to every last 'Blackbird' participant (both time and lack of resources preventing) the chorus echoed by those I *did* talk to amounted to pretty much the same – the so-called horse mutilation probably did not occur; the entire story was probably a hoax; Joe Dormer had got it all wrong.

Or had he?

To date I have been unable to track down the mystery man who supplied Joe Dormer with the details of this case (if he is reading this I would be very happy to hear from him). Presumably Rita Gould still stands by her account although, truth be told, I have been unsuccessful in corroborating her story, too. What I have been able to confirm, however, is that a special-ops military unit (SAS: see File 25) was indeed assigned to the 'Blackbird' operation and was under an express directive to discredit the operation out of hand (as inferred by Corporal Darren Cummings at the time, when he unequivocally told reporters: 'We are here to prove that they [the circles] are caused by people'). It is now evident that this was achieved in as many ways as seemed viable. Only three nights previous to this incident, remember, this same crack SAS unit was probably responsible not only for making the now famous Bratton Castle crop circle hoax (and in a field almost adjacent to where the mutilated horse was discovered) but for making a shivered wreck of George Vernon's nervous system, too. And in any case, if the military was out to put an end to UFO and crop circle fever – which it undoubtedly was – then animal mutilations and crop circle hoaxes would have been the perfect way to do it.

While there is simply not the time or space here to examine in depth the so-called 'cattle mutilation' phenomenon – perhaps one of the most grisly aspects of ufology – I should nevertheless point out that the seemingly deliberate and calculated mutilation of a great number of domestic cattle (cows, sheep, some horses) has indeed been reported over the past few decades by farmers and landowners alike, in particular in the US. In each case the animal seems to have been purposely and precisely delivered of its vital and genital organs and drained of its blood. Indeed, due to the fact that these atrocities have for the most part been performed with such expert dexterity, technologically advanced aliens have been cited as the likely perpetrators. Recently, however, evidence has emerged which points the finger squarely in the opposite direction.

The sheer number of eyewitness accounts that speak of 'military', 'unmarked' and/or 'stealth' helicopters having been observed at mutilation sites is today overwhelming, and would seem to implicate not aliens but the military as prime-suspect mutilators – it seems that, for one reason or another, governments have decided to involve themselves in the perpetration of this strange and grotesque pastime and at the same time disseminate the 'alien cattle mutilation' story as a smokescreen. Contrary to some reports, of course, the technology to achieve the seemingly space-age-style surgery performed on the mutilated animals is readily available, and has been for decades. In this respect it is no secret that the military has been experimenting with laser technology for at least fifty years, some reports say longer. (One source, for example, informed me that he has seen classified documents to the effect that the 'experimental military use of lasers' was under way in Britain 'in the years immediately prior to and during World War One!')

The latest laser technology alone, then, could perform even the most intricate of mutilation operations, no doubt about that.

Which surely points to the fact that, if this mutilation *did* occur, not only did the military have the technology to achieve it, but those whose authority directs the activities of British and US special forces probably had better reason than aliens to carry it out.

In conclusion: sadly the jury must remain out on this one; there is simply not the data upon which to base a reasonable judgement. There are too many holes, too many areas of doubt, too many tracks too well covered. It is not even one hundred per cent certain that the mutilation happened in the first place, though the evidence presented by Joe Dormer seems to suggest that it most likely did. In this respect there is certainly sufficient reason to suspect that – assuming it *did* occur – this grisly act was carried out by the military in an ongoing endeavour to sabotage serious research into the UFO and crop circle phenomena.

It would not have been the first time such a sabotage operation had been deployed. I doubt it will be the last.

DOCUMENT 07

Cosmic Top Secret
Eyes Only Copy One of One

Crop Circles

File 27
Infiltration

Further evidence in support of the fact that not only are the British and US governments deeply involved in the UFO and crop circle phenomena, but that they are doing all in their power to debunk said phenomena in the public eye can be found in the two Files (27 and 28) that I have decided to include here in Document 07. Both involve investigations undertaken by the world's leading crop circle researcher, Colin Andrews.

Testimonies from British farmers and landowners attest to the fact that the crop circle phenomenon has been around for many decades. Some farmers, for example, say that their grandfathers used to talk of 'strange circles' that appeared overnight inexplicably in their fields, as though some unknown circular aircraft (flying saucer?) had landed during the night and had left its impression in the standing crop. Indeed, the earliest reported crop circle of which I am aware dates back to the seventeenth century.

But so far as we are concerned it would be true to say that the modern crop circle phenomenon really kicked in towards the end of the 1980s, when the simple 'circle' patterns that had begun to appear more regularly from 1980 onwards suddenly transformed into what soon became known as 'pictograms', often gigantic and evocative patterns mysteriously 'pressed' into fields of standing crop (mostly wheat, rye, barley, oil seed rape; though these same inexplicable patterns have also been reported in trees, grass, cane and rice, even snow and ice). For the most part the patterns seemed simply to appear out of nowhere (they still do) and, like imprints of some long-forgotten world, seemed to resemble primitive, archetypal images – ancient hieroglyphics, educative geometries and other psychoactive signs and configurations. By 1988 the phenomenon was causing so much public interest that both the British and US governments started to show deep concern about this strange new mystery. Indeed, by 1989 known CIA/MI6 agents had started to infiltrate the crop circle research fraternity in response to the high-level concerns. At the same time MI5 started to monitor the situation seriously from the 'home front' point of view. In 1990 the British Home Office gave the go-ahead for a full-scale disinformation and debunking campaign to be executed via Britain's Security Service (MI5) and implemented via television and the tabloid media. Crop circle hostilities had begun.

Following a series of emergency meetings at a very high level within both the Ministry of Defence and the Home Office, certain 'Fleet Street' editors and journalists in the pay of British (and US) intelligence agencies were 'encouraged' to disseminate stories designed to debunk the phenomenon. Perhaps their most famous – and certainly their most effective

– propaganda exercise in this respect involved the story of how two elderly gentlemen from Southampton known affectionately as 'Doug and Dave' had been responsible for making all the crop circles – more than a thousand of them in one summer alone! – and that therefore the entire phenomenon was a man-made hoax. Doug Bower and Dave Chorley became famous overnight, and considerably richer. It is reported that they were paid £10,000 for their story (a significant amount when one considers the sum that mysteriously 'appeared' in George Vernon's bank account, also £10,000: see Document 06). As a result of this manoeuvre serious crop circle research was irreversibly damaged.

While the MI5-contracted media was busy debunking the phenomenon, CIA/MI6 agents were busy collating information from within the crop circle research community and passing it back to their employers. These agents were also under directive to carry out their own disinformation and debunking schedules. In the summer of 1989, for example, one CIA agent offered Colin Andrews an open-ended 'Swiss bank account'; in return for this lavish offer, Mr Andrews was told that he would have to appear on national television and publicly discredit the phenomenon (see File 28). He refused. Another instance involved a different agent (name on file) who attempted to gain access to several personal files – including Mr Andrews's much sought-after crop circle database – again without success. In response to these setbacks the agency stepped up its operation.

During the years to follow at least four known CIA agents assigned to the 'Aviary' cell (see Document 03, File 13) were fully employed within the crop circle research arena (all names on file). Other field agents have since replaced certain of the original agents who, having been 'rumbled', so to speak, were withdrawn and reassigned (although one of these agents has recently turned up again – she was seen to grace the stage at a crop circle conference in July 1997 – while another now lives in London under the guise of being a freelance science and technology journalist: both names on file). It should be made clear that, as well as the CIA/MI6 and MI5 vanguard, Britain's Defence Intelligence Staff (DIS) and in particular the government's Directorate of Scientific Intelligence (DScI) also played a major role in the infiltration programme – a kind of secret service pincer movement designed to force an entry through front and back doors simultaneously. It worked. DI55 and DI61 are thought to have been the two primary defence intelligence offices involved.

The military, too, were to become an intrinsic part of the phenomenon. For one thing, many crop circles were appearing on military land (mainly in Wiltshire and Hampshire), most of which were either cordoned-off or burnt – often both – by special units assigned to the task. And for another (as detailed in Document 06: 'Operation Blackbird') military chiefs had received directives via MoD channels to find out what could be causing the patterns to appear. While many sceptics suspected that the military were all along responsible for making those crop circles that had not been made by civilian hoaxers, high-ranking military chiefs were scratching their heads in disbelief as, first one and then the next, the patterns continued to invade some of the most secure military-owned lands in Britain.

But it wasn't only the military-owned land that received the special attention of both the Army and the RAF; before too long, wherever crop circles seemed to be appearing most regularly (Alton Barnes in Wiltshire, for example) the military became equally regular visitors. To add to this, many researchers started to report instances of rather severe military harassment whilst they were out in the fields studying the circles. Indeed, perhaps frustrated by their own shortcomings in endeavouring to find answers, by the mid-1990s military units were employing some pretty heavy-handed tactics, especially when the small 'ball-of-light' UFOs began to be seen and filmed in the fields where crop circles regularly appeared. As detailed in the following Case Report, UFOs and crop circles appearing in the same place at the same time was more than the military could tolerate.

File 27: Appendix 01
Case Report: Cosmic Top-X29 Eyes Only
The Military Menace

On 21st July 1994, Colin Andrews was showing a group of eight US-based researchers around some of the most familiar crop circle fields in England. Among this group was a US government scientist who, for security reasons, must remain anonymous. We will call him 'Dr Richard'.

At around midday Mr Andrews and his guests arrived at what is probably the best-known and most prolific crop circle field in the country, the well-known East Field at Alton Barnes in Wiltshire. Having parked up on a hill overlooking both the Vale of Pewsey and the East Field, the team climbed out of the minibus and was straight away confronted by a military helicopter droning overhead. Immediately following this a second helicopter – an Army Gazelle – 'swooped in from the west and started hovering directly in front of us at about sixty to seventy feet in the air'. Still inside the minibus, 'Dr Richard' started to film the incident with his camcorder, while the rest of the team began taking photographs of the helicopters and their occupants. Indeed, as Mr Andrews told me: 'At

Jon King

this point the helicopter was so close to us that we could see the uniformed occupants filming us.'

Mr Andrews takes up the story.

'The craft was bristling with hi-tech equipment – aerials and pods of all kinds. It inched ever closer to us and flew over our vehicle (which was still parked on the public roadway) clearing the roof by no more than forty feet. It then took up position on the opposite side of the road and hovered very close to the hill beside us, a hill called Adam's Grave. The rotor blades were missing the side of the hill by no more than two metres, and the downwash was causing both the vehicle and the hedgerow to bounce around wildly. The scene began to resemble a James Bond movie!

'For several more minutes the helicopter hovered there in front of us, with "Dr Richard" still filming the whole thing from inside the minibus. For some reason the helicopter pilot deemed it necessary to keep an eye on us, even though we were parked on a public highway and doing nothing untoward. This was beginning to look like harassment. It was by now apparent that we were not welcome in Alton Barnes!

'Eventually the helicopter moved off and we thought that perhaps their interest in us was over. We were wrong. Because immediately another helicopter, a Lynx, roared in from the same direction as the first, nosediving in a very dramatic attack fashion as it approached us. It hovered around us for several minutes before performing a long, low manoeuvre across the surface of the wheat field directly below us, narrowly missing another researcher, Steve Alexander, who was carrying his pole and camera into the field. Indeed, Mr Alexander told us he literally had to "duck down" in order to avoid the helicopter blades giving him a short back and sides! We could scarcely believe what we were seeing.

'I have to say that this was unlike any military activity

I had previously witnessed in the area, and I had spent my whole life here, or hereabouts. This area borders the military training ground of Salisbury Plain – it has many military establishments and thousands of acres which are out of bounds to the public. If this was some kind of military training exercise then why were they doing it over public land? Under normal circumstances the military would not dare to dive-bomb the public in this way – it would surely provoke an uproar from the local residents. So what were these Army helicopters doing at Alton Barnes? And moreover, why were they so interested in us?'

It was at this point that the drama suddenly deepened. Mr Andrews explained:

'Camcorder still in hand, "Dr Richard" climbed out of the minibus and suddenly cried out: "What's that over there? *There!* That white object flashing over by the helicopter?" A second or two later we all realized why the military had been so keen to frighten us away from the area.

' "Dr Richard" filmed the second helicopter as it flew away from us and over the large crop formation [in the East Field below] to the far side of the field. As it flew between Woodborough Hill and the crop formation a small white flashing object could be seen hovering just below the top of the wheat. As the helicopter cautiously approached the object remained stationary, but continued to flash pulses of white light. When the helicopter came within about twenty metres of the flashing object it too came to a standstill, its nose towards the object and hovering only a few feet off the ground. For some moments the object remained stationary, just above the ground, and looked very similar – if not identical – to the object filmed by Steve Alexander below Milk Hill in July, 1990. Milk Hill is less than half a mile from the East Field, to the west. Indeed, it is worth pointing out that many small balls of light have been witnessed here – and some filmed – during the last decade or so. It has to be said that it seemed by their menacing tactics that the military were fully aware of this fact.

'Suddenly the object moved. So far as the eye could tell it simply disappeared from the spot where it had been pulsing and flashing and simultaneously reappeared about twenty metres away, and was now stationed to the rear of the helicopter. Seemingly surprised by this "impossible" manoeuvre the helicopter pilot appeared to become confused, and started to rotate his aircraft, as if trying to turn around to face the opposite direction where the object was now pulsing. But then he seemed to change his mind and instead reversed back over the object until it was again pulsing in front of him.

'This manoeuvre gave a good indication of how close to the ground the object was. The helicopter had moved cautiously back over it – the helicopter itself was no more than thirty or forty feet above the field. Another important point is that the object remained completely stationary as the helicopter reversed over it, proving that the light was *not* the reflection of the helicopter's underside anti-collision light. On the contrary, it must have been some form of independent phenomenon.

'Next, as suddenly as all this had begun, it ended. As "Dr Richard" continued to film this incredible event the object suddenly disappeared again, this time, it seemed, for good. We did not see the object again. Seconds later the two Army helicopters flew away and we did not see *them* again, either. It became very evident to us that the helicopters had been called out specifically to monitor the object, whatever it was.'

Having first gained permission from Tim Carson (the farmer who owned the field) Mr Andrews and his team then decided to drive down to where the object had been, but found no trace of either the object itself or anything that could otherwise have caused the illusion of an object having been there. Although a hundred or so metres away they discovered some white plastic containers and bags hanging from fence stakes (used as bird scares) it seemed unlikely that any of these could have been responsible for either the manoeuvres performed by the object or, indeed, for provoking such a military show of strength.

As Mr Andrews told me: 'We could not begin to imagine how any of the bird-scare objects could have reflected and pulsed and manoeuvred in the same manner as the small ball of light.'

And further: 'None of the bird-scare objects were flying loose from their stakes.' Remember, the nearest of the bird scares was at least 100 metres from where the object had been.

I should add that I have seen the video footage shot by 'Dr Richard' and, as Mr Andrews said, the object can be clearly seen to 'disappear' from one place and simultaneously 'reappear' somewhere else. A typical UFO manoeuvre. The highly dangerous and alarming – not to mention *illegal* – manoeuvres of the helicopters can also be clearly seen on the video footage.

File 27: Appendix 02
Case Investigation:
Cosmic Top-X30 Eyes Only
British Land Forces HQ

For security reasons, 'Dr Richard' did not want his name associated with the ensuing debate, so Colin Andrews agreed to handle any interest subsequently shown in the footage. (Indeed, Mr Andrews has shown this footage many times at his lectures, and it has also been shown on the US TV series *Sightings*.)

In an effort to gain answers Mr Andrews also sent a copy of the videotape to Major General Vyvyan, Chief of Staff at the British Land Forces HQ, Erskine Barracks, Wilton, Salisbury, together with a request for an explanation as to the presence of the ball of light and why the helicopter pilots had acted in such a belligerent manner towards himself and his team of researchers. Some time later he received the following reply.

Dear Mr Andrews,
RE: HELICOPTER ACTIVITY
21 JULY 1994
Thank you for your letter of 15 September . . . I do hope you do not mind me replying on Major General Vyvyan's behalf, but as he is on leave at present, I [Major WN Aldridge MBE RRF, Military Assistant to Chief of Staff] thought it best to reply as soon as possible.

I apologise for any delay in replying but the Aviation Branch in the Headquarters here has been trying, unfortunately without success, to positively identify the helicopters involved. Without visibility or knowledge of the aircraft's tail numbers it is not possible to identify individual aircraft . . . [Really? On the video the helicopters are so close they fill the screen — indeed, one can all but read the pilot's name tag, never mind the aircraft's registration number.]

The Lynx and Gazelle featured in your video

were, however, almost certainly from the School of Army Aviation at Middle Wallop . . . [Interesting, then, that they were not displaying the School's colours like every other 'training aircraft' based there — one wonders if Major Aldridge is aware that it is illegal to train pilots from the School of Army Aviation at Middle Wallop in unmarked, 'camouflage' helicopters.]

. . . At the time the aircraft would have been flown by highly qualified Helicopter Instructors from the School and commanded by student Aircraft Commanders . . . the students would have been practising drills for conducting reconnaissance patrols against a well-equipped enemy — tactics that require the close use of ground and vegetation cover; hence the low-flying . . . [Though this area is indeed officially designated a 'low-flying area', according to one RAF helicopter pilot who has also seen the video footage, the type of 'low flying' undertaken in this incident — and clearly demonstrated on the video footage — is only permitted for 'specific purposes' (which do not include training) and only if the area has been 'sealed off from the public', which of course it had not been — indeed, this same RAF helicopter pilot, after viewing the footage with some dismay, confirmed that the helicopters' manoeuvres were certainly 'not indicative of a training exercise'.]

. . . With regard to the possibility of harassment: as stated above the aircraft were being piloted by highly trained and experienced instructors, and they were using the Alton Barnes area as it was free of major obstacles . . . [You mean like . . . PEOPLE?]

. . . I have been assured that a study of the video footage indicates that the aircraft were being operated safely . . . [Not according to the fully qualified RAF helicopter pilot who viewed the footage on my behalf.]

. . . Army helicopter pilots are trained to fly at low level and, whilst hovering or moving slowly, a separation of 2 metres between the rotor blade tips and a slope is quite acceptable . . . [To whom?]

. . . I have also been assured that a Gazelle hovering 70 feet away from a vehicle parked on a public road is similarly not a dangerous activity . . . [No? Pretty damned intimidating, all the same.]

. . . If indeed undue attention was being paid to you and your party I can only assume that it was as a result of natural interest generated by your own filming activities . . . ['Filming activities' were only initiated after one of the helicopters virtually landed on civilian heads!]

. . . You also ask about a flashing light on the ground. No helicopter instructors or student commanders reported seeing any unusual pulsing light on that (or any other) date . . . [Even though one of the helicopter pilots was caught on video chasing it?]

. . . A close study of the video indicates that the 'pulsing light' is almost certainly the reflection of the anti-collision stroboscopic light mounted on the underside of the aircraft.

A similar light is also fitted to the top of each aircraft and is synchronised to flash alternately with the other. As the flashing light on the ground is only apparent when the upper aircraft anti-collision light is off (and therefore the lower one is on) the conclusion drawn here is that it is the chance reflection of the lower anti-collision light from a reflective object lying on the ground — such as a piece of flint, metal or glass (or even water). This assumption is supported by the fact that the pulsing light on the ground disappears when the aircraft moves away . . .

[On the contrary, this assumption is supported by nothing more than the above battery of rhetorical hogwash. Firstly, the 'flashing light on the ground' is *not* 'only apparent when the upper aircraft anti-collision light is off'; it is apparent at seemingly random, intermittent intervals (the intervals between each pulse of light are not at all consistent with those between the helicopter's upper and lower anti-collision lights). And secondly, the video clearly shows the pulsing light to be evident even when the helicopter is a good distance away from it. Indeed, at one point the helicopter reverses a full fifty metres or more over the object while the object remains stationary — how then can it be deemed 'the reflection of the helicopter's anti-collision light'? And by the way, it is absolutely untrue to say that the 'pulsing light on the ground disappears when the aircraft moves away'. Anyone bothering to view the footage themself would see that the

helicopter in question remains in station until
the object disappears, both from sight and — probably — from the military's radar screens, too.]
  . . . I do hope that this information helps to
answer your queries. Please do not hesitate to get
in touch should you need any further assistance.
  Yours sincerely,
  WN Aldridge.

Major Aldridge could indeed have been of further assistance
– he could have retracted the above attempt at a fob-off
and urged his senior officer, Major General Vyvyan, Chief
of Staff, to initiate an immediate, thorough and open inquiry
into this incident. Anything short of this would only serve to
demonstrate the unwillingness of the military to enter into
a public debate about the extreme levels of paranoia and
secrecy surrounding the British government's involvement
with UFO and crop circle phenomena. Indeed, failure to enter
into such a debate would surely only serve to galvanize
public opinion further towards demanding the truth.
  And rightly so.

File 28
Colin Andrews

When I first met Colin Andrews he was still working as an
electrical engineer for local government (Test Valley Borough
Council, Hampshire, England) and had just begun work on
his excellent crop circle video documentary, *Undeniable
Evidence*. The year was 1990 and Colin was riding high
on a wave that promised much: crop circles falling from
the sky like prophetic rain; TV and radio interviews every

other day; a bestselling book that sold in excess of three hundred thousand copies worldwide, enough in itself that he was soon able to give up his job and dedicate himself full-time to researching the crop circle phenomenon. Then came the MI5-orchestrated 'Doug and Dave' debunk campaign. The wave lost its momentum. The world to which Colin had dedicated himself suddenly began to crumble.

Since those heady days Colin has pursued his endeavours as the world's leading crop circle researcher with some tenacity. In the face of jealousy, ridicule and derision aimed at him by many of his so-called 'peers' he has doggedly – and often painfully – stuck to his task, and today still remains the leading figure in the field of crop circle research. However, the fact that he *is* the leading figure has provoked its own comebacks.

For instance, since 1989 Colin has been consistently hounded, intimidated and often threatened by British and US intelligence agencies. So much so that, at one point, he was offered an undisclosed sum of money by the CIA, a 'Swiss bank account' that would have set him up for life. In return he was to denounce publicly the crop circle phenomenon as a hoax. True to his character, he refused. The intimidation of him and the close scrutiny of his work by the intelligence community continues to this day.

I recently spoke to Colin at his new home in Connecticut, USA. What follows is a verbatim transcript of our conversation.

File 28: Appendix 01 Part 1
Case Profile: Cosmic Top-X31 Eyes Only
The Government Hoax Campaign

JK: Colin, how did an electrical engineer become embroiled in the crop circle phenomenon?

CA: Oh, I just couldn't resist it! I'd entered local government in 1974 as an electrical engineer and, following a series of very rapid promotions, I became a senior officer at the Test Valley Borough Council. It was during that period – in July 1983 – when I was driving along a major highway near Winchester, that I saw my first crop circle. In fact it was a 'quintuplet' set of five circles. Together they formed a major pattern in a wheat field at Cheesefoot Head.

JK: And the attraction was instant?

CA: Yes, very much so. I returned that evening with my camera and took the first photograph I'd ever taken of the phenomenon. Having looked very closely at the ground features, the first thing that impressed me was the absolute symmetry, the precision of the formation, and the total lack of damage to the wheat – you know, I couldn't see any tracks or footprints leading in or out of the field. In those days a lot of the formations were like that. Sometimes circles would appear between the tramlines made by the tractors, and there would be absolutely no tracks leading to or from the patterns. This one at Cheesefoot Head was like that. It was very impressive. And it really called for the engineer inside me to fathom how this could possibly have happened.

JK: So how did you set about achieving that?

CA: Over the following days I returned several times to the same area, making contact with the farmers and landowners, and as a result became further impressed with what was happening there. You see, the locals and the farmers were not only telling me that, yes, they had seen the patterns on their land, and that they had been seeing them for a number of years, but they also told me how their fathers before them had also seen the patterns, and that they had been arriving on their land for thirty years or more. Indeed, records of crop circles go back many, many decades. This is not a new phenomenon. Although, I should say, it has certainly evolved very rapidly over the last few years.

JK: What other enquiries did you make?

CA: Well, for one thing I got in touch with the Ministry of Defence, the Army Air Corps at Middle Wallop, and made enquiries there. I also made enquiries with the local police at Winchester and Andover, and it seemed that the phenomenon was clearly known about in those areas.

After this I sought out two other people who had commenced their own research about a year earlier – Pat Delgado and Terence Meaden – and the three of us began meeting regularly. We began working as a team, informing each other of events in our own immediate vicinities and cross-referencing our findings. In 1985 Busty Taylor became involved, and then there were four of us. And that's how it all got started.

JK: There must have been any number of theories in those days – theories about how the patterns were being formed.

CA: Absolutely. Of course, it's a whole lot easier now, looking back over a decade and more of researching the phenomenon, with so many possible causes eliminated from the equation. Nowadays the probable causes consist of maybe half a dozen, no more. That's all we're left with after years of eliminating other possibilities, like whirlwinds, hedgehogs and Doug and Dave.

JK: Nice analogy.

CA: I thought so, yes!

JK: OK, Colin. Seeing as you brought the subject up, what about Doug and Dave? Did they hoax the whole thing as they claimed?

CA: I'll tell you something about Doug and Dave. Firstly, what helped to carry me through the whole Doug and Dave episode was that I knew there were at least a handful of patterns they simply could not have made. In those days – and still today – certain patterns arrived that defied the laws of physics as we understand them. One of those patterns became extremely important to me personally.

I don't understand quite how this works, but I have certainly come to believe that there is an intelligence involved in the making of the crop circle patterns, and that there has been an element of interaction with that intelligence. I know that you have had a similar experience, Jon, and I know that others have also. For me it happened like this.

I had reached the end of my tether in terms of researching something that seemed to be giving up few, if any, solutions. In fact I was almost ready to pack the whole thing in and get back to my normal, fairly comfortable life, when something occurred that has kept me on the case ever since.

One night whilst lying in my bed I wished – almost prayed – for a sign that would take my research at least one step further towards solving the mystery. At this point I was convinced that an intelligence was involved, an intelligence we don't yet understand. With this in mind I visualized a pattern – a Celtic Cross – and I asked, you know, I asked, at a deep level inside me: could this pattern be reproduced, and for convenience sake, could it please arrive close to my home?!

Well, you know, we'd been given the runaround for so long, chasing patterns all over central and southern England. I just thought, well, you know, just for once, *you come to me instead!*

Anyway, the next morning I received a phone call from a local farmer, telling me that he had discovered a new formation next to the double-ringed formation I'd been looking at the night before. When I arrived to investigate the new arrival I could hardly believe my eyes. For one thing it was indeed a Celtic Cross formation, the very pattern I had asked for the previous night. It was the first time ever the phenomenon had produced something of that nature. And secondly, it had arrived in the crop field closest to my home! I was completely overwhelmed. I vowed there and then that nothing would ever convince me that this was a hoax phenomenon, not even Doug and Dave.

JK: Speaking of whom . . .

CA: Yes, quite. Well, now you see why I could never believe that those two had made *all* the crop circles. I never believed that anyway. But now I had gained, at least for myself, proof. As others began to 'fall' around me, succumbing to the whole hoax situation, I became more and more resolute about the phenomenon, largely of course because of my personal experience, of somehow being involved, in some mysterious, interactive sense, with the formation of the Celtic Cross pattern. So when I was confronted by a reporter from the *Today* newspaper who told me about the claims of Doug and Dave, I was ready to challenge them publicly. Especially as one of the claims made by them was that they had made *that* pattern – the Celtic Cross. Indeed, they made this claim to the *Today* newspaper. Apart from the fact that, speaking from a research point of view, this particular pattern was very unusual – in that the lay of the crop was at right angles to the circumference, and included other anomalies which have never been found in man-made circles – I of course was convinced that neither Doug nor Dave could possibly have made this pattern.

So I challenged the two of them to tell me how they had made this pattern. I didn't say anything about what

I'd discovered concerning the unusual floor-lay, nor indeed about my experience. I simply said: 'How did you make that? How *did* you make *that*?' [. . .] They'd been with the *Today* newspaper for a week before our meeting – the paper had already published their claims. The story had hit the headlines on the previous Monday morning, and as anybody in the media knows, if you really want a story to hit, then publish it on a Monday morning. So far as the media is concerned the world goes to sleep on the weekend. So if you can conjure up a story for Monday morning then you know you've got a story that is likely to capture public imagination. This is what people in the business have always told me. It was all so perfectly timed, and of course, the story went worldwide. I don't think there was a television or radio station that didn't cover it. Somebody wanted this story out there. And they made sure they succeeded. We had worked for years trying to encourage serious scientific investigation, and that *one* day, that *one* story, set our programme back many years. It has never fully recovered.

Soon afterwards people started saying things to me like, well, you know, Colin, at least Doug and Dave have spread knowledge of the crop circles abroad; you know, at least they've managed to reach people who otherwise would not have heard about it. Well, that may be true. But they heard about it in a way that made them, from then on, think about the phenomenon as a hoax.[. . .]

JK: Do you think it was all planned from the outset?

CA: There's no doubt in my mind about that. This was one of the – well, I should be careful here – in my opinion this was *possibly* one of the best executed [. . .] planned disinformation programmes, of modern times.

JK: My own information on the dissemination of the Doug and Dave story is that it was indeed a premeditated propaganda exercise perpetrated by the British and US governments and executed via their respective intelligence agencies. Do you agree?

CA: Yes, I do. Indeed, there are three significant events that I can think of right now which have probably been the result of some sort of government planning or involvement.

Firstly, of course, there was 'Operation Blackbird'.

JK: Can you say something about that?

CA: Well, it was a very sophisticated, well-planned, and extremely expensive surveillance operation, the largest of its kind anywhere, whereby we cordoned off acres of land and set up a whole collection of cameras and equipment in order to see if we could catch a crop circle being formed on film. We had more than a million pounds' worth of hi-tech equipment there, some of it on loan, some of it provided by the British Army, some of it paid for by the BBC and Nippon Television [Japan]. It was a highly sophisticated operation set up in conjunction with the media and – in the event – the military, too. It was planned to go on for ten days.

JK: The military were involved?

CA: It turned out that way, yes. Although I don't want to name names, I can say that within the first twenty-four hours – and remember we were on MoD land – two Army officers turned up and volunteered the technical assistance of the British Army. We were asked to leave the site for a confidential meeting with them, which took place in my car. We were offered the assistance of military personnel and equipment, but only if we would collaborate with them. As far as Operation Blackbird is concerned, on the second day, with a huge media presence – I mean, it really was the Fleet Street Circus at its height; even people in the business said that only the Royal Family had pulled more cameras and hype than this; thirty-two major national and international networks were there, bouncing their stories off satellites and beaming them all around the world – we all felt that something had to happen.

And of course, it did. A hoax appeared. I then had to go on live television and tell the world that a triangular UFO had been seen over the field where the hoax had appeared, and that in my opinion, the formation was genuine. Indeed, I was pulled out of my bed to do this! I was really made to look a fool in front of the world.

But what, in retrospect, is so blatantly obvious to me now that the whole thing had been a set-up was this.

In my car, on my way to the scene, I made five telephone calls, which were private calls – no one knew about these calls. I was alone in my car, on a radio telephone. When I got to the site I made an announcement based on what I was told – it was pitch-black; I could see nothing, but I was put under immense pressure to make the announcement. The next day it became very obvious that we'd been set up. The world's media heard me say that we'd had an event – there was a crop formation in the field, UFOs had been seen, we'd got it all on film: we'd had an event!

However, as soon as daylight came I saw that the formation was clearly a hoax. I remember thinking at the time: 'Somebody has set this whole thing up; somebody has infiltrated our operation and knows the technical parameters of the equipment so well that in front of at least twelve infrared and low-light cameras they've managed to execute a major hoax.' The making of this hoax was not captured on film – at least not officially – because it had been made just beyond the design criteria of the equipment installed. Whoever hoaxed that formation knew the equipment inside out – somebody had a very good inside knowledge of what was there.

JK: And you think the British Army or Intelligence may have been behind it?

CA: Well . . . I have to be careful here . . . but two army personnel *had* arrived the day before, as I've said, and had offered their assistance in return for my . . . *cooperation*, shall we say. To add to this, another person – again, I have to be careful here – a person who entered the research arena on that very day, the first day of Operation Blackbird (a person who has since gained an international tag, someone who is well known in the research fraternity) also arrived. And so far as I'm aware, the arrival of this person was the first step in the intelligence community's infiltration of the crop circle research arena.

So this was the first indication to me that 'someone' was very keen to find out about this phenomenon. The military were there. The world's media were there. And also, of course, the government were there, represented by this person, whose name I dare not reveal publicly.

Then came Doug and Dave, and phase two of the disinformation programme got under way.

JK: So why do you think the government would have wanted to infiltrate a research programme which most of the world sees as cranky anyway?

CA: What we have to understand, Jon, is this. The reason the crop circle phenomenon *is* considered cranky, is *because* of the government's carefully executed hoax and disinformation programme. They have deliberately made it seem that way. My personal view is that, even if they knew the cause of the phenomenon, they did not want this information to be shared with or leaked out to the public. I think that somebody – whoever the people are who really run governments, and it certainly isn't who we elect as our representatives – these people feel that we have to be

Jon King

controlled, like children. And I think they are afraid that this, ultimately, by sensing the nature of the mechanism, would lead us to question even such institutions as religion, things that stabilize society so that they can continue to control society. And once you start sniffing in that area, it's highly dangerous to them, to their control.

JK: So you think the Doug and Dave situation was a continuation of that policy?

CA: Yeah, I do. But I'll tell you what, Jon, I think the Doug and Dave thing can be looked at in two parts. One: I think that they could well be two innocent, elderly men who were friends with one another, who'd had a dabble and *did* make *some* crop circles – purely for fun or whatever – and then decided to approach the daily press, off their own backs, make a few bucks. Indeed, they earned around ten thousand pounds for their story. This I find quite possible.

JK: That's a lot of money for a crop circle hoax story.

CA: Yes, it is. But according to my media sources, the *Today* newspaper paid them two large instalments – five thousand and five thousand. Indeed, Doug and Dave threatened to sue for their second payment. They'd had five thousand up front, but the second five thousand, for some reason, didn't come. So they threatened to sue. But they got the full amount in the end.

The second option is that they were used by the British intelligence agencies (although I should point out that Doug and Dave themselves are not, I'm sure, employed by British Intelligence – they're simply not the calibre of the people we're looking at). But they could nevertheless have been used by them. Indeed, the way in which the whole thing was worked supports this probability. For one thing, the intelligence communities in all major countries – certainly in Britain and America – have very good relations with the major editors. Some of these people are paid. The PR people in the intelligence agencies cooperate with them so that they can get the leads on political developments. This information comes through collaboration, cooperation. And once you buy into the major editors, the national newspapers, you've got your stage. I think myself that once Doug and Dave came forward – and I think this is what probably happened – having perhaps been responsible for one or two simple hoaxes in their area, they were then unwittingly used by the intelligence machine to front the government's hoax campaign. Indeed, Doug and Dave themselves may never know that they were used in this way. But what perfect stooges they made! Two old men, sixty-five or thereabouts – if *they* could make crop circles then *anybody* could. It was the perfect plan, very clever.

JK: You said that you thought there were three main phases in the way the disinformation programme unfolded. Operation Blackbird, Doug and Dave . . .

CA: Right. The third phase came along in the guise of someone we both know, Jon (and I'm prepared to go into print on this; they can threaten whatever they like). This person's name was [name deleted by publisher for legal reasons].

[Name deleted], working for the agency who had already put several nails firmly in the coffin of the crop circle phenomenon, arrived on the scene in order to hammer those nails home. They needed to keep the momentum going, and that momentum came in the form of [name deleted], working for the CIA – and that is absolutely fact; I have gleaned information on this man from within the CIA and from people who knew him because he worked on the desk next to them. He'd arrived in Great Britain posing as an American freelance journalist, that was the cover story. *Crap!* [Name deleted] had come to do a job, and he did it very effectively. He came between people, interviewed people, put wedges between fellow researchers [identifying detail deleted by publisher for legal reasons] and all the rest of the stuff. And here's the evidence if you ever needed it.

The five phone calls I made in my car, privately, the ones nobody knew about – [name and identifying detail deleted by publisher for legal reasons] the contents of those five phone calls, and the names of the people I had phoned! How did he know? How could he possibly have known? It was obviously inside information. My phone had been tapped.

And if you want to go even further on this one – and this was clearly overlooked by British Intelligence – I happened to be the guy who signed the invoices, sanctioning payment of the communication system for Test Valley Borough Council. A ten-thousand-to-one chance, but it was nevertheless true. These invoices, of course, included my own radio telephone.

Now, I noticed that throughout the period that covered Operation Blackbird the invoice for my radio telephone simply wasn't there. It seemed, for this period of time, that Test Valley Borough Council were getting my radio telephone calls for free! Very strange. But then, some weeks later, when the invoice finally did arrive in the system, the calls I'd made from my vehicle had been deducted from the bill and stamped by the British government! That phone was bugged! It was taken into a special monitoring system during Operation Blackbird because, for the duration of the operation, in order for them to make that hoax without my knowledge, my movements, my *every* movement, had to be precisely known by them.

And the information they eavesdropped was given to [name deleted] of the CIA.

These, then, are the three major attempts that I know of, made by the intelligence agencies of both Britain and America to debunk and discredit the crop circle phenomenon. There is no doubt in my mind about this.

File 28: Appendix 01 Part 2
Case Profile: Cosmic Top-X32 Eyes Only
The CIA and the Crop Circles

JK: So, Colin. Can you think of any other instances where government agents have become involved in the crop circles research programme?

CA: Yes, yes, I can. One instance in particular comes to mind.

A man who announced himself as working for the CIA back in, I think, June or July of 1989, approached me and said he had been assigned to 'bring me into a plan', or more precisely, '*buy* me into a plan'. He said this was the sole reason he'd come to England – that his assignment was to implement and execute this plan in which I was to be involved.

JK: And did he tell you what this plan was?

CA: He did, yes. He told me that certain individuals, all of whom you know, Jon – Richard Andrews, Terence Meaden, Pat Delgado, to name a few – he told me that the CIA were about to promote each major researcher in turn and then publicly debunk them. He said this was a ploy that was frequently used. He said they would give them a stage, encourage them to declare their hand and, one by one, take them out. He said that I would then be left with a 'role' that he later revealed to me.

JK: How did this man make his approach? How did he contact you?

CA: Well, when he first arrived, Pat and I were asked to go up to Pebble Mill television studios in Birmingham to take part in a programme called *Daytime Live*. It was a kind of live TV debate situation. They were going to air the sequence that contained the mysterious sound detected in a crop formation and recorded by the BBC – the sound that destroyed a hundred thousand pounds' worth of TV camera one sunny afternoon at a crop circle site in Wiltshire! As we came on air, they were running this particular sequence.

Anyway, on the morning of the programme we were in our hotel, and we received a phone call from David Morgenstern of the BBC who said that they had received some communication from a man who claimed he had actually seen a crop circle being formed, and what questions should they ask that would allow them to know if he was telling the truth? So we gave them some questions that we thought would be helpful. When we arrived at the studios we were told that this man had been flown directly in to Birmingham and that we would not be able to meet him because they wanted it to be an absolutely first-time contact on air. As we came on air they panned to the studio audience, and this man described what he'd seen, live on TV.

JK: What exactly did he say?

CA: That he'd been out studying foxes in Scotland, and that one of the foxes on this particular night had refused to follow its regular path which, he explained, was not consistent with the usual behaviour of foxes. I don't know if this is right or not, but it sounded plausible. The fox apparently refused to go any further and instead went back the way it had come. The man then apparently heard some rustling, and then he described the way this circle formed. What he was saying is that the fox had presumably sensed something strange and that after it had scampered off he witnessed the formation of this circle. But the point is that his live TV appearance seemed to legitimize him.

JK: You think this was his way of becoming accepted on the crop circle scene?

CA: Right. From that moment on his being seen in the presence of the crop circle researchers – myself and Pat in particular – became acceptable. It was his 'way in', so to speak.

JK: So what happened next?

CA: Well, some weeks later there was a rap on my door, and when I answered it I immediately recognized the man standing there. It was the 'fox-study' man. He said that he'd come to tell me something . . . he wanted me to get Pat Delgado over to my place because he wanted to talk to both of us.

Pat lived about seventeen miles away. It was late at night but I phoned him and he agreed to come over. When he arrived the man spent all evening into the early hours with both of us, asking question after question. He appeared to be comparing the answers I gave against those that Pat gave. Well, perhaps not surprisingly, Pat eventually grew more and more frustrated, and said to the man: 'Look, exactly what have you come to tell us?' But the man just shook his head, as if to say: 'I'm not ready to tell you yet.' So Pat just stood up and said something like: 'Well, I've got better things to do with my time,' and headed out the door and went home. He was very angry.

The guy accompanied me to the door to see Pat out (I didn't know whether he was going to leave as well – I was rather hoping he would, because I was pretty bloody angry about it, too) but as Pat left and I closed the door the man just spun round on me and said: 'Get your jacket on. I want to tell you something.'

So against my better judgment I went through into the front room and told my wife I was popping out for a few minutes (I wanted to tell her so she didn't become worried). We then went out.

JK: Where did you go at that time of night?

CA: We wandered down towards Andover town centre, then back up Salisbury Road, back and forth, back and forth, questions and more questions, most of a fairly general nature, but none of the questions were about me. Rather they were to do with things like, you know: *Where were the circles? Who were we in touch with? What did we know, particularly about the Russians?* That kind of thing. He was asking every question you could possibly think of that an intelligence agent would probably ask. But the conversation wasn't going anywhere at all. As for myself I was furious, but I didn't quite have the courage to walk away.

JK: But presumably at some point he told you what it was he'd come to tell you?

CA: Yes. When we eventually started to walk back towards my home he stopped on the pavement and said: 'You are now one of us.'

So I said: 'What do you mean by that?'

He said, simply: 'CIA.'

When I asked him for ID he just laughed and said: 'You really think a CIA agent would carry identification?' And then he laughed again.

He told me I would never see his boss, and that he never saw his boss's boss. He said that was the way it worked. He said that from here on in I was 'one of them'. He gave me no say in the matter whatever. He never asked me if I wanted to be associated with the CIA – he just told me that from then on I was to consider myself one of them.

Following this he named a lot of people – most of whom were my colleagues in crop circle research – who were to be eliminated from the research programme (he did not mean that they were to be be killed or anything quite like that, but they were nevertheless to be taken off the stage, so to speak). And they have been. I have watched the process in operation for some years now – a process he openly told me about on that night. And every name he named that night has since been 'got at', and everything that he said *would* happen *has* happened.

JK: Could you give us an example?

CA: Well, for instance, the following year Terence Meaden was never out of the newspapers. Nobody else could get a look in. This is exactly what he told me would happen. But where is Terence Meaden now? Who knows what Terence Meaden's latest ideas are? Answer: no one. Because, presumably, his stage has been taken from him – he's been 'taken out'. Pat Delgado was next, and we all know what happened to him.

[Author's note: sadly, Pat Delgado was so taken in by the 'Doug And Dave' episode, and so distraught because of it, that he retired from crop circle research soon thereafter.]

JK: Do you think there was a reason why you weren't 'taken out', too? Did this man indicate why you should be singled out from the rest?

CA: He did, yes. The CIA guy told me that, so far as they were concerned, I seemed to have a particular affinity and contact with the public. 'You have a way,' is what he said. 'The public identify with you.'

JK: And at the time, of course, you were getting a lot of media coverage.

CA: Yes, I was. There were really only two people in those days, Pat and myself. We'd written a book and it had sold a lot of copies. We were getting a lot of TV and radio coverage. But a decision seemed to be made that night that I was the one. I mean, if you look at it logically, it could have been either one of us. So this man must have been in a position to make a decision. He must have carried some authority within his agency.

JK: Right.

CA: So he chose *me* to go with this 'role' . . .

JK: And what was this 'role'?

CA: Once they had taken these other researchers out of the frame, so to speak, they wanted me to do something for them. He said I was to carry on being Colin Andrews, researching the phenomenon, just doing my thing, and at some point in the near future I would be asked to do one interview which would enjoy maximum, saturated media coverage. During the course of this interview I was to make one statement, and one statement only.

They wanted me to state publicly that the crop circle phenomenon was a hoax. When we got back to my home he said that he would show me how to say it and what to say. In return for this I was offered a bank account in Switzerland, in which would be enough money that I would never need to even think about money ever again. On top of this he said that they were in possession of some kind of 'instrument' which they would send to me within two weeks. He said that this instrument would allow me to identify immediately a real crop circle from a hoax – something that, presumably, could measure some or other microwave residue, or some other residual effect. He told me: 'You will then be in a privileged position, and we will put you right out there as the number one crop circle expert.' He then said that they would send me to a certain college . . . (which I know to be a government establishment, so my ears pricked up at this point) . . . where you will be familiarized with coding structures. I mean, this is an absolute bloody horror story I'm hearing . . . I mean, I was . . . God, no one will ever know how I felt that night.

I was terrified. I even cried. I was completely and utterly bloody freaked. I even saw my daughter the next day and I broke down while I was talking to her, too. I said to her: 'Darling, I want you to forget everything I've ever told you about crop circles. I think I'm in terrible trouble. You know, I'm in bloody trouble.' Of course, she didn't know what I was talking about but I just wanted my family out of it. It took everything I knew to get over that ordeal and carry on a relatively normal life . . .

(At this point Colin took a few moments to himself. It was obvious that the ordeal had affected him very deeply – indeed, that the memory was as painful as the ordeal itself. A short while later we resumed.)

CA: . . . So anyway . . . I was told that there would be another couple of contacts made and that these would be 'voice-only' contacts via the telephone. And sure enough they phoned me, but by this time I'd had time to think about the situation and I'd decided I was going to take his head off, you know. There was no way I was going to give them what they wanted.

JK: So what did you do?

CA: I was given a contact number at the Ministry of Defence and I rang that number and told them that I'd had this approach, but I was told they had no jurisdiction. Can you believe that? A British subject was being harassed by a member of US Intelligence and the MoD had no jurisdiction to protect me! My God! I mean, it really made me ashamed to be British. Anyway, they also told me that I was not to be concerned, that I should simply refuse to cooperate with them. They said that if I refused to go along with it there should not be any danger to me. Hah! I thought: 'Thanks for the invaluable assistance!'

JK: And is that what you did?

CA: In the event, yes. That's precisely what I did. I literally ignored the phone calls. And I guess, in retrospect, it might just have saved my life, the fact that I'd contacted the MoD. Perhaps they have a little more jurisdiction than they admitted to. Perhaps the fact that I contacted the MoD meant that the CIA dared not harm me in any way.

JK: So how did you know which calls to ignore? How did you know it was them?

CA: Oh, it was them, all right. The guy was on the answer machine saying: 'Pick up the phone. Pick up the phone.' But I didn't. I just let it go. Then the voice said: 'Ring me back at this number.' And then they gave a number, but I didn't ring back. A few days later they phoned again, and this time what they said was vile, and frightening. But my answer was: 'Sorry, I'm not playing.' And that was that so far as I was concerned. Like I said, perhaps they knew I'd contacted the MoD. Maybe, just maybe, this was enough for them to leave me alone.

JK: Have you had similar approaches since you moved to America?

CA: Well, nothing quite like that. But I have certainly been approached, yes. A computer analyst at the Pentagon, for example, approached me with a person called [name deleted] Pretty soon this woman, [name deleted], sought [name deleted] out and asked to see her in her office. Now this meant that my new office – which I used to share with [name deleted] – had already been infiltrated by people who we now know for sure were CIA. I have since had several approaches by both of these people.

JK: Sounds like someone was pretty desperate to gain access to your database.

CA: Absolutely. That's the only possible answer. Well, I *know* that's what it was all about. They told me so. For instance, [name deleted], who is an author in the US, offered that I should co-author a book with her and she went to every extreme in order to get me to agree. She wanted to work with me on the project in my office here in Connecticut, which of course would have allowed her unlimited access to my database. But again, I turned the offer down.

JK: Well, thank you for being so frank, Colin. I'm sure you've opened a lot of people's minds about the ways in which the world's intelligence agencies work and about just how seriously they view the UFO and crop circle phenomena. Thanks once again.

CA: My pleasure.

DOCUMENT 08

Cosmic Top Secret
Eyes Only Copy One of One

Classified (Part 1)
Cosmos 2238

File 29
The Wash Incident

Documents 08 and 09 contain five File Reports (29 through 33). While Files 29 through 31 tend to confirm that a high-level UFO cover-up indeed exists in Britain, I have elected to include Files 32 and 33 for the sheer strength of their account. After all, in order for the cover-up scenario to be taken seriously there must first be evidence in favour of a genuine UFO phenomenon. Files 32 and 33 offer up this evidence aplenty.

But first, File 29 – and the night the RAF was placed on high alert . . .

Already famous for being the home of the 1980 Rendlesham Forest (RAF Woodbridge/Bentwaters) UFO incident, in October 1996 East Anglia once again became the centre of a major UFO controversy.

Sightings of strange lights and objects in the skies over East Anglia have been reported on a fairly regular basis throughout the nearly two decades that have elapsed since the Rendlesham Forest incident. But perhaps the most credible – and certainly the best-documented – report was filed by the crew of the *Conocoast* oil tanker, who tracked two sets of 'strange coloured lights' hovering in the sky off the East Anglia coast in the early hours of Saturday, 5th October 1996. This same phenomenon was also witnessed and reported by a civilian pilot, the Great Yarmouth coastguard and officers at nearby Boston and Skegness police stations.

But what is unique about this case is this.

Following an immediate security initiative launched by the MoD and a subsequent request from RAF Kinloss (Scotland) via the Great Yarmouth coastguard, the Skegness police managed to videotape the craft from the roof of their police station. The footage, which shows beyond question that the sightings reported were of some or other unidentified structured aircraft, has since been analyzed and presented as evidence in what has become one of the most discussed and controversial UFO incidents of the past few years.

No doubt due to the sensitive nature of this incident, the MoD tried initially to play it down by claiming that the sighting was nothing more than a combination of lights from the 200ft-high 'Boston Stump' church tower and an electrical storm over the North Sea. However, my own (and others') investigations into this case have led me to a somewhat different conclusion. Like the Roswell 'weather balloon' story, reliable sources in possession of information gleaned from within the Defence Ministry told me that the 'Boston Stump/electrical storm' story was a smokescreen from the outset. According to one source it was a 'fabrication' hurriedly agreed on by 'high-ranking civil servants and military officials on the night in question' (4th/5th October 1996). My source told me that they had been 'called from their beds in the small hours' to deal with a 'high-alert situation' and that, as a consequence, later that same morning front-line MoD spokespersons received a directive from a 'high level within the Ministry' to disseminate the Boston Stump story as a cover for what had really happened.

And what had really happened was that Britain's airspace/defence region had been penetrated by at least one aircraft that remains unidentified to this day.

Witness statements, plus the camcorder footage shot by the Skegness police, together with subsequent statements made by the MoD and further testimonies given in confidence by 'official sources' suggest an altogether different explanation to the official MoD cover story. Namely: that the object(s) seen was/were indeed a UFO or UFOs, and that a covert defence initiative was immediately launched in response to a positive radar echo traced at RAF Kinloss in Scotland. The echo was also traced by NADGE (NATO Air Defence Ground Environment) radar at RAF Northwood and RAF Neatishead in Norfolk.

The question that comes to mind is: Why would the combination of a church tower and an electrical storm provoke a full-scale defence alert across Britain?

File 29: Appendix 01
Case Report: Cosmic Top-X33 Eyes Only Transmission

From the day the sightings occurred, well-known UFO researcher and East Anglia artist David Dane set about investigating the incident. David talked to all of the witnesses concerned, including the crew of the *Conocoast* oil tanker whose report prompted the initial investigation by the MoD. In their own way all of the witnesses told the same story.

To add to this, [name deleted] at RAF Neatishead informed David Dane that an anomalous radar echo had indeed been recorded, but that no quick-response aircraft had been scrambled to intercept the signal. When I spoke to David he told me: 'Having admitted there was an echo on the radar at RAF Neatishead, and considering the quality of the witnesses, it seems extraordinary that the RAF did not intercept. Apparently RAF Neatishead did put in a request for an intercept but this was turned down at a higher level. So you are left with the problem – either they knew what it was or they didn't consider it a threat.'

David went on: 'When I spoke to [name deleted] he explained to me that they felt it was not an obvious threat because the radar at RAF Neatishead was for tracking possible hostile planes coming in from the North Sea. As these objects had appeared out of nowhere, close to the coast and stationary, they did not fit the same parameters as hostile aircraft. And yet the objects sat there for over eight hours and the RAF did nothing.'

David concluded: 'If they thought the object was the effect of an electrical storm, the crew of the oil tanker certainly didn't think so, and these men live at sea. What they told me was just the opposite – that it was certainly not a natural phenomenon. Seeing the video footage has convinced me of the same. So why did the RAF choose to ignore these objects?'

Why indeed?

Proof that the anomalous radar echo was indeed recorded can be found in a transcript of the conversation that took place between coastguards, police, the RAF and the crew of the *Conocoast* oil tanker on 5th October 1996, a copy of which I have on file. Coastguards in Great Yarmouth – whose records show that a Force Four wind was blowing that night, thus ruling out the possibility that the stationary object(s) was a helicopter, a light aircraft, a weather balloon, etc – coordinated the investigation, which spanned the entire East Anglia and north-east coastlines, including the east coast of Scotland. Having received a telephone call from Skegness police at 3:14 a.m. on October 5th, 1996, the Great Yarmouth coastguards suddenly found themselves at the centre of operations.

At 3:14 a.m., the Skegness police reported that they could see a 'red and green rotating light in the sky directly southeast from Skegness.' They further reported that the light seemed 'strange'. The reason they gave for this assessment was that the light was 'stationary' and that it was emitting 'no sound', thus ruling out the possibility that it belonged to an aircraft. Leastways a conventional one. However, as RAF Kinloss reported some twelve minutes later (3:26 a.m.) the light could not have been a star either, nor indeed the result of weather phenomena, as RAF Northwood had by now tracked the object on radar, 'bearing 221 degrees at 16 miles'. The 'electrical storm' theory must surely end here. Indeed, by 3:31 a.m. the radar screens at RAF Neatishead had confirmed a 'couple radar contact' (two independent objects side-by-side); again, both objects were reported as being 'stationary'. To further discount the possibility that these objects might have been terrestrial aircraft, RAF Kinloss then confirmed that there were 'no military aircraft in the area', and further that 'no notified civil flights' were in the area, either. Back in Whitehall I suspect heads began to spin at this point.

At 3:46 a.m. the crew of the *Conocoast* oil tanker joined in the four-way transmission. They confirmed that they too had 'these lights on visual' and went on to describe them as 'flashing red, green and white'. They were unable to identify them as belonging to a conventional aircraft, however, as they appeared 'stationary' and 'approximately one mile high'. In response to an enquiry from the coastguard the *Conocoast* crew then confirmed that they had not seen the objects 'approach', but that so far as they could tell both objects had 'just appeared'. Soon after this (3:53 a.m.) both RAF Neatishead and RAF Northwood confirmed the suspicion that these objects were 'unknowns' when they reported that there was 'no transponder' on either of them, and thus that there was 'no means of interrogation'.

[Note: In this context a 'transponder' is basically a receiver/transmitter which gives out a signal identifying itself as either civilian or military. As there was no transponder on the craft, 'interrogation' – contact and identification – was not possible. Under any other circumstances this situation would have demanded immediate interception by the RAF, but the official line is that no such action was taken. It is anomalies like this one that suggest that some backstairs cover-up is indeed under way at a very high level within the MoD.]

As if to confirm this high-level MoD interest the coastguard then made a very pertinent request. According to the transcript, at precisely 4:17 a.m. he suggested that the Skegness police should 'get video footage' of the craft, 'as the RAF are very interested and may require it later.' The Skegness police responded in the affirmative. I have since seen the footage in question, which indeed shows the strange objects hovering silently over the North Sea near the town of Boston in Norfolk – a fact corroborated by the Boston police, who at 5:17 a.m. reported that they could 'still see the light'.

Four minutes later, at 5:21 a.m., RAF Kinloss confirmed that '[RAF] Neatishead are running a trace on this and cannot explain it'. During this broadcast Flight Lft [name deleted] stated that 'if they are helicopters, they are fast approaching the end of their endurance, as it is well over two hours since the first report, let alone how long they were up there before they were actually sighted'. They were still up there at least six hours later.

Indeed, it was not until 7:20 p.m. that evening that Anglia Radar finally confirmed that the objects had disappeared. At which point they released a most curious statement. 'We are of the opinion that it was Boston Stump,' they said. Evidently they had not been listening in on the transmission.

And neither had they seen the video footage recorded by the Skegness police.

It should be said at this point that information sent to me by a source who must remain anonymous paints a slightly different picture of events.

Contrary to the official MoD line my source claimed that, in response to the anomalous radar echo, a signal classified 'PRIORITY RESTRICTED' was distributed throughout all RAF strike units on the night in question. In brief, the signal stated that two jets, probably Tornados, had indeed been scrambled, and that their flight mission was to intercept the radar-tracked object(s). Witnesses have since revealed that the roar of military jets *was* heard in the vicinity, and that at least one military jet was seen heading up the Norfolk coast towards the sighting location at 9 a.m. on Saturday, 5th October 1996.

Further to this my source claimed that, although one of the pilots 'saw something', the jets were unable to 'catch' the unidentified craft and so returned to their base –

probably RAF Marham. The probability that the jets were scrambled from RAF Marham is based on the fact that Marham houses the closest RAF quick-response strike unit to where the sighting occurred. However, it should also be stated that a 'PRIORITY RESTRICTED' designation is the least urgent of classified signals, 'IMMEDIATE', 'CONFIDENTIAL', 'SECRET' and 'TOP SECRET' constituting the more urgent designations in sequential order. Of course, even higher designations such as 'Q1-7' and 'ULTRA' exist, but these are part of the ABOVE, BEYOND and COSMIC TOP SECRET security designations that do not affect the average rank-and-file military communications personnel or the operations in which they are involved. Thus – assuming that the information I received was correct – this incident did not rank as a particularly high security risk so far as the military was concerned. On the contrary, the indications are that the object(s) in question was known to the signals originator and could even have been the result of a 'HALO' test flight or the test flight of some other highly secret British or US aircraft. Indeed, another very reliable source of mine is of the opinion that a 'PRIORITY RESTRICTED' designation would imply that the scrambled jets were sent up to *escort the test flight* (and not to *intercept a hostile aircraft*), a fact subsequently denied by the MoD.

But whatever the precise details of this incident, the fact remains that in the early hours of 5th October 1996, either a major defence operation or some pre-arranged damage-limitation exercise was indeed initiated as a result of a multiple-witness UFO sighting and an unexplained radar echo traced at RAF Kinloss in Scotland, as well as at RAF Northwood and RAF Neatishead in Norfolk. And by hook or by crook, the MoD seems hell-bent on keeping the details of this operation 'hazy', to say the least.

So the question remains: If the RAF did indeed record a radar echo of an unknown aircraft in our skies, a fact openly admitted to, then what made the relevant authorities decide not to intercept? Do they know what the craft was and who it belonged to, and simply won't tell us? Or are they really able to distinguish between a 'hostile' aircraft and a 'non-hostile' one purely from a radar echo and without being able to 'interrogate' by means of the aircraft's on-board transponder, as claimed by [name deleted] of RAF Neatishead?

And why was a 'PRIORITY RESTRICTED' signal distributed to all RAF strike units on the night in question?

On the other hand, if the RAF *did* intercept – as claimed by at least one inside source – then what's all the bullshit about a church tower and an electrical storm? Indeed, what's all the bullshit about a church tower and an electrical storm anyway?

I'll tell you . . . this secrecy thing is really beginning to bug me!

In response to questions arising from the incident, the MoD remained ambiguous, to say the least. MoD spokesperson Nigel Sergeant, for instance, commented: 'We are trying to prove that it does not represent any sort of security threat, and that it was not an aggressive intrusion into our airspace.'

Further to this, an article in the *Daily Post* (Liverpool: 29 November 1996) entitled *Britain's X-Files Team In A Secret Whitehall Office* quoted an MoD spokesperson as saying: 'We need to keep records because sometimes MPs want to ask Parliament about sightings.' How reassuring to learn that the MoD keeps records of UFO sightings purely to aid in the process of democracy – sterling stuff!

Which brings us to the actions taken in Parliament by the late Martin Redmond, former MP for Don Valley, who by this time was expressing his own concern over the incident.

Mr Redmond openly accused the government of covering up information on this and other UFO incidents, and said that if there was no defence threat, then there was no excuse for secrecy, either. Before his untimely death in January 1997, Mr Redmond had become *the* leading political figure in the struggle to overturn what is now being seen, even in political circles, as a flagrant and unacceptable government cover-up concerning the UFO phenomenon.

On 5th November 1996, Mr Redmond tabled a formal question in the House of Commons to the then Secretary of State for Defence, Nicholas Soames MP. The question read: 'If he will list the reports of encounters by Royal Air Force pilots with unidentified flying craft since 1966 which have not been released to the public; on what grounds they have been retained and if he will make a statement?'

In reply, Mr Soames said: 'The information could be provided only at disproportionate cost.' Which basically means that the government is not prepared to allocate the relatively minimal funds necessary to inform the public about matters it doesn't want the public to know about.

Mr Redmond then asked: 'What is the Royal Air Force's practice as regards investigating sightings of unidentified flying craft which correlate with radar information; if there is a requirement to investigate such phenomena by scrambling aircraft; and if he will make a statement?'

Mr Soames replied: 'Unidentified contacts penetrating UK airspace or the UK air defence region are identified by all means, including interception.'

Here Mr Soames stated quite unequivocally that military (RAF) interception of UFOs is indeed part and parcel of official Defence policy, and this despite consistent denials by the MoD's Secretariat (Air Staff) 2a1 office in this respect. Which of course means that either Mr Soames is lying, or the MoD's Secretariat (Air Staff) 2a1 office is lying. And either way, neither of these official voices will ever be expected to account for deliberately misrepresenting the truth. That is the system. That is what we are up against. And that is why the truth regarding the UFO cover-up will likely remain forever beyond reach – because it is the property of those who operate above the law.

Mr Redmond concluded: 'The answers I've been given lead me to think there is something more to this.' And further: 'The only thing I know for sure is this whole issue is shrouded in secrecy.'

And it is. But why, when according to MoD spokespersons the Ministry collates information regarding UFOs purely so that questions can be asked in the House? In this respect I would suggest that it is high time a concerted effort was made to revolutionize the politics of UFOs – in particular to petition local MPs in order that they can lobby Parliament on our behalf and, like Martin Redmond MP before them, table formal questions in the House of Commons designed to force open the official lid on government secrecy. It is, of course, my belief that most of our lawfully elected representatives are as much in the dark as anybody else regarding the UFO cover-up. But they are nevertheless the ones in a position to do something about it. They are public servants. Let us give them the opportunity to do what they were elected to do – serve the public by informing us of what is going on at the highest levels of government regarding the UFO phenomenon. After all, if in the government's opinion UFOs *do* pose a security threat then surely those most at risk from said 'security threat' have the right to know about it. And that is us. If, on the other hand, the government is content that UFOs *do not* pose a security threat then it has no right to withhold information about the phenomenon from those it is likely to affect the most. Which, once again, is us.

Simply put, this is the premise on which my argument rests.

One further snippet. At the last minute I received some very interesting information from a very reliable source about a civilian pilot who flew his light aircraft from South Norfolk to Yorkshire on the weekend of 5th/6th October 1996 in order to attend a wedding. He flew through Lincolnshire en route. On arrival in Yorkshire he was asked how he had managed to fly through Lincolnshire as air traffic control had been advising all civilian pilots to steer clear of the area. When he asked why he was quietly told: 'Because of reported UFO activity.'

A further testimony, then, that the MoD knew only too well about the UFO activity taking place in this particular area of Britain on the weekend of 5th/6th October 1996, and that measures had been taken to warn pilots of it. The only question is: Was the UFO activity extraterrestrial or military? And no one at the Ministry is about to answer that one!

In conclusion I have to say that, in my opinion, it is a gross miscarriage of humanity that this elite few we call the Defence Ministry should be the ones who decide what we are and what we are not permitted to know concerning the UFO phenomenon – a phenomenon that, after all, may just hold the key to our future and our children's future.

On the other hand, of course, if we are kept in the dark long enough, it might just prove the undoing of us all.

[Note: My special thanks to David Dane and Simon Harris for their invaluable input concerning this case.]

File 30
Cosmos 2238

The re-entry of Cosmos 2238 – a Russian satellite launch-rocket – was officially claimed to have been the cause of numerous UFO sightings in Ireland, Wales and England's South-West on the night of 30th/31st March 1993. However, on investigation it was found that the re-entry (if it occurred at all) occurred between 1:05 a.m. and 1:10 a.m., while independent UFO sightings, including detailed reports from some 19 on-duty police officers, spanned a time-frame ranging from 8 p.m. to 2:40 a.m., and could not therefore have referred to the alleged re-entry. So what *were* these objects reported by so many?

In an effort to unmask this mystery Doug Cooper of Devon UFO Research Organization and Bob Boyd of Plymouth UFO Research Group turned their minds to investigation. Their conclusions were unprecedented in modern-day UFO cases, in particular with regard to the high-level government cover-up currently operating in Britain. Not only did they find major discrepancies in the replies they received from RAF Fylingdales (Britain's top radar-tracking station) but in addition the MoD, in a personal communication to Mr Cooper, admitted that it could not account for the military aircraft seen in the area that night, and that 'while the decay of Cosmos 2238 might explain the high level 1:10 a.m. sightings, it would not explain the other sightings on the night in question'.

Indeed, when all the evidence had finally been weighed

it seemed that either the RAF and the MoD had discovered major difficulties in communicating with each other or, perhaps more likely, *somebody* was telling less than the whole truth.

File 30: Appendix 01
Case Report: Cosmic Top-X34 Eyes Only Police Reports

At 2:20 a.m. on Wednesday, 31st March 1993, Doug Cooper was woken from sleep by a 'phone call from Sgt J. Furneuxe of the Devon & Cornwall Police. Briefly, Sgt Furneuxe reported that an hour earlier (1:10 a.m.) whilst driving towards Dobwalls on the A38, he noticed two very bright lights hovering at about 2,000 ft above the north-west horizon. Knowing the night sky fairly well he immediately realized that they were not stars and that they did not conform to any known aircraft or their navigation lights. At this point he stopped his patrol car and climbed out. For some short while he watched the objects and was then fairly stunned to see them ascend suddenly and speedily to a higher altitude.

Next, the lights seemed to move in an arc over Sgt Furneuxe's position and disappear to the south. At their highest point, about 10,000 ft (this height is based on information obtained from the control tower at Exeter Airport) two 'vapour trails' appeared behind each object; according to Sgt Furneuxe these 'vapour trails' appeared to be 'self-luminous'. At the end of his report Sgt Furneuxe informed Mr Cooper that a number of other police officers had made similar reports to their Operations Room at Exeter.

Shortly after this call Doug Cooper shook the sleep from his eyes and contacted the Ops Room at Exeter Police Station. He was told that they had indeed received a number of similar reports, all from police officers on duty in Devon and Cornwall, and one further report from two officers from the Gwent Police Force in South Wales. At about the same time – 1:10 a.m. – two different police officers, Sgt Mitchell and PC Cotley, were approaching the coastal town of Lynton, North Devon. As they neared the town they noticed two very bright lights approaching from the north across the Bristol Channel. Stopping their patrol car they watched as the lights drew nearer.

But it was as the lights passed overhead that both officers noticed a third, smaller light positioned somewhere between the other two. Sgt Mitchell said that as they passed silently by he got the distinct impression that the lights were attached to a very large object, but he could not make out any shape or other details. As the object moved away from them both officers saw two white vapour-like trails behind each light. Like Sgt Furneuxe they too described these trails as 'self-luminous', but 'not the same as normal aircraft vapours'; more like 'beams of light'. The officers estimated the elevation of the object(s) to be forty degrees to the horizon at an altitude of between 1,000 and 2,000 ft.

It should be noted that, if a spent Russian rocket did indeed re-enter Earth's atmosphere at around 1:05 a.m. to 1:10 a.m. on the night in question then its altitude would have been approximately 85–100 km (about sixty miles, or over 300,000 ft). It is hard to imagine that the officers concerned could have misjudged the objects' altitude by such a ludicrous margin. On the contrary, it is far more likely that these two sightings were associated with other sightings which occurred later that morning, at around 2 a.m., and indeed the previous evening, between 8 p.m. and 11 p.m.

File 30: Appendix 02
Case Study: Cosmic Top-X35 Eyes Only Media Reports

As a result of reports published in two local newspapers (*Honiton News* and *Somerset Gazette*) over the following few days Doug Cooper received a large number of phone calls from members of the public, and from one other police officer who had also seen strange lights and objects in the sky on the night in question. After evaluating these reports it became apparent that, in addition to the initial 1:10 a.m. police reports, there were a number of others to consider. These reports were as follows:

Date: 31/3/93; Event: 'A'; Time: 1:05 a.m.; Place: Innis, Ireland.

Date: 31/3/93; Event: 'B'; Time: 1:10 a.m.–1:17 a.m.; Place: Wales, Cornwall, Devon and Somerset.

Date: 31/3/93; Event: 'C'; Time: 2 a.m.; Place: Bridgwater, Somerset.

Date: 30/3/93; Event: 'D'; Time: 7 p.m.–11 p.m.; Place: North Devon.

Date: 31/3/93; Event: 'E'; Time: 1:30 a.m.; Place: St Ives and Penzance, Cornwall.

Date: 31/3/93; Event: 'F'; Time: Various; Place: Wales, West Country, Avon, Shropshire and South Yorkshire.

Sighting 'A'
Innis, Ireland.
Two Bright Lights

This event occurred at 1:05 a.m. on Wednesday, 31st March 1993, over Innis, Ireland, when two bright lights were observed travelling across the sky. According to the report the lights were seen at high altitude and left white vapour trails in their wake. They appeared to be flying parallel to each other on a south-easterly course.

Evidently this sighting caused some concern to the Irish government; as a consequence fighter aircraft were scrambled to monitor the objects. It seems the operation was unsuccessful, however, as the objects were thought to have been travelling at approximately 3,000 mph – too fast for the jets. Nevertheless this action speaks volumes; it is extremely unlikely that the Irish government would have scrambled fighter jets to intercept an object at 300,000 ft (the approximate height of a rocket re-entry), Russian or not. The flight ceiling of a present-day fighter rarely exceeds 60,000 ft.

Sighting 'B'
Wales, Cornwall, Devon, Somerset.
More Witnesses

At various times between 1:10 a.m. and 1:17 a.m. on Wednesday, 31st March 1993, twelve people (excluding the police officers) reported the sighting of two very bright objects flying across the night sky in a south-easterly direction. With the exception of one they all reported seeing vapour trails, but described them slightly differently. In the main the trails were described as 'white', trailing back from the objects and 'self-luminous'. Again, these reports estimated the altitude of the object(s) as somewhere between 1,000 and 10,000 ft, way too low for the sightings to be confused with the re-entry of a launch-rocket.

Sighting 'C'
Bridgwater, Somerset.
The Military Connection

On Wednesday, 31st March 1993, a group of eel fishermen were fishing the River Parrot near Bridgwater in Somerset. At around 1:30 a.m. they noticed three military-type helicopters flying in an arc from Bridgwater to the nuclear power station at Hinkley Point. This activity was observed for some thirty minutes. At a little before 2 a.m. the fishermen saw two bright orange-coloured lights approaching from the north. As the lights drew closer the fishermen, who had previously thought that the lights were the returning helicopters, realized that in fact they were not – they heard no engine or rotor-blade noises and could see no navigation lights. The objects approached their position at a steady pace, 'not overly fast', and appeared to be at a height of about '800 ft'. On their final approach, in addition to the orange lights, two very bright white lights seemed to be glowing from the rear of the objects.

As they passed silently overhead, one of the fishermen (name on file) thought the objects were joined by some sort of structure, and likened the object to a 'large catamaran'. As the object(s) cleared the fishermen's position two very bright light-sources could be seen at the rear of the craft, throwing 'light-beams' backwards. These were described as resembling 'car headlights'.

Sighting 'D'
North Devon and Somerset.
Two Concordes

During the evening of Tuesday, 30th March, 1993, six independent witnesses reported seeing UFOs 'flying' and 'hovering' over Somerset and North Devon. For the record, the following is one of those reports randomly chosen.

At approximately 9 p.m. a policeman from Bishops Lydeard in Somerset was up on the Quantock Hills, North Somerset. He was with a group of Scouts carrying out some field exercises when his attention was suddenly drawn to a series of bright lights approaching from the north-west. They appeared to be at a height of about 3,000 ft and travelling at a constant speed. As the lights approached, he was able to discern the outline of a large craft which, he said, 'looked like two Concordes flying side by side and joined together'. According to the policeman the lights appeared to be located 'around the object(s)', similar to cabin lights on an aircraft, only much brighter. The object then passed to his left and, after two or three minutes, was lost to sight as it proceeded on a south-easterly course.

[It should be noted that none of the police officers completed sightings report forms for Doug Cooper, even though in the first instance most of them agreed to.]

Sighting 'E'
St Ives And Penzance, Cornwall.
Rockets

A short time before 1:30 a.m. on Wednesday, 31st March 1993, two men living in St Ives, Cornwall, observed two very bright objects flying on a south-south-easterly course over the town. They estimated the objects to be about 2,000 ft up and described them as 'rockets with light-trails'. Both men said the objects were moving very fast and that they were in sight for only five to ten seconds.

Meanwhile, another man in Crowles near Penzance, Cornwall, was himself watching two very bright objects leaving trails behind them and heading south-east at a very low altitude − 2,000 to 3,000 ft. He also observed a third object behind the other two which, he said, was less bright. None of the objects made any noise and the light-trails were, he said, 'thin and straight, like a light-tube'.

At the rear of the two larger objects he also noticed a pink and blue light-source but was unable to say if it was attached. From his southerly position the objects were to the north, and not moving very fast. In fact, he had them in sight for at least two minutes.

This, of course, is at variance with the other two witnesses at St Ives, who said the objects were moving very fast. But as Doug Cooper said in his excellent report, this was probably because they saw the objects overhead whilst the man near Penzance was looking at them from a distance. Indeed, I have to agree with Doug Cooper's conclusion here − that these sightings were in fact of the same two objects but seen from a different location, and therefore from a different line of view.

File 30: Appendix 03
Case Report: Cosmic Top-X36 Eyes Only
The PUFORG Report

Before detailing Sighting 'F' we should take into account at least one of the reports obtained by Bob Boyd of Plymouth

UFO Research Group (PUFORG). In my opinion this is where any idea that the sightings could have been the result of a 'rocket re-entry' becomes null and void.

The most convincing report received by PUFORG came from Judith Kirk of Penzance in Cornwall, as follows:

'I'd been visiting friends, and I arrived home as the 1 a.m. news was starting on the radio. I got out of the car and went towards the house, which is on a dirt track; there are no lights about. I stopped at a gate to look over the landscape, which was moonlit. I was thinking how nice and tranquil it all was when out of the corner of my right eye I saw a couple of objects travelling north to south, not quite overhead. I momentarily thought they were a couple of meteorites, but instead of vanishing quickly they kept on coming.

'They were travelling parallel to each other, very precisely. They were like very big stars, as bright as Sirius and about four times as large. They were about one inch apart as seen by the naked eye and were giving off a vapour trail. The lights were white like stars and the trails were white like fog. The trails came from directly behind the objects and were a single thick trail, not like those given off by large airliners, which are split into two. My first thought was: *'My God! What's that?'* They were obviously some kind of controlled craft, but not like anything I'd seen before. There were no flashing navigational lights, just two extraordinary bright lights which were unusually large and/or powerful, travelling fast.

'As they proceeded, north to south, I noticed there were two other objects accompanying or following the larger two. These were *not* visible in themselves, but were giving off vapour trails, although these were barely visible. As I watched their progress across the sky I tried to relate what I was seeing to something I was familiar with. The closest comparison I can make is that the two smaller vapour trails looked like those seen during the day coming from high-flying smaller jet aircraft – a single jet stream.

'There's nothing I can compare the larger two objects with because they're not like anything I've seen before.'

Judith went on to say that, in her opinion, what she had seen were four intelligently controlled aircraft, and that the 'vapour trails' they left in their wake were extremely 'precise'.

'They looked as if someone had taken a ruler and drawn two dead straight lines across the sky, parallel to the ground,' she said. She also reported hearing a 'muffled rumbling sound coming from somewhere off to the west', and that when the sound started 'dogs living in that direction started barking'.

'It wasn't just one dog,' Judith affirmed. 'It was several. And this continued until the sound subsided. I have listened to and watched aircraft at night since and there is nothing that compares with them in any way. In particular, ordinary aircraft do *not* make dogs bark.'

She concluded: 'I watched the objects fly southward, where they flew into some cloud. The cloud lit up very brilliantly as they flew through it. I thought: "*That is weird!*" Then they went out of my sight.'

According to the report Judith watched the objects for about one and a half minutes in total.

Later that day Judith contacted Westcountry TV and told them about her sighting; they broadcast her report the following day – 1st April. Evidently the presenter was unsure whether it was meant to be a serious article or an April Fool's joke, especially when he discovered the unfortunate coincidence of Judith's name – J. Kirk!

Even so, Judith's testimony remains as convincing as any I have heard.

*   *   *

PUFORG obtained a number of other similar reports, most of which were complete with diagrams drawn by the witnesses. None of the diagrams resembled either conventional aircraft or, indeed, the re-entry of a spent rocket. In each case the reports indicated that the objects seen were at a height of between 1,000 and 10,000 feet, again, far too low for a rocket re-entry. As Bob Boyd of PUFORG commented at the time: 'After investigation, and many reports of similar sightings all over the South-West, we believe the objects to be unexplainable flying objects' – that is, *genuine* UFOs.

File 30: Appendix 04
Case Report: Cosmic Top-X37 Eyes Only Sighting 'F'
Ministry of Defence Reports, 30th/31st March 1993
Plus Independent Report From Retired Airline Pilot

During the course of this investigation Doug Cooper received a report from a gentleman (name on file) who is a recently retired airline pilot. He had phoned Mr Cooper in response to one of the local newspaper articles.

The former commercial airline pilot said that at 1:30 a.m. on Wednesday, 31st March 1993, he observed two jet fighter aircraft travelling at 30,000 ft in a westerly direction and at very high speed – about 1,500 mph. He said the fighters had their afterburners on which indicated to him that they may still have been climbing. As an airline pilot he was well qualified to identify these jets, and was also certain they were of a 'single-engine military' type.

Following this report, Doug Cooper contacted Nick Pope at the MoD, Secretariat (Air Staff) 2a, Room 8245 – the MoD's official 'UFO Desk'. Evidently Mr Pope was most helpful and promised to look into the matter further. Which he did. About an hour later he returned Doug Cooper's call.

Nick Pope said that he had been unable to discover any details regarding these aircraft and was at a loss to explain their presence over East Devon at that time, stating that 'It is unusual for military aircraft to be operating as late as 1:30 a.m.' He added that the MoD had received a number of calls and letters reporting the same kind of lights/objects seen at the same time (i.e. the evening of 30th March and the early morning of 31st March 1993) and that 'while the decay of Cosmos 2238 [the Russian launch-rocket] might explain the high-level 1:10 a.m. sightings, it would not explain the other sightings on the night in question'. Upon request, Mr Pope later sent Mr Cooper a list of these 'other sightings', giving locations, times and directions of travel.

Briefly, the MoD reports covered the period from 8 p.m. on 30th March to 2:40 a.m. on 31st March, and indicated that the objects had been seen as far north as South Yorkshire. They had also been seen in Shropshire and the counties of Cornwall, Devon and Hampshire, all at different times, and in many cases flying in different directions. This information caused Doug Cooper to ask the question:

'Was the information given to me by Nick Pope of the MoD correct? Or was it a deliberate ploy to confuse the issue and try to put me off the scent? I truly do not know.'

If the information received by Doug Cooper *was* correct – and let us for the moment suppose it was – then this means that not only were there UFOs flying and hovering over Somerset, Devon and Cornwall between 8 p.m. and 2 a.m. on the night in question but they were also tracking across the Midlands, South Yorkshire and Hampshire, too. One has to say . . . that was some rocket re-entry!

In contrast to the opinion of Bob Boyd of PUFORG (whose conclusion we will come to in a moment) Doug Cooper is willing to accept that some of the sightings, in particular those that occurred at around 1:05 a.m.–1:10 a.m., could well have been of the Cosmos 2238 satellite launch-rocket as it re-entered Earth's atmosphere. However, he also accepts that the many other sightings reported that night could not possibly have been a rocket re-entry. As Doug himself said:

'On the evening before the re-entry, between 8 p.m. and 11 p.m., objects were seen traversing the North Devon sky and indeed hovering north-west of the same area. In addition it is fairly certain that at 2 a.m. on 31st March an object of some considerable size flew over the River Parrot at Bridgwater, disturbing not only the local fishermen but also the cattle in the adjacent fields. Also at this time we have the mystery of the three helicopters that were seen. They were almost certainly of a military type, but as with the two fighter aircraft over East Devon earlier, their presence has been denied by the MoD. *Why?*

'In association with this we have the sightings at St Ives and Penzance, and other numerous sightings over Cornwall, Devon, Shropshire, South Yorkshire and Hampshire. If these reports are correct then it must be the case that at least one, if not more, unidentified flying objects were active over these areas on the night in question – but what was their purpose?

'In Timothy Good's book *Alien Update*, he cites a number of cases from Russia where UFOs have been observed tracking rocket launches, space flights, and, more importantly, their re-entry procedures. It seems that this activity has been monitored for some years, and that the Russian authorities are fully aware that their space programme has been subjected to some very intense scrutiny by UFOs. For the most part the UFOs appear disc-like and are able to traverse Russian air space at will, and in some extraordinary ways. Additionally, it seems that Britain has also been the victim of such activity. In her book *From Out Of The Blue*, Jenny Randles explores this possibility.

'For example, around the time of the "Bentwaters Incident" (in which both RAF and USAF personnel claimed that a UFO landed at Bentwaters Air Force Base in Suffolk) it is known that the re-entry of a Russian space rocket occurred over the area. Following this, and in addition to the events at the Bentwaters base, a number of UFO sightings were received. Some of the sightings took place before the known re-entry time, and others after. This strongly implies that some unknown craft was present over the area and, as suggested by Jenny Randles, may have been interested in the re-entry.'

Doug Cooper concluded:

'My gut feeling is that UFO(s) were indeed active over the West Country on the night in question, and that they were there to monitor the re-entry of the Cosmos 2238 launch-rocket.'

File 30: Appendix 05
Case Report: Cosmic Top-X38 Eyes Only
RAF Fylingdales

Unlike Doug Cooper's document, the only report PUFORG had for 1:10 a.m. (the time of the alleged re-entry) was from Phillip Young of Truro. PUFORG phoned Phillip and asked if, in his opinion, he had witnessed a rocket re-entry. His answer was to the point and is of note, because Phillip is an astronomer.

'I can't agree with that,' Phillip said. 'What I saw was far too neat. The objects stayed at a fixed position to each other; their speed was constant, as was their brightness. Also, the objects travelled in a very straight line; they were not falling to earth. I don't accept that what I saw was a re-entry.'

So what was it?

By this time, Bob Boyd and the rest of the PUFORG team were beginning to wonder about this 'alleged' rocket re-entry. Doug Cooper had received his information primarily from RAF Fylingdales (Britain's top radar-tracking station in Yorkshire). In order to confirm the information, two weeks later Bob Boyd decided he too would phone RAF Fylingdales. The following is a transcript of his conversation.

'Yes, Mr Boyd, how can I help you?' According to Bob Boyd the man's manner was brusque, unfriendly. Bob explained why he had phoned. 'I can't possibly give you that information,' the man said.

'Why not?' Bob asked.

A short pause, then: 'What's your interest in this, anyway?'

'I'm investigating a UFO report.'

'I'm sure you are (!!)' A longer pause. 'Give me your number, Mr Boyd, and I'll see what I can do and phone you back.'

Bob gave him the number. Forty-five minutes later the man called him back, and for some reason his manner was now totally different, warm, friendly, jovial.

'Ah, Mr Boyd. I have the information you asked for, but I'm afraid it's no use to you because the re-entry came down in the middle of the Pacific.'

'*What? 2238?*'

'Yes, here are the coordinates. It flew north-south and came down at forty-one-point-six degrees north – one hundred and thirty-five degrees west. I just don't see how you got reports of it. It came down on the other side of the world! I'm amazed that they've reported this. How could they see it when it was on the other side of the world?'

'Well, they obviously couldn't have.'

'No, I suppose not. Well, sorry the information is no use to you.'

'Believe me, it's a great help, and very interesting. Thanks very much.'

'Any time, Mr Boyd.'

Naturally Mr Boyd was surprised at this revelation – that in fact Cosmos 2238 had re-entered Earth's atmosphere over the Pacific Ocean and not over the South-West of England. He phoned Doug Cooper, who said he would call the British Astronomical Society. He did. Later Doug Cooper phoned back and told Bob that Fylingdales had got it wrong! The Pacific object, he'd been informed, had been mistakenly given out as 2238 but was in fact 2257, and Fylingdales hadn't yet corrected the information. Bob reminded Doug that Fylingdales had already given *him* the correct information when *he* had phoned them two weeks earlier! Now, two weeks later, the initial 'correct' report had been changed for an earlier 'incorrect' one. Again the question must be asked: *why?*

It should be added that both Bob Boyd and PUFORG, along with the rest of us, remain unhappy with this conflicting information.

'Over the next couple of months,' Bob Boyd told me, 'we tried every avenue we knew, but still we were unable to obtain information on 2238. Because of the time it was taking to get hard facts we decided to leave the re-entry and get on with the report. We already felt that the re-entry did not answer any of the sightings on the night in question, other than the very-high-altitude sightings made at 1:10 a.m. by some of the police officers. The one witness we had that fitted the re-entry's time and altitude [Phillip Young of Truro, astronomer] strongly disagreed that he had seen a re-entry, which we accept.

'We received many more reports, including an official report by the Department of Transport, Energy and Communications (Air Navigation Services Office). In short this report stated that, as well as the objects being seen by many members of the public, they had also received reports from 'civilian and military pilots'. Speaking of the objects, the report said: 'Estimates of their height . . . ranged from several hundred to 25,000 ft.' It is hard to believe that [in the case of trained pilots] an object seen at a height of sixty miles could be mistakenly thought to be, at most, 25,000 feet!

'The MoD accept that UFOs were flying over the South-West of England, Wales and Ireland on the night in question, and admit they are unable to identify them. This is a most remarkable confession. For some reason these particular UFOs 'concerned' them, they said, and were taken 'very seriously' by them. Again, a remarkable confession, one that marks a unique occasion in British UFO investigations.

'But the truly amazing thing is that the MoD said so, publicly!'

[My sincere thanks to Doug Cooper of Devon UFO Research Organization and to Bob Boyd of Plymouth UFO Research Group for allowing me to publish excerpts from their extensive and extremely thorough case notes.]

DOCUMENT 09

Cosmic Top Secret
Eyes Only Copy One of One

Classified (Part 2)
Crash Landing

File 31
UK UFO Crash

It is claimed that in 1947 a UFO crashed near Roswell, New Mexico. The next day high-ranking US Air Force officials openly admitted that indeed a craft of unknown origin had come down at the site, and this unprecedented official government statement was published in the US national press. The day after that, however, the US government changed its story, claiming that in fact the unknown craft was a weather balloon and its radar reflector. Since then the US authorities have changed their story again. They now claim that the unknown craft was a Top Secret Project Mogul spy balloon, and that the 'alien bodies' recovered from the crash site were in fact 'dummies' used in 'high-altitude parachute tests'. The snag here, of course, is that parachute tests are not undertaken from Top Secret spy balloons (see Document 03, File 14).

There were hundreds of eyewitnesses to the Roswell incident, many of whom claimed that they were threatened by US government officials. Some said they were told that if they spoke openly about the crash their families would be murdered. Even so, many of the witnesses continued to tell their stories that, as we have seen, included reports of wreckage material unlike anything found on Earth and alien bodies being seen at the crash site before being transported to supersecret US military facilities. The problem is, of course, when Authority tells the nation *its* side of the story only a small number of people are willing to listen to those who claim otherwise. This, it seems, is human nature.

Despite this sad fact, however, in the summer of 1996 information came my way that pointed to the possibility of a similar incident having occurred in England in 1987. The information further suggested that, like the Roswell incident before it, the UK UFO crash had been cleverly covered up by the military. Although the incident remains 'unsolved' to this day, my own investigations tend to support the fact that indeed an object of unknown origin crashed on the night of 12th/13th October 1987 in Nottinghamshire, England. And whatever it was, it was *not* – as the local press claimed – a 'freak thunderbolt'.

Whatever happened on the night of 12th/13th October 1987, just south of Mansfield in Nottinghamshire, remains a mystery – but it was reported in the local press as being the result of a 'freak thunderbolt'.

The newspaper reports included photographs of partially demolished properties and claims that a 'freak thunderbolt' had caused the considerable damage that had left a number of homes in the Kirkby area of Nottingham uninhabitable. Among the more severely damaged properties was one house in particular that had been virtually destroyed.

On investigation, however, it soon became apparent that this incident had not been caused by a 'freak thunderbolt', nor by any other type of natural phenomenon. Indeed, many people reported seeing at least one UFO (some claimed three) while many more in Mansfield were woken up at 1:30 a.m. by what they described as 'the sound of an explosion'. Somewhat ironically, many of those still awake were watching an old war movie on TV, *The Battle of Britain*. Even more ironic is the fact that, as the 'explosion' resounded, the film had just reached the point where German bombers had started to unleash their payload on a British aerodrome!

Even so, not even the *Luftwaffe* could be blamed for this mystery.

According to personal reports, immediately prior to the explosion household lights came on all by themselves. Other lights (which were already on) exploded, while TV aerials were split in two. As might be expected, insurance companies were inundated with claims for video players and TVs damaged by the so-called 'thunderbolt'. In one street alone forty claims were made, although I have since discovered that a number of these property-damage claims, though investigated, were never met. The reason given was that the government's official Meteorological Office at Bracknell in Berkshire confirmed that there was 'no weather' that night – no cloud, no wind, no rain, no lightning. And no thunderbolts. Indeed, other witnesses told me that they remember the night being still and cloudless, thus ruling out the possibility that the damage was caused by a thunderbolt. This fact, it seems, was seized upon by the insurance companies as a convenient loophole – 'UFO damage' was of course not included in any of the policies, not even in the small print! Thus they refused to cough up.

As local insurance salesman Mike West, who dealt with

many of the insurance claims, revealed: 'It just doesn't make any sense. Every claim that I've dealt with in the last twenty-six years has been logical and reasonable . . . but this defies reason. It [the object] zigzagged across the sky, and people even saw it dive down over the hills . . . I spoke to one old lady who was petrified. She saw it flying straight towards her house. It looped and double-looped and was doing other manoeuvres in the sky. Another man saw it from a distance and described the sky as "suddenly becoming bright red".'

Mr West added that, prior to this incident, he had dealt with numerous insurance claims that had come about as a result of damage caused by lightning and/or thunderbolts. He had never witnessed a case such as this one. On some streets, he said, windows imploded and exploded in alternate houses, a fact seized upon by one local journalist at the time who wrote: 'That was some thunderbolt!'

Some thunderbolt indeed.

Mr West concluded: 'It's as if the whole area was blanketed with electromagnetic radiation.'

To add to this, a local TV and video repairman (whom I will call Bob) told me that all of a sudden the 'lights started to dim' and 'light bulbs fused and started to pop' in his house. The following day he was flooded with calls from people whose video and TV equipment had been damaged by the 'thunderbolt'. When I spoke to Bob, a former military man, he certainly came across as a down-to-earth, level-headed person – 'I'm the type of person who needs to see and measure something before I believe it,' were his precise words. Bob told me that on the night in question, just minutes before the impact, his front doorbell started to ring all by itself. Immediately following this, he said, six light bulbs fused simultaneously and the electrical trip-switch blew. Suspecting a poltergeist – or something of that nature – he began to wonder what on Earth would happen next.

'Suddenly I heard this incredible explosion,' he said, still trying to come to terms with the events that followed. 'My immediate reaction was to race upstairs and make sure my family were OK. I've never heard anything like it. I honestly expected to open my front door and find corpses in the street.'

Bob went on to say that although, during his military days, he had seen 'one or two things he could not explain', the possible existence of extraterrestrial intelligence had never really crossed his mind until he began seriously to investigate this particular case some years later. Even so, he is still not convinced of ET's existence, and thus is still not certain whether or not the crashed object was 'an alien one'. But he *is* convinced that *something* crashed just south of Mansfield, Nottinghamshire on the night of 12th/13th October 1987, that the facts surrounding the crash have been deliberately obscured by government agencies, and that what happened that night has thus far escaped any rational and/or satisfactory explanation. Indeed, Bob is of the opinion that the 'freak thunderbolt' theory is even more ludicrous than the Roswell 'weather balloon' story of 1947. And I have to say I concur.

File 31: Appendix 01
Case Report: Cosmic Top-X39 Eyes Only
Local Investigations

In an effort to gain more information about this incident I contacted local UFO researchers Andrew Emerson and Dominic Beglin. A decade after the event both Andrew and Dominic remain convinced that the incident provoked one of Britain's biggest-ever military UFO cover-ups. Their story follows.

On the night of 12th/13th October 1987, residents reported seeing an object travelling very slowly in a zigzag manner over Mansfield in Nottinghamshire. It was said to be making a 'strange whiny noise, as though it was in some sort of trouble'. Some short while later two more objects were observed coming from the direction of Blidworth, near Sherwood Forest. This was confirmed by some of the insurance claims, which reported objects coming from three different directions and 'colliding in midair' just south of Mansfield.

According to several witness reports, the objects were seen heading towards Kirkby-in-Ashfield when one of them seemed to encounter some kind of difficulty. The UFO then lost power and came down in a large wood near Blidworth. The downed craft appeared to 'bounce' on impact, it was said, creating a violent shockwave that virtually destroyed an entire wood. One report even said that, of the three UFOs, one resembled some kind of craft in difficulty while the other two 'could have been missiles'. Indeed, further investigation found that several eyewitnesses observed a number of 'balls of white light' converging on the UFO as it came down, reminding one of similar eyewitness statements concerning the fate of the TWA800 transatlantic flight that 'blew up' in midair off Long Island, USA in 1996. And then again of the film footage shot from the STS-48 NASA Space Shuttle of a UFO inside Earth's orbit forced to take evasive action against what appears to be have been missile fired at it from Earth. (In this respect one has to ask: Could these 'balls of white light' have been 'missiles'? And if so: Who fired them?) The unidentified craft then 'disappeared into the wood', 'exploded' on impact, and seemingly 'bounced' to a second site where the wreckage finally came to rest at a place known as The Warren, a large wooded area near the privately owned Annesley Hall in Nottinghamshire. Within hours the entire area had been sealed off by police and the military.

At 2:15 a.m., shortly after the 'explosion', seven military helicopters came on the scene. A number of eyewitnesses then watched 'a troop-carrying helicopter [probably a Chinook] surrounded by Gazelles and Lynxes, flying at low speed and scanning the area with powerful searchlights'. These were spotted flying over Normanton, Sutton-in-Ashfield and Kirkby-in-Ashfield. Soon after this, police cordoned off the first site (where the craft had first impacted and 'bounced') erecting road blocks which remained in place for a number of days. It was reported that the Army remained at the second site (the wreckage site) for three to four days.

Where the UFO had first impacted – and seemingly 'bounced' – an intense fire ensued, and the local fire brigade were called in to deal with the blaze. Many trees were burnt down, while others turned to carbon; many remaining trees are still badly burnt to this day. Indeed, even the local Fire Chief was bemused by the nature and intensity of the fire; he commented that he was 'quite surprised to find that the trees facing the fire did not have a mark on them, yet the backs of the trees were smouldering'. This was certainly odd. Especially when added to the further fact that pine cones were found that had seemingly been burnt from the inside out! Could this indicate the presence of some form of intense microwave activity?

When Andrew and Dominic finally investigated the crash site – along with a number of science colleagues – they contended that microwaves might indeed have been the cause of such intense burning, and suggested that the unknown craft had perhaps been powered by some form of electromagnetic propulsion system. The team further calculated that, from the damage left in the wood, the craft would have had a diameter of about sixty feet (this was later confirmed by one eyewitness in particular, who saw the UFO flying low over his house and then coming down in the wood). They also noticed a curious bend in many of the trees left standing – the trees seemed to be bent from the base up to a height of approximately six feet, sometimes a little more, as though they had been 'melted' in the intense heat. A rational explanation for this phenomenon has yet to be offered.

The day after the incident it was reported that 'Army jeeps' and 'heavy military lorries' arrived at the crash site, as Andrew said, 'probably to clear up the wreckage'. To add to this, armed guards were posted to prevent access to the area, while mysterious dark-suited government officials began asking questions of eyewitnesses, in some instances issuing threats and warning them not to say anything about the incident in public. The man who owned the house that had been 'virtually demolished', for example, found a covering of 'metallic dust' on the trees in his garden following the incident. The dust remained for up to three weeks. Two days after announcing his find, two government officials from the DScI (Department of Scientific Intelligence) made themselves known. 'The government officials came up from the DScI,' Andrew said, 'and they took samples of this substance and also threatened this gentleman, telling him to keep quiet about what he knew. This chap has since suffered further threats from an unknown source, mainly by telephone.'

Clearly angered by the whole affair, this man (name on

file) attempted to drive to the crash site in order to ask a few questions for himself. As he parked his car in a neighbouring lay-by, however, he was converged on by four police patrol cars and arrested. He was then taken to the local police station where he was told in no uncertain terms to keep away from the area. He was also told not to talk to anyone about what had happened or he would be prosecuted for 'making obscene phone calls'. This man has since refused to talk to anybody about the incident. Indeed, when I attempted to contact him he refused to confirm or deny any of the above information. Which is a shame. It is alleged that he took colour photographs of the UFO as it approached his house, only seconds before it crashed, and word has since come my way that these photographs are now the possession of the Defence Intelligence Staff.

Andrew further told me that a number of other eyewitnesses had suffered similar threats (certainly I can confirm an irrational reluctance on the part of many witnesses to come forward with information regarding this case). Like others who have investigated the incident Andrew now suspects that some invisible arm of the government/military was responsible for what he considers to be the biggest UFO cover-up this country has ever known. Evidence to this effect can certainly be seen at the crash site today. Over the decade since this incident occurred, top soil and earth has been removed from the crash site down to a level of about nine inches; it has been replaced with clay and covered with fresh topsoil in which new pines and silver birch have been planted. Restoration of the site is now virtually complete.

Which leaves one to ponder the fact that, whoever was responsible for the site's restoration, and whatever their reasons, it is certainly clear that *somebody* wanted the truth regarding this incident covered up.

And then recycled along with the trees.

File 32
1400 Soldiers Of The Royal Marines 41 Commando Group In UFO Encounter

When an ex-Royal Marines regimental sergeant major tells you he has seen a UFO, and that 1400 other Royal Marines saw it too; that his colonel sent up two quick-response Lightning fighters to intercept the UFO; and that more than one hundred rolls of film of the craft were shot and subsequently confiscated by the military . . . it seems reason enough to at least investigate the claim.

So with the help – once again – of PUFORG's Bob Boyd, I did.

On 20th April 1993, Bob Boyd of Plymouth UFO Research Group (PUFORG) was interviewed by local BBC Radio. During the course of the interview Bob happened to mention the fact that, in his opinion, the MoD was in possession of 'conclusive photographic proof of the existence of UFOs'. His statement prompted an unexpected response.

Because some short while later an ex-Royal Marines regimental sergeant major (whom we will call Steve) called to confirm Bob's claim. Steve said that he and 1400 other soldiers of the Royal Marines 41 Commando Group had seen a massive UFO whilst on military manoeuvres in Cyprus in 1971, and that he had photographic evidence to support his claim. When Bob eventually interviewed him Steve gave the following account and, true to his word, produced a set of three astonishing photographs to boot. These, Steve said, were the only photographs out of more than one hundred rolls of film to have escaped confiscation. The rest, he said, ended up in the MoD's X-File archive.

Steve takes up the story.

'We were doing what is known as a night move. What happens is you move a Command HQ from one place in the field to another in darkness. One of my jobs was to control that move. So I would depart, set up a new location, and then the unit would have to move to me . . .

'Shortly before eight p.m. we drove to a new location. There was a particularly bad piece of track on the way there, and so I dropped off a young marine and told him to stay on this track and direct the unit when they came . . .

'At about eight o'clock a very bright light appeared behind the crest of a hill, maybe a thousand metres away. Initially I thought it was the headlights of a car on full beam, situated behind the hill. As this was a night move I got on the radio, gave my call sign and told them to turn their lights off. But the light just got stronger, so I transmitted again: 'Negative lights'. As I was transmitting my orders this light rose over the crest of the hill, still a thousand metres away, and I said: "It's not bloody headlights, it's a flare!"'

Steve went on: 'I thought at first it was a mortar flare, and I was pretty concerned because we were in a carob grove, which is dry trees, and if a flare lands amongst them you've got major problems . . . There were about twenty of us looking at this light when suddenly we realized it *wasn't* a flare. You couldn't relate it to anything else you'd seen. This was a massive thing, about the size of a golf ball at arm's length, at a forty-five-degree angle. It had no obvious sign of movement. The main mass of light was almost spherical, but it was putting out so much radiance it looked like nothing you'd ever seen before. It was like a burning ball of light, like if you lowered the sun to ground level and looked at it. It was awesome.

'We could also see other lights in amongst it, or we thought we could. Not obvious lights. They weren't like porthole lights with little people waving at you. Just indications of other lights, the same colour as the main one. This burning ball of brilliance coming overhead with lights shaped sort of like a cross at the centre . . .'

Steve then recalled the 'young marine' he had left behind in order to guard the 'particularly bad piece of track' they had come across. Steve had ordered the marine, a corporal, to remain behind and direct the other members of the unit as and when they arrived. Due to the sudden appearance of the UFO, however, the corporal had uncharacteristically deserted his post. Steve explained:

'Remember the marine corporal we'd left guarding the track? Well, all of a sudden this guy came over the hill doing about six hundred miles an hour! This is in full kit, and Cyprus is a hot, sticky place. "Can you see that?" he said. We told him we could. "Thank Christ for that!" he said. It wasn't until that happened we realized that, by being in a group of people . . . it wasn't as frightening as it [must have been for him] alone. I mean, for a marine corporal to disobey my orders and bugger off, then it was something! To run away from something is a serious offence, let's not disguise the fact. He deserted the post I'd given him.'

Steve went on to explain that everybody on the exercise, about 1400 men, also saw the strange 'light'.

'We had radio sets and we could hear the transmissions of other people talking about the light. At one stage the following dialogue took place between a "call sign", which is a unit, and a commanding officer, "Sunray". There was a little bit of chat about the light and then Sunray said: "It must be a flying saucer, ha! ha!". These were the words he used.'

According to Steve the soldiers continued to watch the UFO for about twenty-two minutes. 'We were all professional observers,' he stressed. 'I carry powerful binoculars, night glasses . . . that light took twenty-two minutes to disappear out of sight of the binoculars, to the right of the Moon.'

When questioned about the light – its altitude, its speed, its flight characteristics – Steve said that no impression of sound, movement or speed could be detected. Having no yardstick by which to compare the light, he said, it was simply impossible to measure its size and capabilities. 'I've been trained for twenty-seven years to judge distances but I couldn't tell you if it was a thousand metres high, five thousand metres high, fifty miles high . . . I'm also a professional parachutist so I know distance in the air, but I couldn't tell you how far away or how high it was.'

Similar comments have been made by many UFO witnesses.

The next morning, Steve said, talk of the sighting was paramount among both soldiers and civilians at the base. Indeed, it soon became apparent that virtually everyone had seen the UFO. However, Steve also said that the military had already started to claim that the UFO – which had hovered above the 1400 commandos for twenty-two minutes, remember – could be easily explained. Steve was told that NASA had launched a Mariner probe the previous day and *that* was what the soldiers had seen.

'I rang Aquitiri and asked to speak to the station Met Officer,' Steve explained, 'but I couldn't get hold of him. The lines were burning. So I contacted my opposite number and spoke to him. He said the switchboard had been jammed solid with calls about the light. Then he said: "It was the Mariner shot, that's what we were all watching." Later that morning the colonel sent for me and instructed that all sub-units were to write a report, and anyone who had taken photographs was to hand them in as part of the research into this Mariner thing. This was done.

'Next I went to draw ammunition. I used to lodge my ammunition in a compound. Everyone I saw said: "Did you see the light?" And I'd have to stop and chat about it.

'I went down there [to the ammunition compound] and was talking to the blokes about it. One bloke told me he'd come out of the mess, drunk, footless! He'd managed to get to his car, and had tried to start it, when he looked up and saw what *we*'d seen. He said he became stone-cold sober in seconds! He raced back inside the mess and went 'Ga! ga! ga!', and they all ran out and watched the light.'

The soldiers weren't the only ones to witness the UFO; locals on the island saw it, too. But to them it bore a significance all its own.

'The locals believe a light, a bright light like this one, means the coming of the new Messiah,' Steve explained. 'When I went for my ammo, locals who worked in the ammunition dump told us that the entire village had seen the light and that it was part of their religion of Christ, and that they were all praying in the streets, thinking that the Boss Man had arrived again!

'It wasn't just a few people. It was reported in the local press, so it could easily be checked. You could dead easy get a check on it.'

[I tried in vain. Although I approached various news agencies, including the Cyprus News Clipping Agency in my endeavours to corroborate Steve's story, I was told that no records had been kept from the year in question, 1971. Convenient, one wonders? Or an unfortunate fact of life? It should be said that Steve remains adamant that the local media did indeed cover the story, and in a big way.]

Steve went on: 'I started collating the reports and listening to other people talking about it. Echo company on the left-hand side of the island had observed it, maybe ten minutes earlier than we had. The light came from west to east, halfway across the island, then we watched it come over the mountain and fly south. I didn't know they had Mariner craft that could turn angles and then disappear!'

Steve said that a lot of material was subsequently submitted to the military investigation that followed the incident, including photographs and negatives. 'There was a large quantity of films handed in,' Steve recalled. 'I would say over a hundred rolls of film.' But it wasn't until Steve visited his colonel some few weeks later that he was informed of the results of the investigation. To his surprise, the 'Mariner' story had been dropped.

'About two or three weeks later I went for my morning sherry with the colonel. He said: "That UFO's been confirmed."

'So I said: "What UFO?"

'"Didn't I tell you?" he said. "It came back confirmed. It was a UFO."

'Prior to this the colonel hadn't given me the full brief. I was responsible for running the unit and he would normally have been dead straight with me. On this occasion, for some reason, he'd had a top-level meeting with his company commanders, but he hadn't told me the full story.'

According to the colonel, two quick-response fighters – Lightnings – had been scrambled from Aquitiri Air Base to intercept the UFO. But to no avail.

'In the centre of Cyprus is a place called the Troodhos Mountains, on top of which they've got the most sophisticated radar in the world. The dishes are called "golf balls" because of their appearance, and are maybe three to four hundred feet in circumference. They're used to monitor U2 flights and long-range radar transmissions.

'There's a fighter base at Aquitiri and it's a very sophisticated fighter base. On RAF bases abroad they always have QRF [Quick Response Fighters] burning internally. On an operational base you always have the latest aircraft there, ready to go.

'I was told by the colonel that the "golf balls" up on Troodhos had traced the UFO early on. Now you never get a single plane going off QRF, you always get two. He said they put two Lightnings up, which are capable of about twelve hundred miles an hour. Even so, according to the colonel, the Lightnings couldn't touch it.

'The UFO must have been a fair old height,' Steve marvelled. 'The Troodhos radar would have picked it up at some distance, yet the Lightnings couldn't get near it doing twelve hundred miles an hour. If you ask me how fast the UFO was going I'd say it was almost stationary, and still the Lightnings couldn't touch it.

'But none of the facts relate. It doesn't fit with anything you've ever seen before. I would be very interested in seeing what the Lightnings saw. They would have been put up early enough by radar to get within good distance of [the UFO]. They all carry cameras on board so they would have triggered the cameras if nothing else. These would be cine cameras.'

So the RAF would certainly have been able to study the film in depth following the incident.

But there were other cameras present, too. According to Steve the UFO was also filmed by an official naval photographer who had been assigned to photograph anti-tank guns in action.

'These photos I've given you were taken by a naval publicity photographer. In the middle of the island was the support company which was firing the weapons. The photographer was with this company. He was using tripods set up for night-firing. It wasn't just a hit-and-miss affair with a guy with a camera. This was one of the few occasions when a guy was there with a proper set of equipment. This guy was photographing what are known as "wombats" and "nobats". They're anti-tank guns and they have an open breech called a venturi. When the round fires the propellant burns out the back in a big flash, so when you see them they look very dramatic. That's what these cameras were set for.

'When the light appeared the photographer put his camera on it. I imagine these are the only three surviving photos. He gave me a set of the prints; that's what these are. They're time exposures, so they don't show the ball of light as such, but its trail across the sky. Lots of the people who saw this are still serving. You'll find that the senior officers like me have gone, but lots of the younger ones will still be serving.

'There was no cover-up on the base because it fitted with the Mariner thing, but we all knew it wasn't that. What was surprising was that it didn't make the English press. It's amazing where you've got at least a thousand or more trained observers all looking at the same object – plus you've got the whole small isolated community of Cyprus seeing it, and the event being reported on their radio and in their media – and yet it never got any press coverage here!

'I just heard you by accident on the radio and what clicked in my mind was when you said that you knew the MoD had got something on these lines. I thought: "I'll tell him about the photos." Otherwise they would have just lain there forever.'

File 32: Appendix 01
Case Review: Cosmic Top-X40 Eyes Only PUFORG Comment

'Needless to say we were amazed at Steve's account of this remarkable sighting and subsequent events. As he stated, he is a trained observer and his account shows this and his consternation at what he was seeing. It is obvious the sighting remains vivid in his mind to this day. It was an enthralling report to listen to.

'There is little we can add except some points about the photographs. There were, according to Steve, originally five or six photos, and though the missing ones would have been of value, the others, which Steve has given to PUFORG, are a very welcome addition to our files.

'There are three 6'×8' b/w prints, each showing a bar of light. They are time-lapse shots of approximately 5–6 minutes.

'Photo No. 1

'This shows the object nearest the camera. We cannot account for the double bar of light on this shot, unlike the other two photos that both show a single bar of light. It cannot be caused by camera movement, as the dust illuminated by the object is perfectly clear with no sign of movement or double exposure.

'Photo No. 2

'This shot shows the lights of Dekalia Garrison on the horizon and gives an excellent perspective of the sighting.

'Photo No. 3

'Here the object is furthest from the camera. The dust is still plainly visible. This shot is of note because there are four fainter trails beneath the main light following the same path as the UFO. These smaller lights appeared a couple of minutes into the time exposure and remained parallel with the main light for the rest of the shot. They increase in brightness along their path.

'Though we do not have the negatives our photographic analysts said that the trails are definitely not a blemish or a scratch – they are definitely photographic images. Under magnification the trails are seen to be irregular, as if there was a slight wavering in the flight of these lights. Two of the trails are quite clear but the other two can only be seen under magnification. Three trails appear to be moving in the same direction as the UFO but the fourth looks as if it is approaching the main light head-on. With the other trails they start dim and get brighter. The fourth is dim as it nears the main UFO trail and becomes brighter underneath it . . .'

'. . . We have known that since the 1950s at least, the MoD and similar Defence establishments around the world have had conclusive photographic proof of the existence of UFOs. And the photographic evidence must be quite stunning. On this one spectacular sighting alone, not only were there jets involved – and undoubtedly filming – but the MoD received over one hundred rolls of film of the UFO as well as reports of the event from officers in the field. To repeat, the photographic evidence held by the authorities must be quite stunning.

'We contacted the MoD in London and asked if they could give us any further details of this case, and if it would be possible to see any of the other photographs handed in. In an otherwise helpful reply Nick Pope of the MoD said that unfortunately the case was too old for him to be able to help.

'"The files for 1971 would have been sent to the Public Records Office a long time ago," he told us, "and are covered by the terms of the Public Record Act, remaining closed

337

from public viewing until thirty years after the last action was taken."

'This report from Steve is unique. The huge number of "active" armed forces personnel as witnesses is without precedent, and this must be one of the only UFO reports ever recorded to have UFO photographs taken by a serviceman while on a major exercise.'

Both myself and PUFORG are greatly indebted to Steve for his courage in coming forward with this story. And, by the way, if there is anyone out there who might be able to help corroborate Steve's story (perhaps you were a member of the Royal Marines 41 Commando Group stationed in Cyprus in 1971, or maybe you know someone who was; or perhaps you managed to obtain further photographs of the event) I would be very pleased to hear from you.

File 33
M5 Encounter

During the summer of 1996 I was invited to meet a couple who claimed they'd had a bizarre encounter with a UFO whilst travelling on the southbound carriageway of the M5 motorway. At their request, and due to the fact that they had both held extremely sensitive government posts, I agreed not to publish their names. We will call them Julie and Tom.

On a quiet Sunday morning in June (1996) I drove to a location in the Welsh countryside where I had arranged to meet the couple. I found Tom sitting in the sun, in a beer garden, supping a pint. Julie was sitting opposite him with her hands cupped nervously around a half-empty glass of bitter lemon. The scene was little short of idyllic.

My immediate impression was that Julie and Tom were, well, 'average people', I guess: sincere, friendly, down-to-earth, and above all else deeply concerned that their story should be told accurately and not sensationalized in any way. They mentioned that they had already been courted by two major television companies and a national newspaper, but that they had graciously declined the offers for fear that their story might be misrepresented. Whatever their reasons for agreeing to talk to me it was clearly not for financial gain.

Indeed, Julie and Tom had waited more than six years to tell their story; they were now ready to face the devil, so to speak. And face the devil they did. What follows is their own personal account of their own remarkable encounter – an encounter that, I was soon to discover, had changed their lives completely.

File 33: Appendix 01
Case Report: Cosmic Top-X41 Eyes Only
Abducted

It was May 1990 and Julie and Tom were looking forward to their summer holiday with their two children, Karen, aged eight, and Jane, aged six. They had booked a caravan in the tiny Cornish fishing village of Looe. Tom says he's the kind of person who always tries to miss the main rush of holiday traffic, either setting off very early or very late. As the children had woken up extra early this particular morning, excited at the prospect of their holiday by the sea (Julie and Tom further encouraged by the fact that they had packed the car the night before) the family decided to head off into the predawn darkness. The time was approximately 3:15 a.m.

Having crossed the Severn Bridge they caught the slip

road that filtered them south along a deserted M5 motorway. It was now closing on 4 a.m.; dawn was yet to break. The unpopulated roads meant that they were making good time – there were few heavy lorries on the roads this night, fewer cars. Had they known, however, what this night held in store for them they would never have continued their journey into its twilit silence. And had they not continued their journey, of course, they would never have had such a story to tell as this one . . .

Tom: 'It was between four and four-fifteen in the morning and still dark when we came to some bollards in the road where we had to change lanes. I noticed a very powerful bright light to the left of us, in a field about three hundred yards away. I remember feeling fresh and awake, not at all tired.

'At first I thought the light was probably to do with some building work going on over there, until it started to rise slowly up in the air. Then I thought it must be attached to a lift in a tower or something, but as I thought that it started moving towards us. So I thought, well, it must be a helicopter . . .'

Julie: 'We were still driving along as normal but looking at this bright light, which wasn't pointed directly at us but we could see it was moving. Then, in a second, it was hovering right by us. It didn't fly over towards us – suddenly it was just there, by the side of the car. I said to Tom: "No, you're not dreaming, Tom. It's a UFO!"'

Tom: 'I'd been watching this light out the corner of my eye. Well, I was driving, you see, and I had to keep one eye on the road. But suddenly the light was right on us, only it wasn't a light as we first thought, it was some kind of craft with a very powerful light on it. The next thing we knew *all* the lights came on!'

Julie: 'We could see it very clearly now. It was hovering very close to the car. It was metallic, a sort of dull, dark-grey, and had a blue-and-white strobe light flashing. Along the bottom there was a row of red lights that weren't flashing. They were just on, glowing . . .'

Tom: 'Well, I can tell you at this point I started to panic. My foot was hard down on the accelerator. I just wanted to lose that thing. By now the kids were screaming in the back seat, but as I put my foot down it kept pace with us perfectly . . .'

Julie: 'It was huge, about the size of two very large houses joined together and less than thirty feet from us. I was just praying for it not to hurt the kids . . .'

Tom: 'The thing was simply gliding through the air, silently, no noise whatsoever, keeping perfect pace with the car. I remember the time because afterwards we realized the car's quartz clock had stopped. It was quarter past four. The clock has never worked since.'

Julie: 'I remember thinking that maybe we'd lost some time. We seemed to be further down the road than we should have been. And it had been quite dark before the UFO came . . .'

Tom: 'The next thing I know it's dawn – it's light and we're driving along the road and my main concern was the kids in the back. By this time they were silent. We couldn't get a word out of them . . . I felt like I was in shock. I mean, one minute I'm at the bollards in relative darkness and the next it's light and we're miles further down the road.'

At this point I emptied my glass. It was my round. I disappeared inside and bought the drinks. When I came back out I sat myself down and asked a few pertinent questions . . .

*　　*　　*

341

JK: 'Where were you when you first saw the light, can you remember?'

Julie: 'Yes, there was a sign for the River Axe, I remember that.'

JK: 'And when you realized it was dawn?'

Julie: 'We were just near the sign for the Huntspill River.' [These two points are about eight miles apart, between junctions 21 and 23.]

I then asked: 'What was the last thing you remember?'

Julie: 'I remember thinking: "We are all God's creatures, please don't harm us." Then I felt a pulling sensation on the top of my head and everything went blank. The next thing I knew I was sitting with my head down and my hands on my lap and it felt wonderful to be in my body. The strange thing was I thought how nice it was that it fitted me like a glove.'

Tom: 'When we arrived at the caravan [in Cornwall] I tore a sheet of paper into four pieces and we each separately drew what we had seen.' At this point Tom produced four near-identical drawings of the UFO – the only minor difference being the number of red lights on the bottom.

JK: 'How did you feel when you arrived?'

Tom: 'Well, we were all deeply shaken and violently ill. We all had chronic diarrhoea and vomiting sickness. I tell you it was awful. But it was all worth it in the end. Our lives have changed so dramatically'

JK: 'In what way? Can you be specific?'

Tom: 'Well, where do I start? My life's changed completely. I felt different from that moment on, really. I began to find ordinary situations and people boring – all my old friends, I just couldn't socialize with them any more. It all seemed so superficial. I feel sad about the fact that we've lost all our old friends but we just couldn't talk to them any more.

'I remember one instance in particular, getting into a

conversation about politics with some of my colleagues, some of the most high-ranking dignitaries and government officers in the country. I just broke into the conversation and said: "It doesn't make any difference if Labour or Conservative get in because we're all governed by the ONE anyway. We are all being scrutinized." Well, as you can imagine, it made a few jaws drop, I can tell you!'

Julie: 'I remember one quiet afternoon sitting out in the back garden and just asking, "Who is God?" and "Who made us?" and "Where were we all going?" and feeling sure that I would get an answer soon. That was just before all this happened.'

JK: 'How did the children react to the encounter?'

Tom: 'Well, they still don't talk about it much. But what we have noticed is that they have become so creative – we are amazed at some of the things they can do, considering their ages.'

JK: 'Did any of you find strange marks or scars on your body after the incident?'

Julie: 'I've had this red mark on my head ever since [Julie showed me a small red circle on her scalp] and it's really tender. It often feels really hot and hurts when I think too deeply about things.'

Tom: 'There's nothing like that on me, no.'

JK: 'Do you think you were abducted?'

Tom and Julie: 'We don't really know – we can't really remember. All we know is the lights came on and the next thing we know is we're miles further down the motorway.'

JK: 'Have you ever undergone hypnotic regression to try and find out what might have happened during your time-loss period?'

Julie: 'No. I'm too frightened. I think they hurt me. I think I went on board and I think they hurt me in some way. I don't want to remember that. My life has changed so much for the better since the experience that I'd prefer to focus on that.'

Tom: 'I know it might sound crazy but since the experience we've both become more aware of the spiritual side of things. I love trees and standing stones, and I find I give far more time to my photography now than I ever did. The kids, too, have become very talented with their hands.'

Julie: 'We're not the sort of people to sit around indoors and do nothing. We're always on the move, visiting Avebury and Silbury Hill and other ancient sites.'

Tom: 'I've never photographed a UFO, but I'd dearly love to. In fact, I know that one day I will, and it won't be a fuzzy light in the distance or anything like that. I just know that that's my prime mission in life now, to photograph a UFO that nobody will be able to dismiss. Of course, I had my camera with me when we experienced our encounter, but the last thing on my mind at the time was to take a photograph of it! But next time it'll be different. Next time I'll be ready.'

I came away from my meeting with Tom and Julie feeling strangely uplifted, and yet a little drained as well. I would say the uplifting feeling was something to do with being able to look them squarely in the eye as they told me their story, and to feel the sheer energy and sincerity which I felt was everywhere in them – that, plus the way they seemed to have transformed what had undoubtedly been a nightmarish and nerve-jarring ordeal into something very positive. It is not so easy to account for the 'drained' feeling.

Oddly enough, Julie phoned me a couple of days later and said that she too had felt drained after our meeting. Perhaps it was nothing more than the intensity of sharing such an extraordinary experience with two people who clearly believed every word they said. That, and the unforgiving strength of that Taffy Valley beer!

[My sincere thanks to Julie, Tom and their two children for allowing me to publish their remarkable account. I wish them every happiness for the future.]

DOCUMENT 10

Cosmic Top Secret
Eyes Only Copy One of One

Mind Control

File 34
The Abductors:
Technological Hypnosis
And the Government Abduction Programme

In June 1997, former head of the Pentagon's Foreign Technology in Army Research and Development, Colonel Philip J. Corso, finally confirmed what so-called conspiracy theorists like myself have been claiming for years (see Document 06, File 23). In his book *The Day After Roswell*, Colonel Corso unequivocally stated that the US-based military-industrial complex was in possession of acquired alien technologies, and that said technologies had been gleaned from reverse-engineering the mechanics of recovered alien spacecraft. Colonel Corso, a man of impeccable credentials who admitted to being in charge of the US government's 'alien technology' programme during the 1960s, went on to reveal that technologies gleaned from the Roswell crash (and other similar incidents) became the precursors for today's laser technology, fibre optics, computer hardware/microchip technology, super-tenacity fibres and night-vision equipment . . . plus a host of still-secret, still-classified technologies including various psychotronic devices capable of translating human thoughts and emotions into electronic signals, and vice versa. It is these 'still-secret, still-classified' technologies to which our attention will be given in Document 10.

A 1991 nationwide (US) survey commissioned by the Bigelow Holding Company and conducted by the highly reputable Roper Organization found by extrapolation that literally millions of Americans considered themselves to be UFO abductees – that they had been abducted by aliens and experimented on. Thousands more similar accounts have been reported and logged worldwide.

Many of those questioned said that their experiences were plainly horrific. Many (an estimated 14,800,000), for example, bore physical scars that had seemingly appeared overnight and that neither they nor close friends – nor even relatives – could explain. Under examination some of the scars proved to be the result of 'implant operations' – tiny electrode-type 'microchip' devices surgically implanted, in some cases just beneath the skin, in other cases in the inner ear, in the nasal cavities, in the eye, even in the brain. Some of these implants have since been surgically extracted and appear in essence to be extremely sophisticated integrated circuits – or, more simply put, electronic receiver-transmitters, chip-sized, like space-age radio tags. Indeed, on initial examination the implants seemed so sophisticated, and so exotic, that it was thought they could not possibly have originated on Earth. They were thus seen to represent incontrovertible proof that aliens from another world were abducting people and implanting them with microscopic bits of off-planet technology. And, for the most part, the UFO research community swallowed this conclusion.

In further support of this theory the survey and other investigations found that many 'abductees' bore painful memories of small grey alien creatures who they claimed had stolen them from their beds or their daily routines and had taken them aboard their 'spaceships'. The small grey aliens – these days known more simply as 'greys' – had then performed medical-style operations on them.

To counter this, other reports stated that the so-called greys seemed subordinate to taller, more 'humanoid' figures, and that indeed it was the 'humanoid' aliens (often described as wearing 'white coats' and 'white masks' – like 'surgeons' – and sometimes even speaking with American accents) who actually performed the operations. In these instances the smaller greys, it was claimed, seemed little more than automaton helpers, clone-like creatures responding to commands given by the humanoids like a robot responds to its programme. It should also be said that those who remembered anything at all about their ordeals only seemed able to recall the details through something of a drug-like haze, as though they had been under some kind of psychotropic/psychotronic influence whilst in the aliens' custody. Others reported hallucinogenic after-effects that lingered in their minds like LSD flashbacks, even to this day. Still others complained of recurring nightmares, headaches, diarrhoea and vomiting.

In conclusion: investigations found that, while only a small proportion of abductees seemed able to give fairly vivid descriptions of their abduction environment – the inside of the 'spacecraft', its technological parameters, its flight capabilities, etc. – a relatively large proportion were able to give detailed accounts of the surgical procedures performed on them and the cold, clinical atmosphere of the environment in which these procedures were performed. Common to virtually all cases were the clone-like greys and the taller humanoids.

On the face of it, then, the suggestion is that an advanced alien species with unknown motives has journeyed to Earth in order to conduct genetic experiments/implant operations on a less evolved galactic species: humans. OK, it's possible, I guess. But let me offer you an alternative scenario.

File 34: Appendix 01
Case Inquiry: Cosmic Top-X42 Eyes Only Smokescreen

A growing body of evidence now suggests that some of the 'still-secret, still-classified' acquired alien technologies referred to by Colonel Philip J. Corso are today being used in some insidious electronically induced 'human behaviour' experiment, and that the so-called 'alien abduction' phenomenon is the smokescreen behind which much of this experiment is being carried out.

A mass mind-control programme, the evidence says, is currently being perpetrated on specifically targeted sectors of the international community by covert military and intelligence agencies such as the CIA. A relatively minor part of this exercise (though no less insidious for that) involves the systematic programming of the collective mind with often grotesque and menacing images of aliens (a process achieved via media and advertising channels, plus television dramas such as *Dark Skies*, *The X Files* and blockbuster movies such as *Independence Day*). The growth of the idea that aliens are hostile and therefore a threat to national and global security is thus facilitated. And so the UFO/ET phenomenon – together with its attendant new technologies – remains the exclusive property of the military.

Another – and certainly more pernicious – aspect of this same operation involves flooding the airwaves with extremely-low-frequency (ELF) pulse-modulated microwave signals (ELF is the end of the frequency-spectrum at which the human brain responds and functions). When these microwave signals are fine-tuned to match known behavioural frequencies they induce chemical reactions in the target-victim's brain that in turn engender specific moods and/or states of mind (see File 35). This can be achieved with the same devastating effect whether the target-victim is an individual, a group or even a nation. The target-victim thus becomes a pawn in the hands of the remote-controller.

But perhaps the most sinister aspect of this mind-control/human-behaviour operation involves what has become known as the 'alien abduction phenomenon'. Evidence now points to the fact that, not only is the so-called alien abduction phenomenon the product of government, and not alien, activity, but that the entire alien abduction scenario is a government invention, a 'smokescreen' used to conceal the genetic research and electronic mind-control programmes carried out by covert military-industrial scientists. At the same time, of course, this propaganda exercise serves to reinforce the fear factor in public attitudes and reactions to the extraterrestrial presence – a double rap. The idea that some quasi-military special forces unit is abducting innocent people so that black-budget government scientists can carry out their genetic research and mind-control experiments on them is, of course, quite absurd, at least on the face of it. But the evidence is there just the same.

I recall your attention, for example, to the ordeal faced by 'Mark' and the five other British soldiers who were zapped by a beam-weapon projected from a UFO whilst on night manoeuvres on Salisbury Plain (see Document 06, File 24). This beam-weapon rendered the soldiers senseless. 'Mark' is now convinced that he and his colleagues were used as guinea pigs in some covert government mind-control experiment.

And, then again, there was the similar ordeal faced by George Vernon (Document 06, File 25). George, remember, heard a voice in his head that guided him undetected into the restricted military zone where Operation Blackbird was taking place (a secure area cordoned off by the British Army and hundreds of thousands of pounds' worth of hi-tech military surveillance equipment – yet George was still able to slip the net: how?). He was then approached by what appear to have been 'black-ops' military personnel who were able to control his mind like a puppeteer controls his puppet. Evidence that certain 'suicide bomb' terrorists and political assassins are also victims of government mind-control operations is now overwhelming.

But if any one of the above seemingly absurd notions holds any truth at all then the question surely arises: What possible motive could the military-industrial complex have for conducting mind-control experiments on the innocent public?

Read on . . .

File 34: Appendix 02
Case Study: Cosmic Top-X43 Eyes Only
MK-ULTRA
Remote Control

The following evidence is based largely on abductee testimony (in particular the numerous anachronistic and out-of-character features found in many abduction accounts) plus

CIA admission to the effect that its scientists have indeed been active for nearly fifty years in the research and development of 'behaviour control' techniques and technologies.

Over the past few years the CIA has – to some meagre extent – finally confessed to its involvement in parapsychological and psychotronic research and development programmes. For example, as a strictly defensive response to Chinese 'brainwashing' of US prisoners of war during the Korean War (1950–1953) the agency says that its scientists were directed to undertake a series of mind-control experiments under the code name MK-ULTRA (subsequently MK-SEARCH). This highly secret 'black' programme was initiated in 1953 and included research into electric-shock treatment; human irradiation tests; the effects of various drugs (in particular LSD), ultrasonic devices and microwave frequencies on the human brain; and perhaps more pertinent so far as we are concerned, electrode implants surgically inserted in the human body for the purpose of what has become known as 'remote hypnosis', or 'remote influencing'. Indeed, this 'remote control' programme was to become one of the most notorious – and plainly evil – CIA operations ever known. Though many documents concerning the programme were destroyed by former CIA Director Richard Helms (when he left office in 1973), nevertheless the surviving archive files tell the story clearly enough.

That certain sectors within the US-based military-industrial complex are in possession of technologies capable of inducing a so-called 'alien abduction' scenario is now beyond doubt. With a minimum of forty-five years' research behind it the CIA's remote-control technologies must be as far in advance of ordinary microwave transmitters as UFOs are in advance of the Wright Brothers. Indeed, evidence now suggests that at least some so-called alien abduction cases are the result of technologically induced 'screen memories' – false mental impressions created by CIA and other quasi-government/military scientists in order to cover up their mind-control and genetic research activities. State-of-the-art technology and/or the use of drug-induced/drug-augmented hypnosis would be easily sufficient to generate such 'screen memories'.

Holographic and virtual-reality modes, for example, could be utilized to present the abductee with life-like 'sci-fi' sounds and images to create the impression of an 'on-board experience'. While under the influence of psychotropic drugs and/or technologically induced psychotronic effects, the sounds and images would appear to the abductee as real as nightmares. Recalling such an experience in future dreams or under hypnotic regression would only add to its authenticity – on 'waking up' from the ordeal the victim would indeed believe that he or she had been abducted by aliens and experimented on.

Before we turn our eyes to the skies in search of the abduction perpetrators, then, I suggest we first look a little closer to home – in the deep and cavernous bowels of military requirement, for one. After all, that the military is in possession of this technology is no longer in question; that covert military-industrial agencies are implicated in the perpetration of this phenomenon is equally evident. But what of the motive? What possible reason could the military have for abducting people, performing genetic experiments on them and/or implanting them with microscopic receiver/transmitters? According to author, Martin Cannon, modern warfare theorists claim they might have the answer.

Some of the world's leading modern warfare theorists claim that the reason US military-industrial programmes may well be responsible, at least in part, for the so-called alien abduction scenario is to do with what they term 'requisite military requirement'. Top theorists say that military ambitions to create a 'non-thinking soldier', for example, in particular someone who is able to suffer the traumas of psychotronic and chemical/biological warfare without displaying reaction to the effects (or, indeed, to the very thought of having to do battle under such abominable conditions) are reason enough to justify such programmes. Indeed, these ambitions know no bounds. The soldier of the future, they say, must by necessity be a remote-controlled automaton-like entity who responds only to commands transmitted via his 'chip-in-brain implant'. He must be numb to all else. His thoughts, his desires, even his own intracerebral neuronic impulses must be overridden by remote electronic commands. While theorists agree that this same level of control can be facilitated chemically with the use of mind-altering, mind-controlling drugs (a process dubbed 'narco-hypnosis' by CIA scientists), the ability to monitor and control technologically the neuronic commands and responses of the soldier in the field via the remote stimulation of his implant would be far more predictable and effective. Thus it is towards the development of more and more sophisticated 'remote hypnosis' technologies that the British and US governments' most covert scientists are today working (and have been for a minimum of forty-five years).

When you consider that, together with the CIA-sponsored drugs trade and the development of new and often breakneck technologies, the world's black-budget economy subsists largely on the spoils of war – on the covert sale of arms, the nuclear defence industry and the protection of oil-rich nations such as Kuwait – and when you further consider that this economy is orchestrated by the unseen engineers of civil and international conflict anyway, a picture begins to emerge in which the need for the non-thinking soldier becomes a paramount requirement. When the soldier in the field begins to question the motives for his part in any given conflict, for example, political or otherwise, the war machine grinds to a halt. The outcome of wars is planned from the outset: Vietnam is the prime example of a 'wrong outcome'. It was not planned that way. The black-budget spin doctors messed up. Which is why Vietnam is still a symbol of the downfall of presidents. 'We do not want another Vietnam on our hands,' all presidents say, at one time or another. All presidents say this because a 'wrong outcome' throws the economy into turmoil – careers are ruined; lives are lost. Such a situation cannot be permitted.

In his excellent paper on this subject, *The Controllers*, Martin Cannon explains how Vietnam showed us that soldiers are first and foremost human beings, and that, despite the barrage of propaganda hurled at them, human beings will sooner or later perceive the difference between a war based on genuine national security interests and one based on political manoeuvring. As Mr Cannon writes: 'To forestall this realization, or to render it irrelevant, military planners must withdraw the human combatant and replace him with a new species of warrior.'

And further: 'The soldier of the future will not discern; he will merely do. He will not be a butcher; he will be the butcher's *knife* – a tool among tools, thoughtless and effective.'

The mind-controlled, non-thinking soldier.

Another reason for suspecting that the so-called alien abduction phenomenon could be the result of some covert government/military agenda falls once again in the category of requisite intelligence and/or military requirement. The CIA, for example, is said to employ technologically based mind-control techniques as a way of creating torture-proof agents, such as those assigned to extremely sensitive and highly dangerous counter-intelligence missions 'behind enemy lines'. The remote control of pre-programmed assassins such as Sirhan Sirhan (see Document 03, File 13) who was framed by the FBI for the assassination of Robert Kennedy must of course be a further consideration.

Yet another reason for suspecting that the abduction phenomenon could be government-sponsored is, of course, the possibility that the victims concerned are being used for genetic research. These days, the theory that aliens are abducting humans (and mutilating cattle) in order to study our genetic make-up and/or to extract certain chromosomes and DNA codes is as popular as roast on Sunday. Indeed, many abductees have reported the artificial extraction of sperm and ova during their experiences, and the fact that the 'aliens' are busy splicing together human and alien genetic materials in their efforts to engineer some hybrid monster. I argue, however, that the only entities in sore need of genetic enlightenment are humans and, more specifically, military-industrial scientists involved in highly immoral eugenics programmes and other genetic research and cloning procedures. Indeed, as we speak animals and their organs (and, for all we know, humans and *their* organs, too) are being cloned for human transplant in secret government laboratories, some say for the good of humanity. Insiders, on the other hand, say it is primarily for the purpose of providing longevity to the elite and their kin (in the form of replaceable spare parts – hearts, livers, kidneys, fresh brains programmed with an 'entire lifetime's experiences' courtesy of British Telecom and its newly developed 'Soul Catcher 2025' implant). Still others claim that the Nazi dream of genetically engineering a new 'Aryan' race did not die with Hitler in 1945 but is today being continued by CIA scientists who learned their trade from Third Reich henchmen such as Klaus Barbie (the 'Lyon Butcher') and Holocaust mastermind Otto von Bolschwing. It is now no secret that top Nazi officials and scientists were smuggled out of Germany towards the end of World War II instead of facing war crimes charges (see Document 03, File 10). As part of a massive covert operation code-named 'Operation Paperclip' these unspeakable monsters found a new life and new 'specimens' in post-war America. So-called alien abductions and cattle mutilations would indeed have provided – and would continue to provide – the necessary DNA and bodily parts (as well as the perfect cover) for this abominable research. Indeed, my contention is that this is almost certainly the case – that extraterrestrials are not responsible for the so-called alien abduction scenario (at least not all of it) but that humans are being surreptitiously abducted from their daily routines by covert military and/or intelligence units and experimented on by black-budget government scientists. As fantastic as this may seem, the evidence speaks louder than one's desire to believe otherwise.

File 34: Appendix 03
Case Study: Cosmic Top-X44 Eyes Only
Stimoceiver
RHIC-EDOM

As briefly mentioned above, neuroscan imaging, X-rays, magnetic resonance imaging (MRI) and surgical extractions have certainly borne out abductees' claims that they have been mysteriously implanted with minute foreign objects. But are these implants evidence of alien technology?

In the late 1950s/early 1960s an eminent neuroscientist

named Jose Delgado invented what he called a 'stimoceiver', a minute electrode capable of receiving and transmitting electronic signals via FM radio waves. A stimoceiver implanted in the brain via the sinus cavities, for example (a common abductee scenario) will act as a powerful stimulant when activated by FM radio waves. This arrangement is indeed capable of wielding a surprising degree of control over the victim's cerebral functions and responses from some considerable distance. For the present moment, whether or not such devices are being used by the military is not the question. The point is that these miniature devices exist: they are part of human/terrestrial technology, and they have been for at least forty years. It seems absurd that aliens capable of technological feats as yet inconceivable to us (such as interstellar and/or intergalactic, possibly even hyperspatial travel) would resort to such 'Stone Age' technologies as receiver/transmitter microchips.

A further point to be considered is the rather disturbing fact that many abductees recall not only being taken on board 'spaceships' but being taken to underground military bases where their implant operations are often carried out. Interestingly – on a par with *alien* abduction reports – these *military* abduction reports also tell of automaton-like small grey creatures with large black wrap-around eyes who seem both witless and emotionless, and taller 'humanoid' aliens, again often described as wearing surgeons' clothing and being able to talk in the abductee's native tongue, in some cases even using native slang. While it is by no means beyond the bounds of possibility for technologically advanced aliens to have mastered the human language – quirks, traits, warts and all – such testimony nevertheless poses the possibility that the 'humanoids' are in fact true humans, and not aliens. Since the reports seem to imply that the operations are carried out at underground military bases it would be reasonable to conclude that these humans are in fact military personnel, most likely military-industrial scientists assigned to covert mind-control and/or genetic research programmes. Though abhorrent in the extreme, the idea is not as ludicrous as it might at first seem.

After all, if military-industrial agencies are indeed working towards perfecting their 'stimoceiver' and other 'chip-in-brain implant' capabilities then guinea pigs would certainly be needed. Hence the abductions. And what better cover story for this insidious operation than to create an 'alien-abduction-and-implant' scenario? What better way to disguise the fact that the supersecret black-operations military are the real abductors, military-industrial scientists the true implanters?

On the other hand, of course, if there *is* a race of bad-dude aliens out there and they too are conducting genetic experiments on humans then the cover story is even more viable – it is already in place. There would be no need for the perpetrators to invent a new one. Rather, it would be far wiser to simply hide behind the existing one and blame it on the aliens.

Which, the evidence seems to suggest, could well be the game plan to date.

Yet another major feature in the so-called alien abduction scenario is that of missing time, or 'time-loss', suggesting that the aliens might possess some kind of supernatural power capable of erasing periods of time from the abductees' memory. But is there any evidence to suggest that advanced terrestrial technology could in fact produce this same result? I think there is.

Perhaps here I should stress the fact that the abduction experience in itself bears all the hallmarks of a hypnotically engendered state (maybe this is why hypnotic regression can be such an effective tool in unlocking and releasing the experience from memory.) Hypnosis, whether chemically or electronically induced, is a key to the enigma of time-loss.

For many years now it has been known that the CIA possesses and employs a rather pernicious technology called 'RHIC-EDOM'. It is claimed that the combined effects of RHIC (Radio Hypnotic Intracerebral Control) and EDOM (Electronic Dissolution Of Memory) can and does induce states of hypnotic trance/remote influence and memory loss. Utilizing the implanted stimoceiver as its point of stimulus RHIC remotely controls the subject's intracerebral functions and responses while EDOM, by jamming the synaptic transmissions in specific areas of the subject's brain, is the mechanism that creates the missing-time scenario. Necessary neural transmissions are prevented from taking place along selected neuro-canals thereby rendering the subject 'memory-less' – the subject's memory is simply erased from consciousness. The result? No memory of the abduction or of how long the implant operation may have taken. As if from a bad dream the victim 'wakes up' from the experience wondering where on Earth they are and what has happened to them. And why minutes, often hours (sometimes days) have gone by without explanation.

Again, this is twentieth-century terrestrial technology, no aliens required.

File 35
Project Pandora
ELF Pulse-Modulated Microwaves

Though many of the CIA's mind-control records were destroyed in 1973 by its former Director, Richard Helms, the surviving evidence suggests that the programme lives on – not only in the US but in Britain, too. And that it has done for several decades.

In order to demonstrate the fact that remote mind-control technology (RMCT) indeed exists – that it is not the figment of some wildly paranoid imagination – and that it exists at a very advanced operational level, I intend here in File 35 to call upon the assistance of one or two specialists in this field. Not the least of these is Tim Rifat, Britain's top RMCT expert.

According to Mr Rifat, electronic mind-control as a new class of weapon became operational in 1965. It was then, after eighteen years of researching and developing acquired alien psychotronics, that the US government finally mastered (at least to some degree) the aliens' ability to stimulate thought and emotion via remote electronic stimulus. It was then also that the now-infamous CIA-funded 'Project Pandora' was initiated, in which the effects of carefully modulated microwave radiation were used to influence brain functions. The chief researcher on this project was one Dr Ross Adey.

In an interview conducted for *UFO Reality* magazine, Tim Rifat told me:

'Dr Adey's research at the Brain Research Institute of the University of California demonstrated that there was a way to control human behaviour and reaction by using "pulse-modulated microwave electromagnetic [EM] radiation". Pulse-modulated microwaves were found to be especially useful as the carrier for mind-control signals as they were able to pass through the cranium, which is rather resistant to low-level EM. The pulse-modulated microwave carrier-beam could then be used to carry signals, rather like radio signals can be frequency- or amplitude-modulated to carry music or speech.

'One of the aims of the research was to be able to place sounds and speech in the victim's brain. This intracerebral hearing could be used to drive the victim mad, as no one else would be able to hear the voices transmitted but the victim himself. Further research was carried out to see what conditions were needed for the transmission of data directly into the victim's brain using microwave carrier-beams. This reaction was found to be dependent on the frequency, amplitude and dose of the microwave radiation used. By mimicking natural brain frequencies the human brain could be controlled remotely by use of pulse-modulated microwave beams modulated in such a way as to carry these vital frequencies. A thorough understanding of the leap forward in mind-control technology has to be appreciated; in one jump the CIA learnt how to control human behaviour and thoughts by use of microwaves. This is called ELF pulse-modulated microwave remote mind-control technology; or, more simply, just remote mind-control technology (RMCT). These days, of course, RMCT has developed into an abhorrent class of weapons, one which is frequently used by the CIA, as well as by MI5 and MI6.'

No doubt the KGB and other more covert agencies, too.

In support of Mr Rifat's claims, American RMCT expert Anna Keeler says that this 'abhorrent class of [microwave] weapons' has been proven to cause 'leukemia, skin cancer, cataracts and various forms of emotional illness', as well as being able to 'induce heart seizures; create leaks in the blood/brain barrier, which would allow neurotoxins in the blood to cross and cause neurological damage or behavioural disorders; and . . . produce auditory hallucinations or microwave hearing, during which the person can hear tones that seem to be coming from within the head or from directly behind it'. In Jim Keith's superb book *Secret and Suppressed* Anna Keeler goes on to suggest that words transmitted via low-density microwaves or radio frequencies could be used to remotely influence unwitting victims. She explains how in 1984, for example, a US House of Representatives report stated that a large number of stores across America had been subliminally transmitting high-frequency words – above the range of human hearing – in an attempt to reduce shoplifting. Evidently the exercise was very successful. Results showed that shoplifting had been reduced by as much as eighty per cent. As Anna Keeler concluded: 'Surely, the CIA and military haven't overlooked such useful technology.'

Indeed not. In accord with Anna Keeler's findings, Dr James Lin of Wayne State University remarked: 'The capability of communicating directly with humans by pulsed microwaves is obviously not limited to the field of therapeutic medicine.' And further, Dr R. O. Becker, twice Nobel Prize nominee for his research into bio-electromagnetism, was even more explicit when he wrote of the 'obvious applications in covert operations designed to drive a target crazy with "voices"'.

Once again I recall your attention to the experience under-gone by George Vernon, who suffered no less than three nervous breakdowns following his Operation Blackbird ordeal (see File 34 above, and Document 06, File 25). I should also remind you here of my allusions to the use of 'sleeper agents' for covert political and other high-profile assassinations, such as Robert Kennedy, Martin Luther King . . .

. . . Princess Diana?

'Drive faster,' the voice in his head seemed to whisper. 'Drive faster . . .'

*   *   *

Next I asked Tim Rifat to explain something of the RMCT weapons arsenal currently being used by the intelligence community, both in the US and in Britain.

'The electronic RMCT weapons system falls into a number of classes,' he explained. 'The simplest employs microwaves at low amplitudes, 10,000 microwatts per centimetre squared, to cause performance decrements and disorganization. This is used to make subversives ill.

'It was found that beaming microwaves at people made them fatigued – their immune system, after an initial boost, became highly depressed in function. The victim suffered neurological damage which affected his/her mentation and ability to perform. Premature ageing, cancer-stimulation and blood-cell irregularities, as well as cataracts in later life, all added to the long-term damage done to victims by US and UK intelligence agencies.'

And these techniques are being used by the intelligence agencies today?

'They are, yes. Referred to as "hot spots", the irradiation of victims' homes with microwaves is carried out on a large scale. Organizations which irritate the authorities have their buildings turned into a hot spot by microwave rigs so that staff all suffer "sick building syndrome", caused by microwave damage. Or the staff of the target organization have their behaviour changed to cause discord. This technology is so successful that MI5 use it frequently – they will microwave anybody or any organization which in any way alarms them. Beware, they are easily alarmed!

'If this doesn't work, the next step is increasing the field-intensity of the microwaves to cause local hot spots in the victim's body areas which have poor circulation, such as the eyes and the gall bladder. The microwaves heat up these tissues as they don't have the blood circulation to carry away the excess heat. The victim feels nothing but sustains acute and chronic illness in these areas. Intelligence organizations in the West use this technology to disable what they call "permanently subversive elements", ones they cannot scare off.

'The Greenham Common Women are examples of this. These women were systematically irradiated with microwaves to make them ill, symptoms of which included vertigo, retinal bleeding, burnt face (even at night), sleep disturbances, nausea, loss of concentration, palpitations, memory loss, disorientation, migraines, paralysis, faulty speech-coordination, irritability and anxiety attacks. These are standard symptoms of microwave attack at low-intensity, non-thermal exposure. US victims are called "wavies".'

So how exactly do microwaves bring about these effects?

'When ELF-modulated microwaves are used, they are keyed to distinctive patterns of brainwaves called "preparatory sets", which exist for every mechanical gesture the body makes. There are also specific "excitation potentials" which exist for specific emotional states – excitatory reactions, subliminal stress, behavioural arousal, enhanced suggestibility by inhibition of higher functions and patterned behaviour – all of which are controlled by intelligence operatives. This technology is used by the CIA and MI5 to modify the behaviour of "high-profile subversives", for example. Discrediting well-known people who are causing problems for the elite is achieved by subjecting them to pulse-modulated microwaves which carry hysteria encoded as ELF excitation potentials. This makes the troublesome high-profile person display behaviour which discredits them. Examples of this methodology are, allegedly: David Icke, Fergie, and the late Princess Diana . . .

'. . . Outside environmental reinforcement by use of media

agents in league with MI5 assures that the high-profile person's mind-controlled hysterical outburst will be put in the worst possible light to discredit them. In this way high-profile subversives who cannot be fitted-up in the normal way by Britain's police, or taken out by assassination squads such as "Pegasus", are made harmless to the establishment.'

On occasion, however, it would seem that to discredit the 'high-profile subversive' is simply not enough, in particular when she poses such an obvious and direct threat to the constitutional status quo.

'Drive faster,' the voice in his head seemed to say. 'Drive faster . . .'

File 35: Appendix 01
Case Study: Cosmic Top-X45 Eyes Only Alien Abduction

'It has been reported that a triangular black UFO either piloted or accompanied by US black-ops military personnel fired a beam at British soldiers which paralyzed them (see Document 06, File 24). This technology is quite well known.

'Neurological research has found that the brain has specific frequencies for each voluntary movement, called "preparatory sets". When you pick up a cup of tea there is a specific preparatory set for this action. A pulse-modulated microwave beam carrying an ELF signal which is identical to the one in the motor neurone centre of the brain is used to jam the abductee's motor coordination. This technology is similar to television interference wherein the TV is snowed-out by the jamming from a more powerful signal at the same frequency.

'In the case of abductees their motor neurone excitation potentials are swamped by a bigger signal carried by a microwave carrier-beam which literally swamps the brain so that it cannot control the body. Pulse-modulated weapons – which broadcast the ELF preparatory sets of the motor cortex at the victim – will paralyze the subject of the abduction without killing them, as breathing and heartbeat are involuntary actions controlled by another set of frequencies in another part of the brain. Once the abduction victim has been paralyzed they can be taken aboard government/alien craft. Mind-control technology has progressed so quickly because the US and UK Secret Governments have had a never-ending supply of abduction victims which they have used for neurological brain vivisection – to obtain preparatory sets and excitation potentials, the code for the pulse-modulated mind-control weapons.

'Undamaged experimentation victims are then brain-wiped to clear all short-term memories from their consciousness. This is relatively easy, as the technology is quite well-developed.'

File 35: Appendix 02
Case Study: Cosmic Top-X46 Eyes Only Memory Loss

'When you remember something it is first stored in your short-term memory. After approximately twelve hours this short-term memory is converted in the brain to long-term memory, after which you remember this information for the rest of your life. If this conversion from short-term memory to long-term memory does not occur, the data is lost. A simple example is forgetting the description of a person you saw involved in a crime incident. It is well known that witness evidence is highly suspect. People do not remember consciously (in any efficient manner) what they do not make special efforts to remember, such as car number plates – even though they saw them for a moment.

'The CIA-funded scientists found that microwave radiation could interfere with this transfer of memories from short- to long-term memory. Microwave/RF radiation of a specific frequency of 450MHz could interfere with the calcium efflux events (the transfer of calcium into or out of synapses – the connections between brain cells) and by this means the memory of people could be interfered with. Memories were lost when people were irradiated with these frequencies.

'More advanced electronic RMCT used ELF-modulated masers for long-range penetrative invasive EM mind-control. Together with Doppler-shifted interrogative RMCT masers, the victim's brain-states can be analyzed at a distance and the "subversive" can be modified at a distance. Developments on this technique and the use of low-frequency EM radiation to see through walls has allowed intelligence agencies in the US to make useful inroads on the path to "synthetic telepathy" – the electronic scanning of victims' brains by monitoring the electromagnetic emissions from people's brains and using, among other things, the P300 brainwaves (as measured on an EEG) to read the victims' subvocalized thoughts. Sony has for five years ploughed millions of yen into researching this area. In *New Scientist* a recent article described how Japanese scientists were beginning to electronically read the P300 brainwaves so that computers could scan the brain for verbal content.

'This research has, at present, been able to match up only a handful of words which are passing through the subject's brain. However, there has been much anecdotal reference to a supersecret part of the US military which has developed means of electronically scanning the brain to read the subvocalization which passes through the mind. Synthetic telepathy, the ability to electronically scan subversives' brains, would be a valuable tool for the US military that, since the fall of the Soviet Union, fears its own population more than those of its enemies.'

And people say *conspiracy theorists* are paranoid!

Finally I asked Mr Rifat the sixty-four-thousand-dollar question: Where in his opinion did this technology originate? His reply was unequivocal.

'The rapid development of this mind-control technology by the US and UK military/intelligence community indicates that there may indeed have been some reverse-engineering from captured aliens and their craft [as revealed by Colonel Philip J. Corso – see File 34 above and Document 06, File 23] or knowledge-transfer in exchange for bases of operation such as Area 51.'

And the White House, Parliament, the Vatican . . .

. . . Some deal.

Files 34/35: Addendum
Data Review: Cosmic Top-X47 Eyes Only
Brave New World

The idea that some covert arm of the military-industrial complex is using human specimens in order to perfect its technological goals (some say political goals, too) is both hideous and unbelievable. Yet the evidence suggests that this may well be precisely what is happening.

Literally thousands of people in Britain and America believe that they have been abducted by aliens. They believe this because they have managed to access memories of being abducted by 'beings' who appear identical to the stereotypical 'grey' alien, the same little bug-eyed monster that has been thrust into the public face by what I believe to be a very clever, very stealthy, very insidious and very deliberate government propaganda programme.

To add to this, a very high percentage of abductees recall the fact that they have been implanted and/or experimented on during their abduction experiences. Surgical extractions, plus comprehensive medical and psychological tests carried out under strict laboratory conditions, only tend to confirm that the abductees' claims are indeed genuine – except for one rather crucial factor.

A rapidly mounting body of evidence now suggests that the 'abductors' are far more likely to be British and/or US military special forces than aliens and, likewise, the 'experimenters' are far more likely to be black-budget government scientists than interstellar travellers. And further, this same body of evidence also points to the fact that the victims' recollections of 'bug-eyed aliens' as the perpetrators of their abduction ordeals are nothing more than technologically induced 'screen memories', a technique developed – according to Colonel Philip J. Corso – as a result of the CIA and other covert government agencies reverse-engineering acquired alien technology.

In short, the indications are that employees of your government and mine, under the guise of being 'alien abductors', are responsible for secret Nazi-like experiments perpetrated on the innocent public – that's us: you and me. What the motive is – *exactly* – is yet to be determined. But if the more radical conspiracy theories are to be believed then some horrific backstairs stratagem is under way, one that involves the microchipping of a critical-mass number of humans with a view to creating some imminent *Brave New World* scenario wherein the masses become remotely controlled automatons programmed to serve whatever agenda the elite has chosen to sanction. And furthermore, such an agenda would seem to include the summary cloning (genetic engineering) of human 'spare parts' (organs) with a view to offering longevity to the elite few while their automaton servers (that's us, remember, the ones providing the spare parts) become ever more mindless pawns in the game.

A staged 'alien invasion', the most die-hard conspiracy theorists say, facilitated by a technodelic mix of holographically projected aerial phenomena and strategically deployed UAVs (Unmanned Air Vehicles) would be the desired end game. Why? Because such an *Independence Day* scenario would engender fear enough in the global population that the immediate and urgent establishment of some saviour-like though totalitarian New World Order/One World Government would not only be welcomed by the frightened masses, it would be downright demanded by them.

And thus the conspiracy theorists' worst nightmare – the Brave New World/New World Order scenario – would finally be achieved.

Absurd? Abhorrent? Well, yes, of course it is. But so is the thought of government scientists injecting pregnant women with plutonium, simply to measure the effect. As is the thought of government scientists releasing deadly viruses into the environment, simply to measure the effect. As is the thought of government scientists subjecting 'guinea pig' populations to the effects of radiation, simply to measure the effect . . . .

. . . And as is the thought of government scientists developing remote mind-control technology (RMCT), implanting that technology in unsuspecting victims and simultaneously inventing the so-called 'alien abduction' scenario as a convenient smokescreen.

At least three out of the four above examples are indisputable facts. And to judge by the evidence now available, the fourth must be worth at least an each-way bet.

DOCUMENT 11

Cosmic Top Secret
Eyes Only Copy One Of One

Deep Underground (Part 1)
Alien/Government Bases

File 36
Tunnels and Cities

A vast network of tunnels, cities and joint alien/government bases lies deeply hidden beneath the surface of the Earth. So say the latest conspiracy theories. But what evidence is there to support such a seemingly absurd claim? And, moreover, what could be the motive behind the construction of such an alien/government netherworld . . . ?

According to former US special forces operative and geological-cum-structural engineer Phil Schneider – who, before his tragic and mysterious death in January 1996 helped build underground complexes at Area 51, Nevada; Dulce, New Mexico; and Denver, Colorado, among others – a complex deep-underground tunnel system has been under construction in the United States since at least the 1950s. Indeed, this tunnel system is now – forty years on

– rumoured to criss-cross continental North America like a massive underground railway network, linking more than one hundred deep-underground facilities that are said to be operational in the US alone. (Others are said to exist in Britain, Sweden, Switzerland, France, Germany, Australia, South Africa, the Middle East, Israel and Russia – some even say in Antarctica, too.)

But what hard evidence is there to support such claims?

In his excellent book, *Underground Bases and Tunnels: What is the Government Trying to Hide?* US black projects investigator Dr Richard Sauder PhD claims to have uncovered official documentation that reveals the US government's plans for 'deep underground, elaborate tunnel systems' and 'secret underground government installations'.

According to Dr Sauder, recently uncovered US government documents reveal that the US Army Corps of Engineers has been heavily involved with the construction of underground facilities since the 1960s. Indeed, an official US Army Corps of Engineers report published in 1985, entitled *Literature Survey of Underground Construction Methods for Application to Hardened Facilities*, concludes:

'Since adequate technology is available to construct hardened underground facilities under virtually any ground conditions, the main constraint in construction projects remains economic viability rather than technical feasibility.'

In other words, if the money is available, then the technology to construct hardened underground facilities is also available. And with at least $600 billion a year being made available for black-budget projects (in the US alone) then I'm sure a nickel or two could be spared for the US Army Corps of Engineers to dig holes in the ground. Big holes in the ground. Holes big enough, for example, to accommodate the massive North American Aerospace Defense Command

(NORAD) facility built into the belly of Cheyenne Mountain in Colorado. NORAD is probably the largest and most covert radar-tracking station in the world.

And inside the massively gutted Cheyenne Mountain is where it lives.

'I must deviate a little because several of the most interesting facilities that have been designed and constructed by the Corps are classified,' said Deputy Director of Engineering and Construction for the US Army Corps of Engineers, Lloyd A. Duscha, in a speech entitled *Underground Facilities for Defense – Experience and Lessons*. According to Dr Sauder the Deputy Director goes on to reveal the Corps' involvement – back in the 1960s – 'in the construction of the large NORAD facility beneath Cheyenne Mountain in Colorado'.

'As stated earlier,' Duscha told the underground construction conference, 'there are other projects of similar scope which I cannot identify, but which include multiple chambers up to fifty feet wide and 100 feet high using the same excavation procedures mentioned for the NORAD facility.'

As Dr Sauder himself concludes: 'You will probably not find a more honest admission anywhere by a military officer that the Pentagon has in fact constructed secret underground installations.'

Dr Sauder goes on to present officially documented evidence of a highly covert deep-underground construction programme initiated as far back as the early 1950s. The documents reveal not only that the US government has been planning and constructing deep-underground facilities for over forty years, but also that it has the technology to do so. As well as the possibility of hi-tech laser-boring machinery having been developed for the task, capable of boring large distances in a very short time, it is also suggested that electron-beam, plasma, microwave, ultrasound and nuclear subterrene methods might also have been developed and employed. Though some of these technologies may sound more like the fantasies of a 1960s sci-fi novelist, nevertheless this information is contained in an official US government document that dates back to 1974. The appropriate departments have had more than twenty years to develop these technologies and put them to use.

Indeed, all the evidence suggests that this is precisely what they have done.

If the idea of plasma, microwave or laser-boring machines seems too far-fetched, however (even though the documents clearly show that, as far back as the early 1970s, various US government departments were already researching and developing these technologies), then what about the more conventional means?

Flame-jet tunnelling, for instance, or nuclear subterrene. Both of these methods are well within our technological capabilities, and have been for some time. The idea of flame-jet boring machines dates back – according to the officially released documentation – at least as far as the 1960s. It takes little wit to calculate, then, that the US authorities have had at least thirty years to perfect and upgrade this method. In effect – and in short – the flame-jet method (as described by United Aircraft Research Laboratories in 1968) involves the use of high-power, high-temperature flame-jets that cut into the rock-face as the cutting head rotates. However, this still leaves the problem of rock and muck disposal.

Not so with the nuclear subterrene. Developed at Los Alamos National Laboratories in New Mexico, the nuclear subterrene simply melts its way through the rock and soil like a hot knife through butter. No debris. No disposal problem. That is, of course, assuming the designs and patents obtained by Dr Sauder have indeed been developed to the point that they are today in use. Dr Sauder himself does not speculate in this respect. What he does say, though, is that the nuclear subterrene employs a 'compact nuclear reactor that circulates liquid lithium from the reactor core to the tunnel face, where it melts the rock. In the process of melting the rock the lithium loses some of its heat. It is then circulated back along the exterior of the tunnelling machine to help cool the vitrified rock as the tunnelling machine forces its way forward. The cooled lithium then circulates back to the reactor where the whole cycle starts over. In this way the nuclear subterrene slices through the rock like a nuclear powered, 2,000 degree Fahrenheit earthworm, boring its way deep underground.'

I strongly recommend that you read Dr Richard Sauder's book, *Underground Bases and Tunnels: What is the Government Trying to Hide?* In it you will find the documented evidence of which I speak – documented evidence of the deep-underground construction programme responsible for the hundreds of military-industrial deep-underground facilities worldwide.

The technology exists. The documents exist. The tunnels exist. The underground bases are real. But where are they?

And moreover, what are they being used for?

File 37
The Network

It is alleged that there are 129 fully equipped, fully operational deep-underground facilities scattered across the United

States. Below is a brief summary detailing the whereabouts and operational parameters of just a few of the more notorious among them . . .

File 37: Appendix 01
Case Study: Cosmic Top-X48 Eyes Only
White Sands
Los Alamos
Dulce

It is rumoured that the Los Alamos National Laboratories deep-underground facility and the White Sands Proving Ground deep-underground facility could well be one and the same dungeon. Los Alamos is where the US government developed the first atomic bomb; White Sands is where they tested it.

While White Sands Proving Ground (part of the Kirtland AFB complex) is one of America's primary testing grounds for new weaponry, Los Alamos National Laboratories is undoubtedly one of the US government's primary secret technology and scientific experimentation facilities. It is situated in New Mexico. At least, the above-ground Los Alamos facility is situated in New Mexico. The deep-underground Los Alamos facility, on the other hand, via an elaborate tunnel system running the breadth of Arizona, is thought to reach as far north and west as southern Nevada. It is not out of the question, then, that the Los Alamos/White Sands/Dulce and the Area 51/S-4 deep-underground complexes merge some place east of Las Vegas (for information on Area 51 and S-4 see Briefing Document).

According to some reports, at least one live alien was a 'guest' at Los Alamos in 1952. If the reports are to be believed it was kept in a sub-facility known as Complex 111 – or more simply C111 – reportedly the first deep-underground facility built at Los Alamos. Some say that C111 is the largest deep-underground facility in the world, but this is debatable. Nevertheless it is said to be approximately one mile square and deep enough to withstand a five megaton nuclear blast, directly overhead.

Among the goings on at Los Alamos today are experiments in the fields of particle physics, gravity-wave propulsion, electron-beam weaponry, laser-beam weaponry, geophysics, psychotronics, mind-control and other 'human behaviour' programmes. According to Dr Richard Sauder PhD (see File 36) it is possible that parts of the Los Alamos facility go down as far as a mile. Perhaps even further. This would certainly seem to be the case with the Dulce facility, the hub of the New Mexico deep-underground complex located at the outer edge of the Los Alamos facility. Here, according to former US Special Forces operative Phil Schneider, who helped construct the facility, the US military is not the only occupant. There are aliens down there, too.

Various reports, including Schneider's, speak of an alien underground base at Dulce. Indeed, Schneider claims that in 1979 US Special Forces (Delta Force) and select FBI units engaged in underground warfare against the aliens, who are reported to have occupied the base for centuries but were only discovered when the US government began extending the Los Alamos facility to include what is today known as the Dulce deep-underground complex. Whether or not some kind of peace settlement has ever been negotiated with the Dulce aliens, or any deal struck, I do not know. What *is* apparent is that countless UFO sightings are reported in this area, almost on a daily basis. But then, the same can be said for most of the state of New Mexico.

What we don't know, of course, is who the UFOs belong to – the Americans or the aliens?

For all our sakes, let us pray it's not the Americans.

File 37: Appendix 02
Case Study: Cosmic Top-X49 Eyes Only
Lockheed
McDonnell
Northrop

The Lockheed Martin, McDonnell Douglas and Northrop facilities situated in southern California are perhaps the largest of America's deep-underground installations.

The Lockheed facility is better known as the Hellendale facility as it is situated next to what used to be Hellendale auxiliary airport, only a few miles from Hellendale itself. Here the F117A Stealth fighter was born, along with rumours of on-site 'acquired alien technology' projects and other 'black' corporate programmes.

Alien 'guests' have been reported at this facility (as 'technical advisers', to quote one source) and a plethora of UFO sightings, too. There are even reports of abductees being taken underground here, being experimented on, experiencing missing time and waking up with strange marks on their skin. More what one would have expected of the Los Alamos facility, surely, or White Sands, or even Area 51. But then again, similar reports have been received regarding those facilities, too.

A feature common to these three facilities is the presence of strange runway-like constructions that command the eye from the air ('runways that are not runways', as they have been described, because they are not used by aircraft) and the Lockheed facility is no exception. Built into these 'runways' are large diamond-shaped doors through which huge, space-age-type pylons rise from somewhere underground. The pylons are adorned with what some commentators have referred to as 'detachable attachments', largely disc-shaped devices that have been seen to hover silently when beamed with electromagnetic radiation. Indeed, it seems that some quite intense electromagnetic and/or electrogravitic research is being carried out here with a view to developing new and exotic propulsion systems. If they haven't already done so.

Palmdale, California, barely a stone's throw from Los Angeles, is the home of the McDonnell Douglas facility. Once again, this facility boasts similar 'runways' that are not utilized by aircraft and the same diamond-shaped doors through which the same space-age-type pylons rise from underground. Protruding from the pylons are the same strange 'detachable attachments' at which electromagnetic radiation is beamed. According to eyewitnesses these attachments resemble UFOs – discs, some circular, others elongated – and once again have been seen to hover silently and glow a variety of different colours during flight tests. It is almost certain that the 'UFOs' are unmanned.

The Northrop facility, like its two ugly sisters, looks like some squeaky-clean deserted space-age airport with runways that serve no obvious purpose and pylons plus attachments that rise up out of diamond-shaped doors. Once again, this facility indulges in some kind of electromagnetic-cum-electrogravitic propulsion research and boasts an impressive array of radar and microwave dishes. Northrop, of course, is the company responsible for the construction of the radar-invisible Stealth B2 bomber.

Like the facility at S-4 (Area 51) the Northrop deep-underground facility is said to plummet an incredible forty-two levels below ground. What goes on down there is anybody's guess. For all we know they could be constructing an entire fleet of non-conventional aircraft. Which is all well and good if we're *all* to be included in the plot – if we get one each. But it is far from good if what is really going on down there is some exclusive boys'-club venture intended to furnish the already rich and powerful with even more wealth and power. Indeed, to my mind that would be immoral and wholly unacceptable.

But what is even more unacceptable is this.

Associated with the Northrop facility is an abundance of UFO sightings and abduction experiences – UFOs that glow during flight tests; abductees who recall being taken deep underground and tampered with.

Which only makes me wonder: If it really is aliens who are abducting people, then is it not strange that they should choose to take their victims to military-industrial R&D facilities, deep underground, in order to perform their experiments?

Or maybe the abductors aren't alien after all . . .

File 37: Appendix 03
Case Study: Cosmic Top-X50 Eyes Only Underground Overview

To list all the known deep-underground facilities in the United States would require a great deal of both time and effort, and indeed, a mighty tome to contain them all. But for those of you interested to know where at least some of the major facilities are (to add to the ones mentioned above) here's a short menu.

*   *   *

Fort George Meade, Maryland: home of the National Security Agency (or Big Brother, as this formidable listening agency is otherwise known). It is known that at least a ten-acre deep-underground facility exists here, stacked with row on row of the world's most sophisticated computer-monitoring and surveillance equipment. From this seat of unrivalled power the NSA listens in on most – if not all – of the world's communications systems, be they telephone (who did *you* call last night?), telex, fax, radio, TV, microwave, you name it. They probably even tune in to most telepathic communications, too!

Fort Belvoir, Virginia: home of the US Army Corps of Engineers. Fort Belvoir is a mere hop-and-a-skip from Fort Meade – no distance at all by deep-underground graviton train! The Army Corps of Engineers, remember, are the ones who dig the holes in the ground. And by all accounts they're very good at it.

Edwards Air Force Base, Southern California: rumoured to house its own fleet of unconventional aircraft. UFOs have been frequently spotted over or near this base, and for a good many years. Indeed, it was here that former US Air Force Colonel and NASA astronaut Gordon Cooper formed part of a small unit of men who witnessed and filmed a disc-shaped craft hovering over the base. According to Colonel Cooper the film was sent to Washington DC, never to be seen again.

But there are even wilder claims associated with this base. On 20th February 1954, for example (when the base was still known as Muroc Air Force Base), President Eisenhower is said to have signed a formal treaty here with a visiting alien embassy (see Document 03, File 12 and Document 13, File 41). The meeting is said to have been attended by Franklin Allen of the Hearst media and publishing empire;

Edwin Nourse of Brookings Institute (financial adviser to President Truman, Eisenhower's predecessor); well-known US metaphysician Gerald Light; a Los Angeles Catholic Bishop by the name of MacIntyre and, of course, President Eisenhower himself. It is this treaty – the Greada Treaty – claims former US Naval Intelligence man Milton William Cooper that gave formal permission to the alien visitors to utilize bases deep inside the Earth.

According to a letter written by Gerald Light following the meeting, the aliens were other-dimensional in quality. '. . . The reality of "other-plane" aeroforms is now and forever removed from the realms of speculation . . .' he wrote with some emotion. And further: 'During my two days' visit I saw five separate and distinct types of aircraft being studied and handled by our Air Force officials – with the assistance and permission of the Etherians!' It was no doubt Mr Light's metaphysical background that inspired him to refer to the aliens as 'Etherians'.

So there we have it. It would not surprise me in the least to learn that the deep-underground facility here is part of a much larger complex that includes access to the nearby Lockheed Martin, McDonnell Douglas and Northrop deep-underground facilities, and that the 'Etherians' still have a hand in what goes on down there!

Wright-Patterson Air Force Base, Ohio: likely alien autopsy site and home of the most famous (infamous) secure hangar in the world: Hangar 18. Here it is that the US government's Foreign Technology Division is headquartered. Here it is also that the crashed Roswell disc plus an unknown number of alien bodies were delivered before being taken to Groom Lake and then to S-4 (Area 51), Nevada. This is more than pure fantasy; it is more than just conspiracy theory. It is the testimony of some of the highest-ranking and most reputable former military, intelligence and special-projects personnel in America, including former Roswell Army Air Field Staff Intelligence Officer Major Jesse A. Marcel; former National Security Council adviser and head of the US government's Alphacom Team, Dr Michael Wolf; former black-projects engineer Bill Uhouse (Jarod 2); former US Air Force officer Colonel Edward Strieber; and former US Army Intelligence officer on the staff of General Douglas MacArthur and head of the Pentagon's Foreign Technology in Army Research and Development, Colonel Philip J. Corso.

And even if all the above turn out to be disinformation agents, it is nonetheless certain that a massive deep-underground facility code-named S-3 exists here, directly beneath Hangar 18.

Mount Weather, Bluemont, Virginia: COG (Continuity of Government) Command Centre. Construction of this deep-underground facility was initiated as far back as 1936 by the US Bureau of Mines. According to former employees, Mount Weather is an underground city of impressive proportions. Buried deep inside the earth the facility is equipped with such amenities as private apartments, dormitories, streets and sidewalks; cafeterias and hospitals; a water purification system; a power plant; general office buildings; a small lake fed by fresh water from underground springs; a massive transport system and its own TV and satellite communications system. Like any Ultra Top Secret government facility, Mount Weather, it seems, is a world unto itself.

Mount Weather is also the Operational Command Center for more than 100 deep-underground Federal Relocation Centers. Most of these are concentrated in Pennsylvania, West Virginia, Virginia, Maryland and North Carolina, and include fifty top-secret deep-underground COG Command

Posts, each one linked to the other forty-nine – plus Mount Weather itself – via satellite communications systems and underground wave relays. Together this network of underground facilities constitutes the backbone of America's Continuity of Government programme.

It is here, to this unfeasibly large though highly secret hole in the ground that, in the event of some or other national emergency, the President and a specified number of key officials would be relocated. Among other Federal agencies represented here is the DMPSA (Defense Mobilization Planning Systems Agency) whose special-ops teams would be responsible for the relocation procedures in the event of such an emergency. The special-ops teams are constantly updated with continuity schedules, war directives, military codes, and other essential, classified data. In the event of an emergency, the President would be in safe hands.

Or would he?

An article written by Richard Pollock for the American journal *The Progressive Magazine* in 1976 claims that a 'parallel government-in-waiting' is already housed here, permanently, and that it includes the Office of the President and the Vice President to boot. Having personally interviewed several very high-ranking government officials working at Mount Weather, Pollock revealed that a minimum of nine Federal Departments are housed at this Ultra Top Secret facility, each with its own official Head appointed by the White House and addressed as 'Mr Secretary'. Unlike their above-ground counterparts in Washington DC, of course, the Mount Weather officials serve an 'indefinite term' in office. Which means that they do not have to face re-election (but then, they were never elected in the first place). Policies formulated at Mount Weather – like the appointments of the Department Heads – are done so without the consent of the Senate.

Indeed, without the consent of the American people whom they represent . . . in a covert sort of way.

Denver Airport, Colorado: New World Order Command Centre. It is rumoured that many of the Ultra Top Secret science and technology programmes formerly carried out at Area 51 have recently been transferred to the massive deep-underground facility now in operation beneath the newly-built Denver Airport. Hence the timely release of the 1996 blockbuster *Independence Day* which – despite the producers' arguments to the contrary – would never have been granted release had Area 51 still been centre-stage. Of this much I am convinced.

The airport itself was the cause of some protest from the outset; the local community did not want this airport built. Indeed, one source claims that a very high-ranking Denver official was paid $1.5 million by the CIA 'to help get this project through'. Someone wanted this airport built, and they wanted it built very much. Why?

Former US special forces operative and geological-cum-structural engineer Phil Schneider, who helped in the construction of the Denver facility, claimed he knew the answer.

Before his death Schneider claimed that he had helped in the construction of a staggering 88-square-mile deep-underground base here. He said the base is 2.5 miles deep and that it contains a 4.5-square-mile deep-underground city. During the last year of construction, Schneider said, the main thrust of the work was to connect the airport's own underground complex to the deep-underground New World Order facility several hundred feet further down. Indeed, the airport is a veritable shrine to New World Order symbology: engraved on the airport's dedication stone, for example, are Masonic symbols (including the Nazi 'Black Sun' symbol) and the words *New World Airport Commission*. Is someone trying to say something here?

Describing the new multibillion-dollar facility, *Pandora's Box (Volumes I & II)* author Alex Christopher told Radio KSEO host Dave Alan: 'The dedication stone for the Denver airport has a Masonic symbol on it. A whole group of us went out to the airport to see some friends off and see this capstone [dedication stone] . . . It sits at the south-eastern side of the terminal which, by the way, is called the Great Hall, which is what Masons refer to as their meeting hall. And on this thing it mentions the "New World Airport Commission". I have never heard of that, have you?

'. . . It also has a thing that looks like a keypad on it . . . [My source] told me that this keypad-looking area looked like a form of techno-geometry that is alien-oriented, and that it had something to do with a "directional system" . . . that functioned as a homing beacon to bring ships right in to the Great Hall . . .

'. . . In the same general area . . . there are some most unusual designs on the floor that are all Masonic in nature, which lead right back to the "Black Sun" . . . which goes back to Nazi symbology.'

Christopher, who managed to gain access to the airport's 'active area' underground, goes on to describe unusual levels of electromagnetic radiation emanating from even deeper underground. She also describes two 'huge shafts large enough to fit a two-lane highway' inside them and a 'very technical building complex with interlocking tunnels' that is mysteriously buried underground and connected to the main concourse by a tram tunnel. Christopher also says that she conducted interviews with 'several people who worked on the project' and who 'saw things that scared them so badly they won't talk about it'.

It should be pointed out that one of Alex Christopher's main sources regarding the Denver facility was Phil Schneider, the special-ops engineer who helped to construct this and other underground facilities at Area 51, Nevada, and Dulce, New Mexico. Appalled at what he finally discovered regarding the agenda underpinning the deep-underground programme (which he had worked on for some years) Schneider promised to release all the information he had gleaned over the years and post it on the Internet. This promise was made publicly. Before he had the chance to fulfil his promise, however, Schneider committed suicide.

Or did he?

The fact is that in January 1996 Phil Schneider was found dead; the way in which he died resembled a 'Special Forces' military-style execution in every respect. We are of course expected to believe that, only a short time before he was due to post this wealth of information on the Net, Schneider double-tied a catheter (some reports say a piano wire) around his own neck and strangled himself. I am no medical expert, but I doubt whether this mode of 'suicide' is very popular. I doubt whether it is even possible. It seems certain Phil Schneider had a helping hand, then . . .

Appendix 03: Addendum 01
Case Profile: Cosmic Top-X51 Eyes Only
A Final Testimony

. . . I intend here to interpose an addendum to Appendix 03 in the form of this edited version of a lecture given by Phil Schneider in May 1995. I hope I am not infringing anyone's copyright by including this lecture. It is my wish by so doing to introduce you to the mind of someone by whose word I am presenting evidence and upon whose testimony I am resting a portion of my own argument; someone who would otherwise remain anonymous.

It is also my fervent belief that this man's final testimony should not go unpublished.

Overview

'. . . To give you an overview of basically what I am . . . I started off and went through engineering school. Half of my school was in that field, and I built up a reputation for being a geological engineer as well as a structural engineer with both military and aerospace applications. I have helped build two main bases in the United States that have some significance as far as what is called the New World Order. The first base is the one at Dulce, New Mexico. I was involved in 1979 in a firefight with alien humanoids, and I was one of the survivors. I'm probably the only talking survivor you will ever hear. Two other survivors are under close guard. I am the only one left that knows the detailed files of the entire operation. Sixty-six Secret Service agents, FBI, Black Berets and the like, died in that firefight. I was there . . .

'. . . Part of what I am going to tell you is going to be very shocking. Part of what I am going to tell you is probably going to be very unbelievable, though instead of putting your glasses on I'm going to ask you to put your "scepticals" on . . . do your own homework . . .

'. . . The first part of this talk is going to concern deep-underground military bases and the black budget. The black budget is a secretive budget that garners twenty-five per cent of the Gross National Product of the United States. At least this amount is used in black programmes, like those concerned with deep-underground military bases. Presently, there are one hundred and twenty-nine deep-underground military bases in the United States . . .

'. . . They have been building these one hundred and twenty-nine bases day and night, unceasingly, since the early 1940s. Some of them were built even earlier than that. These bases are basically large cities underground connected by high-speed magneto-leviton trains that have speeds up to Mach Two. Several books have been written about this activity. Richard Sauder, a PhD architect, has risked his life by talking about this. He worked with a number of government agencies on deep-underground military bases . . .

'. . . The average depth of these bases is over a mile, and they again are basically whole cities underground. They all are between two-point-six-six and four-point-two-five cubic miles in size. They have laser drilling machines that can drill a tunnel seven miles long in one day. The black projects sidestep the authority of Congress, which as we know is illegal. Right now, the New World Order is depending on these bases. If I had known at the time I was working on them that the NWO was involved, I would not have done it. I was lied to rather extensively.'

Greada Treaty

'Back in 1954, under the Eisenhower Administration, the federal government decided to circumvent the Constitution of the United States and form a treaty with alien entities. It was called their "1954 Greada Treaty" . . . slowly the aliens altered the bargain until they decided they wouldn't abide by it at all. Back in 1979 this was the reality, and the firefight at Dulce occurred quite by accident . . .

'. . . I was involved in building an addition to the deep-underground military base at Dulce, which is probably the deepest base. It goes down seven levels and is over two-point-five miles deep. At that particular time we had drilled four distinct holes in the desert, and we were going to link them together and blow out large sections at a time. My job was to go down the holes and check the rock samples, and recommend the explosive to deal with the particular rock. As I was headed down there, we found ourselves amidst a large cavern that was full of outer-space aliens, otherwise known as Large Greys. I shot two of them. At that time there were thirty people down there. About forty more came down after this started, and all of them got killed. We had surprised a whole underground base of existing aliens. Later, we found out that they had been living on our planet for a long time, perhaps a million years. This could explain a lot of what is behind the theory of ancient astronauts.'

UFOs
Stealth Technology

'. . . I didn't get really interested in UFO technology until I started work at Area Fifty-One, north of Las Vegas. After about two years recuperating after the 1979 incident, I went back to work for Morrison and Knudson, EG&G and other companies. At Area Fifty-One they were testing all kinds of peculiar spacecraft. How many people here are familiar with Bob Lazar's story? (See Briefing Document.) He was a physicist working at Area Fifty-One trying to decipher the propulsion factor in some of these craft . . . I am not a very good speaker, but I'll keep shooting my mouth off until somebody puts a bullet in me, because it's worth it to talk to a group like this about these atrocities . . .

'. . . There are other problems. I have some interesting 1993 figures. There are twenty-nine prototype Stealth aircraft presently. The budget from the US Congress five-year plan for these is two hundred and forty-five point six million dollars. You couldn't buy the spare parts for these black programmes for that amount. So we've been lied to. The black budget is roughly one point three trillion dollars every two years. The US Congress never sees the books involved with this clandestine pot of gold. Contractors of Stealth programmes: EG&G, Westinghouse, McDonnell Douglas, Morrison-Knudson, Wackenhut Security Systems, Boeing Aerospace, Lorimar Aerospace, Aerospacial in France, Mitsubishi Industries, Rider Trucks, Bechtel, I.G. Farben, plus a host of hundreds more. Is this what we are sup- posed to be living up to as freedom-loving people? I don't believe so . . .

'. . . Still, sixty-eight per cent of the military budget is directly or indirectly affected by the black budget. Star Wars relies heavily upon Stealth weaponry. By the way, none of the Stealth programme would have been available if we had not taken apart crashed alien discs. None of it. I believe our government officials have sold us down the drain – lock, stock and barrel. Up until several weeks ago I was employed by the US government with a Ryolite-thirty-eight clearance factor – one of the highest in the world. I believe the Star Wars programme is there solely to act as a buffer to prevent alien attack – it can have nothing to do with the Cold War,

which was only a toy to garner money from all the people –
for what? The whole lie was planned and executed for the
last seventy-five years.'

Drugs
Delta Force
Guardians of Stealth

'. . . Here's another piece of information for you folks. The
Drug Enforcement Administration and the ATF rely on Stealth
tactical weaponry for as much as forty per cent of their
operations budget. This in 1993, and the figures have gone
up considerably since. The United Nations used American
Stealth aircraft for over twenty-eight per cent of its collective
worldwide operations from 1990 to 1992, according to the
Centre for Strategic Studies and UN Report 3092 . . .

'. . . The Guardians of Stealth. There are at least three
distinct classifications of police that guard our most well-kept
secrets. Number one, the Military Joint Tactical Force (MJTF),
sometimes called the Delta Force or Black Berets, is a multinational tactical force primarily used to guard the various Stealth
aircraft worldwide . . .

'. . . By the way, there were one hundred and seventy-two
Stealth aircraft built. Ten crashed, so there were at last
count about one hundred and sixty-two. [Name deleted
by publishers for legal reasons] signed them away about
six weeks ago to the United Nations. There have been
indications that the Delta Force was sent over to Bosnia
during the last days of the Bush administration as a covert
sniper force, and that they started taking pot shots at each
side of the controversy in order to actually start the Bosnia

conflict . . . that would be used by succeeding administrations for political purposes.'

World Trade Center Bombing

'. . . I was hired not too long ago to do a report on the World Trade Center bombing. I was hired because I know about the ninety-some-odd varieties of chemical explosives. I looked at the pictures taken right after the blast. The concrete was puddled and melted. The steel and the rebar was literally extruded up to six feet longer than its original length. There is only one weapon that can do that – a small nuclear weapon. That's a construction-type nuclear device. Obviously, when they say that it was a nitrate explosive that did the damage, they're lying, one-hundred per cent, folks . . .

'. . . The people they have in custody probably didn't do the crime. As a matter of fact, I have reason to believe that the same group held in custody did do other crimes, such as killing a Jewish rabbi in New York. However, I want to further mention that with the last explosion in Oklahoma City, they are saying that it was a nitrate or fertilizer bomb that did it. First, they came out and said it was a one-thousand-pound fertilizer bomb. Then, it was one thousand five-hundred. Then two thousand pounds. Now it's twenty thousand. You can't put twenty thousand pounds of fertilizer in a Rider Truck . . .

'. . . Now, I've never mixed explosives, *per se*. I know the chemical structure and the application of construction explosives. My reputation was based on it. I helped hollow out more than thirteen deep-underground military bases in the United States. I worked on the Malta project, in West Germany, in Spain and in Italy. I can tell you from experience that a nitrate explosion would have hardly shattered the windows of the federal building in Oklahoma City – it would have killed a few people and knocked part of the facing off the building, but it would never have done that kind of damage. I believe I have been lied to, and I am not taking it any longer, so I'm telling you that *you*'ve been lied to.'

Black Helicopters

'. . . The black helicopters. There are over sixty-four thousand black helicopters in the United States. For every hour that goes by, there is one being built. Is this the proper use of our money? What does the federal government need sixty-four thousand tactical helicopters for? I doubt if the entire military needs sixty-four thousand, worldwide. I doubt if all the world needs that many. There are one hundred and fifty-seven F-117A Stealth aircraft loaded with LIDAR and computer-enhanced imaging radar. They can see you walking from room to room when they fly over your house. They see objects in the house from the air with a variation limit of one inch to thirty thousand miles. That's how accurate it is . . . I worked in the federal government for a long time, and I know exactly how they handle their business.'

Earthquake Device
AIDS
Alien Humanoids

'. . . The federal government has now invented an earthquake device. I am a geologist, and I know what I am talking about. With the Kobe earthquake in Japan [1995] there was no pulsewave as in a normal earthquake – none. In 1989 there was an earthquake in San Francisco. There was no pulsewave with that one, either. It is a Tesla device that is being used for evil purposes . . .

' . . . The black-budget programmes have subverted science as we know it. Look at AIDS, invented by the National Ordinance Laboratory in Chicago, Illinois in 1972. It was a biological weapon to be used against the people of the United States. The reason I know this is that I have seen the documentation by the Office of Strategic Services, which by the way is still in operation to this day, through the CDC in Atlanta. They used the glandular excretions of animals, humans and alien humanoids to create the virus. There is absolutely no defence against these germs – none. They are a biological weapon of terrible consequence . . .

' . . . Saddam Hussein killed three point five million Kurdish people with a similar biological weapon. Do we, the people of this planet, deserve this? No, we don't, but we are not doing anything about it. Every moment we waste we are doing other people on the planet a disservice . . .

' . . . I will tell you one thing. If I keep speaking out like I am maybe God will give me the life to talk my head off. I will break every law that it takes to talk my head off. Eleven of my best friends in the last twenty-two years have been murdered. Eight of the murders were called "suicides" . . . I cut up my security card and sent it back to the government, and told them if I was threatened – and I have been – that I was going to upload one hundred and forty thousand pages of documentation to the Internet about government structure and the whole plan. I have already begun that task. Thank you very much.'

A special thanks to Phil Schneider, whose death is an ugly

reminder of the kind of animal we are dealing with. May it not be in vain.

File 37: Appendix 04
Case Study: Cosmic Top-X52 Eyes Only
Pine Gap

Pine Gap: and finally to different shores . . . to the land Down Under, in fact, and perhaps the most disquieting – and certainly the most secretive – US/British deep-underground facility in the world: Pine Gap.

According to a French document written by researcher Lucien Cometta and translated into English by Dr John Gille, there are three Ultra Top Secret deep-underground bases in Australia, all financed and owned – ostensibly – by the US government, and populated by the British and US military. The first is to be found at a place called Nurranger, near Woomera, South Australia; the second is hidden somewhere in New South Wales. The third – and by far the largest – is located near the southern slopes of the MacDonnell Range of mountains in the centre of Australia, some small distance west of Alice Springs. This facility is known as Pine Gap.

Pine Gap is completely underground, some say with 'barely visible entrances to the surface'; it is officially known as *The Joint Defense and Space Research Facility* (JDSRF). Although this title might lead one to assume that the primary purpose of this facility is to research and develop space defence technology, according to my own sources – plus the findings of private researchers like Jimmy Guieu – the real purpose of the so-called JDSRF is to research and develop electromagnetic propulsion systems and psychotronic weaponry. Reports of luminous white discs and bright red spheres in the skies over Pine Gap and the surrounding area are manifold and commonplace, and would tend to support the electromagnetic propulsion theory. Indeed, several locals claim that they have actually seen 'white discs' being unloaded from large US transporter planes at the airports which serve the facility. The discs, they say, are always around thirty feet in diameter and carry the USAF emblem.

Also at the facility is an enormous nuclear generator that is used to supply the high levels of energy needed to service some kind of newly developed transceiver. It seems, too, that there is an extremely high-voltage plasma accelerator in use here – the most sinister utilization of such an accelerator would be to produce a Death Ray or, more simply put, a plasma gun. (In this respect it is interesting to note that the 1991 NASA video footage, which shows a UFO in Earth's upper atmosphere taking evasive action against what appears to be a missile – some experts say a *plasma* missile – fired at it from Earth, was taken from the STS-48 NASA Space Shuttle *Discovery* while in orbit over . . . you guessed it: *Australia*.) Plasma and particle-beam weaponry, of course, forms the mainstay of cutting-edge warfare technology – which is why the powers-that-be can get away with selling us their nuclear disarmament scams. With these kind of 'bullets' they no longer need nuclear weapons.

Other reports speak of a massive deep-underground residential facility here, as yet largely unoccupied; even so, ready for use. In my efforts to discover who may have invested in a slice of this exclusive property, and why, one or two very unexpected names came to light. Indeed, I stumbled across one name in particular which, should the rumour be true and the facts officially released to the British public, would incite a civil revolution overnight. No doubt about that.

Before revealing the name of this mysterious luminary, however, perhaps we should first take a look at the alleged deep-underground programme currently operating in Britain. After all, if the Americans are up to no good you can bet your last dollar bill the Brits will be close on their heels.

And by all accounts they are.

DOCUMENT 12

Cosmic Top Secret
Eyes Only Copy One Of One

Deep Underground (Part 2)
Aliens And Hybrids

File 38
RAF Rudloe Manor

America's Area 51 is not the only Ultra Top Secret deep-underground facility to accommodate alleged alien/government genetics and technology programmes. Similar programmes are operating in Britain. This, at least, is the claim of those who work, or have worked, at Britain's most top-secret deep-underground military installations. And to judge by the evidence thus far uncovered, such a claim may not be so absurd as it might at first seem.

It has long been rumoured that Salisbury Plain in Wiltshire may be the primary site for a British deep-underground military-industrial facility. Others are suspected at Harwell, Aldermaston, Greenham Common, Porton Down, Boscombe Down, RAE Farnborough, RAF Woodbridge/Bentwaters, BAe Warton, RAF Chicksands, Machrihanish, Rudloe Manor.

The list is endless. But as far as my own research is concerned, the most whispered-about facility is undoubtedly the alleged deep-underground complex simmering beneath Salisbury Plain.

According to my investigations – which included interviews with former and still-serving military and defence personnel, as well as a number of civilians employed at military establishments – one of the major entrances to the Salisbury Plain facility is to be found at RAF Rudloe Manor in Wiltshire. Without wishing to give away too many national security secrets (which is not the purpose of this exercise) Rudloe Manor is home to the Controller Defence Communications Network (CDCN), officially described as a 'tri-service unit controlling worldwide defence communications', which essentially means that, as well as providing voice and data communications for the MoD, the Army, the Royal Navy and the RAF, Rudloe Manor is the hub of all defence data-trafficking and radio relay-processing for the combined British/NATO military machine, worldwide. Whatever does or does not go on here, one thing is clear: this facility is the most highly top-secret military communications establishment in Britain.

Documents uncovered as long ago as the 1970s (and others since) clearly show that RAF Rudloe Manor is not only Britain's primary contingency seat for Government in times of war and/or other national emergencies (known officially as the National Seat of Government, or NSG, Britain's answer to Mount Weather – see Document 11) but also that the base serves as the nerve centre for nuclear missile deployment and military/intelligence communications relays.

But what is even more pertinent to our own investigation is this. The Rudloe Manor complex, known in intelligence circles as 'The Citadel', houses the government's primary data-gathering agency for the investigation of all anomalous aerial phenomena – i.e. UFOs – in Britain. Even GCHQ (Government Communications Head Quarters), often thought of as Britain's most senior – and secretive – government listening post, reports back to a 'central computer' housed at Rudloe Manor's mysterious CCC department (commonly known as Corsham Computer Centre). It is not publicly known what CCC's real code name is, or indeed, what really goes on beneath its scrubbed concrete floors. What is known, however, is that lurking somewhere beneath CCC's main building complex is an underground bunker containing, among other things, at least one entrance to an even deeper-level 'superbunker' that is accessed only by personnel carrying extremely high security clearances. And of these, none is permitted to say what goes on down there.

File 38: Appendix 01
Intelligence Report:
Cosmic Top-X53 Eyes Only
MI5/MI6
Low Flying Complaints

Another highly secretive facility housed at the Rudloe Manor complex is known as P&SS (Provost & Security Services), home of the RAF Police and an operational MI5 cell (MI5: Britain's Security Service concerned with the country's internal security). It is also thought that MI6 (Britain's Secret Intelligence Service concerned with counter-intelligence operations at home and abroad) together with a British-based CIA cell utilizes an 'unauthorized' office within this complex. According to one source, this is where all data regarding UFO reports is finally collated and processed. If a British 'Mulder and Scully' team exists in real life, this is probably where it operates from.

To add to this, and despite official denials to the contrary, Rudloe Manor's Low Flying Complaints department handles all reports of UFO sightings/encounters and 'unknown aerial phenomena' in Britain. But that is not all. According to an inside source (as well as information received from my own intelligence sources, including Stealth, plus one other very reliable source, name on file) all data gathered at Rudloe Manor is then passed on via the base's Air Commodore and P&SS (MI5/MI6) to a high-level DIS (Defence Intelligence Staff) department at Whitehall – possibly DI55 and/or DI61. This officially non-existent DIS office, buried away somewhere in the bowels of the MoD's London citadel, is where the meatiest of all UFO/ET data is sifted and logged, before finally being duplicated and sent on via MI6/CIA channels to its final destination: America!

According to my information, the Chain of Command stemming from Rudloe Manor's Low Flying Complaints department does not end, as perhaps one might have expected, with the base's Air Commodore. And what is even more disturbing is the fact that it does not end at Whitehall, either. Rather, all Low Flying Complaints (UFO) information gathered at Rudloe Manor ends up somewhere in the United States, possibly Washington DC, more likely Langley, Virginia, home of the CIA. It is just as likely, of course, that relevant bits of data are syphoned off en route and end up buried away somewhere in a vault inside Fort George Meade, Maryland, home of the US government's primary and most secretive intelligence-gathering agency, the National Security Agency (NSA). It is also possible that the US Air Force Office of Special Investigations (AFOSI) is involved, along with US Naval Intelligence, US Army Intelligence, the Defense Intelligence Agency (DIA) and heaven only knows who else. The point, though, is that all UFO/ET data gathered on British soil by serving British military personnel – data that is collated and classified under the jurisdiction of *Britain*'s Official Secrets Act; data which is paid for by the *British* taxpayer; data which is kept secret from the *British* taxpayer for the very reason that it contains information pertinent to *Britain*'s national security – ends up in America.

Why?

And speaking of America . . . my sources also informed me of top-level meetings that occur at Rudloe Manor involving very high-ranking military personnel from Britain, America and Canada – and other more mysterious characters who seem by their descriptions to resemble the infamous 'Men in Black'. These characters, it is said, turn up in unmarked vehicles with tinted windows and are invariably dressed in black suits and ties. It is likely they are US intelligence operatives, most likely NSA.

The meetings, which occur on a fairly regular basis, are said to include high-level deliberations on the management of the information gathered (a kind of British MJ-12 operation). Again, despite consistent denials to the contrary, it would seem that the British and US military/intelligence alliance is very interested indeed in the UFO phenomenon. And to judge by some of the accounts received from serving military personnel (plus, of course, others received from everyday civilian witnesses) one can only wonder if there is another, unseen, off-planet member forming part of this alliance, too.

File 38: Appendix 02
Intelligence Report:
Cosmic Top-X54 Eyes Only
Britain's Area 51

According to my information – in particular that gleaned from my source who actually works at Rudloe Manor, plus one other who wishes to exercise the utmost anonymity, plus Stealth – there exists at least a 25-square-mile underground complex beneath the top-secret Rudloe Manor base. My hunch is that it may even be bigger than that.

Information alluding to a complex underground tunnel system which stretches in its entirety from London to the West Country (where Rudloe Manor is situated) is available from most libraries (see, for example, *Beneath The City Streets* by Peter Laurie, 1979 edition). The system was built either during or some time prior to World War Two, and was intended as a direct underground link between the Government in Whitehall and the National Seat of Government (NSG) in times of war or emergency, which is of course the Rudloe Manor complex (or at least the deep-underground pit lurking beneath The Citadel's official 'above-ground' façade). Indeed, one underground bunker at Rudloe is affectionately known to some of the resident personnel as 'Maggie's Den', referring of course to Britain's Prime Minister of the 1980s, Margaret Thatcher. During World War Two it is known that Churchill often worked out of a bunker that exists somewhere beneath the Rudloe Manor complex. It is rumoured also that the Monarchy has its own bunker close to Rudloe Manor, and a dedicated underground rail-link from London to the West Country, although this may be little more than a contingency arrangement as it is known that the Royals would be flown out of the country should a serious national emergency arise. (More later.)

That the underground complex exists is not in question – as I have said, this information is publicly available. What *is* in question, however, is the nature of the projects carried out beneath Salisbury Plain and, moreover, who is conducting them. The tunnels and bunkers that make up the official complex, although of course underground, could not be considered in the same light as, say, the American deep-underground facilities I detailed in Document 11. Nevertheless they are there, and would provide the perfect cover for a deeper, more extensive underground facility where highly covert R&D programmes could indeed be carried out.

My sources informed me, for example, of deep-underground vaults where huge volumes of electrical and scientific equipment are being stored, as well as an underground hangar stocked to brimming with what appear to be 'personal files'. I was also told that certain areas within the underground complex are strictly off-limits to all personnel without extremely high security clearances. Indeed, security at Rudloe Manor is as high as you might expect at any Ultra Top Secret establishment. SAS squads are sent in regularly to test the base's inner security and, as yet, have never managed to force their way in.

According to one source, although the outer gates are patrolled only by the regular MoD Police – or 'mod-plods', as they are known – the inner security guards are fully armed and trained to kill. As my source told me: 'The ones who guard the perimeter, they're just the mod-plods. But the real security guards are mean bastards; they mean business. Unlike the guards at other military establishments these guys are armed with live rounds, and they'll use them. You wouldn't want to mess with them.'

So what exactly are they guarding?

For those who are unfamiliar with Salisbury Plain, it is a vast sprawling area of some thousands of acres, and is home to many highly secret MoD compounds and military lands and bases. Many crop circles have arrived on this land, yet only a handful have been made known to, and accessible to, the public. Many formations have been burned within minutes of their discovery. Many UFO sightings have been reported here, too – though, again, most have been denied, covered up, or otherwise explained away by the military. Indeed, as almost any grass-roots UFO or crop circle researcher will tell you, the military has been keeping a very close eye on the development of these two phenomena here, in particular over the past seven or eight years. Why?

Perhaps this next report might have something to do with it.

On Sunday, 11th February 1996, at around 5:30 p.m., two friends of mine were driving home from Alton Barnes in Wiltshire where they had been visiting for the weekend. They had just joined the A303 from the A345, heading west, and had reached the crest of the hill that looks down on Stonehenge when in the distance, some two hundred or so feet above the north-west horizon, one of them saw a very bright silver-blue light suddenly rise up into the sky. It remained hovering for only a few moments before it descended rapidly and dipped back down behind the horizon. According to their account, the light was about five or six times the magnitude of, say, Venus on a good night.

The lightform then repeated the same manoeuvre, only this time its colour was luminous orange, or amber. Again it hovered in the sky and performed a small series of very rapid 'jagged' manoeuvres before again dipping down behind the horizon. By this time both friends were certain that what they were seeing was neither a flare (common to Salisbury Plain, especially when troops are on night manoeuvres) nor the headlights of a conventional aircraft, nor indeed the lights of *anything* conventional. They kept their eyes peeled.

Next, the lightform simply 'appeared' in the sky at about the same height as it had first ascended to (about 200 ft above the horizon). Its size in the sky, they said, was approximately that of a large, luminous football (where Venus might be estimated as being about the size of a golf ball, at best a tennis ball). It was again silver-blue, and extremely bright. It simply 'blipped' into view, remained there for 'a second or two', and then 'blipped' out again. A few moments later it appeared again:

'As we watched in disbelief,' one of the witnesses told me, 'the object rose up again from behind the horizon, performed a small series of rapid, jagged manoeuvres beneath the low cloud cover and then dipped back down out of sight. It repeated this same manoeuvre one more time before dipping back down behind the horizon again, this time for the last time. Although we took a swift right off the A303 and across the Plain in pursuit of the object, we did not see it again that evening.'

What I found particularly interesting about this report was that the manoeuvres the lightform was performing, and the way it was performing them, sounded very similar to those of craft caught on film over Area 51, Nevada. On Michael Hesemann's excellent video *UFOs: Secrets of the Black World*, for example, craft can be seen in the form of bright white lights dancing and jigging above Area 51's 'test-flight' zone. I don't know about you, but I have yet to see an army flare perform a 'series of rapid jagged manoeuvres', much less simply 'blip' into view at 200 ft, and then 'blip' out again. Could Salisbury Plain be Britain's Area 51?

According to some of those who have worked at Area 51, of

course, the lightforms seen (and filmed) hovering and darting above the desert there are in fact acquired alien spacecraft being test-flown by America's 'top gun' pilots. Considering 'Mark's' harrowing ordeal (Document 06, File 24) and George Vernon's equally chilling report (Document 06, File 25), both of which occurred on Salisbury Plain, something tells me this same acquired alien technology may now be operating in Britain.

One further nugget in support of this hypothesis arrived on my desk in the form of a letter (for the sake of privacy I have withheld the young man's name). See what you make of this.

Dear Jon,

I live quite near RAF Rudloe Manor. Around 12:30—1:00 a.m. last July, I think it was the 17th or 18th, I couldn't sleep and for some reason got up and looked out of the window. As I looked out I spotted what looked like an orange ball of light hovering about 100 ft over the base. I stared at the light for a few minutes and I couldn't believe my eyes as it started to flash blue, green, white and orange, and started to dance in the sky and manoeuvre like no aircraft I have ever seen.

I quickly ran into my dad's bedroom and woke him up, as I couldn't believe what I was seeing. He came in and looked, and he was just as surprised as I was. We ran through the possibilities of what it could be: a plane, satellite, weather balloon, planet; and it couldn't have been any of these because of the incredible way it was moving. So we grabbed a pair of binoculars we

have (not expensive ones, I hasten to add) and
went outside to get a better look.

It looked like a bright diamond shape with a
hazy blue green light all around it. Through the
binoculars it was unbelievable. We watched for
about another half an hour as it made its way
towards Bath and out of sight.

We have seen this strange light a few times
since, and are absolutely baffled as to what it
is . . .

One thing's for sure: someone at RAF Rudloe Manor knows
exactly what it is. But they, of course, aren't telling.

File 39
Remote Viewing

In a final attempt to glean at least some information about a
possible deep-underground facility beneath Salisbury Plain,
I thought it might be interesting to conduct a remote-viewing
experiment.

Not that such an experiment could ever be classed as
conclusive. But remote viewing is nevertheless a technique
employed by both the British and American intelligence
communities (and some US police departments), a technique
recently revealed by the likes of former US government
remote viewers Ingo Swann, Major Ed Dames, Sgt Mel
Riley and Major David A. Morehouse. In short, these
former 'psi-spies' were used by the CIA/DIA to psychically
locate strategic enemy targets such as top-secret military
installations that could not be found by conventional means.

They were used to 'psychically spy' on Saddam Hussein during the Gulf War, for example – to 'psychically locate' Iraqi troop positions and Scud missile sites as well as to keep a psychic eye on the movements of the Iraqi dictator himself and, where possible, psychically influence his decision-making. Their sole qualification for the job was that they all displayed 'innate psychic tendencies'.

According to the official party line, during the dark days of the Cold War US intelligence agencies (the CIA prime among them) discovered that the Soviets were employing psychics to 'remote view' tactical and strategic US military targets. These operations were funded by the KGB. Further investigations led the CIA to discover that the Soviet psychics were also capable of homing in on individual targets, such as field agents, case officers, even prominent politicians and other leading figures, some with their fingers on strategic buttons. The KGB psychics were reportedly able to remotely scramble electronic interception and surveillance equipment as well as bring about mental and physical ill-health to the US operatives and other military and political personnel. Something had to be done to counter the situation.

In 1972 CIA scientist Dr Hal Puthoff was given the task of overseeing what was to become known as the US government's psychic warfare programme, serially code-named 'Grill Flame', 'Center Lane', 'Sun Streak', and finally – and currently – 'STARGATE'. At the time Puthoff was working at the CIA-sponsored Stanford Research Institute (SRI) in California – arguably the US government's second-largest think-tank – where he was involved in the development of a top-secret laser and beam-weapon capability. Other hi-tech defence-related projects were – and still are – also researched and developed at SRI. In 1972, under the directorship of Puthoff (and one other CIA scientist also seconded from SRI's laser and beam-weapon department, Russel Targ) a budget of $70 million was awarded to SRI for research into psychic warfare. With a self-confessed interest in parapsychology Puthoff was considered the ideal man for the job. Both he and Targ deemed ESP the most likely form of the paranormal to produce results.

In the first instance civilian psychics were employed, well-known New York psychic Ingo Swann being one of the first to take part in the programme. Indeed, Swann was so successful, and impressed his employers so much, that he soon became 'head teacher' of the SRI remote viewing programme under Puthoff. According to Puthoff, Swann was able to pinpoint strategic and top-secret military targets simply by focusing his mind on any given area or location, often working with nothing more than random map coordinates. Having 'found' the target in his mind's eye he was then able to 'remote view' the place – scan through top-secret files and more often than not give a detailed description of the installation and its personnel. He boasted a near-perfect success rate. It wasn't long before Swann was 'finding' and 'viewing' targets unknown even to his CIA employers.

Recounting his most horrific remote-viewing operation, Swann said that suddenly he found himself looking at what appeared to him to be a top-secret prison camp patrolled by military-type guards and surrounded by electrified perimeter fences.

'I then came upon an elevator,' he said in 'Jon King's X-File Document' (*UFO Reality*, June/July 1996). 'I thought, "Well, it can't be going up, so it must be going down". So I went underground, and found that the place was in fact a biological research installation. There were horses, pigs, monkeys . . . all being subjected to biological and chemical tests. And then I found the humans, who were also being experimented on.'

Swann shed tears as he recalled: 'It was the most dreadful thing I have ever seen. I wept for at least an hour before I could get it back together.'

Perhaps the most chilling aspect to this account is that the installation was later found precisely where Swann said he had 'seen' it. It was, as Swann had said, some kind of top-secret facility where humans and animals were being experimented on. According to Swann, two years after he had given the information, the installation was destroyed by US Special Forces.

Due to the success of his own involvement, Ingo Swann was then given the task of training military personnel in the art of remote viewing. Among the military psychics was Sergeant Mel Riley of the US Army, who was attached to the programme from 1978 until he retired from military service in 1990. According to Riley, who boasted a history of psychic experiences, those who most excelled at remote viewing were artists, visionaries and risk takers – in short, those who seemed to possess a natural psychic tendency and those who seemed less than keen to conform to social and military disciplines.

'We came from a lot of different backgrounds in the military and intelligence fields,' Riley said, 'field agents, case officers, that kind of thing. Most of us had very interesting backgrounds – some had undergone near-death experiences, one had been badly shot up in Vietnam, and quite a number could recall early experiences with what they believed to be UFOs.'

Another senior military official, Major General Ed Thompson, Asst Chief of Staff for Intelligence, US Army, 1978–1981, who was also involved with SRI's psychic warfare programme, claims:

'Remote viewing is still a worthwhile pursuit, for the same reasons that I thought it was originally. There's something there, we can't explain it, but it works. There are a lot of things it can do.'

Indeed, Thompson's is an opinion shared by former CIA Director (1977–1981) Admiral Stansfield Turner, who is likewise convinced that information gleaned by the remote viewers remains priceless. 'As far as the future of parapsychology in intelligence is concerned,' he said in 1995, 'no intelligence organization would turn their backs on such a valuable source of information. Were I in the CIA today I would still want them [the psychics] to monitor what is going on.'

There is every reason to believe that they (the psychics) still *are* monitoring what is going on – that the CIA's remote viewing programme is still very much alive. And, moreover, that it works.

File 39: Appendix 01
Case Report: Cosmic Top-X55 Eyes Only
'Q'

Military remote viewers, of course, undergo a strict and rigorous training period, there is no question about that. But much of what that training entails is now public knowledge and, in any case, the basic qualification for any remote viewer remains that of an innate psychic ability, as the late Edgar Cayce, for example, demonstrated, often with stunning accuracy. The training is to do with honing rather than developing this psychic ability. The ability is already there.

With this in mind, I invited a proven British psychic (whom I will call 'Q') to see what could be found beneath Salisbury Plain (although it should be said that Q did not know that

Salisbury Plain was to be the focus of our endeavour, nor did he know we were looking for underground bases or alien technology programmes, not until we had completed several sittings – for the record, all Q was told before the experiment began was that I required him to see what he could 'find' at certain random map coordinates). The results, collated from several different sittings which, for the sake of clarity, I have edited together, were startling to say the least, and were as follows.

Focusing in the first instance on his 'target' coordinates (consisting of two sets of four random digits, the SRI-proven 'key' for homing the psychic eye in on the given target), Q started to describe a 'large expanse of open countryside' where he said he could see 'stationary tanks', 'war games' and a 'quarry-like structure'. In response to my command: *Describe your environment in more detail*, he replied:

'A small building. There's a small building standing on its own, inside some sort of compound.'

What kind of compound?

'An area . . . fenced-off . . . other buildings around . . . but this one's on its own. It seems significant.'

Describe the building.

'It's like . . . like an outbuilding, I suppose, or a workman's hut. But it feels empty . . . there are no workmen inside.'

You can see inside?

'I can now, quite clearly, yes. There's nothing inside, except a door that leads out . . .'

Out where?

'No, not out, down. Down some steps to a slightly larger area, still empty, no people . . .'

Empty?

'Quite empty.'

Is there anything at all? Can you scan around?

A moment or two passed, then: 'There's another door, or gate, like an iron lattice-work gate . . . wait a minute . . . it seems to lead into a small area, a room . . . no, not a room, an enclosure . . . no, a lift, you know, an elevator.'

Step into the elevator. Where does the elevator take you?

'Down . . .'

Down?

'. . . Into some kind of basement area, yes . . .'

Describe the basement area.

A small pause; Q mumbled something inaudible. No further reply.

Describe the textures within this environment.

A moment, then: 'Mmm, artificial lights . . . sparse . . . quite dark . . . not too dark to see, but dimly lit . . . and harsh, brick, stone, cold. It's not very nice down here.'

Can you hear any sounds?

Q shook his head. 'No, not really, not *sounds* . . . but I can sense activity . . . a sense of activity . . .'

Activity?

'In the air . . .'

What kind of activity?

'Thinking . . . brain activity . . . electrical activity . . . there's some kind of field, some kind of energy field, like electronic, magnetic, electromagnetic . . . preventing me from seeing clearly. It makes me feel nauseous.'

Q readjusted in his seat, breathed deeply, refocused. Then: 'Beyond the energy field, an area . . . a rather small area . . . oh, and there are men, like soldiers . . . black uniforms . . . others in white coats. There are soldiers here, military . . .'

What do they do?

Q shrugged. 'Guard the area, presumably.'

The soldiers?

'The soldiers, yes.'

And the white coats?

This time a long pause, then Q shook his head. He could not see what the white-coated people were doing.

A moment later I asked Q to step back and take an overview, through the eye of an eagle, so to speak. A few minutes passed, then he said: 'I can see a series of corridors, tunnels, well-lit criss-crossing tunnels, leading to other areas, sealed areas. I cannot see precisely where they lead to . . . the corridors lead to other areas . . . the tunnels appear to go very deep into the earth.'

Can you follow the tunnels?

'It's difficult.' Minutes passed in silence, until finally Q shook his head. 'I don't seem able to follow the tunnels,' he said.

What about the corridors?

'Yes . . . they just connect the rooms, the different areas . . .'

What else can you see around you?

'There's nothing much on this level . . . but the corridors and the entrances to the tunnels.'

No colours?

'Some, yes . . . deep-red, electrical, UV [ultra-violet] . . . like a mix of UV and deep-red or infra-red, with the smell of electricity. Not much light, though. Just the entrances to the tunnels, like several holes in the darkness, filled with light . . . and the corridors, [with] one or two people in them, going from one room to the next, like offices . . . and another elevator, presumably to take you back up, or further down . . .'

And the soldiers? What happened to the soldiers and the people in white coats?

Q screwed his eyes tight, but gave no reply.

At this point Q had to snap back to beta and take a rest. He was visibly disturbed by what he had sensed and discovered thus far. I asked him if he wished to call it a day, but he said he would take one further look after he had rested for a minute or two. Which he did.

A short while later: *Where are you now?*

'I'm penetrating one of the tunnels . . . it's well-lit, quite warm, but it still seems strange, vacant, sort of eerie . . .' Then: '. . . I'm coming out of the tunnel . . . it seems to come out in some kind of sealed area, with guards, smoking . . .'

Smoking?

'One of the guards is smoking a cigarette . . .'

In the tunnel?

'No. In the street. There's a street with a pavement . . . the guards are on the pavement.'

Are you still underground?

'Oh, yes, quite definitely . . . I think I'm down on a deeper level, though.'

Describe the guards.

'Military . . . soldiers . . . black uniforms with berets . . .'

Are they the same kind of soldiers you saw before?

'I think so, yes.'

Can you see what they are guarding?

'I can see what looks like the entrance to a big warehouse kind of place, a factory, or a laboratory . . . I can see inside . . . so clean . . . very clean areas with people in white coats and overalls, all working . . .'

What are they doing? How are they working?

'In groups, some on their own. And there are benches . . .'

What about the textures?

'Harsh . . . hard . . . steel and chrome . . . and glass . . . I can sense glass, or perspex, or something of that nature. Glass containers . . . and I can see people bending over benches, chrome and wood, some standing, some on stools. It's all very stern . . .'

Stern?

'The atmosphere, yes. Stern, oppressive, like an over-bearing air of authority . . . it looks like a normal laboratory situation but it all feels so very heavy, oppressive, you know, almost like the atmosphere of a very strict schoolroom, a very tight regime . . . there is real fear here . . .'

Can you say something more about the glass? You said you could sense glass, or perspex, and you mentioned glass containers . . .

A moment, then: 'Bottles . . . glass bottles, jars . . . and tanks . . . glass tanks. There are glass jars with ahhh . . . with what look like cultures growing in them, and tanks lined up against a wall . . . blue . . .'

Blue?

'. . . Like a blue liquid with forms or specimens suspended in them, like a laboratory, you know, specimens, preserved in blue liquid . . . is it blue? . . . oh, my God, they're like . . . well, they're like human forms, biological forms or specimens . . . aliens or hybrids or something engineered, something made, you know, genetically. They look sort of human . . . but, well, they're so ugly, grotesque things . . . *Jesus* . . . I can't look at them any longer . . .'

Q shivered, slowly shook his head and opened his eyes. 'I think I'm done,' he said, and rubbed the horrors from his eyes with the heels of his hands.

While I was burning up inside with the desire to know more about this underground laboratory, it was of course Q's mental and emotional health that demanded priority. By the time he'd completed several hours' remote viewing (on several separate, intense occasions) he seemed very drained, disturbed, less keen to revisit the nightmarish netherworld simmering beneath Salisbury Plain than at first he had been. It was clearly time to call a halt.

I was not disappointed. He had, after all, more than satisfied any expectations I might have had prior to conducting the experiment. Although he hadn't found any crashed and recovered alien spacecraft, nor indeed any other substantive signs of acquired alien technology, he had nonetheless remotely viewed what appeared to be a deep-underground facility (complete with 'human forms, biological forms or specimens . . . aliens or hybrids or something engineered' suspended in 'blue liquid' in 'glass tanks') at the location described by the coordinates I'd given him. Curiously, these coordinates – though random so far as he knew – were in fact those corresponding to the Imber Ranges on Salisbury Plain, where the 'stationary tanks' and 'war games' he had described at the beginning of our first sitting can be found on a regular basis. Indeed, of all the military 'Danger Zones' demarcated on Salisbury Plain, the Imber Ranges form the only area 'permanently closed' to the public.

Of course, this is a long way from conclusive proof, and unlike the British and US intelligence machine I did not have the means to confirm this information one way or the other. There were no Special Forces units at my disposal to force a way in – no way for me to gain entry, even to the ranges, much less to the elevator that Q claimed to have seen operating from inside the 'workman's hut', nor even to the 'tunnel' that led him from the ranges to wherever the laboratory was located.

Food for thought, even so . . .

File 39: Appendix 02
Intelligence Report:
Cosmic Top-X56 Eyes Only
The Commodore's Daughter

Two final points.

One: following our last sitting, Q told me that he'd also

sensed the storage of a 'significant database' while he'd been viewing underground. What he meant exactly even he could not say. But he stressed the fact that he'd had the strongest sense of some kind of 'significant database' being stored somewhere in the place he had just viewed. We joked that it could have been where the government's 'X Files' were stored.

Two (and far more pertinent): not long after our last sitting some information came my way that seemed to corroborate Q's description of an underground laboratory. And of what he'd seen going on in that laboratory. I had, of course, already gleaned a fair knowledge of what might be going on beneath our streets from my own sources. But this next piece of information served to bolster that knowledge even further. It is as follows.

Shortly after my sittings with Q I received a letter from someone claiming he had very sound contacts in both the intelligence (MI6) and security (M15) services. Indeed, this person – who must remain anonymous – claimed that some of his contacts were 'longstanding friends'. Without going into too much irrelevant detail, the reason this person contacted me, he said, was to offer me 'a piece of friendly advice' concerning an article I had written for *UFO Reality* magazine (an article about Salisbury Plain being a likely site for a British deep-underground military-industrial facility, curiously enough, and which included impressions from Q's initial remote viewing of Salisbury Plain). My correspondent told me in no uncertain terms that, in his opinion, and in the opinion of some of his MI5/MI6 buddies, I had been led up the garden path by my sources regarding the deep-underground facility beneath Rudloe Manor and Salisbury Plain. Though my information was partly correct, he said (indeed, correct enough that he had written to me and warned me against publishing a 'genuine national security issue'), it was, in the main, incorrect.

'You are quite correct in stating that there is a vast, underground complex in Wiltshire', he informed me, and indeed went on to say that this underground complex is 'the largest in the United Kingdom' and that it is 'extremely secure'. However, he added that 'Neither the Corsham [Rudloe Manor] complex, nor any other underground Government facility in the United Kingdom has any connection whatsoever with UFOs, captured aliens or their craft'. I wrote back and thanked him for his concern. I also told him that I thought he was wrong.

Though this information (plus other valuable snippets he seemed willing to share) was in itself of sincere interest to me, further information received from the same source in a subsequent communication fairly claimed my sanity. By this time I had sat with Q (during remote viewing sessions) on a number of occasions, and this new information seemed to correlate too closely with Q's descriptions of an 'underground laboratory' for coincidence to win the day. To add to this, I had of course already received information from my own main intelligence source, Stealth, about similar operations under way at several government facilities, either on or beneath British soil. Before that, however, and with my correspondent's express permission, I will relay to you the same story he relayed to me. Apart from one or two minor edits (to protect his identity) the story is told verbatim.

Dear Mr King,

Many thanks for your very interesting letter . . . I stated in my original letter that . . . . . . One of my roles . . . is to attend functions and speak about [certain] activities. One such invitation was arranged by a good friend of mine a couple of years ago, and involved an after-dinner speech in a large hotel . . . I cannot remember the name of the organisation I was addressing, but my audience seemed to consist of a large number of retired former professional men, both civilian and military . . .

When the formalities were over, and we headed for the bar, my host literally tugged at my sleeve and led me away from the room. He was a very senior serving Royal Navy officer (a Commodore, I think), and he was *extremely* nervous and agitated all of a sudden. What he told me follows.

This man's daughter worked for the Scientific Civil Service (Department or Branch not specified), having graduated with flying colours in Genetics. She had effectively been head-hunted for the post. He and his wife had become increasingly concerned over the previous year or so that said daughter was becoming more and more introverted and unhappy with her work. Her (non-service) friends had virtually lost touch with her and she seemed to be worried about something but would not open up to her family. Given the likely security clearance her father would hold, this in itself suggests the poor girl was virtually paranoid. Matters had come to a head the previous Christmas when she had stayed with her parents, only to find she had woken the whole house with the most 'blood-curdling screams' my host had ever heard, and that included his service in the Falklands War.

Under very close questioning, it eventually emerged that she had been suffering unspeakable nightmares for months, solely as a result of her work. The scenes she described to her father, and which he relayed to me, subsequently appeared in an episode of 'The X Files' I happened to see. Large tanks of strange-coloured liquids with equally strange alien-type 'beings' suspended in them, linked to monitors, and other equipment, in a huge warehouse-type laboratory. The man's daughter, on medical advice, tendered her resignation but this was refused on the grounds that she had been too intimately involved with the project (whatever it was) and would be a security risk if she were to walk out. This was of course quite unfair, since she would still have been bound by the Official Secrets Act. She had in fact done her damnedest *not* to release the information which was so troubling her.

My host was clearly worried and stated quite unequivocally that he believed his daughter's life was now in danger. From whom and for what reason he did not say. Nor did I ever discover why he had chosen to impart this information to *me*, who, after all, had been engaged through a mutual friend to offer a lively and amusing account . . . to a group of professional persons at their annual dinner. The only possible explanation I can think of is that in the process of being introduced to my host, earlier in the evening, I had mentioned that I worked at . . .

I listened sympathetically, but could offer

```
little in the way of constructive advice, since
I hadn't a clue whom to contact or where to start
trying to verify his story. All my usual sources
drew complete blanks. Maybe yours will have more
success, since they seem, from what you say,
to be rather more intimately involved in this
particular area.
   Yours sincerely . . .
```

Having read this letter in full I was grateful and gobsmacked, both at once – grateful for the information; gobsmacked that it correlated so precisely, not only with Q's remote viewing information, but with information I had already received from my own sources, including my main intelligence contact, Stealth.

According to Stealth, highly secret genetic and mind-control programmes are indeed being carried out at British-based military-industrial facilities, deep underground – facilities so secret, he says, and information regarding their purpose so highly classified and tightly compartmentalized that even the highest-ranking military, intelligence and other government personnel have little (if any) idea of their existence, much less of what goes on in them. Stealth also implied that these experiments were responsible for the so-called 'alien abduction' phenomenon – that he had seen briefings to the effect that this phenomenon was a govern-ment propaganda exercise used as a smokescreen behind which its own black-budget scientists dabbled in genetics, eugenics, cloning and mind-control. He strongly implied that 'human guinea pigs' were being used here, unwittingly, in particular for research into what he called 'human behaviour in response to electronic remote influencing', in other words 'implant and mind-control'. Indeed, without actually saying it he implied that perhaps 'Special Forces' military were abducting people so that military-industrial scientists could experiment on them, implant them and, while they were under drug- and/or technologically-induced hypnosis, fill their minds with 'screen memories' of aliens so that when they came to they would think – assuming they remembered anything at all – that they had been abducted by aliens rather than soldiers (see Document 10). He called it 'the perfect cover', so crazy that no one would ever believe it anyway. No one would ever *want* to believe it. He said that he did not know the complete agenda behind the programme, whether or not the aliens were hands-on involved (or whether they were just being sold as 'the patsies'), and neither did he know the precise locations of the 'several facilities' where these obscenities were taking place. (Information received from other sources, however, points to an alleged deep-underground military-industrial facility in Berkshire – with entrances at Aldermaston and Greenham Common – as a possible primary site.) Though he reiterated that he did not know the full extent of the agenda behind these programmes, Stealth reminded me that one of its chief aims was to implant certain selected individuals – some civilian, most former military and intelligence personnel with known mental/emotional debilities and/or sexual hang-ups – with the latest mind-control technology. These 'implantees', he reiterated, are known in intelligence circles as 'sleeper agents' (see Document 03, File 13).

Another source (non-intelligence, though someone who holds a sensitive government post) says that he knows several people currently employed at British underground facilities where acquired alien technology and genetics programmes are being carried out. This source also names Berkshire as one of several possible primary sites; others include Harwell in Oxfordshire, RAE Farnborough in

Hampshire and two sites in Scotland. I regret that this is all I am permitted to say regarding this source of information, other than that it is a notably reliable one.

For the record, however, one other contact of mine – who also holds a very sensitive government post – claims to know someone who once worked at a deep-underground facility in Berkshire where, he alleges, these kind of programmes have been carried out for decades. He further confirmed that the facility is compartmentalized into an unknown number of sub-facilities and that the programmes carried out there include eugenics, clone-production and hybridization. He stated quite unequivocally that some of the programmes required the participation of either 'captured' or 'engineered' extraterrestrials. Make of that one what you will. He also claims that buried somewhere beneath RAE Farnborough in Hampshire is a facility stuffed full with files/records on secret-technology projects dating back many decades, and that some of the records refer specifically to 'reverse-engineered alien technologies' and 'crashed and recovered alien vehicles'. I should add here that one other – entirely independent – source (former RAF) told me that he was once part of a special unit assigned to destroy 'secret-technology' files stored beneath RAE Farnborough. I am, of course, unable to substantiate this information.

There is, however, one other similar story in circulation that stems from the lips of a man called Barry King. Known also as 'The Voice', Mr King claims to be a former employee (security guard) at a top-secret underground facility that he says exists beneath the village of Peasemore in Berkshire. In their attempts to engineer the 'perfect human', King says, government scientists are busy creating 'programmable life forms' at this facility. He was quoted in an interview conducted for *Truth Seekers Review* (May/June 1996) as saying: 'They have these life forms in jars, lined up in rows, and there are loads of them – rows and rows. To look at them is very spooky, very frightening. The situation is out of control . . .'

He added: 'We got the technology from the aliens. They gave it to us. It's not a friendly arrangement . . . Our military wanted to get the technology and information and then stab the aliens in the back. The aliens . . . are trying to get genetic material from us . . . For this they need humans. We are business to them. The military are letting them do this to a degree, but there are more military abductions than alien.'

Barry King claims that certain factions within Britain's Defence Intelligence Staff (DIS) are unhappy that these programmes are now being carried out in Britain, and so are endeavouring to 'leak' this information out into the public domain. For this reason they have agreed to protect Mr King from any recriminations he may otherwise have faced for speaking publicly about these matters. In return for his protection, however, he must refrain from publishing certain photographs he claims to possess – photographs taken by DIS operatives and given over into King's safe keeping; photographs that allegedly depict parts of the deep-underground Berkshire complex and its diabolical secrets; photographs that could put this debate to bed, once and for all, should they ever surface in the public domain. To date, they have not.

And so there we have it. I do not, of course, expect you or anybody else to simply 'believe' the above without question, but to judge for yourselves the evidence and correlations presented and to draw your own conclusions. Whether or not there actually is a massive deep-underground R&D facility beneath Peasemore (Aldermaston/Greenham Common) in Berkshire, or indeed Salisbury Plain in Wiltshire, must for the time being remain open to further investigation. We have no way of proving the matter one way or the other. But the fact that a sizeable underground complex of bunkers and tunnels exists beneath RAF Rudloe Manor, possibly fanning out to include areas beneath Salisbury Plain, is not in question. It is a matter of public record. And in any case, underground facilities of one kind or another exist at many highly secure British military bases: it would be more out of the ordinary for there *not* to be an underground facility at such a sensitive installation as Rudloe Manor. During the course of my own investigations I have interviewed and spoken with many still-serving and former military personnel, none of whom deny the existence of underground facilities beneath high-security military bases (there is rumoured to be a massive deep-underground complex beneath RAF Woodbridge and Bentwaters in East Anglia, for example, home to what must surely be Britain's best-known and best-documented military UFO incident to date, the Rendlesham Forest Incident, which occurred in December 1980).

The question is therefore not: Do underground facilities exist? Rather: Are there supersecret underground facilities in Britain that are being used by the British-based military-industrial complex to research and develop acquired alien technologies and/or to experiment in eugenics, cloning and hybridization? Do any of these programmes demand the unwitting participation of human guinea pigs? Does this demand precipitate a further demand, that of abducting people, experimenting on them and implanting them with microscopic bits of acquired alien technology?

And if so, is it then the very propagation of these pro-grammes that has spawned a need to create the so-called alien abduction scenario as a smokescreen behind which these activities can be carried out?

If the answer to even one these questions is, staggeringly, *Yes*, then once again, the integrity of the military-industrial complex – and thereby the government – is called very profoundly into question.

After all, the military requirement to possess new technologies in advance of the enemy, so to speak, the need to develop and deploy capabilities beyond those of the next superpower, is one thing. To my mind this is a purely logical – if primitive – state of affairs.

However, the deliberate use (and abuse) of unwitting citizens in order to attain higher and higher levels of technological superiority is utterly unacceptable. More than this. It is a criminal act, a crime equal to human rights abuse and its perpetrators should be brought to book for that. It is indeed such a crime because – whatever the scheme, whatever the agenda – it serves to elevate the elite few to worlds of untold potential while the rest of us are kept on some evolutionary leash like so many medicated sheep. If only a tiny proportion of 'military' UFO reports are genuine – UFOs observed over highly sensitive military bases; UFOs observed by serving military personnel; serving military personnel being used as guinea pigs in genetic/mind-control experiments and/or psychological warfare exercises; unwitting civilians being used by the military in the same way – then either the military-industrial complex is, in its own right, in possession of technology some thirty to fifty years in advance of anything we know about (which in itself is highly suspicious, and utterly unacceptable – the elite on a rollercoaster, the sheep on a leash) or some outside, possibly off-planet source is feeding our governments technological enlightenment in exchange for something we have and it wants. (This latter scenario, of course, would certainly demand the high levels of secrecy currently being employed.)

And either way, within the precincts of a free and democratic socio-political system such as that supposed to exist in Britain there are questions that demand answers. Satisfactory answers.

As yet, no such satisfactory answers are forthcoming.

DOCUMENT 13

Cosmic Top Secret
Eyes Only Copy One of One

Deep Underground (Part 3)
The Unseen Agenda

File 40
Satellite Government

In his book *Beyond Top Secret*, Timothy Good tells us: 'It has become increasingly evident to me that the above-Top Secret facts about this multifaceted [UFO] subject are restricted to a relatively small group of individuals within the military and scientific intelligence community – a group which, in the US at least, operates outside the normal and legal parameters of government.'

Indeed, the evidence speaks for itself.

My own investigations into this 'relatively small group of individuals', for example, has shown me beyond question that such a group indeed exists, and moreover that it exercises a power not just, as Timothy Good says, beyond the 'normal and legal parameters of government', but beyond the moral and extremely vulnerable parameters of human rights. And more than this. It is becoming increasingly evident that this *relatively small group of individuals'* own unseen agenda lies behind every major administrative policy governing the western world.

In other words, the people we elect to Government are in effect no more than puppets. Sure, they debate policies and make decisions in what appears on the surface to be an open and democratic forum. And so long as the policies they debate and the decisions they make remain within the parameters of this *relatively small group of individuals'* unseen agenda then the system is seen to work and everything remains hunky-dory. But what, in truth, *is* this *relatively small group of individuals?*

Who really makes Policy?

According to retired black-ops engineer Bill Uhouse (Jarod 2), who claims to have worked on secret government projects for more than thirty years (from the mid-1950s through to his retirement in the late 1980s), in 1953 a satellite government was set up in order to liaise with a visiting alien civilization. Its primary purpose was to form a kind of alien/US New World Administration alliance, while the CIA/MJ-12 directive was to keep this alliance secret. Indeed, as mentioned in Document 02, File 05, this may well be the truth behind the Majestic-12 schedule (see also Document 06, File 23); on the other hand, of course, it could just as well be the usurping of it.

Uhouse claims that four aliens survived a UFO crash in Arizona in May 1953 and that the still-living aliens were taken to the supersecret deep-underground facility, S-3, at Wright-Patterson Air Force Base in Dayton, Ohio, America's first 'Area 51'. The aliens were said to be around four feet tall with two eyes, two ears, a nose and a small round mouth, and though vaguely humanoid in appearance, their arms were said to be 'longer than normal'. The 'guests', Uhouse further claims, were subsequently transferred to a similar underground facility at Area 51 (where Uhouse himself worked). This facility is now known as S-4. Here it was, Uhouse says, that alien/government communications were first established. According to several sources the transfer of operations, prisoners and artefacts from Wright-Patterson to Area 51 began at some point in 1954.

Uhouse, of course, is not the only insider to make such claims. Former US Naval Intelligence man Milton William Cooper, for example, says that he has seen documents to the effect that at least 600 aliens were at one time resident at Area 51. Indeed, according to Cooper, the construction of this new alien facility (S-4) was the direct result of the first government/alien treaty – the Greada Treaty – which he insists was signed by a reluctant President Eisenhower and a visiting alien embassy on 20th February 1954, at Muroc Air Force Base (now Edwards AFB) California. In brief, this treaty meant that the aliens could now utilize secret bases on Earth (in particular in the US); in return they would furnish the US government – and *only* the US government – with new and advanced technologies. Also agreed, Cooper says, was that the aliens would not directly interfere in human affairs and, likewise, 'we' would not interfere in theirs. However, he further reveals that there *were* certain areas of enterprise in which both the US government and the alien visitors would collaborate, namely: secret alien/government genetics and technology programmes scheduled to be carried out in the newly constructed deep-underground facilities across North America, particularly those in the American South-West – the Four Corners area of Colorado, Utah, Arizona and New Mexico – plus others in southern California. If Cooper's (and Uhouse's) information turns out to be correct, of course, then from 1954 onwards the secrecy machine would certainly have demanded new levels of stringency. And security.

Hence the need for a satellite government.

Indeed, by this time (1954) the so-called 'alien problem' had reached meltdown, and was – perhaps understandably – causing some serious amount of concern among certain echelons of government, in particular, of course, the military and scientific intelligence communities. It had already been decided that all information concerning the aliens (knowledge of the newly signed treaty in particular) should be compart-mented and classified at the highest possible security level – COSMIC TOP SECRET – and that such information should be the sole possession of a small but powerful group within the government. It was at this time, according to Uhouse and others, that President Eisenhower sanctioned the formation of a satellite government headed by none other than then Vice President Richard Nixon. The satellite government's mandate was to manage all affairs relating to the newly signed treaty and to interface with the official US government for support only. Exchange of information regarding the alien situation was forbidden.

As Uhouse explained: 'Nixon did it right by establishing the satellite government. This provided cover for the visitors plus a totally new concept for protecting all information relating to this subject.' From this point on any military or intelligence personnel involved in the alien programme were reassigned via covert CIA/MJ-12 channels to the command of the satellite government.

The question now, of course, is: Does this satellite government still exist? And if so, does it still operate in conjunction with this visiting alien civilization? Does this satellite government still sanction and oversee the covert alien/government technology schedules rumoured to be taking place in some of the many deep-underground R&D facilities across America (and to some lesser extent in Britain)? And perhaps more to the point: Just what, exactly, are those schedules all about?

One wonders how many of our legitimately elected representatives to Government know what is really going on behind their backs.

Much less beneath their feet.

File 40: Appendix 01
Case Profile: Cosmic Top-X57 Eyes Only
Noah

In my efforts to find out more about this shameful scenario I came across some interesting information regarding the so-called Secret Government and its attendant agendas. In particular I stumbled on something that has been appropriately dubbed by some *Project Noah's Ark*. With more money being spent on this project than any other it is likely that it constitutes the Secret Government's most prized agenda of all – its biggest, most secretive undertaking ever. Assuming 'Noah' to be none other than the Secret Government itself (or at least that Government's hub) and the 'Ark' to be the elaborate system of deep-underground installations dotted around the planet (together with a possible complex of bases on the Moon), the question arises: What is the real motive behind *Project Noah's Ark*? Why is this project necessary? What does Noah know that the sheep have yet to learn?

And moreover: Who the hell *is* Noah, *exactly*?

*　　*　　*

As I have asserted before, the so-called Secret (Satellite) Government is no fiction. It is not the product of some wild and paranoid imagination. On the contrary, it is the product of the post-Second World War intelligence agency boom, at least to some large degree. Through the eyes of this new and secretive (and many-headed) hydra the world's US-based financial and industrial giants suddenly saw that the once uncharted and disparate globe of nations had suddenly become a village, small enough that it could now be managed from the comfort of one's armchair. Or somebody else's. The CIA's. With both the victors and the victims of the biggest war the planet had ever known ludicrously indebted to the world banks (and so to the elite, who generously financed both sides during the hostilities) and with only one rival superpower to contend with, world control became a doddle. More than this: it became a requirement for survival. From the late 1940s onwards the US-based Secret Government became the Beast who would be Noah. And the military-industrial complex set about building this Beast's Ark.

It is important we remember, however, that this Beast is not some all-powerful, all-seeing coherent group of cigar-smoking businessmen who sit regularly together and plan the takeover of Mother Earth. Human nature simply does not work like that. On the contrary, like its shadow (the elected Government) the Secret Government is a power-thirsty conglomeration of busy little cliques, a kind of sour-smelling pot-pourri of agendas and sub-agendas all vying for control, yet bound together (somewhat precariously, I would say) under a single common ambition: to ensure the survival, not only of the game, but of each member's stake in it. There are covert military cells whose agendas come together only for the sake of maintaining the national security system, behind which their own little power-perches thus remain intact. There are covert intelligence cells whose agendas come together only for the sake of some common global administrative ambition. And there are organized crime cells and high-powered corporate cells who serve each other's interests only for the sake of ultimate control and manipulation of world affairs. Noah is a multifaceted animal.

But more than this. Lurking somewhere behind the scenes of national and international government, Noah reigns supreme.

Policy affecting each and every one of us is decided by this cabalistic mishmash of international financiers, multinational industrialists, high-ranking military and intelligence chiefs and very senior civil servants. (Add to the pot the godfathers of organized crime – and one or two, shall we say, influential families, or 'Houses', as they prefer to be known – *plus* a sordid soup of military-industrial backbenchers thrown in for good measure – and we begin to get at least the broadest outline of who Noah actually is: of who actually makes Policy.) This Policy is then filtered out into the public sector via the so-called democratically elected Government, itself of course no more than a public face for the non-elected secret one. And though diverse in the extreme, the non-elected secret one is comprised essentially of those who manage – or are otherwise able to manipulate – the global economy. 'Give me control over a nation's currency, and I care not who makes its laws,' said Secret Government architect Mayer Amschel Rothschild when formulating his plan of 'economic inductance'. And Mayer Amschel Rothschild, of course, was right: his descendants have been running the world for decades.

The skill, of course, is to play the economy as you might a chess game. In this respect strategies are cast and moves made (behind the scene of each crime); a knight for a bishop, a rook for a queen: and who but the game-players know the strategy – what is really being done, what each move represents? In reality, of course, it's whether a Left-Wing or a Right-Wing Government would best execute the next appropriate move in the game – a Socialist Government to take us into a European Federal State, and so aid in the process of centralizing global power; a Republican Administration to lead us in time of war, and so help to refurbish the arms-trade coffers and buoy up the funds for next year's black budget. Socialism or Capitalism: two faces, one agenda. Communism or Fascism: two sides, one game. And in this game the kings and the queens and the rooks and the bishops are the shepherds who herd the flocks – the illusion-givers, the dream-sellers . . .

. . . The pawns, of course, are the sheep; the ones who buy those dreams.

And all the while the Chess Master remains unseen, unburnt by the fires of nationalism, unscathed by the losses of war (indeed, enriched by such losses, for both conqueror and conquered alike will be his debtors come the war's end). And so untouched by the ebb and the flow of socio-political evolution is he that it would appear he has no existence but that of a god, a Chess Master. We the electorate (the flock), of course, must simply sit back and accept the game as it is played by proxy – the moves planned in our name; the decisions made on our behalf – in boardrooms and bedrooms alike. This is the system; we have little choice but to comply with this system. For one thing it makes us powerless; we do not have the resources by which to muster the power sufficient to challenge it. It decaffeinates us, makes us weak, in mind and soul and verve. It puts down the revolution in all of us (before it has even begun) and so makes of us a body of *yes* people: *yes* to the lies; *yes* to the spies; *yes* to the grubby dollar bills. Yes to the system.

In this respect it is a cleverly orchestrated form of social medication.

But then it has to be. Any serious challenge to this system would be regarded as an affront to the inner Policy-making machine, which in turn would be tantamount to an assault on the Empire – the Economy – itself. Unacceptable. To those who pull the strings of world government, remember, economics equals religion – or, said another way: money equals power; it is the meat by which they subsist, their creed. A serious glitch, therefore, in the mechanism of the official 'Stock Market' economy would carry serious implications for the unofficial, black-budget one – *it* would falter, too. Secret empires would fall and power cells crumble. This situation could never be tolerated. Indeed, this is why such emphasis is piled upon the fate and the fluctuations of the world's stock market shares and index numbers. As Mayer Amschel Rothschild knowingly inferred, control of a nation's (a world's) economy is control of its policies, and control of policy is absolute government.

There are no two ways about that.

In addition to this, of course . . . somewhere amongst the moves and the countermoves, the manoeuvres and the mates and the checkmates . . . there is the question of our *own* economy, our *own* money.

In the so-called modern world we have a system whereby we are legally bound to contribute to the national budget. This contribution – which in its purest form is a fair and a viable one – is commonly called, simply, 'tax'. Each person donates a portion of their own income to the Treasury and trusts that their appointed representatives at this Treasury will spend their money wisely, and in a way that is beneficial to the whole nation. While most will no doubt feel disgruntled that, in reality, this does not happen, the sad fact of the matter is that the purchase of a nuclear warhead in lieu of a new cancer research centre is almost irrelevant compared with what becomes of our 'unseen taxes'. The implications of this latter scenario are vast indeed.

In America alone, for example, untold billions of tax-payers' dollars are spent every year on black-budget projects such as advanced technology programmes, unpublished defence, space and aeronautics programmes, the covert construction of deep-underground military installations, etc. To some lesser extent a similar situation exists in Britain – but where does this money really come from?

While we are told on the one hand that vast cuts are necessary in areas of health, education and welfare (that the country is carrying a huge budget deficit, and that, as a result, those who need help the most – the sick, the young, the socially dependent – cannot have it: there are simply not the resources), at the same time more money than can be conceivably imagined is being creamed off and funnelled into projects that serve the agendas of an elite few. (Indeed, the black budget currently consumes around $650 billion a year in the US alone. That's $1.3 trillion every two years. A trillion dollars is a thousand billion. A billion dollars is a thousand million. One per cent of this inconceivable sum is a million satisfied Third World bellies. Plus some.) Like all else involving the motives and activities of this shady elite, this situation is, quite simply, unacceptable.

File 40: Appendix 02
Case Study: Cosmic Top-X58 Eyes Only
A Twentieth-Century Ark

So what does all this have to do with Noah?

The biblical story tells us that, under instruction from God, Noah set about constructing an Ark on which he was to survive an impending catastrophe, him and his beasts. It is now suspected that a twentieth-century 'Ark' is under construction and that it is intended to ferry the elite to some safe and indestructible haven where the tendrils of impending doom cannot and will not ever reach. Does this imply, then, that the Secret Government has been, like Noah before it, forewarned by . . . *God?*

(Or rather that, all those centuries ago, Noah was in fact forewarned by . . . *aliens?*)

As detailed in Document 11 (File 36) recently unearthed official documentation has revealed that a multibillion-dollar black programme is indeed under way in the US, involving the construction of a deep and hi-tech underground network of military-industrial installations. Some reports say that this network is literally undermining the geological substructures of entire continents, not the least of which is the continent of North America. So what is this deep-underground network all about? And moreover, why is it funded by *black* money? Why is it all so secret?

According to some conspiracy theorists, of course, the answer is all too apparent. 'It's a latter-day Noah's Ark,' they say. 'The Secret Government has been warned of some impending end game – alien invasion, pole shift, the strike of a passing comet or asteroid – and they're busy making provision for it. When the proverbial finally hits the fan they'll all dive underground, or head for outer space, while we surface mortals will be left to face the music.'

Hmmm . . . I suppose it's possible. Unlike Noah, however, I somehow doubt that the Secret Government – as fat and powerful as it undoubtedly is – has a direct hotline to 'God'. While it is no secret that the CIA keeps an active eye on the latest 'prophecies, channellings and ET bulletins' relating to the immediate future (and indeed, employs its own in-house psychics and channellers to double-check prophecies relating to the present day), it is unlikely that such enormous sums of money would have been spent building an underground Ark based purely on the speculations of prophets – indeed, on what must surely be considered by the scientific intelligence community as, at best, flimsy and unsubstantiated information. If the rumours are true then there must be an alternative source of information – an alternative to the New Age oracle.

It is, of course, possible that the motives behind the deep-underground programme are no more sinister than pure logic. For one thing, it is cheap real estate. Rather than purchase more and more land for the construction of more and more Research & Development centres – which in itself would be extremely expensive – why not simply burrow beneath the land you already own? And for another, it is sound defence policy. No matter how well disguised and guarded they may be, above-ground top-secret facilities can always be detected by enemy spy planes and satellites. If you are below ground, however – a thousand feet, a mile, two – it is far less likely that your secrets will show up on enemy screens. It should be remembered that the Nazi V2 rockets were built in underground munitions factories during World War Two. For this reason they remained undetected by Allied forces.

Even so, a growing body of evidence seems to suggest

another, more sinister motive. According to those with an inside view – Alex Christopher, Philip J. Corso, Robert Dean, William Cooper, Whitley Strieber, to name a few – the more covert departments within the US administration are well aware of what they term 'the alien presence' and that this 'alien presence' knows of a massive and imminent global event – indeed, that this 'alien presence' is doing its damnedest to *warn us of the threat*. Some say this event will take the form of extraterrestrial contact, while others expect a cataclysm, both in terms of the geological environment and our own social and psychological edifices. Perhaps it will be all of these. But the point is that this same body of evidence says that government foreknowledge of this event may well be the reason for all the underground activity.

Whitley Strieber, for example – whose uncle, Colonel Edward Strieber [USAF], spent much of his career at Wright-Patterson AFB – says in his book *Breakthrough*: '. . . individuals formerly at Wright have alluded to a top-secret scientific paper that alleges that the ability of the visitors to enter our reality is mediated by the degree to which we acknowledge their existence, and that the 'invasion' can be literally held at bay by orchestrated denial and general disbelief.'

The implications of this statement could, of course, fill a book, all by themselves. If the scientific intelligence community is aware that any full-bodied ET approach – 'invasion' – can be 'mediated by the degree by which we acknowledge their existence', it implies that somehow it has gained knowledge of how the extraterrestrials operate (i.e. on more subtle levels of mind and reality). This in turn implies that any mass-scale ET approach can only be facilitated via some or other level of ET/human interaction, implying of course that such interaction be 'telepathic', 'psychic' or 'intuitive': in any event spontaneous and wired-in.

On the other hand, of course, if only one of the testimonies given by so many former employees at supersecret under-ground facilities is true (that they have witnessed alien life forms either working with or being held by the US government) then this further implies that some or other level of ET/human interaction has already taken place (it could even have taken place as long ago as 1954, of course, when it is alleged that the Greada Treaty was signed), and that the reason, therefore, the US-based Secret Government is making provision for some imminent global event is because it has been informed of such an event by the extraterrestrials themselves.

(Who knows, this may even have been where the original Noah got *his* information.)

Hence the construction of *Noah's Ark*.

File 41
The Flood

According to former intelligence operative John Coleman, there are very strong financial links between the Pine Gap deep-underground facility (see Document 11, File 37) and the Club of Rome, an inconceivably rich and powerful group of faceless individuals who comprise one of the Secret Government's most notorious power cells. In this respect the Club of Rome's allegiance is unequivocally pledged to a consortium that, effectively, controls and conduits all international finance. This consortium is known as the Committee of 300.

It is said that much of the funding for the Pine Gap facility either originated with or was laundered via this group, and that this same situation continues today. Indeed, thanks to the courage of inside sources such as John Coleman and high-ranking Australian civil servant Peter Sawyer, and the conviction of investigators such as Alex Christopher and former US Special Forces operative Phil Schneider, there is now sufficient evidence to conclude that most – if not all – black-budget funding is administrated by, or via, this unseen consortium: the Committee of 300. It is the Elite of the elite, so to speak.

But what is perhaps the most startling revelation concerning this group is that, according to several sources – including John Coleman, Alex Christopher and US conspiracies author Jim Keith – the Committee of 300's 'chain of command' does not stop with presidents and prime ministers, nor even popes; nor indeed with the Rockefellers or the Rothschilds of this world. And neither does it stop with *any* of the highly influential Bilderberg Policy Group associates who make up the majority of the Committee's membership. Rather, it goes all the way back to what John Coleman claims is the most influential family – 'House' – in the world: the House of Windsor, where indeed it does stop.

Which in effect means that, if the evidence so far uncovered is correct, and the documents uncovered by Coleman genuine, the highest office in the masonically structured Secret Government 'Cabinet' is the Office of the Monarch of England. Which in turn, of course, means that the supreme head of the Secret Government New World Order Consortium, the Committee of 300 (at least on the face of it, at least its figurehead) is none other than Queen Elizabeth II, the richest, most powerful woman in the world.

File 41: Appendix 01
Case Review: Cosmic Top-X59 Eyes Only
Earth Changes

In support of this seemingly unbelievable claim, recently uncovered information points to the fact that the Queen (or a body acting on her behalf) has, under an assumed name, been busy buying up land and property in Colorado, where America's own 'Pine Gap' is now located (beneath the newly constructed Denver Airport – see Document 11, File 37). According to US conspiracies investigator Alex Christopher, the Queen and her 'House' seem to be preparing for some imminent 'global event' and the consequent establishment of what has become known as the New World Order – the emergence of the Secret Government into the public arena in the form of some totalitarian Third Reich-style regime: the long-prophesied One World Government.

'The information,' Christopher said, 'covers how the major corporations, railroad and banking concerns in this country [US] were set up through a "trust" that was originally known as the *Virginia Company* . . . And that brings us right up to today, because we are still looking at everything falling under that trust system, going back to the Crown of England . . .

'. . . All of them are doing the bidding, and it goes back to their secret societies and the establishment of the New World Order, which all leads back to the House of Windsor.'

Christopher goes on to say:

'There has been, in this country, for a long time, a grooming process whereby people carry on the bidding of the Crown of England. That is one of the things the system involving the Rhodes Scholars was set up to achieve. Cecil Rhodes set it up to groom people for this task, to carry the United States into the New World Order. It appears from what I have been able to find out that the Crown of England has had this very skillfully planned for hundreds of years, and it could be possible that they have been privy to information that not many of us have been for a long, long time, about the chaos involving Earth changes that is coming.

'It is my understanding that England is not going to make it through the changes, so they set up a whole new Empire over here. That goes back to some of the things we discussed before, about lands being bought up in Colorado . . .'

When the latest scientific – geological, meteorological, etc. – findings are considered against this theory, the idea that Earth changes (brought about by sudden and massive seismic, volcanic and oceanic activity) may well be imminent becomes a plausible one. Indeed, the idea that information concerning this possibility is presently in the hands of the elite (while at the same time being hidden from the rest of us) becomes equally plausible. Many top scientists, for example, are finally coming round to the idea – slowly, complainingly – that regular, periodic 'earth-crust displacements' could be the real driving force behind the Earth's topographical evolution: that every so many thousands of years the Earth's crust 'slips' on its own molten interior, without warning, thereby causing spontaneous widespread destruction by way of volcanic eruptions, massive hurricane-force winds and equally massive earthquakes, land shifts and tidal waves. Indeed, there is a growing body of evidence that suggests that such a displacement occurred as recently as 10,000 years ago.

In the 1950s Professor Charles Hapgood (whose work was lauded by Albert Einstein) found by analyzing thousands of radiocarbon datings of climatic events that: (a) a crustal displacement may have occurred as many as three times over the past 100,000 years; (b) each time, an advanced civilization unknown to modern scholars – its language; its art, its science

– could have been, in the blink of an eye, obliterated from the slate of history; and (c) the last displacement occurred at the end of the last Ice Age, around 10,000 years ago, the result of Earth's seemingly natural, periodic and purgative geological cycle. This theory says that civilizations come and go like weekends, and that top government scientists may now be able to predict the cyclic arrival of 'Monday morning'. The disturbing factor so far as our present civilization is concerned is that, in geological terms, the weekend is coming to a close: it is now late Sunday evening.

Maps from antiquity (compiled by Admiral Piri Reis in 1513, and Oronteus Finaeus in 1531, the latter drawn from source maps dating back beyond 4000 BC) form no less impressive a part of this same body of evidence. The reason? They depict precisely the topographical land mass of Antarctica, and the land mass of Antarctica, remember, lies under several thousands of feet of ice. Indeed, it was not until a comprehensive seismic survey was carried out in 1949 that it became possible to so precisely map the land mass beneath that enormous ice-bulk. But someone did. And they did it more than 6000 years ago. How?

There can be only one possible answer: when the maps were drawn up Antarctica was ice-free, and visited – if not populated – by a civilization at least equal to our own in terms of science and technology. The technical ability to so accurately depict the lines of latitude and longitude contained on the maps is alone proof enough of this.

As many leading-edge scientists and geologists are now beginning to realize, and as both Hapgood and Einstein postulated more than forty years ago, at some point in recent history (around 10,000 years ago) the land mass of Antarctica was further north than it is today (about 2000 miles further north, most agree). And because it was, it enjoyed a far more temperate climate than it does today. But in order for this to hold true, Hapgood theorized, a massive displacement of the Earth's crust must have occurred around the end of what we are these days prone to call the last 'Ice Age', even though the very term 'Ice Age' could turn out to be the misnomer of the epoch. When the 'earth-crust displacement' theory is finally proved correct in the eyes of orthodox science – which one day very soon it surely must be – then orthodox scientists will be forced to accept that glacier paths found on continents such as Africa, for example, are not the result of great swathes of ice creeping slowly south from the Arctic Circle (or north from the Antarctic Circle) but of land masses being hurled towards the polar regions during Earth changes brought on by sudden and massive crustal displacement activity. In other words, the mountain comes to Mohammed, proving that soon the idea of 'ice ages' will be as outmoded as the one about the Earth being flat.

Anyway, the point so far as we are concerned is this: if scientists such as Charles Hapgood and Albert Einstein were convinced of the 'earth-crust displacement' phenomenon as long ago as the 1950s, and further, that the military-industrial complex has thus had as long to study the pros and cons of this phenomenon as it has had to reverse-engineer alien artefacts, then why did we hear nothing further of it until Graham Hancock's 1995 masterpiece *Fingerprints of the Gods* hit the bookstands and reminded us all of Earth's true history? Why are our children not being taught this theory in school? Why were *we* not taught this theory in school? If government scientists have for forty years and more been able to study and evaluate the planet's cyclic-cataclysm scenario then what do they know about this crucial phenomenon today? What do they know that they don't want *us* to know? Indeed, who is to say they haven't by now cracked the code entirely, and so are able accurately to predict events within this cycle, a bit like long-ranging a weather forecast? After all, the ancients seemed able to predict their own destructions accurately enough – the story of Noah alone is evidence of this, never mind the countless other similar 'myths' and 'legends' worldwide, all of which accurately depict the arrival of 'the last days' or 'the end times' in terms of global flood and catastrophe. So why not us? Especially when you consider that there is now a vast body of evidence to suggest that ancient artefacts such as the Mayan Calendar and the Egyptian Pyramids embody precisely this information – that they were purpose-built by previous Earth civilizations to inform future Earth civilizations about the planet's cyclic behaviour: how civilizations come and go; how the Earth undergoes a series of 'beginnings' and 'end times' in cyclic fashion; what astronomical and other signs to look out for as indicators that another such 'end time' is upon us. And, by the way, according to the Mayan Calendar the present Earth cycle comes to an end on 23rd December AD 2012. Some traditions predict it sooner than that.

In light of this information, then, the following question comes reluctantly – though unavoidably – to mind: When we see how plainly and unashamedly the governments have consistently lied to us, about all manner of things (not least something of such planetary significance as the presence of an extraterrestrial intelligence), do you imagine for one minute that they would tell us if they *were* in possession of such secrets, such arcane knowledge as this? That they *did* know of some massive and imminent global destruction? That they *had* decoded the Pyramids? The Mayan Calendar? The Dead Sea Scrolls? The apocalyptic scriptures secreted away in the vaults of the Vatican? Or would they more likely make provision for their own survival and at the same time seek to maintain social equilibrium by keeping the evidence to themselves – keeping stum about the main event? After all, the chances are that provision can only be made for the survival of a limited number anyway, and included among that number must, of course, be the world's elite – kings, queens, presidents and popes, our most enlightened academic and military minds, etc. – plus, of course, a few spare seats for the rich and the famous.

Now all I'm saying here is . . . put yourself in *their* shoes – what would *you* do, assuming *you* had the means? Purchase a ticket and keep stum? Or give up your seat and tell the world?

Human nature, right . . . ?

Further evidence to support the crustal displacement argument can be found in that mammoths, bison, sabre-tooth tigers, horses, antelopes and any number of other mammals, many with their bellies full of fruit and vegetation uncommon in the present-day version of their habitats, have been discovered 'snap-frozen' in regions of Siberia, Alaska and other northern territories. It is as though when they died they were enjoying a meal several thousand miles south of their death beds. This is, of course, not possible. Indeed, to great minds like that of Albert Einstein this can mean only one thing: sudden and instant global cataclysms in the form of crustal displacements have indeed occurred, more than likely on a regular basis.

Of Professor Hapgood's findings, Einstein wrote: '. . . The very first communications . . . I received from Mr Hapgood electrified me. His idea is original, of great simplicity, and – if it continues to prove itself – of great importance to everything that is related to the history of the Earth's surface.'

And further: '. . . At each point on the Earth's surface . . .

many climatic changes have taken place, apparently quite suddenly.'

Unlike other cataclysm theories, then – the 'big freeze' theory; the 'pole shift' theory; the 'polar meltdown' theory; 'global warming'; 'alien invasion' – the 'earth-crust displacement' theory says that the cyclic destruction of Earth's civilizations and environments is both sudden and massive, and far more frequent than orthodox history has thus far seemed prepared to accept. It could also, of course, scientifically account for the world's 'myths' and 'legends' about the ubiquitous Flood. Indeed, when comprehensively studied (and with an open mind) it is the only theory that can even begin to describe accurately our lost history – the apparent 'loss-without-trace' of technologically advanced civilizations and continents, Mu, Atlantis, etc.; the possible intervention of extraterrestrials. In this respect I would urge anyone who has not yet done so to read Graham Hancock's *Fingerprints of the Gods* (Heinemann, London, 1995). It is a spellbinding read.

Assuming the possibility, then – even if only for this argument – that information regarding these cyclic devastations is secretly available, perhaps stashed away in some CIA vault or Vatican catacomb or similar-type archive somewhere; and more than this, that it has either been rediscovered by at least forty years of intense scientific research or passed down, codified, one age to the next and secreted away in the treasure troves of kings and presidents alike . . . then the words of Alex Christopher, though still extreme in their import, take on a nonetheless more viable and poignant character:

'. . . It appears from what I have been able to find out that the Crown of England has had this very skilfully planned for hundreds of years, and it could be possible that they have been privy to information that not many of us have been for

a long long time, about the chaos involving Earth changes
that is coming . . .'

File 41: Appendix 02
Intelligence Report:
Cosmic Top-X60 Eyes Only
The Red Book

One other scenario, of course, would be if this information
told a slightly different story. What if, for example, instead of
warnings of global cataclysms, the codified data told of a race
of extraterrestrial visitors who periodically returned to Earth
in order to upgrade the genetic evolution of its progeny? And
further, what if this data had not been passed down at all,
but had been acquired from our alien makers themselves;
stolen or gifted, either way?

Evidence is now emerging that suggests that the CIA
may well be in possession of such information – information
gleaned, not from catacombs or archives or science, nor
even from ancient calendars or pyramids, but from something
which has become known in intelligence circles as the *Red
Book*, a sort of extraterrestrial 'compact disc' containing a
holographic narration of both our history and our future. Its
sister disc, the *Yellow Book*, is also reported to be in CIA/Big
Brother hands and to contain a similar holographic diary of
events. The source of this information is said by US researcher
and author Dr Richard Boylan PhD to be a deep-cover CIA
agent known as Beltway Throat. My own sources have been
unable to confirm or deny the existence of the discs, but
according to Beltway Throat the CIA 'acquired' them from
a 'captured' rather than an 'invited' alien visitor.

In short, bits of the information contained on the 'discs'

allegedly refer to a major event due to occur at some point in the near future – an event that may well involve the public arrival of an extraterrestrial civilization and/or some global land shift or polar shift or crustal displacement-type cataclysm. What is even more unnerving is the fact that the schedule said to be contained on the discs concurs with independent information gleaned from UFO contactees and channellers, as well as with that gained by some of the US government's most proven remote viewers – i.e. that some major geological catastrophe is imminent and that it involves the participation of UFOs and ETs in some as yet unspecified way. With this in mind, then, the lies and the secrets underpinning the military-industrial complex's deep-underground programme together with those underpinning NASA's deep-space programme begin to make sense – deep-underground bases to counter the alien invasion; deep-space (Moon?) bases to escape the crustal displacement.

The scenario becomes more bizarre by the moment.

File 42
Pine Gap Revisited

And so back to Pine Gap.

What links this information to the Australian deep-underground facility at Pine Gap is that, along with the new Denver facility – and possibly one or two others – it is heavily rumoured that Pine Gap will be the primary seat of world government in the event of Earth changes, alien invasion or some other world-threatening situation.

Evidence to support this fact once again comes from several independent sources, not the least of which is Peter Sawyer, a former high-ranking Australian civil servant who recently exposed the fact that a vast intelligence-gathering facility has been constructed – and is operational – in Australia's capital city, Canberra. The facility is known to house a vast array of the world's most advanced satellite-linked computers – the computers, he claims, are plugged in to every bank, post office, telephone exchange, private telephone, every arrival and departure desk, every state welfare computer system, indeed, every private and government business complex in Britain and the United States, as well as Australia.

He concluded that the Canberra complex is the pivotal data-storage centre for information gathered on every private citizen in the western world. Remember, this information comes not from the lips of a conspiracy theorist; Peter Sawyer was a very senior civil servant in the Australian government.

To add to the above . . . Sawyer's in-house investigations also revealed that the vast new Parliament building in Canberra – far beyond the needs of national administration; most of it buried underground – is intended as *the* primary seat of New World Administration. (It is said that underground links to Pine Gap are already operational, and that Pine Gap will be the global 'White House', so to speak, Canberra the global 'Parliament'.) Presumably, with Britain and America too vulnerable to mutiny by their respective populations, Australia has been purposely selected by the Committee because of its sparse population and its distance from the rest of the world. Put quite simply, Australia is the safest country to retreat to. (It is rumoured among British intelligence circles, for example, that the Queen would be ferried to Australia in the event of a national emergency. What those rumours do *not* say, however, is that she would be flown to Pine Gap as the leading representative of the New World Order.)

But until it becomes necessary (for whatever reason) for the NWO to rear its ugly head (following whatever 'event' is on the way) the Pine Gap deep-underground retreat will, presumably, remain open and ready for business. As well as a place being reserved for every member of the Committee of 300 at the new deep-underground facility in Denver, Colorado, the primary NWO residence in the event of alien invasion (fake or otherwise), Earth changes or indeed some other global catastrophe would almost certainly be the supersecret deep-underground facility in the centre of the Australian wilderness – Pine Gap – where the Queen's private apartments are said to be ready and waiting . . .

Debriefing Document

You would be forgiven for expecting me to sum things up here by declaring my consummate belief in the imminent takeover of the world by a joint alien/Secret Government junta; that this junta may achieve its *coup d'état* by staging a fake 'alien invasion' and simultaneously be seen to save the world, *Independence Day*-style, thereby lulling the masses into a false sense of servitude; that some insidious *Brave New World* scenario would then be implemented wherein the remote-controlled masses would become segregated into social tiers, their chip-in-brain implants keeping them wired in to electronic instruction from Big Brother; that Nazi-style stormtroopers would patrol the streets and enforce the whim of this new regime upon the souls of the meek and the mighty alike; that bad-dude aliens would suddenly crawl out of their holes in the ground and force us to eat radioactive fruit and veg, infected beef, chemically-fattened poultry; force us to drink contaminated water; breathe polluted air; swim in seas full of piss and shit . . .

(But hang on a minute . . . it's like that already, isn't it?)

. . . You would be forgiven for expecting me to sum things up in this way, but you would be wrong.

On the contrary, instead of adding to this nightmarish thought-pool and going off on a line about the establishment of the New World Order according to the Secret Government (the takeover of the world by the Rothschilds, the Rockefellers, the Black Nobility and its front groups –

the United Nations, the Council on Foreign Relations, the Royal Institute for International Affairs, the Round Table, the Bilderberg Group, P2 Masonry, the Club of Rome, the all-powerful Committee of 300, etc., etc., etc.), I intend here to inject a modicum of positive energy: a little hope.

Frankly, I don't see such an open takeover as viable. There is simply no need. The abovementioned organizations are doing a fine job of running the world for themselves even now – why should they wish to ruin a good thing by stepping out into the open and declaring the unseen agendas which, up to now, have served them so well? Surely the fabric of successful covert government depends on that government remaining covert. Of course, moves towards making their job all the easier by creating a Federal US/European Union centralized in Washington and Brussels are now well under way; the election of Tony Blair and his revamped middle-class socialist party has taken care of that, certainly from the British point of view. And bearing in mind the fact that the Black Nobility – and thereby the Secret Government – is, according to former intelligence operative John Coleman and others, headed by the House of Windsor, the British point of view is exceedingly crucial. With the handover of Hong Kong in 1997 the sun may finally have set on the obsolete British Empire, but in the seedy upper echelons of covert world government the Empire still reigns supreme. Make no mistake.

That aside, and whatever one's disposition regarding Secret Government conspiracy theories and alien/government pacts, inside investigations have certainly led me to believe that there is an altogether different New World Order scenario to be considered here, one whose agenda is derived not from megalomania but from evolutionary necessity. It is this scenario I wish to put to you here.

*   *   *

Throughout the course of this book I have alluded to the fact that the US-and-British-based military-industrial administration (and, of course, its attendant intelligence agencies) is extremely aware of and indeed concerned about the metaphysical-cum-paradigm-shift aspect of the UFO phenomenon -- that at its core said phenomenon is an expression of some inner, collective and ongoing shift in consciousness that is destined to culminate with the arrival of a new and as yet unseen reality: an extraterrestrial reality. The big white chiefs know the phenomenon is real, manifest, that its precepts are beyond those governing the purely human experience – the human paradigm – and that therefore it represents a quantum-leap potential in the evolution of human mind and artifice. In this respect it is seen as a major threat to the structures and agendas that uphold the present social, political and economic mindset (see Document 03, File 13).

Hence the 'powers-that-be' perceive the phenomenon as a 'threat to national security', and hence they classify it at the highest possible security level: COSMIC TOP SECRET.

In short, those who currently wield the power do not want the paradigm shift to happen – they do not want *any* paradigm shift to happen, much less one directly pertinent to the imminent spiritual and psychological 'upgrade' of the very people they presently control. Prevention of the paradigm shift is thus paramount. And so far as the 'powers-that-be' are concerned, remember, such a paradigm shift is represented in the form of the UFO phenomenon and the attendant human expectation of some imminent extraterrestrial contact. Thus to ridicule and debunk the phenomenon in the public eye – while at the same time garnering all relevant information – is the agreed-upon policy.

I recall your attention here, for example, to the passage from

Whitley Strieber's book *Breakthrough: The Next Step* (quoted in Document 13, File 41) in which he states: '. . . Individuals formerly at Wright [Wright-Patterson AFB] have alluded to a top-secret scientific paper that alleges that the ability of the visitors to enter our reality is mediated by the degree to which we acknowledge their existence, and that the "invasion" can be literally held at bay by orchestrated denial and general disbelief.'

To my mind this is the most staggering official statement yet disclosed.

Indeed, it would seem from this statement that the 'powers-that-be' have realized the fact that the UFO phenomenon is an interactive one – that ET and his fleet of elusive ships are here precisely because some inner human need has beckoned them, like some intergalactic beacon pulsing SOS signals to the farthest reaches of reality. Indeed, expanding this line of thought one might further postulate that the UFO phenomenon has become so manifestly evident today for no more complex reason than that sufficient people are now ready to experience it – as though the Earth itself were alive and alert to the fact that evolution's 'missing link' was about to show its face once again, and in passing seed a new and higher echelon of life beyond the strictly human one, in the same way as – at some point in the past – it seeded a new and higher echelon of life beyond the strictly animal one, hence the still unexplained arrival of *Homo sapiens*. In this respect I believe the *'orchestrated denial and general disbelief'* policy recommended by the scientific intelligence community is an ongoing tactic employed by the authorities in order to forestall the arrival of such an evolutionary upgrade: prevention in advance of its coming.

To add to this . . . in Document 10 I presented a summary of evidence to the effect that the CIA and the Secret Government are involved in mind-control programmes. As reluctant as you or I might be to accept some of the tales that have emerged from the bowels of the military-industrial agenda, that the British-and-US-based military-industrial complex is engaged in psychotronic research pertaining to the direct control of human behaviour is now cold hard fact, as confirmed by Dr Chris Winter of British Telecom's Artificial Life team when commenting on the development of BT's *Soul Catcher 2025* implant. Indeed, chip-in-brain implants, microwaves, HAARP and other mind-control technologies now form part of an insidious battery of 'non-lethal weapons' used, among other things, for stimulating human thought and consciousness to resist its own natural inclination – in other words, for tuning our brains to revolt against our own natural instincts and intuitions. The natural inclination of human consciousness, of course, is always towards its own progressive evolution – its own growth, expansion and transformation. A succession of periodic paradigm shifts – perhaps marked by sudden and dramatic earth-crust displacements, perhaps by the periodic return of our genetic 'forebears' (ET) – is certainly evidence of this evolutionary upgrade occurring on a cyclical basis (see Document 13, File 41).

Based on the overwhelming evidence thus far available, then, it is my contention that human consciousness and civilization is once again on the verge of some massive evolutionary leap, and that by its nature this leap implies some level of involvement with extraterrestrial intelligence(s). Perhaps because this leap promises that human awareness will – virtually overnight – evolve to the point where it can no longer be controlled by current technological means, the 'powers-that-be' do not want the masses informed of its imminence. On the contrary, if they cannot prevent the paradigm shift occurring then they will do – and are doing – all in their power to keep knowledge of it under wraps: to conceal it from public attention until such time as they are able to successfully 'reverse-engineer' its warp and weft and so are better able to manipulate its eventual coming to pass.

Hence all the official secrecy surrounding the UFO phenomenon.

One final aspect to be considered here takes us back to the Roswell incident and its inherent implications regarding alien/government collusion. Are the governments working with aliens? Is there some alien/government treaty that is being kept secret from the rest of the world?

The simple answer, of course, is: *No*, the governments are not working with aliens. Although the evidence leans heavily towards the fact that at least one extraterrestrial intelligence is indeed taking a keen interest in our affairs, and that according to US Special Forces Command Sgt Major Robert O. Dean and others, the governments and NATO are fully aware of this fact, there is nevertheless little – if any – real evidence to suggest that some fiendish alien race is endeavouring to invade our world with the help of the world's governments. Were this the case then the dastardly deed would by now have been done, the so-called 'invasion' successfully accomplished and recorded in the annals of Earth's brief history, of this much I am utterly convinced. Indeed, the only real evidence to be had regarding alien/government involvement is to be found in the new and extremely high-technology defence measures currently being developed and deployed in anticipation of alien invasion. Which in turn, of course, tends to support Sgt Major Dean's claims that certain NATO chiefs are indeed aware of the extraterrestrial presence and that they are endeavouring to prevent open contact with the visitors by a range of various means – including the implementation of the '*orchestrated denial and general disbelief*' policy recommended by the US scientific intelligence community plus the further implementation of more direct military measures . . . like bringing down the visitors' craft with pulsed electromagnetic radar effects and particle-beam weaponry, and either killing or capturing the 'alien' occupants. This, I believe, is what happened at Roswell in New Mexico in July 1947. The subsequent leap forward in military technology is certainly evidence that this was a genuine extraterrestrial incident; it is evidence, too, of the governments' endeavours to reverse-engineer the alien technologies on offer as a result of the Roswell recovery, as confirmed by former US Army Intelligence officer and head of the Pentagon's Foreign Technology in Army Research and Development, Colonel Philip J. Corso. In this respect it would seem that Roswell marked the beginning of the Technological Age.

It is my conclusion, then, that fifty years ago (1947) the 'powers-that-be' started to become aware of two new and intrinsically interactive phenomena:

(a) the extraterrestrial presence;

(b) its implications regarding the possibility of an imminent social, political and economic (and technological) paradigm shift – a shift which they did not and do not fully comprehend, nevertheless one in which, even today, they detect the inherent dangers of social mutiny.

If we assume for the present that the evolution of consciousness is no random event but follows instead a preset sequence of events built in to some potentially conscious evolutionary programme (perhaps what we might call the 'collective unconscious') then we can further assume that there is a natural though preprogrammed schedule that regulates the arrival of each successive paradigm shift. Certainly it would seem that the ETs are working to a similar schedule that could result in full and open contact with the human race, and that any subsequent and mutual human/ET cohabitation scenario will naturally create its own New World Order. However, the evidence also suggests that the upper echelons of secret government are aware of such a schedule and are working towards its disruption and ultimate prevention. They have their own ideas about which New World Order they would prefer to see in place, and it is not the mutually interactive human/ET one. Not unless, of course, they can control it. Which they cannot.

I believe this is the reason that the military-industrial complex and the intelligence communities are hell-bent on keeping the phenomenon in the realms of the weird and the wacky, while at the same time they are constantly endeavouring to stay one step ahead by keeping the truth in a box marked 'Classified'. The biggest problem facing them, of course, is that human consciousness simply cannot be classified. Not in its purest expression. Not by anybody. Not even the CIA.

Which brings us to the following conclusion.

While the truth that is 'out there' may well be contained in some CIA vault or secret government X-File archive, the truth that is our purest consciousness, our purest mind – our living soul – can only blossom to the point where we are ready to meet and cohabit with beings of a higher order – ETs, if you will – and so together build a more highly evolved echelon of social, political and economic reality wherein the exploration of both inner and outer space will be the encouraged and accepted norm.

This is what I mean by the term 'paradigm shift'. This is what I mean by the term 'New World Order'.

And that's what they're afraid of.

Bibliography

BEYOND ROSWELL, Michael Hesemann and Philip Mantle (Marlowe & Co., 1997) ISBN: 1-56924-781-1

UFOs: Secrets Of The Black World (Video Documentary) Michael Hesemann (Contact: Ark Soundwaves of Glastonbury, PO Box 1395, Glastonbury, Somerset, BA6 9FE UK)

A COVERT AGENDA: The British Government's UFO Top Secrets Exposed, Nicholas Redfern (Simon & Schuster UK)

THE CONTROLLERS: Mind Control And Its Role In The Alien Abduction Phenomena, Martin Cannon (Feral House, 1996) ISBN: 0-922915-32-6

EUROPE'S FULL CIRCLE: Corporate Elites and the New Fascism, Rodney Atkinson (Compuprint Pub, 1996) ISBN: 0-9525110-0-2

FINGERPRINTS OF THE GODS: A Quest For The Beginning Of The End, Graham Hancock (Mandarin, 1996) ISBN: 0-7493-1454-0

ABOVE TOP SECRET: The Worldwide UFO Cover-Up, Timothy Good (Grafton Books, 1989) ISBN: 0-586-20361-3

BEYOND TOP SECRET: The Worldwide Security Threat, Timothy Good (Pan Books, 1997) ISBN: 0-330-34928-7

ALIEN LIAISON: The Ultimate Secret, Timothy Good (Arrow Books, 1992) ISBN: 0-09-985920-3

SECRET AND SUPPRESSED: Banned Ideas And Hidden History, edited by Jim Keith (Feral House, 1993) ISBN: 0-922915-14-8

BEHOLD A PALE HORSE, Milton William Cooper (Light Technology Pub, 1991) ISBN: 0-929385-22-5

The Conspirator's Hierarchy: THE COMMITTEE OF 300 (Fourth Edition) Dr John Coleman (WIR, Joseph Holding Corporation, 1997) ISBN: 0-9634019-4-7

UNDERGROUND BASES AND TUNNELS: What Is The Government Trying To Hide? Dr Richard Sauder PhD (Gazelle Books, 1997) ISBN: 0-932813-37-2

TOP SECRET/MAJIC, Stanton T Friedman (Michael O'Mara Books, 1997) ISBN: 1-85479-203-2

SECRET SOCIETIES: And Their Power In The 20th Century, Jan

van Helsing (Contact: Ewertverlag, SL, Muhlentannen, 14-D-49762, LATHEN, Germany) ISBN: 3-89478-654

THE DAY AFTER ROSWELL, Col Philip J. Corso (Ret) with William J Birnes (Pocket Books, Simon & Schuster, 1997) ISBN: 0-671-00461-1

BREAKTHROUGH: The Next Step, Whitley Strieber (HarperCollins, 1995) ISBN: 0-06-017653-9

THE CIA'S GREATEST HITS, Mark Zepezauer (Odonian Press, 1994) Contact: Odonian Press, Box 32375, Tucson AZ 85751, USA. Tel: 520 296 4056 or 800 REAL STORY. Fax: 520 296 0936. E-mail: odonian@realstory.com.

REVELATIONS: Alien Contact And Human Deception, Jacques Vallee (Souvenir, 1992) ISBN: 0-285-63073-3